Lecture Notes in Computer Science 7167

Commenced Publication in 1973
Founding and Former Series Editors:
Gerhard Goos, Juris Hartmanis, and Jan van Leeuwen

Editorial Board

Jörg Kienzle (Ed.)

Models in Software Engineering

Workshops and Symposia at MODELS 2011
Wellington, New Zealand, October 16-21, 2011
Reports and Revised Selected Papers

 Springer

Volume Editor

Jörg Kienzle
McGill University
School of Computer Science
3480 University, McConnell Eng. 318
Montreal, QC, H3A 0E9, Canada
E-mail: joerg.kienzle@mcgill.ca

ISSN 0302-9743   e-ISSN 1611-3349
ISBN 978-3-642-29644-4   ISBN 978-3-642-29645-1 (eBook)
DOI 10.1007/978-3-642-29645-1
Springer Heidelberg Dordrecht London New York

Library of Congress Control Number: 2012935552

CR Subject Classification (1998): D.2, D.3, F.3, K.6, I.6, H.4

LNCS Sublibrary: SL 2 – Programming and Software Engineering

Typesetting: Camera-ready by author, data conversion by Scientific Publishing Services, Chennai, India

Printed on acid-free paper

Springer is part of Springer Science+Business Media (www.springer.com)

Preface

The MoDELS conference series is the premier conference series for model-based software and systems engineering, and covers all aspects of modeling, from languages and methods to tools and applications. The 2011 edition of MoDELS took place in the beautiful port city of Wellington, the capital of New Zealand, during October 16–21, 2011. Like in the past years, the conference hosted several satellite events, i.e., eight workshops, two symposia and seven tutorials, on the first three days of the conference. The events took place in the stunning National Museum of New Zealand "Te Papa," which allowed the participants to discover the vibrancy of the Maori culture in between the sessions.

Following tradition, the workshop and symposia organizers invited the authors of the selected best papers of their event to revise and extend their contributions for publication in these proceedings. In addition, this LNCS volume also includes for each workshop and symposium a summary of the event. The summaries and papers are presented in this book in the following order:

- Doctoral Symposium
- Educators' Symposium
- Variability for You - VARY
- 5th International Workshop on Multi-Paradigm Modeling - MPM'11
- Experiences and Empirical Studies in Software Modelling - EESSMod 2011
- 6th International Workshop on Models@run.time
- Workshop on Model-Driven Engineering, Verification and Validation - MoD-eVVa 2011
- Comparing Modeling Approaches Workshop - CMA 2011
- Models and Evolution - ME 2011
- 4th International Workshop on Model-Based Architecting and Construction of Embedded Systems - ACES-MB 2011

I would like to thank everyone involved in making the satellite events such a success: Thomas Khne, the General Chair, who took care of all the local arrangements for the three days of the satellite events; the members of the Workshop Committee (Lionel Briand from University of Oslo - Norway, Robert France from University of Colorado - USA, Jeff Gray from University of Alabama - USA, and Hans Vangheluwe from University of Antwerp - Belgium), who worked diligently to ensure the highest quality for the workshops; and Arnor Solberg and Jürgen Dingel, the Workshop Co-chairs of MoDELS 2010, who generously shared their past experience with me.

January 2012   Jörg Kienzle

Table of Contents

5th International Workshop on Multi-Paradigm Modeling

First International Workshop on Experiences and Empirical Studies in Software Modelling

6th International Workshop on Models@run.time

Model-Driven Engineering, Verification and Validation

Comparing Modeling Approaches Workshop

Models and Evolution Workshop

4th International Workshop on Model-Based Architecting and Construction of Embedded Systems

Doctoral Symposium
at MoDELS 2011

Joerg Evermann[1] and Ivan Porres[2]

[1] Memorial University of Newfoundland, Canada
jevermann@mun.ca
[2] Åbo Akademi University, Finland
Ivan.Porres@abo.fi

The doctoral symposium (DocSym) of the 14th International Conference on Model Driven Engineering Languages and Systems (MODELS 2011) provided an opportunity for doctoral researchers to present and discuss their research, and to gather feedback from peers and experienced researchers in the field.

The goal of the DocSym is to provide a forum in which PhD students can present their work in progress and to foster the role of MODELS as a premier venue for research in model-driven engineering. The symposium aims to support students by providing independent and constructive feedback about their already completed and, more importantly, planned research work. The symposium was accompanied by prominent professors in the field of model-driven engineering who will actively participate in critical discussions.

The 2011 DocSym is the 8th doctoral symposium at the MODELS conference and continues a tradition of mentoring and guiding young researchers that began with the doctoral symposium at the 2004 UML conference in Lisbon and was then held annually at the MODELS conferences in 2005 (Jamaica), 2006 (Genoa), 2007 (Nashville), 2008 (Toulouse), 2009 (Denver), and 2010 (Oslo).

Participation in the DocSym is a competitive process. This year, we received 10 high quality submissions by PhD students from all over the world and accepted 6 for admission to the DocSym. This highly competitive admission highlights the growth of the field of model driven engineering and the continuing interest of future researchers in this area. The submissions that we received showed a wide range of topics in the field of model driven engineering, ranging from formal methods to model evolution and transformation and to modelling for embedded and mobile devices. The six accepted papers are the following:

- **Henning Agt** (Technische Universität Berlin, Germany) — Supporting software language engineering by automated domain knowledge acquisition
- **Regina Hebig** (Hasso Plattner Institute for Software Systems Engineering, Potsdam, Germany) — An approach to integrating model management and software development processes
- **Muhammad Atif Quereshi** (University of Technology, Sydney, Australia) — Interoperability of software engineering metamodels
- **Andreas Vogelsang** (Technische Universität München, Germany) — A hierarchical model for structuring functional requirements and their dependencies

J. Kienzle (Ed.): MODELS 2011 Workshops, LNCS 7167, pp. 1–3, 2012.
© Springer-Verlag Berlin Heidelberg 2012

- **Timo Wegeler** (Fraunhofer Institut für Rechnerarchitektur und Softwaretechnik, Germany) — Towards quality assurance of DSL engineering processes
- **Magdalena Widl** (Vienna University of Technology, Austria) — Formal methods in software model evolution

The published proceedings required an even more restrictive choice. Only two of the six accepters papers, those by Henning Agt and Muhammad Atif Quereshi, were chosen for inclusion in the proceedings. This represents a highly competitive 20% acceptance rate for the published proceedings.

Submissions were invited from PhD students who have settled on a PhD topic, but are still sufficiently far away from completion to be able to take full advantage of the given feedback (typically, this means that, at the time of the symposium, students should be at least one year away from completion). Submissions should describe research-in-progress that is meant to lead to a PhD dissertation. In contrast to regular academic papers that describe completed work, the submissions for the DocSym were asked to focus on descriptions of

- Problem: The problem the research intends to solve, the target audience of this research, and a motivation of why the problem is important and needs to be solved.
- Related work: A review of the relevant related work with an emphasis of how the proposed approach is different and what advantages it has over the existing state of the art.
- Proposed solution: A description of the proposed solution and which other work (e.g., in the form of methods or tools) it depends on.
- Preliminary work: A description of the work to-date and results achieved so far.
- Expected contributions: A list of the expected contributions to both theory and practice.
- Plan for evaluation and validation: A description of how it will be shown that the work does indeed solve the targeted problem and is superior to the existing state of the art (e.g. prototyping, industry case studies, user studies, experiments).
- Current status: The current status of the work and a planned timeline for completion.

The submissions were judged on originality, significance, correctness and clarity. Each submission received at least 3 reviews. Again, the criteria for reviewing the papers differed from those that are typically applied to completed research papers. Specifically, the review committee used the following criteria:

- Overall quality of the submission itself (e.g., clarity, and precision, relative to the stage of the research)
- Adequacy of the problem statement, the solution description, the expected contributions, the plan for evaluation, and the review of related work.
- Originality of the proposed solution

- Significance and relevance of the problem and proposed solution to both theory and practice in model-driven engineering

For this year's DocSym, we decided to invite last year's DocSym participants as reviewers. We believe this provides an opportunity for these young researchers to gain valuable experience in reviewing and evaluating papers and also brings a different perspective to the reviews, as the reviewer's own DocSym experience was still fresh in their minds. Every paper was also reviewed by one or both of the DocSym organizers. We thank the following reviewers for providing their time and expertise to help with this year's DocSym:

- Alexander Bergmayr (University of Vienna, Austria)
- Mauro Luigi Drago (Politecnico di Milano, Italy)
- Quratulann Faroow (Technical University Ilmenau, Germany)
- Fabian Gilson (Facultés Universitaire Notre-Dame de la Paix, Namur, Belgium)
- Dieter Mayrhofer (Technical University of Vienna, Austria)
- Catia Trubiani (Universitá degli Studi dell'Aquila, Italy)
- Dragos Truscan (Åbo Akademi, Finland)
- Lijun Yu (Colorado State University, USA)

The doctoral symposium was held on October 17th and a range of senior, experienced researchers in the field of model driven engineering volunteered their time to serve as discussants for the presented research. Each participating student was asked to prepare a 20 to 25 minute presentation of their research proposal. This was followed by a discussion of the proposal by an assigned mentor and by other participants. We thank the following faculty members for their time and expertise:

- Colin Atkinson (University of Mannheim, Germany)
- Juergen Dingel (Queens University, Canada)
- Marian Petre (The Open University, UK)
- Wolfram Schulte (Microsoft Research, USA)
- Bran Selic (Malina Software Corp., Canada)

Finally, we wish to thank the general chair of the MODELS 2011 conference, Thomas Kühne, and the workshop chair, Jörg Kienzle, with whom we worked closely, for their support and help in many different ways during, before, and after the DocSym.

Supporting Software Language Engineering by Automated Domain Knowledge Acquisition

Henning Agt

Technische Universität Berlin
Einsteinufer 17, 10587 Berlin, Germany
henning.agt@tu-berlin.de

Abstract. In model-driven engineering, domain-specific languages (DSLs) play an important role in providing well-defined environments for modeling different aspects of a system. Detailed knowledge of the application domain as well as expertise in language engineering is required to create new languages. This research work proposes automated knowledge acquisition to support language engineers in early language development phases. We describe an iterative approach in which DSL development benefits from formalized knowledge sources and information extraction from text supporting domain analysis and metamodel construction. We show how the acquired knowledge is used to guide language engineers and how knowledge acquisition is adapted according to modeling decisions.

1 Introduction and Problem Statement

Model-driven engineering (MDE) proposes systematic use of models as primary development artifacts for software system construction. These models describe different aspects of a system on a higher level of abstraction using particular modeling languages (e. g., UML or domain-specific languages (DSLs)). MDE aims at generating source code from the developed models and, as a consequence, reducing the effort at manually creating source code with programming languages. On the one hand, it has been shown that modeling and code generation increases productivity of software development projects [17], especially if developers can use ready-to-use domain-specific modeling languages [19] and language workbenches. On the other hand, if the available modeling languages do not suit the particular aspect to be modeled or they are not even available for a certain domain at all, additional initial language development effort neutralizes the productivity gain [16].

Creating new modeling languages requires expertise in language engineering, such as finding the right abstractions, creating metamodels and the correct usage of generalizations/specializations and aggregations. Assuming that language engineers have these competencies, these techniques are usually applied to different application areas and industrial sectors. These engineers are required to have detailed knowledge of the domain in order to create modeling languages. Assembling domain knowledge is a time-consuming manual process (e.g. talking to domain experts and reading specific documentation).

J. Kienzle (Ed.): MODELS 2011 Workshops, LNCS 7167, pp. 4–11, 2012.

As far as modeling techniques and programming are concerned, current state-of-the-art language workbenches, such as Eclipse Modeling Project, Spoofax and MetaEdit+, offer a lot of support in terms of metalanguages, model editors, transformation engines and code generators to build domain-specific languages and domain-specific tools. With regard to the actual content and meaning of the abstract syntax of a language, very limited assistance is provided.

In particular, the research question we are addressing is *"Can the development of domain-specific modeling languages be improved by automated knowledge acquisition?"*. To answer this question we consider the following: (1) *Where does the required knowledge come from?* Semantic knowledge bases and ontologies are an important source and this knowledge can also be obtained from text. (2) *How can the necessary knowledge be acquired automatically?* We propose the construction of queries from terms and relations in a model and their execution against multiple knowledge bases. (3) *How can the acquired knowledge be used to improve modeling?* We suggest that guidance through domain visualization and checking for semantically incorrect content leads to better quality models. (4) *How does model evolution effect knowledge acquisition?* In each step of a modeling process guidance shall be adapted according to the changing content of a model.

Section 2 discusses existing work related to this proposal. Section 3 explains our iterative approach for domain knowledge acquisition and modeling guidance. Section 4 describes the current status of this work and concludes the paper.

2   Related Work

This research proposal works on the connection of several research areas. We summarize the most important works in the following categories:

Software Language Engineering. The relatively new field of software language engineering [18] deals with methodologies and tools for the design of new modeling languages. Typical tasks in language engineering are abstract and concrete syntax design and semantics specification [9]. Systematic development of DSLs is discussed by Mernik et al. [21]. They identify several patterns for each DSL development phase. Strembeck and Zdun [24] describe activities for a DSL engineering process. In our research work we focus on metamodel-based [4] abstract syntax modeling as one of the most important early-stage activities of language creation in which classes, attributes and relationships of the language are defined. Current state-of-the-art techniques of modeling language design are presented by Selic [23].

Ontologies in Model-Driven Engineering. The use of ontologies in model-driven engineering has been investigated from different perspectives. Ontological foundations for metamodeling and modeling languages have been analyzed by Guizzardi [13], Evermann et al. [7] and Henderson-Sellers [15] with regard to the relation between conceptualizations, metamodels and ontologies. Results of the MOST project [29] show the advantages of bridging ontology languages and modeling languages under a common metamodel and offering reasoning services for structural and behavioral modeling. Tairas et al. [26] show how ontologies improve the domain analysis phase of DSL development. Also, the connection between ontologies and MDE has been studied vice versa. Gasevic et al. [12] describe how ontology engineering benefits from methods of model-driven development. We focus on exploiting existing formalized knowledge to find suitable terms and relations for the abstract syntax of domain-specific languages.

Model Extraction From Text. In recent years a lot of research has been carried out to automatically create ontologies and knowledge bases with information extraction methods [6]. The field of knowledge harvesting [30] aims at automatically creating large scale knowledge bases by extracting facts from semi-structured and unstructured natural language text. For example, the YAGO [25] and DBpedia [5] projects show that large ontologies with millions of facts can be created automatically with high accuracy.

In the software engineering domain, requirements engineering still heavily relies on text documents. Natural language analysis is used in this field to automatically create early software design artifacts from textual specifications. Important works in this area are based on semantic annotations and semantic role labeling [28], use case parsing [32] and extraction of conceptual models [27]. Natural language processing (NLP) is also being applied to create process models from text [11]. We believe that these activities and the increasing amount of formalized knowledge can significantly support the creation of modeling languages in terms of model quality and the reduction of the time needed to create them.

3   Proposed Solution and Contribution

This PhD thesis aims at developing methods and tools to guide language engineers during the early stages of the creation of domain-specific languages using automated knowledge acquisition. Figure 1 shows the concept of the proposed EXAMINE system (**Ex**tracting information for Software Language Eng**ine**ering). Our approach incorporates an iterative process with three steps. Each of the steps is associated with tools that support the activity and artifacts that are produced or consumed, respectively.

During **Model Refinement**, the language engineer develops the DSL and modifies its abstract syntax. Usually, an existing *Language Workbench* is used to carry out this task. The objective of the EXAMINE system is to build services for modeling environments that provide modeling assistance. In order to provide this assistance, the necessary knowledge of the appropriate domain has to be acquired based on the terms of a created model.

The goal of **Knowledge Acquisition** is to automatically query existing knowledge bases, such as ontologies and lexical databases for semantically related concepts by using the content of a model. In case the results are insufficient, the system tries to extract the required knowledge from text corpora. Querying and result integration is handled by the *Extractor*.

In the **Modeling Guidance** step, the obtained knowledge is processed to guide the engineers with the help of domain exploration and modeling advice. Furthermore, the *Model Advisor* also checks for semantic mismatches between the created model and the acquired knowledge.

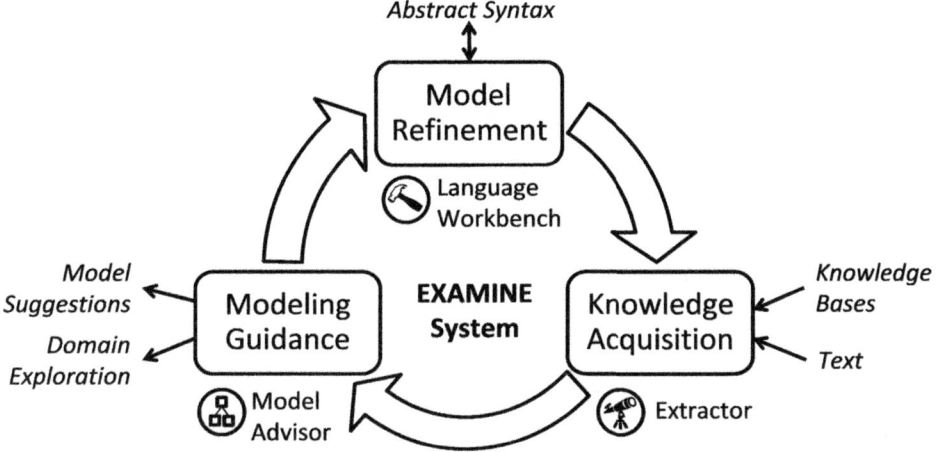

Fig. 1. Concept and Iterative Approach of the EXAMINE System

In the transitions between the steps, the EXAMINE system **adapts** itself according to the modeling decisions made by the engineer (e.g. adding, changing and removing elements). The system also considers that the language engineer can directly use information from the acquired knowledge for the created model and that he can deselect information which he is not interested in.

In the following sections each of the steps is described in more detail.

3.1 Model Refinement

Current state-of-the-art modeling language design is based on language work-benches [10] that offer tools and languages for almost all DSL development phases. Nevertheless, for identifying and modeling domain concepts and relations, tool support is very limited [21].

In our approach, language engineers use existing language workbenches for abstract syntax design and make modeling decisions in a familiar environment. On top of that, services are offered that interact with the modeling environment in order to provide the engineers with domain knowledge and to give advice and corrections. These services can help in various places: thesauri for class name auto completion, graphical visualization of domain concepts and relations and drawing the user's attention to semantically incorrect parts of the model.

Furthermore, the approach enables connection of acquired domain knowledge with the abstract syntax, thus explicitly describing the semantics of a modeling language. For example, the TwoUse approach [22] is a possible solution to link models and domain knowledge contained in ontologies.

3.2 Knowledge Acquisition

In order to provide modeling assistance to language engineers, first, we propose automated querying of semantic knowledge bases. There exist several types of information sources that contain a variety of domain and conceptual knowledge: foundational ontologies (e.g. DOLCE, UFO), upper ontologies (e.g. SUMO), lexical databases (e.g. WordNet [8], FrameNet), manually created ontologies (e.g. Cyc), automatically constructed knowledge bases (e.g. YAGO [25], DBpedia [5]) and knowledge bases created by community effort (e.g. Freebase). The formalized knowledge has been significantly increased over the past years, also supported by the Linked Open Data Initiative.

Starting from a few initial terms contained in a created model, the *Extractor* component of the EXAMINE system constructs queries for knowledge bases (e.g. in SPARQL) to derive an initial top term ontology. In further modeling steps, the more the model is refined, the more specific the queries become. To achieve this, (1) a translation of the model content into queries is required, (2) the queries are executed against several sources, (3) the results are integrated (e.g. based on already existing owl:sameAs relations) and (4) an intermediate ontology specific to the information need is compiled.

In case existing knowledge bases do not provide enough information with regard to the targeted domain, we also address the acquisition of knowledge from unstructured information sources, such as natural language text corpora. Natural language processing relies on linguistic analysis pipelines in order to do tokenization, part-of-speech tagging, parsing, named entity recognition and information extraction tasks on top of that. In our approach, we are especially interested in deriving conceptual knowledge from text: concepts and different types of relations (i.e. hypernym/hyponym and meronym/holonym relations). For example, many approaches that learn taxonomic relations from text use Hearst patterns [14] which consider syntactic patterns between noun phrases. Another state-of-the-art mechanism is Open Information Extraction [6] that extracts any type of relation between entities.

3.3   Modeling Guidance

Once the required domain knowledge is obtained, the *Model Advisor* processes the results and assists the language engineer in the further development of a model. We propose the following kinds of assistance: (1) a graphical and naviga-ble visualization of the domain concepts and relations, (2) suggestions on what should be included in the developed model, and (3) identification of possible semantic mismatches between the model and the acquired knowledge.

Graphical information visualization [20] is one method to provide exploratory access to domain knowledge. We intend to use a representation of the acquired domain knowledge that is familiar to the language engineer (e.g. generating class diagrams or semantic networks and hiding the URI-based subject-predicate-object statements of knowledge bases). Providing suitable excerpts and high-lighting information according to the model content is a challenge in that area.

During the modeling process the language engineer should receive suggestions on what he might include in the model by determining missing classes and re-lations (e.g. *"You created the classes 'patient' and 'doctor'. You may also add 'nurse' and 'hospital'."*). Of course, this example is a very simple way of making a suggestion. The goal of the model advisor is to develop more sophisticated methods for doing that. Giving this advice is similar to topic suggestion [31].

Finally, existing formalized domain knowledge can be used to detect semantically incorrect parts of a model (e.g. 'nurse' is a subclass of 'doctor'). In a first step, we exploit WordNet's hypernym/hyponym and meronym/holonym relations to verify subclasses and aggregations in a model. In subsequent research we also aim at detecting incorrect associations, cardinalities and attributes.

3.4 Adaptation

Our approach considers, firstly, that knowledge acquisition and modeling guidance should be adjusted according to the evolving content of the models. For example, if an engineer deletes a class from his model it should not be suggested by the model advisor again and again. In a first step, a systematic catalog of basic model operations (such as adding, changing and removing a class or an association) and their impact on the iterative process will be defined.

Secondly, the EXAMINE system reacts to the amount of information contained in a model. If a model contains just a few terms the domain exploration should start with a domain overview. The more elements are added to the model, the more details can be acquired and the more specific queries can be executed.

Finally, integrating acquired knowledge directly into a model is considered as positive user feedback. Due to the fact that current state-of-the-art methods of knowledge acquisition (especially NLP) still lack high accuracy, knowledge acquisition can be iteratively improved through user feedback.

4   Current Status and Outlook

This research effort is still at an early stage. The idea of automatically providing guidance for language engineers using knowledge bases and ontologies was developed from the author's previous work in the area of using semantic technologies for model-based software integration [2] and development of domain-specific languages [1] and from the author's interest to work on the connection of different research areas. First results on automatically querying an RDF version of WordNet and generating guidance models have been published at the DSM'11 Workshop [3].

The expected contributions from this PhD thesis are methods for automated domain knowledge acquisition and modeling guidance based on the acquired knowledge. The methods will be implemented by the *Extractor* and the *Model Advisor* component of the EXAMINE system as described in Section 3. The results of this research work shall enable language engineers to create models more efficiently and at higher quality.

The presented concept was developed in the context of the research project BIZWARE[1], a collaboration of two academic and eight industrial partners to

---

[1] This work is partially supported by the Bundesministerium für Bildung und Forschung BMBF under grant number (Förderkennzeichen) 03WKBU01A.

investigate the potential of domain-specific languages and model-driven engineering for small and medium enterprises. The industrial partners are software companies working in different domains: healthcare, production/logistics, facility management and publishing.

Currently, our approach is analyzed by performing the iterative process manually for small domain models in the healthcare and facility management domain in collaboration with domain experts of our industrial partners. From that we expect to refine and improve the proposed method. We also survey the coverage of existing knowledge bases and lexical-semantic databases for developing these models, thus estimating the degree of automation that can be achieved.

References

1. Agt, H., Bauhoff, G., Kutsche, R.-D., Milanovic, N.: Modeling and Analyzing Non-Functional Properties to Support Software Integration. In: Salinesi, C., Pastor, O. (eds.) CAiSE Workshops 2011. LNBIP, vol. 83, pp. 149–163. Springer, Heidelberg (2011)
2. Agt, H., Bauhoff, G., Kutsche, R.D., Milanovic, N., Widiker, J.: Semantic Annotation and Conflict Analysis for Information System Integration. In: Proceedings of the MDTPI at ECMFA (2010)
3. Agt, H., Kutsche, R.D., Wegeler, T.: Guidance for Domain Specific Modeling in Small and Medium Enterprises. In: SPLASH 2011 Workshops. ACM (2011)
4. Atkinson, C., Kühne, T.: Model-Driven Development: A Metamodeling Foundation. IEEE Softw. 20, 36–41 (2003)
5. Auer, S., Bizer, C., Kobilarov, G., Lehmann, J., Cyganiak, R., Ives, Z.: DBpedia: A Nucleus for a Web of Open Data. In: Aberer, K., Choi, K.-S., Noy, N., Allemang, D., Lee, K.-I., Nixon, L.J.B., Golbeck, J., Mika, P., Maynard, D., Mizoguchi, R., Schreiber, G., Cudré-Mauroux, P. (eds.) ASWC 2007 and ISWC 2007. LNCS, vol. 4825, pp. 722–735. Springer, Heidelberg (2007)
6. Etzioni, O., Banko, M., Soderland, S., Weld, D.S.: Open information extraction from the web. Commun. ACM 51, 68–74 (2008)
7. Evermann, J., Wand, Y.: Ontology based object-oriented domain modelling: fundamental concepts. Requir. Eng. 10, 146–160 (2005)
8. Fellbaum, C.: WordNet: An Electronic Lexical Database. The MIT Press, Cambridge (1998)
9. Fowler, M.: Domain Specific Languages. Addison-Wesley, Boston (2010)
10. Fowler, M.: Language Workbenches: The Killer-App for Domain Specific Languages? (2005),
   http://www.martinfowler.com/articles/languageWorkbench.html
11. Friedrich, F., Mendling, J., Puhlmann, F.: Process Model Generation from Natural Language Text. In: Mouratidis, H., Rolland, C. (eds.) CAiSE 2011. LNCS, vol. 6741, pp. 482–496. Springer, Heidelberg (2011)
12. Gasevic, D., Djuric, D., Devedzic, V.: Model Driven Architecture and Ontology Development. Springer-Verlag New York, Inc. (2006)
13. Guizzardi, G.: On Ontology, ontologies, Conceptualizations, Modeling Languages, and (Meta)Models. In: Proceeding of the 2007 Conference on Databases and Information Systems IV: Selected Papers from the Seventh International Baltic Conference DB&IS 2006, pp. 18–39. IOS Press, Amsterdam (2007)

14. Hearst, M.A.: Automatic acquisition of hyponyms from large text corpora. In: Proceedings of the 14th Conference on Computational Linguistics, COLING 1992, Stroudsburg, PA, USA, vol. 2 (1992)
15. Henderson-Sellers, B.: Bridging metamodels and ontologies in software engineering. J. Syst. Softw. 84, 301–313 (2011)
16. Hudak, P.: Modular Domain Specific Languages and Tools. In: Proceedings of the 5th International Conference on Software Reuse, ICSR 1998. IEEE Computer Society, Washington, DC (1998)
17. Kelly, S., Tolvanen, J.P.: Domain-Specific Modeling: Enabling Full Code Generation. Wiley-IEEE Computer Society Press (March 2008)
18. Kleppe, A.: Software Language Engineering: Creating Domain-Specific Languages Using Metamodels. Addison-Wesley Longman Publishing Co., Inc., Boston (2009)
19. Kosar, T., Oliveira, N., Mernik, M., Pereira, M.J.V., Crepinsek, M., da Cruz, D.C., Henriques, P.R.: Comparing general-purpose and domain-specific languages: An empirical study. Comput. Sci. Inf. Syst. 7(2), 247–264 (2010)
20. Mazza, R.: Introduction to Information Visualization, 1st edn. Springer Publishing Company, Incorporated (2009)
21. Mernik, M., Heering, J., Sloane, A.M.: When and how to develop domain-specific languages. ACM Comput. Surv. 37, 316–344 (2005)
22. Parreiras, F.S., Staab, S.: Using ontologies with UML class-based modeling: The TwoUse approach. Data Knowl. Eng. 69(11), 1194–1207 (2010)
23. Selic, B.V.: The theory and practice of modern modeling language design for model-based software engineering. In: Proceedings of AOSD 2011, pp. 53–54. ACM, New York (2011)
24. Strembeck, M., Zdun, U.: An Approach for the Systematic Development of Domain-Specific Languages. Softw. Pract. Exper. 39, 1253–1292 (2009)
25. Suchanek, F.M., Kasneci, G., Weikum, G.: Yago: A Core of Semantic Knowledge. In: 16th International World Wide Web Conference (WWW 2007). ACM Press, New York (2007)
26. Tairas, R., Mernik, M., Gray, J.: Using Ontologies in the Domain Analysis of Domain-Specific Languages. In: Chaudron, M.R.V. (ed.) MODELS 2008. LNCS, vol. 5421, pp. 332–342. Springer, Heidelberg (2009)
27. Thonggoom, O., Song, I.-Y., An, Y.: EIPW: A Knowledge-Based Database Modeling Tool. In: Salinesi, C., Pastor, O. (eds.) CAiSE Workshops 2011. LNBIP, vol. 83, pp. 119–133. Springer, Heidelberg (2011)
28. Tichy, W.F., Körner, S.J., Landhäußer, M.: Creating software models with semantic annotation. In: Proceedings of ESAIR 2010. ACM, New York (2010)
29. Walter, T., Parreiras, F.S., Staab, S., Ebert, J.: Joint Language and Domain Engineering. In: Kühne, T., Selic, B., Gervais, M.-P., Terrier, F. (eds.) ECMFA 2010. LNCS, vol. 6138, pp. 321–336. Springer, Heidelberg (2010)
30. Weikum, G., Theobald, M.: From information to knowledge: harvesting entities and relationships from web sources. In: Proceedings of the Twenty-ninth ACM SIGMOD-SIGACT-SIGART Symposium on Principles of Database Systems of Data, PODS 2010, pp. 65–76. ACM, New York (2010)
31. West, R., Precup, D., Pineau, J.: Automatically suggesting topics for augmenting text documents. In: Proceedings of the 19th International Conference on Information and Knowledge Management, CIKM 2010. ACM, New York (2010)
32. Yue, T., Ali, S., Briand, L.: Automated Transition from Use Cases to UML State Machines to Support State-Based Testing. In: France, R.B., Kuester, J.M., Bordbar, B., Paige, R.F. (eds.) ECMFA 2011. LNCS, vol. 6698, pp. 115–131. Springer, Heidelberg (2011)

Interoperability of Software Engineering Metamodels

Muhammad Atif Qureshi

School of Software, Faculty of Engineering and Information Technology,
University of Technology, Sydney, PO Box 123, Broadway, NSW 2007, Australia
atif@it.uts.edu.au

Abstract. Several metamodels have been proposed in the software engineering literature recently. For practical usage, it is important to ensure that these metamodels can be used in an interoperable fashion. In this paper we present an approach as a part of our PhD research in the same direction. Our methodology is based on the study of analogous characteristics among metamodels, ontologies and schemas. We have adopted ontology merging and schema matching techniques and apply them to the domain of metamodels to assist in creating interoperable metamodels. This methodology is applied and presented here with an illustrative example in which we show the results of merging two of the OMG metamodels: the Organization Structure Metamodel (OSM) and the Business Process Modelling Notation (BPMN).

Keywords: Interoperability, metamodels, ontologies, merging techniques.

1   Introduction and Problem Overview

Several metamodels have been introduced over the last few years in the literature and through standards committees, focusing on different parts and characteristics (e.g. process, product, measurement and organizational) of the software development life-cycle. These metamodels have typically been developed independently of each other within the standards organization with shared concepts being only "accidental".

Furthermore, it is noted that these metamodels are not static in nature. Over the years, new versions are introduced that, typically, extend the scope of the focus domain. For instance, the scope of UML moved from object technology to include component technology and, later, to include execution semantics for code generation capabilities. This leads not only to an increase in size [1] but also, typically, to an increased complexity of the metamodel involved. This complexity is compounded when more than one metamodel needs to be used during the life cycle of a software development project. It is not easy for different key players of software development, key players such as method engineers, methodologists and analysts, to either comprehend or control this compounded complexity. We therefore propose that there is a need to formulate a way in which these metamodels can be used in an interoperable fashion. Interoperability of metamodels can be seen either as a merger or alignment of metamodels. Both merger and alignment of metamodels require finding the similarities between pair of metamodels through matching/mapping.

J. Kienzle (Ed.): MODELS 2011 Workshops, LNCS 7167, pp. 12–19, 2012.

A greater degree of interoperability needs to be sought for a more widespread adoption of metamodels in the wider software engineering community [2], either in terms of mappings between pairs of metamodels or by the direct merging and integration of a number of such metamodels. This need is further endorsed by the rise of industry interest in model driven software engineering (MDSE) [3]. A recent example is the change in OMG's (Object Management Group) OMA (Object Management Architecture) to MDA (Model Driven Architecture) [4] as well as the various conferences on the topic [5]. This interoperability may also reduce their joint complexity, hence making them easy to understand and use.

Therefore this research is focused on how to ensure that these software engineering metamodels are interoperable. It is important to note that every metamodel depicts not only the syntax of its specific domain of focus but also its semantics – this is especially important when we consider interoperability. Our project seeks first to identify similarities, syntactic, structural and semantic, between pairs of metamodels and then determine whether a merger is possible or the metamodels need to be aligned.

2   Related Work

The problem of metamodel interoperability is comparatively new [5], so the literature still lacks comprehensive approaches for metamodel interoperability. Thus, rather than inventing a new technique, it was feasible to investigate the interoperability in the field of study that has characteristics similar to metamodels (e.g. ontologies and schemas) and investigates the possibility of 'technology transfer'. Ontologies and metamodels have some common characteristics [6, 7] since both are models [8]. Ontologies improve not only the semantics of a metamodel [9] but experience with ontology mergers also provide a potential way in which these metamodels can be bridged with each other to be interoperable.

The growing use and development of ontologies have raised the problems of overlapping concepts, increased size and increased complexity, making it difficult to manipulate ontologies. Solutions suggested in the literature are mapping, alignment and merging of ontologies. Many researchers have explored ways to map and/or merge ontologies. In the following paragraphs, we briefly summarize these approaches.

Mohsenzada *et al.* [10] have presented an algorithm to merge two ontologies. They have categorized ontologies as global and local and worked on the merging of local ontologies without the help of a global ontology. The semi-automated algorithm SMART for ontology merging [11] is a five step approach. Some of these steps are performed automatically (*Initial List, Automatic Updates*) and some are performed manually by the user (*Load, Select Operation*). Formal concept analysis (FCA) has also been used [12] to merge two ontologies in a bottom-up fashion, an approach that is based on three steps: developing formal contexts based on linguistic analysis, merging of two contexts and building up a concept lattice, and finally semi-automatic ontology creation.

The general concept of ontology mediation can be classified as ontology mapping, ontology alignment or ontology merging [13], the first of which was illustrated by using a mapping language with the help of the automated tool OntoMap. Other

existing approaches and frameworks for ontology merging and alignment have been
discussed in [14] and some areas are highlighted where work still remains to be done.

As noted above, since both metamodels and ontologies have similarities, we propose that the merging techniques that have been devised and applied extensively in
the domain of ontologies might be equally efficacious for facilitating metamodel interoperability. The following section explains our methodology based on not any single
ontology merging technique but on the steps common to almost every ontology merging technique.

3   Proposed Solution

Figure 1 presents our proposed solution (as a BPMN diagram) for metamodel interoperability. We start after selecting the two metamodels as an input and then perform
three different activities (syntactic analysis, semantic analysis and structural analysis)
either parallel or in sequence. These activities are elaborated in following paragraphs.
Each of these activities will result in a separate list of concepts (by concept we mean
the conceptual classes in the metamodels) from both metamodels.

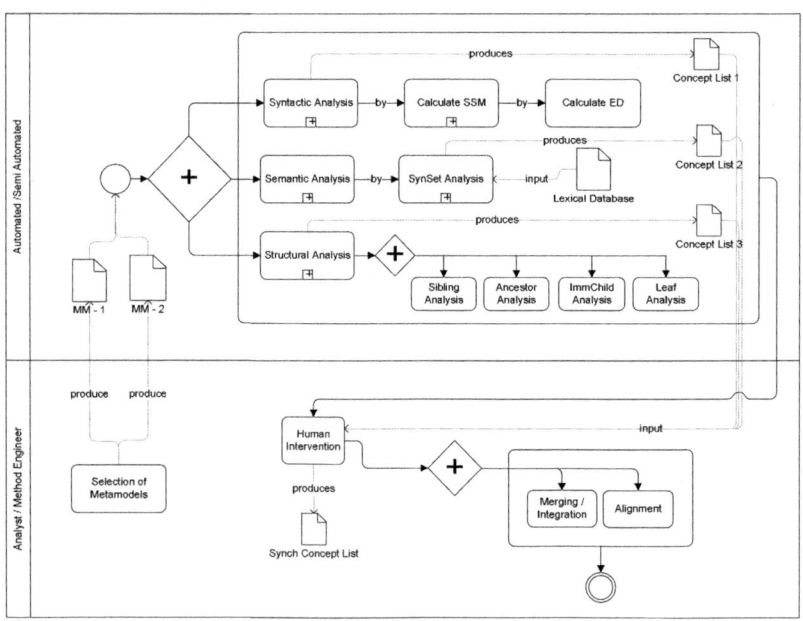

Fig. 1. Methodology for Metamodel Interoperability

Syntactic similarity between the concepts of two metamodels is checked by calculating SSM (Syntactic Similarity Measures) [15]. SSM is calculated using edit dis-
tance formula (ED) proposed by [16].

$$\text{SSM}\left(S_i, S_j\right) = \max\left(0, \ \frac{\min\left(|S_i|, |S_j|\right) - \text{ED}\left(S_i, S_j\right)}{\min\left(|S_i|, |S_j|\right)}\right) \tag{1}$$

where ED counts the number of token insertions, deletions and substitutions to transform one lexical string S_i to another S_j, viewing each string as a list of tokens. The syntactic similarity presented here is based on the names of the conceptual classes and can be further fortified by comparing the attributes of these classes as well. After calculating SSM for each concept in both metamodels, the concepts that are the same or have a strong similarity are listed for further evaluation. Small values of ED indicate greater similarity between pair of concepts. SSM values are then calculated using Equation 1. The values of SMM range from 0 to 1, where 1 indicates that the two concepts are exactly same and 0 means there is a bad match. After calculating SSM for each concept in both metamodels, the concepts that are the same or have a strong similarity are listed for further evaluation.

Structural similarity is measured using the schema matching technique used in [17, 18]. Structural similarity of two concepts $C1$ and $C2$ is calculated based on the structural neighbors of $C1$ and $C2$. Structural neighbors of a concept $C1$ are ancestors($C1$), siblings($C1$), immediateChild($C1$) and leaf($C1$). The structural similarity is obtained in function of partial similarities as follows:

structSim(C1,C2) = ancSim (C1,C2)*ancCoef

+sibSim (C1,C2)*sibCoef

+immChildSim(C1,C2)*immChildCoef

+leafSim(C1,C2)*leafCoef
$$\tag{2}$$

where, $0 \leq ancCoef < 1$, $0 \leq sibCoef < 1$, $0 \leq immChildCoef < 1$, $0 \leq leafCoef < 1$, and $ancCoef + sibCoef + immChildCoef + leafCoef = 1$.

These partial similarities are then calculated by mean values of all the neighboring concepts. For example, the similarity between the ancestors of two concepts C1 and C2 can be calculated using following equations.

$$\text{ancSim} = \frac{\sum_{i=1}^{|ancestor(C1)|} \left(\sum_{j=1}^{|ancestor(C2)|} M[i][j]\right)}{|ancestor(C1)| * |ancestor\ (C2)|} \tag{3}$$

where M is the matrix containing SSM values for all concepts in ancestor set of both C1 and C2.

The concepts of both metamodels will be further investigated for semantic similarity. Semantic similarity is checked by identifying, using any lexical database, meanings and synonyms of concepts in metamodels and comparing them. Each concept and its synonyms in one metamodel are checked against each concept and its synonyms in the other metamodel (Eq. 4). The purpose of semantic similarity is to check whether the concepts appearing similar from previous steps are really similar in the context of the two metamodels. This analysis can be further supported by identifying and comparing the homonyms and hypernyms of the concepts.

$$semSim = \frac{\sum_{i=1}^{|synSet(C1)|} (\sum_{j=1}^{|synSet(C2)|} M[i][j])}{|synSet(C1)| * |synSet(C2)|} \tag{4}$$

The final step requires human intervention and has to be performed by the analyst. First task at this stage is to synthesize the concept lists emerging from previous steps. The overall similarity is calculated (Equation 5) for all pair of concepts.

$$\begin{aligned} Similarity\ (C_1, C_2) = {} & SSM(C_1, C_2) * synCoef \\ & + SemSim\ (C_1, C_2) * semCoef \\ & + StructSim(C_1, C_2) * structCoef \end{aligned} \tag{5}$$

Values of coefficients (e.g. synCoef) in equation 5 have the same conditions as the coefficients in equation 2 and are to be decided by the analyst and depends upon the importance (for analyst) of some similarity measure. For example assigning synCoef = 0.4 means that the analyst has weighted the syntactic similarity 40% of overall similarity. The synthesized list of the concepts, which have values of overall similarity greater than the threshold value (set by the analyst), represents the correspondences or mapping points in both metamodels. Another important consideration at this stage is to look into the definitions of the matched concepts in the specifications of both metamodels. For example a pair of concepts matched may have different definitions as per their original specifications.

The next important step for the analyst is to decide about the integration/merging or alignment of metamodels. This decision is based on the number of factors that an analyst has to keep in mind like the percentage of number of conceptual elements matched, tool support, compatibility of old models with models produced from merged metamodel. Keeping all these factors in mind we can say that the actual interoperability of metamodels cannot be fully automated task and requires a strategic human intervention for right decisions.

The next section presents the application of this framework on a pair of metamodels BPMN (Business Process Modelling Notation Metamodel) [19] and OSM (Organizational Structural Metamodel) [20].

4   Current Status and Plan

Our overall research topic focuses on how to ensure that metamodels are interoperable. Our broader aim is to investigate the utility of creating a fully merged (from multiple current metamodels) single comprehensive metamodel that would form the basis for situational metamodel engineering (SMME: [21]).

As a first step towards such a metamodel suite, we have started, quasi-arbitrarily, with two metamodels (BPMN and OSM) endorsed by a single organization (OMG).

The reason is (1) they are fairly well known but also, and probably more importantly, (2) one might conjecture that models emanating from a single organization would have more inter-coherence than pairs of conceptual models from different organizations. Figure 2 presents the mapping of concepts from both (OSM and BPMN) metamodels which were identified as candidate concepts for mapping after all steps discussed in section 2.

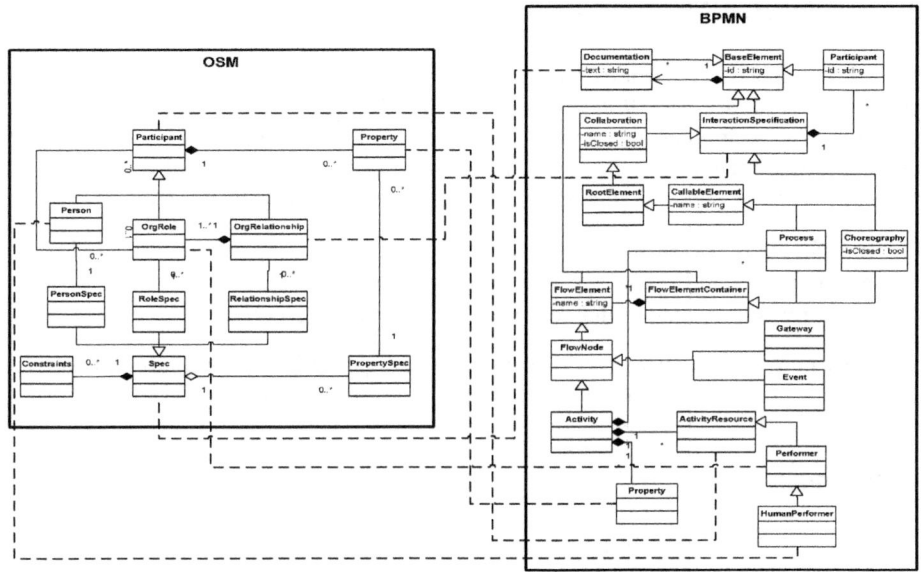

Fig. 2. Mappings of OSM and BPMN

Syntactic checks were made for all 11 concepts of OSM and more than 150 different concepts of BPMN. The concepts were extracted from XMI (XML metadata interchange) specifications of these metamodels. Semantic checks were carried out using a lexical database WordNet [22]. WordNet is a registered trademark for Princeton University and contains more than 118,000 word forms and 90,000 different word senses. Approximately 115 different synonyms were found for the concepts of BPMN and OSM and were compared with each other. For structural similarity, the concept lists along with their parents were used as an input to a code written to calculate structural similarity between concepts. More than 3800 different permutations of structural similarity were computed for the concepts of OSM and BPMN. Based on all these similarity computations, a list of candidate concepts was finalized. The concepts in this list were further investigated manually as per their definition in metamodel specifications. These concepts were synthesized and were finalized for mapping (Figure 2).

Besides the mapping of BPMN and OSM, the mapping of some agent oriented metamodels, ADELFE [23], GAIA [24] and PASSI [25], is in progress. Future work aims to identify similar mappings and mergers, first with other OMG metamodels such as ODM [26], SMM [27] and SPEM [28] and secondly with metamodels from other standards bodies such as ISO e.g. the metamodel given in [29]. Such work requires more detailed analysis of the topology of each metamodel viewed as a graph i.e. focusing not only on the concepts but also on the relationships between the concepts. It is also interesting to speculate whether, in addition to borrowing merging techniques from the ontology domain, metamodel interoperability may also benefit from consideration and utilization of a higher-level or foundational ontology [8, 30, 31].

5   Expected Contribution

This research will be a milestone for several key players in software development community who are or will be interested to use different metamodels. This will provide them a comprehensive and comparatively simple metamodel as compared to using multiple metamodels in a standalone fashion. In the long run, this research will be helpful for the software engineering community as a whole because of

- Significant contributions to the body of software engineering knowledge
- Expected reduction in the complexity of metamodels
- Provision of better and comprehensive metamodel(s).

This research will be an important step towards a potential research area in software engineering and will contribute to recent initiatives in the same direction [5].

References

1. Henderson-Sellers, B., Qureshi, M.A., Gonzalez-Perez, C.: Towards an Interoperable Metamodel Suite: Size Assessment as One Input. International Journal of Software and Informatics (2011) (accepted for publication)
2. OMG: large volume of emails in online discussion groups during 2009 (2009)
3. Bezivin, J., Gerbe, O.: Towards a Precise Definition of the OMG/MDA Framework. In: Proceedings of the 16th IEEE International Conference on Automated Software Engineering. IEEE Computer Society (2001)
4. OMG: MDA Guide, version 1.0.1. omg/2003-06-01 (2003)
5. Bézivin, J., Soley, R.M., Vallecillo, A.: Proceedings of the First International Workshop on Model-Driven Interoperability. ACM (2010)
6. Gonzalez-Perez, C., Henderson-Sellers, B.: An ontology for software development methodologies and endeavours. In: Ontologies in Software Engineering and Software Technology, pp. 123–152. Springer, Berlin (2006)
7. Bézivin, J., Vladan, D., Dragan, D., Jean-Marie, F., Dragan, G., Frederic, J.: An M3-Neutral Infrastructure for Bridging Model Engineering and Ontology Engineering. In: Interoperability of Enterprise Software and Applications, pp. 159–171. Springer, London (2006)
8. Henderson-Sellers, B.: Bridging Metamodels and Ontologies in Software Engineering. Software and Systems 84 (2011) (in press)
9. Devedzić, V.: Understanding ontological engineering. Communications of the ACM 45, 136–144 (2002)
10. Mohsenzadah, M., Shams, F., Teshnehlab, M.: A new approach for merging ontologies. Worlds Academy of Science and Technology, 153–159 (2005)

11. Noy, N.F., Musen, M.A.: An Algorithm for Merging and Aligning Ontologies: Automation and Tool Support. In: Sixteenth National Conference on Artificial Intelligence (AAAI 1999). AAAI Press, Orlando (1999)
12. Stumme, G., Maedche, A.: FCA-MERGE: Bottom-Up Merging of Ontologies. In: International Joint Conference on Artificial Intelligence (2001)
13. de Bruijn, J., Ehrig, M., Feier, C., Martíns-Recuerda, F., Scharffe, F., Weiten, M.: Ontology Mediation, Merging, and Aligning. In: Semantic Web Technologies (2006)
14. Predoiu, L., Feier, C., Scharffe, F., Bruijn, J.d., Martin-Recuerda, F., Manov, D., Ehrig, M.: State-of-the-art survey on Ontology Merging and Aligning V2. EU-IST Integrated Project (2005)
15. Maedche, S.: Comparing Ontologies - Similarity Measures and a Comparison Study. Institute AIFB, University of Karlsruhe, Internal Report (2001)
16. Levenshtein, V.I.: Binary codes capable of correcting deletions, insertions and reversals. Soviet Physics Doklady 10, 707–710 (1966)
17. Chukmol, U., Rifaieh, R., Benharkat, N.A.: EXSMAL: EDI/XML semi-automatic Schema Matching Algorithm. In: Seventh IEEE International Conference on E-Commerce Technology (CEC 2005) (2005)
18. de Sousa Jr., J., Lopes, D., Claro, D.B., Abdelouahab, Z.: A Step Forward in Semi-automatic Metamodel Matching: Algorithms and Tool. In: Filipe, J., Cordeiro, J. (eds.) Enterprise Information Systems. LNBIP, vol. 24, pp. 137–148. Springer, Heidelberg (2009)
19. OMG: Business Process Modelling Notation Beta1. v 2.0. OMG (2009)
20. OMG: Organization Structure Metamodel. 3rd Initial Submission. OMG (2009)
21. Hug, C., Front, A., Rieu, D., Henderson-Sellers, B.: A method to build information systems engineering process metamodels. Journal of Systems and Software 82, 1730–1742 (2009)
22. Miller, G.A.: WordNet: A Lexical Database for English. Communications of the ACM 38, 39–41 (1995)
23. Bernon, C., Gleizes, M.-P., Peyruqueou, S., Picard, G.: ADELFE: A Methodology for Adaptive Multi-agent Systems Engineering. In: Petta, P., Tolksdorf, R., Zambonelli, F. (eds.) ESAW 2002. LNCS(LNAI), vol. 2577, pp. 156–169. Springer, Heidelberg (2003)
24. Zambonelli, F., Jennings, N., Wooldridge, M.: Developing multiagent systems: The Gaia methodology. ACM Trans. Softw. Eng. Methodol. 12, 317–370 (2003)
25. Bernon, C., Cossentino, M., Gleizes, M.-P., Turci, P., Zambonelli, F.: A Study of Some Multi-agent Meta-models. In: Odell, J.J., Giorgini, P., Müller, J.P. (eds.) AOSE 2004. LNCS, vol. 3382, pp. 62–77. Springer, Heidelberg (2005)
26. OMG: Ontology Definition Metamodel V 1.0 (2009)
27. OMG: Architecture-Driven Modernization (ADM): Software Metrics Meta-Model (SMM). FTF - Beta 1 (2009)
28. OMG: Software & Systems Process Engineering Meta-Model Specification (2008)
29. ISO: Software Engineering Metamodel for Development Methodologies (2007)
30. Guizzardi, G.: On Ontology, Ontologies, Conceptualizations, Modeling Languages, and (Meta)Models. Frontiers in Artificial Intelligence and Applications 155, 18–39 (2007)
31. Guizzardi, G.: Ontological Foundations for Structural Conceptual Models. Telematica Instituut Fundamental Research Series (2005)

Software Modeling in Education: The 7th Educators' Symposium at MoDELS 2011

Marion Brandsteidl[1] and Andreas Winter[2]

[1] Vienna University of Technology, Austria
marion.brandsteidl@tuwien.ac.at
[2] Carl von Ossietzky University, Germany
winter@se.uni-oldenburg.de

Abstract. The Educators' Symposium (EduSymp) focuses on discussing teaching the usage of software modelling techniques throughout all phases of a software development process to software engineers at universities and software industries. Collocated with the ACM/IEEE International Conference on Model-Driven Engineering Languages and Systems (MODELS), EduSymp provides the opportunity to discuss new ideas and approaches in the wide area of teaching modelling within the software modelling community to gain new insights and ideas. Besides paper presentations the 7th EduSymp, held in October 2011 in Wellinton, New Zealand, also comprised an inspiring keynote about challenges and opportunities in teaching modelling as well as an active discussion on skills and competencies to be educated in modern modeling education.

1 Overview

Modeling systems plays an important role in todays software development and evolution. Modeling provides goal-oriented abstractions in all phases of software development, which require deep knowledge on modeling techniques and broad experiences in applying these techniques. Although most computer science curricula include some modeling education and therefore provide the basic building blocks for modeling, meta-modeling, and model transformation, the whole spectrum of modeling in software engineering is rarely captured, even a curriculum on modeling is not available to define education standards in modeling.

Collocated with the ACM/IEEE International Conference on Model-Driven Engineering Languages and Systems (MODELS), the Educators' Symposium (EduSymp) focuses on the wide topic of software modeling education ranging from experience reports and case studies to novel pedagogical approaches.

The 7th edition of the EduSymp concretely addressed approaches

- to teach modeling and meta modeling foundations,
- to teach model driven software development and evolution approaches, and
- to integrate model driven technologies into modern computer science curricula, to students in software engineering programs, and to experienced software developers in industries.

J. Kienzle (Ed.): MODELS 2011 Workshops, LNCS 7167, pp. 20–24, 2012.
© Springer-Verlag Berlin Heidelberg 2012

2   Contributions

EduSymp 2011 received 13 papers which have gone through a rigorous review process and finally, 7 papers were presented. The papers have been selected based on the novelty of the ideas or solutions, the impact of modeling during software development education, and relevance to the topics for the symposium. Robert France presented his broad insights in teaching modeling in a keynote on "Teaching Student Programmers How to Model: Opportunities & Challenges". The symposium also included an intensive discussion on skills and competencies to be educated in modern modeling education. This discussion was introduced by a stimulating position paper by Martina Seidl and Peter Clarke on "Software Modelling Education".

In the following, the abstracts of the presented papers and the keynote give a glimpse on the wide variety of topics discussed at the EduSymp 2011. The complete proceedings of the 7th Educators Symposium are made available at Electronic Communications of the European Association of Software Science and Technology (ECEASST).

Avoiding OCL Specification Pitfalls
Dan Chiorean, Ileana Ober and Vladiela Petrascu

This paper discusses about teaching software modeling by using OCL specifications, in the context in which the web represents the main source of information. The raise of the interest for models induced a higher need for clear and complete specifications. In case of models specified by means of MOF-based languages, adding OCL constraints proved to be an interesting answer to this need. Several OCL examples posted on web include hasty specifications, that are often dissuasive with respect to complementing models with OCL specification. OCL beginners, and not only, need to know how to avoid potential specification traps.

Our proposal is based on a complete and unambiguous description of requirements, that represents the first step towards good OCL specifications. The work highlights several major aspects that need to be understood and complied with to produce meaningful and efficient OCL specifications. This approach was tested while teaching OCL at Babes-Bolyai University of Cluj-Napoca.

Mismatches between Industry Practice and Teaching of Model-Driven Software Development
Jon Whittle and John Hutchinson

EAMDE was a 12 month research project, investigating how industry uses model-driven software development (MDSD). Using quantitative and qualitative research techniques, experiences were collected on the adoption and application of MDSD in 17 companies. The study highlighted examples of good and bad practice that lead to success or failure with MDSD. Some of these practices appear to have ramifications on the way that MDSD, and software modeling more generally, is taught within universities. This paper presents three of the key findings relevant to education: (1) A significant number of successful MDSD companies build their own modeling languages and generators, suggesting a re-orientation of education away from UML notation to fundamental modeling principles; (2) MDSD is generally taught top-down, whereas industry success is more likely when MDSD is applied bottom-up; (3) successful application of MDSD requires skills both in abstract modeling and compilers/optimization; however, these skills tend to be separated in standard CS curricula.

Model Correctness Patterns as an Educational Instrument
Azzam Maraee, Mira Balaban, Arnon Strum and Adiel Ashrov

UML class diagrams play a central role in modeling activities. Given the difficulty in producing high quality models, modelers must be equipped with an awareness of model design problems and the ability to identify and correct such models. In this paper we observe the role of class diagram correctness patterns as an educational instrument for improving class diagram modeling. We describe a catalog of correctness and quality design (anti)-patterns for class diagrams. The patterns characterize problems, analyze their causes and provide repairing advice. Pattern specification requires an enhancement of the class diagram meta-model. The pattern classification has a major role in clarifying design problems. Finally, we describe an actual experiment of using the catalog for teaching modeling.

Models and Clickers for Teaching Computer Science
Matthias Hauswirth

Many courses in a computer science curriculum, from computer architecture over programming languages to operating systems, discuss complex and intricate mechanisms and systems. Engineers who develop such mechanisms and systems (e.g. an operating system) use models to deal with their complexity. Instructors who teach the concepts behind those mechanisms and systems often implicitly use models to make those concepts more approachable: they present simplified abstractions and draw diagrams to focus on the essential.

In this position paper we propose to make this implicit use of models explicit. We propose to use models as a teaching tool in all courses where they are helpful, not just in a course on models or model-driven development. Moreover, we present an infrastructure, the Informa Clicker system, that provides support for integrating models into an interactive classroom. Using Informa, instructors can ask students to describe arbitrary concepts by creating and submitting simple models directly in the classroom, and they can ask students to evaluate their peers' models. The resulting models and evaluations allow instructors to quickly spot aspects of the modeled concepts that students misunderstood, and to clarify these misunderstandings within the same lecture.

Our hypothesis is that this use of Informa improves the student's learning as well as their modeling skills. We plan to test this hypothesis in future work.

Threshold Concepts in Object-Oriented Modelling
Ven Yu Sien and David Weng Kwai Chong

Proponents of the object-oriented (OO) paradigm frequently claim that the OO paradigm is "more natural" than the procedural paradigm because the world is filled with objects that have both attributes and behaviors. However students in higher education generally experience considerable difficulty in understanding OO concepts and acquiring the necessary skills in object-oriented analysis and design. This paper proposes OO modelling to be a set of threshold concepts and describes a study that sought to improve undergraduate students learning of OO modelling by adopting concept maps as "stepping stones" to facilitate the development of analysis class and sequence diagrams.

Teaching MDE through the Formal Verification of Process Models
Benoît Combemale, Xavier Crégut, Arnaud Dieumegard, Marc Pantel and Faiez Zalila

Model Driven Engineering (MDE) and formal methods (FM) play a key role in the development of Safety Critical Systems (SCS). They promote user oriented abstraction and formal specification using Domain Specific Modeling Languages (DSML), early Validation and formal Verification (V&V) using efficient dedicated technologies and Automatic Code and Documentation Generation. Their combined use allow to improve system qualities and reduce development costs. However, in most computer science curriculae, both domains are usually taught independently. MDE is associated to practical software engineering and FM to theoretical computer science. This contribution relates a course about MDE for SCS development that bridges the gap between these domains. It describes the content of the course and provides the lessons learned from its teaching. It focuses on early formal verification using model checking of a DSML for development process modeling. MDE technologies are illustrated both on language engineering for CASE tool development and on development process modeling. The case study also highlights the unification power of MDE as it does not target traditional executable software.

Teaching Modeling–An Initial Classification of Related Issues
Ludwik Kuzniarz and Jürgen Börstler

Modeling is an important skill needed in both science and engineering domains. In software engineering, in particular, models are ubiquitous artefacts. The development, manipulation and understanding of models is therefore an important learning objective. The paper describes motivations and an outline of an re-search project aimed at to classifying issues related to the teaching and learning of modeling together with some initial research results.

Position paper: Software Modelling Education
Martina Seidl and Peter Clarke

Model-driven engineering (MDE) is a promising paradigm to deal with the ever increasing complexity of modern software systems. Its powerful abstraction mechanisms allow developers to focus on the essential challenges hiding away irrelevant aspects of the system under development. Within the last few years, noticable progress has been made in putting the vision of MDE into practice, where the activity of textual coding is substituted by modeling. With matured concepts and stable tools available, MDE becomes more and more ready to be applied in software engineering projects.

Nevertheless, the best available technology is worthless, if it is not accepted and used by the developers. Also in MDE profound training is needed to fully exploit its power. In this paper, we discuss the efforts taken in educational environments to promote the application of modeling and MDE technologies for the software development process and discuss several challenges which still have to be faced.

Keynote: **Teaching Student Programmers How to Model:**
Opportunities & Challenges
Robert France

In my experience, students with some programming expertise (or students who believe they are programming experts) tend to view software modeling with great skepticism. They often feel that modeling adds accidental complexity to the software development process as they perceive it.

While we should acknowledge that there may be some elements of truth in their views (new methods, tools and techniques do bring additional baggage that can initially contribute to accidental complexity), we, as educators, should also try to leverage such skepticism in an opportunistic manner. In this talk I'll present some thoughts on how we can leverage such skepticism and also discuss some of the challenges of teaching students how to discover and use "good" abstractions in their models.

3   Thanks

Thanks to all authors who considered EduSymp 2011 for sharing and discussing their thoughts and submitting a paper. Our deepest thanks also go to Robert France, Martina Seidl and Peter Clarke for supporting EduSymp with their additional presentations. Many thanks also go to Jeff Gray, who presented Martina Seidl and Peter Clarkes paper. We would also like to express our gratitude to the program committee who supported excellent and timely reviews, which will provide significant hints to improve and extend the already much elaborated submitted papers.

The list of the international program committee is shown below:

– Colin Atkinson	– Michael Godfrey	– Karl Reed
– Jordi Cabot	– Martin Gogolla	– Jean-Paul Rigault
– Peter J. Clarke	– Øhystein Haugen	– Patricia Roberts
– Ira Diethelm	– Gerti Kappel	– Martina Seidl
– Jean-Marie Favre	– Ludwik Kuzniarz	– Ven Yu Sien
– Robert France	– Jochen Ludewig	

Our thanks also include the additional reviewers (Christina Dörge, Malte Dünnebier, Elena Planas, Lars Hamann, and Manuel Wimmer).

Finally, we like to thank the organizers of MODELS 2011 in Wellington for providing brilliant support for organizing the 7th Educators' SymposiumModels.

Using Constraints
in Teaching Software Modeling

Dan Chiorean[1], Vladiela Petraşcu[1], and Ileana Ober[2]

[1] Babeş-Bolyai University, Cluj-Napoca, Romania
{chiorean,vladi}@cs.ubbcluj.ro
[2] Université Paul Sabatier, Toulouse, France
ober@irit.fr

Abstract. The paper[1] presents an approach to teaching software modeling that has been put into practice at the Babeş-Bolyai University of Cluj-Napoca and Paul Sabatier University in Toulouse. This aims at persuading students of the advantages deriving from the usage of rigorous models. The development of such models, which relies on the Design by Contract technique, is a must in the context of the Model-Driven Engineering paradigm. Another goal of our approach is for students to acquire core software modeling principles and techniques, allowing them to identify and avoid various types of pitfalls enclosed by the modeling examples posted on web. Following a decade of use and teaching of OCL, we have concluded that starting with a defense of the necessity and advantages offered by the use of constraints (an "inverted curriculum" approach) is a far more efficient teaching method compared to a pure technical introduction into the language itself.

Keywords: rigorous modeling, OCL specifications, meaningful specifications, efficient specifications, model understanding.

1 Introduction

In MDE (Model-Driven Engineering), "models are not only the primary artifacts of development, they are also the primary means by which developers and other systems understand, interact with, configure and modify the runtime behavior of software" [9].

The final goal of MDE technologies is to generate easy maintainable applications in various programming languages, such as Java, C#, C++, and so on. This requires starting from complete and unambiguous models, specified by means of rigorous modeling languages. The current technique used to specify languages is metamodeling. Irrespective of the abstraction level involved (meta-meta, meta or model level), in order to achieve rigorous model descriptions, the use of constraints (assertions) is a must.

The use of assertions in software development is promoted by the Design by Contract technique. In [11], the author identifies four applications of their use,

---

[1] This paper is an extended version of [7].

J. Kienzle (Ed.): MODELS 2011 Workshops, LNCS 7167, pp. 25–39, 2012.

namely: help in writing correct software, documentation aid, support for testing, debugging and quality assurance and support for software fault tolerance.

Working with assertions is therefore a core technique that model designers must manage. Despite this, practice shows that Design by Contract is not yet employed at its full potential. This may be due to both the lack of relevant examples showing the advantages of using concrete constraint languages (such as OCL) and the availability of a large number of examples which, at best, cause confusion among readers. An experience of over ten years in teaching OCL to computer science students (at both bachelor and master levels) has allowed us to conclude that, apart from providing positive recommendations (books, papers, tools), warning potential OCL users on the pitfalls enclosed by negative examples is mandatory. As web users, students are exposed to both clear, well-written documents and to documents containing various drawbacks, on whose potential occurrence teachers have the duty of raising warnings. However, merely showing that particular models or specifications are inadequate or even incorrect with respect to the purpose they were created for is not enough. Presenting at least one correct solution and arguing on its advantages is a must.

Complementing models with OCL is meant at eliminating specifications ambiguities, thus increasing rigor, reaching a full and clear definition of query operations, as well as promoting Design by Contract through the specification of pre and post-conditions.

The development of models and applications takes place as an iterative incremental process, allowing return to earlier stages whenever the case. Enhancing models with OCL specifications facilitates their deeper understanding, through both rigor and extra detail. Whenever the results of evaluating OCL specifications suggest a model change, this change should only be done if the new version is more convenient compared to the previous ones, as a whole. The use of OCL specifications should contribute to the requirements validation. An application is considered as finished only when there is full compliance among its requirements, its model, and the application itself.

The remaining of this paper is organized as follows. Section 2 explains the reasons why teaching OCL through examples integrated in models is more advantageous compared to the classical way of teaching OCL. In Section 3, we argue on the necessity of understanding the model's semantics, which is the first prerequisite for achieving a good specification. Section 4 emphasizes the fact that we need to consider several modeling solutions to a problem and choose the most convenient one with respect to the aspects under consideration. Section 5 shows the role of OCL in specifying the various model uses, while Section 6 justifies through an example the need of using snapshots for validating specifications. The paper ends with conclusions in Section 7.

2   Teaching OCL through Examples Integrated in Models

There are various ways of teaching OCL. The classical approach emphasizes the main language features: its declarative nature and first order logic roots, the type system, the management of undefined values, the collection types together with their operations and syntax specificities, and so on [6], [4]. Many of the examples used to introduce collections employ expressions with literals, which are context-independent and easy to understand.

OCL is a textual language which complements MOF (Meta Object Facility)-based modeling languages. The students' interest in understanding and using the language increases if there are persuaded of the advantages earned from enriching models with OCL specifications. To convince students of the usefulness of OCL, the chosen examples should be suggestive in terms of models and enlightening in terms of earned benefits. That is the reason why we have considered more appropriate taking an "inverted curriculum"-type of approach, by introducing OCL through examples in which the OCL specifications are naturally integrated in models. Unfortunately, along with positive OCL specification examples, the existing literature offers also plenty of negative ones, starting with the WFRs (well-formedness rules) that define the static semantics of modeling languages. The negative examples may wrongly influence students' perception. Therefore, we argue that a major issue in teaching OCL to students is explaining them the basic principles that should be obeyed when designing OCL specifications, principles that should help them avoid potential pitfalls.

Two modeling examples that have been probably meant to argue for the use and usefulness of OCL (taking into account the title of the paper in question) are those presented in [15]. The examples and solutions proposed by this article provide an excellent framework for highlighting important aspects that should be taken into account within the modeling process. In the second semester of the 2010-2011 academic year, we have used these examples in order to warn students on the pitfalls that should be avoided when enriching models with OCL specifications.

3   Understanding the Model's Semantics

A model is an abstract description of a problem from a particular viewpoint, given by its intended usage. The design model represents one of the possible solutions to the requirements of the problem to solve. It is therefore essential for the students to realize the necessity of choosing a suitable solution with respect to the aspects under consideration. The first prerequisite for designing such a model is a full understanding of the problem at hand, reflected in a thorough informal requirements specification. Nygaard's statement "Programming is Understanding" [16] is to be read as "Modeling is Understanding", since "Object-oriented development promotes the view that programming is modeling" [12]. Understanding is generally acquired through an iterative and incremental process, in which OCL specifications play a major role. This is due to the fact that "if you don't understand something, you can't code it, and you gain understanding trying to code it." [16]. To be rigorous, "understanding" is only the first mandatory step to be accomplished in both programming and modeling. Finding the problem solution and describing it intelligibly must follow and take advantage of problem understanding. The informal specification of constraints is part of model understanding. Whenever constraints are missing from the initial problem requirements, they should be added in the process of validation and refinement of the informal problem specification.

To illustrate these statements, we will use one of the modeling examples from [15] (shown in Fig. 1), which describes parents-children relationships in a community of persons. The model requirements description is incomplete with respect to both its intended functionalities and its contained information. In such cases, the model specification, both the graphical and the complementary textual one (through Additional Operations - AOs, invariants, pre and post-conditions), should contribute to enriching the requirements description. The process is iterative and incremental, marked by repeated discussions among clients and developers, until the convergence of views from both parties.

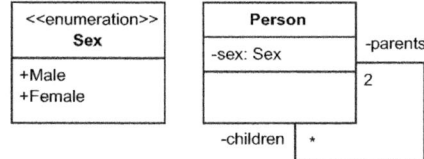

Fig. 1. Genealogical tree model [15]

The proposed solution should allow a correct management of information related to persons, even when this information is incomplete. Unknown ancestors of a particular person is such a case (sometimes not even the natural parents are known). For such cases, the model provided in [15] and reproduced in Fig. 1 is inadequate, due to the infinite recursion induced by the self-association requiring each person to have valid references towards both parents. Snapshots containing persons with at least one parent reference missing will be thus qualified as invalid.

Both this problem and its solution, consisting in relaxing the `parents` multiplicity to 0..2, are now "classical" [5]. Partial or total lack of references (1 or 0 multiplicity) indicates that either one or both parents are unknown at the time.

The only constraint imposed in [15] on the above-mentioned model requires the parents of a person to be of different sexes. Following, there is its OCL specification, as given in [15].

```
self.parents->asSequence()->at(1).sex<>self.parents->asSequence()->at(2).sex
```

The technical quality of formal constraints (stated in either OCL or a different constraint language) follows from the fulfillment of several quality factors. Among them, there is the conformance of their behavior to their informal counterparts, the intelligibility of their formal specification, the debugging support offered in case of constraint violation, the similarity of results following both their evaluation in different constraint-supporting tools and the evaluation of their programming language equivalents (code snippets resulted from translating constraints into a programming language, using the constraint-supporting tools in question)[2]. Based on these considerations, the above specification, although apparently correct, encloses a few pitfalls:

1. In case at least one parent reference is missing and the multiplicity is 2, the evaluation of WFRs should signal the lack of conformance among the multiplicity of links between instances and the multiplicity of their corresponding association. To be meaningful, the evaluation of model-level constraints should be performed only in case the model satisfies all WFRs. Unfortunately, such model compilability checks are not current practice. In case the `parents` multiplicity is 0..2 and one of the parents is left unspecified, the model will comply with the WFRs, but the constraint evaluation will end up in an exception when trying to access the missing parent (due to the `at(2)` call).

2. In case there are valid references to both parents, but the sex of one of them is not specified, the value of the corresponding subexpression is `undefined` and the whole expression reduces to either `Sex::Male <> undefined` or `Sex::Female <> undefined`. This later expressions provide tool-dependent evaluation results (`true` in case of USE [1] or Dresden OCL [14] and `undefined` in case of OCLE [10]). The results produced by OCLE comply with the latest OCL 2.3 specification [13]. However, as the topic of evaluating undefined values has not yet reached a common agreement, students should be warned on this.

3. Moreover, in case one of the parents' sex is undefined, the code generated for the above constraint will provide evaluation results which depend on the position of the `undefined` value with respect to the comparison operator. According to the tests we have performed[3], the Java code generated by OCLE and Dresden OCL throws a `NullPointerException` when the `undefined` value is located at the left of the `<>` operator, while evaluating to `true` in case the `undefined` value is at the right of the operator and the reference at the left is a valid one. As we are in the context of the MDE paradigm, which relies extensively on automatic code generation, the results provided by the execution of the code corresponding to constraints is an aspect that has to be taken into account when judging the quality of the formal constraints in question.

4. The OCL expression would have been simpler (not needing an `asSequence()` call), in case an ordering relation on `parents` had been imposed at the model level.

Similar to most of the activities involved in software production, the specification of assertions is an iterative and incremental process. That is why, in the following, we will illustrate such a process for the considered family case study. For the purpose of this section, we will work with the model from Fig. 1, assuming

---

[2] Apart from the technical issues involved in evaluating the quality of assertions, there is also an efficiency issue, concerned with aspects such as the efficiency of the assertion specifications themselves, the amount of undesirable system states that can be monitored by using assertions, as well as their level of detail.

[3] The corresponding Java/AspectJ projects can be downloaded from [2].

though that the multiplicity of the `parents` reference has been set to 0..2, so as to avoid infinite recursion.

Ordering the `parents` collection with respect to sex (such that the first element points to the mother and the second to the father) allows writing an invariant that is more detailed compared to the one proposed in [15] for the constraint regarding the parents' sex. Following, there is the OCL specification we propose in this respect, when both parents are known. In case of invariant violation, the debugging information is precise, allowing to easily eliminate the error's cause.

```
context Person
 inv parentsSexP1:
  self.parents->size() = 2 implies
   Sex::Female = self.parents->first().sex and
   Sex::Male = self.parents->last().sex
```

When any of the parents' sex is `undefined`, the invariant above evaluates to `false` in Dresden OCL and to `undefined` in OCLE. In similar circumstances, both Java code snippets generated for this invariant by the two tools return `false` when executed. Therefore, this invariant shape overcomes the drawbacks of the one from [15] previously pointed at items 1, 3 and 4. The triggering of a `NullPointerException` by the generated code in case of absence of one of the parents' sex has been avoided by placing the defined values (the `Sex::Female` and `Sex::Male` literals) on the left-hand side of equalities.

The solution to the problem mentioned at item 2 above comes from obeying to the separation of concerns principle. In order to avoid comparisons involving `undefined` values, whose results may vary with the OCL-supporting tool used, the equality tests of the parents' sex with the corresponding enumeration literals should be conditioned by both of them being specified. Such a solution is illustrated by means of the invariant proposal below.

```
context Person
 inv parentsSexP2:
  self.parents->size() = 2 implies
  ( let mother = self.parents->first() in
    let father = self.parents->last() in
     if (not mother.sex.oclIsUndefined() and not father.sex.oclIsUndefined())
     then mother.sex = Sex::Female and father.sex = Sex::Male
     else false
     endif
  )
```

The invariant above evaluates to `false` when any of the parents' sex is `undefined`, as well as when they are both defined but set inappropriately (the first parent's sex is not `Sex::Female` or the second is not `Sex::Male`, as previously established by the ordering rule). The evaluation results are the same for both the OCL constraint and its Java equivalent, irrespective of the tool used, OCLE or Dresden OCL. Therefore, this last invariant shape provides solutions to all pitfalls previously detected for its analogue from [15].

Yet, a correct understanding of the model in question leads to the conclusion that the mere constraint regarding the parents' sex is insufficient, despite its explicit specification for each parent. As rightly noticed in [5], a person cannot be its own child. A corresponding OCL constraint should be therefore explicitly specified.

```
context Person
  inv notSelfParent:
    self.parents->select(p | p = self)->isEmpty()
```

However, restricting the age difference among parents and children to be at least the minimum age starting from which human reproduction is possible (we have considered the age of sixteen) leads to a stronger and finer constraint than the previous, that may be stated as follows.

```
context Person
  inv parentsAge:
    self.parents->reject(p | p.age - self.age >= 16)->isEmpty()
```

In the above expression, each `Person` is assumed to own an `age` attribute. In case both the contextual instance and its parents have valid values for the `age` slot, the `reject(...)` subexpression evaluates to the collection of parents breaking the constraint in question.

The fulfillment of this constraint could be also required at any point in the construction of the genealogical tree. Assuming any parent to be created prior to any of its children, this restriction could be stated by means of the precondition included in the contract below.

```
context Person::addChildren(p:Person)
  pre childrenAge:
    self.children->excludes(p) and self.age - p.age >= 16
  post chidrenAge:
    self.children->includes(p)
```

The conclusion that emerges so far is that the lack of OCL specifications prohibiting undesired model instances (such as parents having the same sex, self-parentship or the lack of a minimum age difference among parents and children) seriously compromises model's integrity. The first prerequisite for models to reach their purpose is to have a complete and correct specification of requirements, and to deeply understand them. An incomplete specification reveals its limits when trying to answer questions on various situations that may arise. Specifying and evaluating OCL constraints should enable us to identify and eliminate bugs, by correcting the requirements and the OCL specifications themselves. Moreover, in the context of MDE, care should be taken to the shape of constraint specifications, ensuring that their evaluation using OCL-supporting tools provides identical results to those obtained by executing their equivalent code generated by those tools. Another conclusion, as important, is that the model proposed in the analyzed paper does not fully meet the needs of the addressed problem[4] and we are therefore invited to seek for a better solution.

---

[4] In case there is a single parent specified, we have no means to check whether the sex has been set appropriately, according to its role (mother or father) and we may need extra attributes (e.g. age) for specifying finer constraints.

4   Modeling Alternatives

A model equivalent to that of Fig. 1, but which is more adequate to the specification of the required constraints, is the one illustrated in Fig. 2. The model in question contains two recursive associations: one named MotherChildren, with roles mother[0..1] and mChildren[0..*] and the other FatherChildren, with roles father[0..1] and fChildren[0..*].

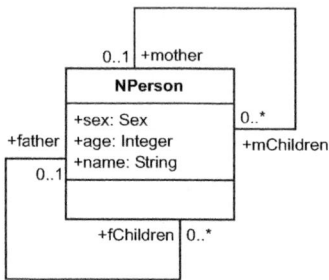

Fig. 2. An alternative model for expressing parents-children relationships

Within this model, the constraint regarding the parent' sex can be stated as proposed below.

```
context NPerson
 inv parentsSexP1:
  (self.mother->size() = 1 implies Sex::Female = self.mother.sex) and
  (self.father->size() = 1 implies Sex::Male = self.father.sex)
```

Compared to its equivalent constraint stated for the model in Fig. 1, the above one is wider, since it also covers the case with a single parent and checks the sex constraint corresponding to the parent in question. As previously pointed out, the problem with the initial model (the one in Fig. 1) is that we cannot count on an ordering when there is a single parent reference available. The parent in question would always be on the first position, irrespective of its sex. As opposed to this, in Fig. 2, the parents' roles are explicitly specified, with no extra memory required. When at least one parent's sex is **undefined**, the evaluation of this invariant returns **undefined** in OCLE and **false** in Dresden OCL, while the execution of the corresponding Java code outputs **false** in both cases. Given the invariant shape, the identification of the person breaking it is quite straightforward, therefore the problem can be rapidly fixed.

An alternative invariant shape, providing the same evaluation result in both OCLE and Dresden OCL, for both OCL and Java code is the one below.

```
context NPerson:
 inv parentsSexP2:
  (self.mother->size() = 1 implies
   (let ms:Sex = self.mother.sex in
     if not ms.oclIsUndefined() then ms = Sex::Female
     else false endif )
  ) and
```

```
(self.father->size () = 1 implies
 (let fs:Sex = self.father.sex in
  if not fs.oclIsUndefined() then fs = Sex::Male
  else false endif)
)
```

With respect to the second constraint, we propose the following specification in context of the model from Fig. 2.

```
context NPerson
 inv parentsAge:
  self.mChildren ->reject(p | self.age - p.age >= 16)->isEmpty() and
  self.fChildren ->reject(p | self.age - p.age >= 16)->isEmpty()
```

The `parentsAge` invariant above uses one of the specification patterns that we have proposed in [8] for the *For All* constraint pattern. If we were to follow the classical specification patterns available in the literature, the invariant would have looked as follows.

```
context NPerson
 inv parentsAgeL:
  self.mChildren ->forAll(p | self.age - p.age >= 16) and
  self.fChildren ->forAll(p | self.age - p.age >= 16)
```

A simple analysis of these two proposals reveals that the `parentsAgeL` invariant shape is closer to first order logic. However, in case of constraint violation, this does not provide any useful information concerning those persons breaking the invariant, as the first one does. The specification style used for the `parentsAge` invariant offers model-debugging support [8], a major concern when writing assertions.

The corresponding pre and post-conditions are similar to their equivalents from the previous section, therefore their specification could be left to students, as homework.

5   Explaining the Intended Model Uses

Any requirements specification should include a detailed description of the intended model uses. In case of the model under consideration, it is important to know what kind of information may be required from it. Is it merely the list of parents and that of all ancestors? Do we want the list of ancestors ordered, with each element containing parents-related information, in case such information is available? Do we only need information regarding the male descendents of a person?

In case of the initial model in which the recursive association is ordered, the list of all ancestors of a person can be easily computed as follows.

```
context Person
  def allAncestors():Sequence (Person) =
    self.parents ->union(self.parents.allAncestors())
```

The evaluation result for the constraint above is correct only if we assume the genealogical tree as loop-free. This latter constraint is implied by the one restricting the minimum age difference between parents and children. In the absence of this assumption, the OCL expression's complexity increases.

A simpler alternative for this case employs the semantic closure operation on collections. This operation, now included in OCL 2.3, has been implemented in OCLE ever since its first release and returns a set.

```
context Person
  def allAncestors():Sequence(Person) =
  (Sequence{self}->closure(p | p.parents))->asSequence()
```

The advantages offered by the modeling solution proposed in Fig. 2 are clear in case we are interested to compute all ancestors of a person, specifying explicitly which of them are unknown (not stored in the database). Following, there is a possible OCL query to be used in this purpose, that employs the tuple type.

```
context NPerson
  def tParents: TupleType(ch:NPerson, mo:NPerson, fa:NPerson) =
  Tuple{ch = self, mo = self.mother, fa = self.father}

  def allTParents: Sequence(TupleType(ch:NPerson, mo:NPerson, fa:NPerson)) =
  Sequence{self.tParents}->closure(i | Sequence{i.mo.tParents, i.fa.tParents})
                      ->asSequence()->prepend(self.tParents)
```

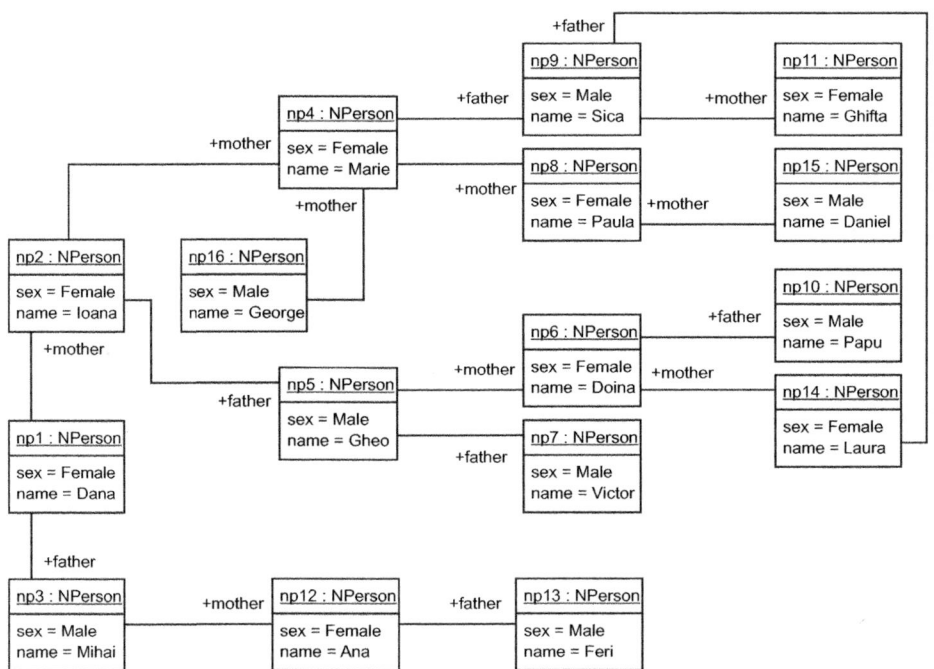

Fig. 3. Sample snapshot of the model from Fig. 2

Evaluating in OCLE the family tree presented in Fig. 3, we obtain:

```
Sequence{Tuple{np1,np2,np3,}, Tuple{np2,np4,np5}, Tuple{np3,np12,Undefined},
   Tuple{np4,np8,np9}, Tuple{np5,np6,np7}, Tuple{np12,Undefined,np13},
   Undefined, Tuple{np8,Undefined,Undefined}, Tuple{np9,np11,Undefined},
   Tuple{np6,Undefined,np10}, Tuple{np7,Undefined,Undefined},
   Tuple{np13,Undefined,Undefined}, Tuple{np11,Undefined,Undefined},
   Tuple{np10,Undefined,Undefined}
}
```

Since the members of each tuple are (child, mother, father), in this particular order, the analysis of the above evaluation result allows an easy representation of the corresponding genealogical tree.

With respect to a potential query meant to compute all descendants of a person, the only difference between the two proposed models concerns the computation of a person's children. In this respect, the model in Fig. 1 already contains a **children** reference, while in case of the one from Fig. 2, a corresponding query needs to be defined, as shown below.

```
context NPerson
  def children: Set(NPerson) =
  if self.sex = Sex::Female
  then self.m_children
  else self.f_children
  endif
```

6   Using Snapshots to Better Understand and Improve the Requirements and the Model

One of the primary roles of constraints is to avoid different interpretations of the same model. Therefore, the specification process must be seen as an invitation for a complete and rigorous description of the problem, including the constraints that are part of the model. The model must conform to the informally described requirements, even before attaching constraints. In case this condition is not fulfilled, the constraints specification process must ask for additional information, meant to support an improved description of requirements, a deeper understanding of the problem, and by consequence, a clear model specification.

Despite its importance, as far as we know, this issue has not been approached in the literature. That is why, in the following, we will try to analyze the second example presented in [15], concerning a library model. This example aims to model the contractual relationships between a library, its users and companies associated with the library. The only informal specification provided is the following: "In this example, we'll assume that the library offers a subscription to each person employed in an associated company. In this case, the employee does not have a contract with the library but with the society he works for, instead. So we add the following constraint (also shown in Figure 10): ...".

First of all, we would like to remind the definition of a contract, as taken from [3]: "A binding agreement between two or more parties for performing, or refraining from performing, some specified act(s) in exchange for lawful consideration." According to this definition and to the informal description of requirements, we conclude that, in our case, the parts in the contract are: the user on the one

hand, and the library or the company, on the other hand. As one of the involved
parts is always the user, the other part is either the library (in case the user is
not employed in any of the library's associated companies), or the company (in
case the user is an employee of the company in question).

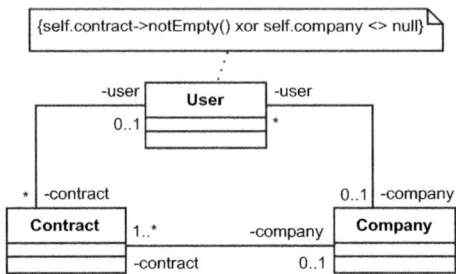

Fig. 4. The library model from [15], Figure 10

Regarding the conformance among requirements, on the one side, and model,
on the other side (the class diagram, the invariant presented in Figure 10 and
the snapshots given in Figures 12 and 13 of [15]), several questions arise. Since
a thorough analysis is not allowed by the space constraints of this paper, in the
following, we will only approach the major aspects related to the probable usage
of the model. In our opinion, this concerns the information system of a library,
that stores information about library users, associated companies, books, book
copies and loans. The library may have several users and different associated
companies.

Since the Library concept is missing from the model proposed in [15], we
have no guaranty that, in case the user is unemployed, the second participant
to the contract is the library. Moreover, in case the user is employed, the invariant proposed in [15] does not ensure that both the user and the corresponding
company are the participants to the contract. As a solution to this, we propose an improved model for the Library case study (see Fig. 5), as well as two
corresponding invariants, in the context of Contract and User, respectively.

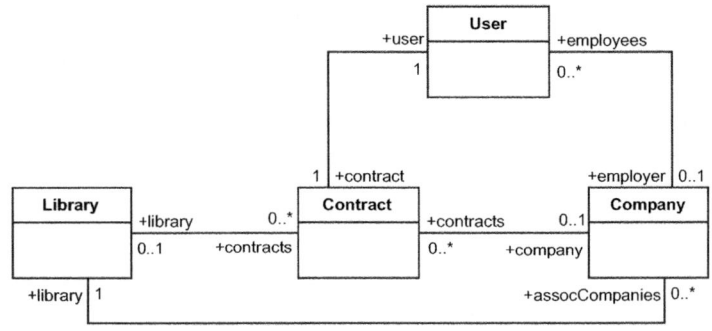

Fig. 5. A revised version of an excerpt of the library model from [15]

```
context Contract
 inv onlyOneSecondParticipant:
  self.library->isEmpty() xor self.company->isEmpty()

context User
 inv theContractIsWithTheEmployer:
  if self.employer->isEmpty()
  then self.contract.library->notEmpty()
  else self.employer = self.contract.company
  endif
```

The above constraints forbid situations like those from Fig. 6 (in which the user u1 has a contract c1 both with the library l1 and the company comp1) and Fig. 7 (in which the user is employed by comp3, but its contract c2 is with comp2). These undesirable model instantiations are not ruled out by the invariant proposed in [15] in the User context.

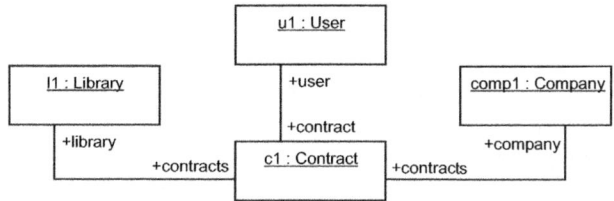

Fig. 6. The user has a contract with both the library and the company

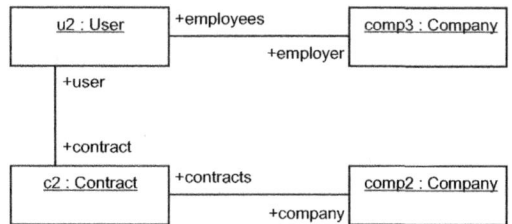

Fig. 7. The user is employed by comp3, but its contract c2 is with comp2

Even more, in Figure 12 from [15], contractB65 and contractR43 have only one participant, company80Y, a stange situation in our oppinion. Also, in the same figure, if userT6D is unemployed by company80Y, and, by consequence, contractQVR is between userT6D and the library, we cannot understand why company80Y (which does not include among its employees userT6D) has a reference towards contractQVR between userT6D and the library.

Unfortunately, as stated before, our questions do not stop here. In Figure 10 from [15], a user may have many contracts, but in the requirements a different situation is mentioned. In the class diagram of Figure 10, all role names are implicit, fact that burdens the inteligibility of the model.

In this example, the snapshots meant to be used for testing have supported us in understanding that the requirements are incomplete and, by consequence, so are the model and the proposed invariant. In such cases, improving the requirements is mandatory.

7 Conclusions

The building of rigorous models, which are consistent with the problem requirements and have predictable behavior, relies on the use of constraints. Such constraints are not stand alone, they refer to the model in question. Consequently, the model's accuracy (in terms of the concepts used, their inter-relationships, as well as conformance to the problem requirements) is a mandatory precondition for the specification of correct and effective constraints. In turn, a full understanding of the model's semantics and usage requires a complete and unambiguous requirements specification. Requirements' validation is therefore mandatory for the specification of useful constraints.

The examples presented in this paper illustrate a number of bugs caused by failure to fulfill the above-mentioned requirements. Unfortunately, the literature contains many erroneous OCL specifications, including those concerning the UML static semantics, in all its available releases. Having free access to public resources offered via the web, students should know how to identify and correct errors such as those presented in this article. Our conclusion is that the common denominator for all the analyzed errors is *hastiness*: hastiness in specifying requirements, hastiness in designing the model (OCL specifications included), hastiness in building and interpreting snapshots (test data).

There are, undoubtedly, several ways of teaching OCL. The most popular (which we have referred as the "classic" one, due to its early use in teaching programming languages), focuses on introducing the language features. OCL being a complementary language, we deemed important to emphasize from the start the gain that can be achieved in terms of model accuracy by an inverted curriculum approach. In this context, we have insisted on the need of a complete and accurate requirements specification, on various possible design approaches for the same problem, on the necessity of testing all specifications by means of snapshots, as well as on the need to consider the effects of a particular OCL constraint shape on the execution of the code generated for the constraint in question.

However, the teaching and using of OCL involves a number of other very important issues that have been either not addressed or merely mentioned in this article, such as the specifications' intelligibility, their support for model testing and debugging, test data generation, language features, etc. This paper only focuses on the OCL introduction on new projects, with a closer look on training issues, this is why we have not detailed on the above mentioned topics.

Acknowledgements. This work was supported by CNCSIS - UEFISCSU, project number PNII – IDEI 2049/2008.

References

1. A UML-based Specification Environment,
   `http://www.db.informatik.uni-bremen.de/projects/USE`
2. Frame Based on the Extensive Use of Metamodeling for the Specification, Implementation and Validation of Languages and Applications (EMF_SIVLA) - Project Deliverables, `http://www.cs.ubbcluj.ro/ vladi/CUEM_SIVLA/deliverables/EduSymp2011/workspaces.zip`
3. InvestorWords, `http://www.investorwords.com/1079/contract.html`
4. The OCL portal,
   `http://st.inf.tu-dresden.de/ocl/index.php?`
   `option=com_content&view=category&id=5&Itemid=30`
5. Cabot, J.: Common UML errors (I): Infinite recursive associations (2011),
   `http://modeling-languages.com/`
   `common-uml-errors-i-infinite-recursive-associations/`
6. Chimiak-Opoka, J., Demuth, B.: Teaching OCL Standard Library: First Part of an OCL 2.x Course. ECEASST, vol. 34 (2010)
7. Chiorean, D., Ober, I., Petraşcu, V.: Avoiding OCL Specification Pitfalls. In: Proceedings of the 7th Educators Symposium: Software Modeling in Education at MODELS 2011 (EduSymp 2011). Electronic Communications of the EASST, vol. xx, 10 pages. EASST (2011)
8. Chiorean, D., Petraşcu, V., Ober, I.: Testing-Oriented Improvements of OCL Specification Patterns. In: Proceedings of the 2010 IEEE International Conference on Automation, Quality and Testing, Robotics - AQTR, vol. II, pp. 143–148. IEEE Computer Society (2010)
9. France, R., Rumpe, B.: Model-driven development of complex software: A research roadmap. In: 2007 Future of Software Engineering, FOSE 2007, pp. 37–54. IEEE Computer Society, Washington, DC (2007),
   `http://dx.doi.org/10.1109/FOSE.2007.14`
10. LCI (Laboratorul de Cercetare în Informatică): Object Constraint Language Environment (OCLE), `http://lci.cs.ubbcluj.ro/ocle/`
11. Meyer, B.: Object-Oriented Software Construction, 2nd edn. Prentice Hall (1997)
12. Nierstrasz, O.: Synchronizing Models and Code (2011), Invited Talk at TOOLS 2011 Federated Conference, `http://toolseurope2011.lcc.uma.es/#speakers`
13. OMG (Object Management Group): Object Constraint Language (OCL), Version 2.3 Beta 2 (2011), `http://www.omg.org/spec/OCL/2.3/Beta2/PDF`
14. Software Technology Group at Technische Universität Dresden: Dresden OCL,
   `http://www.dresden-ocl.org/index.php/DresdenOCL`
15. Todorova, A.: Produce more accurate domain models by using OCL constraints (2011), `https://www.ibm.com/developerworks/rational/library/accurate-domain-models-using-ocl-constraints-rational-software-architect/`
16. Venners, B.: Abstraction and Efficiency. A Conversation with Bjarne Stroustrup - Part III (2004), `http://www.artima.com/intv/abstreffi2.html`

Mismatches between Industry Practice and Teaching of Model-Driven Software Development

Jon Whittle and John Hutchinson

School of Computing and Communications
Infolab21, Lancaster University, UK
{j.n.whittle,j.hutchinson}@lancaster.ac.uk

Abstract. EAMDE was a 12 month research project, investigating how industry uses model-driven software development (MDSD). Using quantitative and qualitative research techniques, experiences were collected on the adoption and application of MDSD in 17 companies. The study highlighted examples of good and bad practice that lead to success or failure with MDSD. Some of these practices appear to have ramifications on the way that MDSD, and software modeling more generally, is taught within universities. This paper presents three of the key findings relevant to education: (1) A significant number of successful MDSD companies build their own modeling languages and generators, suggesting a re-orientation of education away from UML notation to fundamental modeling principles; (2) MDSD is generally taught top-down, whereas industry success is more likely when MDSD is applied bottom-up; (3) successful application of MDSD requires skills both in abstract modeling and compilers/optimization; however, these skills tend to be separated in standard CS curricula.

Keywords: model-driven software development, education.

1   Introduction

EAMDE was a twelve month empirical research project, beginning in October 2009, that aimed to investigate how industry applies model-driven software development (MDSD) in practice. The original motivation behind EAMDE was that, whilst there are some clear benefits to MDSD (such as increased productivity through code generation), there are also some potential drawbacks (such as increased training costs or difficulties in integrating legacy code). The project aimed to discover what factors – technical, organizational and social – lead some companies to succeed with MDSD, whereas others fail.

The methodology was to apply quantitative and qualitative research methods to understand when, how and why companies do or do not succeed with MDSD. A three pronged approach was followed: (i) a questionnaire widely disseminated to MDSD practitioners, which received over 400 responses; (ii) in-depth interviews with 22 MDSD professionals from 17 different companies; (iii) on-site studies observing MDSD in practice. In particular, the in-depth interviews were recorded and

J. Kienzle (Ed.): MODELS 2011 Workshops, LNCS 7167, pp. 40–47, 2012.

transcribed, resulting in over 150,000 words describing rich and detailed experiences of the application of MDSD spanning many years and covering a wide range of MDSD knowledge (our interviewees had more than 360 years of software engineering cumulative industrial experience).

The study was intended as an exploratory one, from which key themes would emerge to suggest more formal research hypotheses. Results from the study have previously been described [1, 2]. In addition, however, some of the themes that emerged relate to the way that MDSD, and software modeling more generally, is taught in universities.

This paper reports briefly on three key findings from the EAMDE study that suggest a reconsideration of the way that modeling is taught. For each, we present the finding, illustrate it using examples from our interviews, and suggest an alternative educational approach.

2   Greater Emphasis on Domain-Specific Modeling

A key observation from our study is that MDSD may be much more widespread than is generally believed. We have found that some form of MDSD is practised widely, across a diverse range of industries (including automotive, banking, printing, web applications etc.) and in companies of varied size. The questionnaire respondents, for example, (all of whom were MDSD practitioners) were employed in a range of different roles (37% developers, 36% project managers) and represented a good spread of size of company with respect to the number of people involved in software development (e.g. 53%<100 and 20%>1000).

Perhaps surprisingly, a significant number of MDSD examples from our study followed domain-specific modeling paradigms. Around 46% of questionnaire respondents used in-house or vendor-provided domain-specific modeling languages (DSLs). Interview data shows that a very successful approach is to develop small DSLs for narrow, well-understood domains. Practical application of domain modeling is pragmatic, where DSLs (and accompanying generators) are developed sometimes in as little as two weeks. Hence, much MDSD success is 'hidden' – in the sense that there is very widespread use of mini-DSLs, often textual, and that there may be many such mini-DSLs used within a single project: one interviewee reported on the use of multiple XML-based DSLs to generate 70% of a system, for example.

This evidence of practice has ramifications on the way that modeling is taught. Most modeling courses tend to focus on UML and, furthermore, emphasize the presentation of notation rather than principles. This occurs perhaps because it is straightforward to teach notation – an OMG standard exists that describes the notation explicitly and therefore offers a clear path to follow both for textbook writers and educationalists. In contrast, there are relatively few books that teach modeling principles. Our study suggests that, although UML may be an important language to learn, it may be more beneficial to focus on underlying modeling skills. The prevalence of DSLs points to the need for developers with skills in modeling that may be divorced from any specific knowledge of UML notation.

Note that this does not necessarily mean a switch to focus on the notational details of a particular metamodeling framework. Rather, we would advocate an emphasis on getting students to understand the key concepts in a domain and using DSLs to show how such concepts can be structured and organized. Most UML books put notation first and concept structuring is either only secondary or hidden entirely. Although much more limited, books on DSLs (e.g., [3]) seem to do a better job of teaching general principles of (domain) modeling.

The following quote from one of our interviewees is illustrative of the kind of difficulties that a focus on notation can bring.

What we found is when we taught UML, we'd be teaching about classes and inheritance relationships etc., and there'd be no practical use of this then you'd give an exercise and of course it would be done badly... And what we basically realised is we were spending much much more time discussing the semantics of the language...so we scrapped the course completely... we went out, we bought 4 boxes of the monopoly board game... We gave them this, we said go model the game using these concepts.... We reintroduced the core of UML, class diagrams, in about an hour and then we had people get on with it. We set this up so they would spend 7/8 hours – a whole day – just modelling, playing with the concepts, so they could write down things and then actually work with the sort of physical version of this actually using the monopoly pieces, and actually exploring the concepts within this simple board game – it's quite a challenging board game

3   Teach MDSD Bottom-Up Rather Than Top-Down

Following on from the previous section, our findings lead us to believe that successful MDSD practice tends to be driven from the ground-up. MDSD efforts that are imposed from high-level management typically struggle. As a result, there are fewer examples of the use of MDSD to generate whole systems. Rather than following heavyweight top-down methodologies, successful MDSD practitioners use MDSD as and when it is appropriate and combine it with other methods in a pragmatic fashion. Those companies that do succeed invariably do so by driving MDSD adoption from the bottom-up: that is, small teams of developers try out aspects of MDSD, which in turn leads them to recognize reusable assets, and eventually MDSD propagates upwards to the organisation as a whole. The following quote from our interviews is typical:

Yes, yes of course we started just with a few components and we started I think around [the year] 2000 with the first component and now I think 50-60% of all our code is from re-used building blocks but in the beginning it was only 5% or 10%

This way of working suggests that developers find it easier to get to grips with MDSD when they use it to refactor existing assets from the ground-up rather than trying to abstract from above. In turn, it suggests that modeling should be taught bottom-up rather than top-down.

A typical course in software modeling (and in software engineering, more generally) teaches in a top-down fashion in which requirements models are first developed and are then iteratively refined into architecture, design, code, etc. Students often have a great deal of difficulty proceeding in this manner because it requires formulating abstractions of a system before the concrete details are understood [4].

Given that success in industry seems to be associated with bottom-up introduction of MDSD, we advocate an approach to teaching MDSD that mirrors this practice. Although as yet we have no concrete proposals for such a course, one can imagine a programming-focused module that starts with an existing system and asks students to develop slightly different versions of some features of the system. This process could then be used to discuss the merits of defining reusable assets and abstracting from those assets by defining a modeling language and code generator. The advantage of such a course over most existing modeling courses would be that abstraction skills are introduced and nurtured using very specific, concrete examples, which give students a handle on the difficult topic of abstraction.

4   Integrate Abstraction and Compiler Skills within CS Curricula

As we have seen previously, successful MDSD companies often develop in-house domain-specific languages and code generators, or, in some cases, they extend or modify off-the-shelf tools. In the interviews, we heard of two ways of achieving this task: either use separate developers, one for modeling and one for writing a generator that could produce optimized code, or use a single developer capable of carrying out both developing a DSL and writing a decent generator for it. The following quote is indicative of the former approach:

> …they couldn't optimize the generated code so the way they had to do it was asking the hardware guys to have more hard disc, more memory, because of the tool. So beforehand we had very small memories and we'd been using C and we were very clear about the memory map and each engineer has a clear view on how much memory space they can use. But this case we cannot do something with the generated code so we simply ask the hardware guys to have more hard disc.

The interviews tend to suggest that the second way of working is more successful. In other words, companies that are successful with MDSD tend to have MDSD 'gurus' within the organization who possess a combination of skills in both abstraction (modeling, metamodeling, DSLs, etc.) and compiler/optimization. It is interesting to note, however, that these two skill sets – abstraction/modeling and compiler/optimizations – tend to be quite far apart in typical CS curricula. Although it may be common for a compiler course to be included as a core module, taken by all CS students, software engineering is typically taught very separately from this and usually does not make much reference to it, if any. The danger is that students specializing in software engineering receive only very basic training in compiler/optimization skills, which may cause problems when applying MDSD in practice, as the following quote illustrates:

The tool itself is very inefficient. But I also developed a lot of CASE tools whilst I was at the university as a PhD student, but if somebody asks me how to optimize your code from your CASE tool, then I don't know how to do that!

Based on our study, we would argue that perhaps abstraction and compilation/optimization techniques ought to be taught together in an integrated fashion. Although further study is needed to validate this hypothesis, such an idea would radically alter the way that software engineering is taught and would skill-up a new generation of developers capable of both abstracting in a problem space and transitioning to a solution space in an efficient manner.

5   Additional Findings on MDSD Education and Training

The previous three sections have outlined three key education-related findings in our study and have shown how these findings uncover mismatches between industry practice and current educational philosophies; we proposed, in each case, a way of changing modeling education practice to address these mismatches.

In this section, we briefly mention some other, less significant, results from our study related to MDSD education and training. Our questionnaire was designed to be a broad-brush investigation of factors that affect MDSD success. In particular, however, a significant part of the questionnaire was designed to unravel well-known points of contention regarding the use of MDSD. As with any new technology, there are a number of influencing factors that shape how effective MDSD will be when applied. Some of these factors have a clear positive impact on success criteria such as productivity and maintainability. Such positive influences, however, are balanced by potential negative influences from the same or competing factors. One reason why the idea of MDSD has caused heated debates over recent years is because we do not yet fully understand in which contexts the positive influences outweigh the negative ones. As a simple example, code generation in MDSD appears, at first glance, to have a positive effect on productivity. But the need to integrate generated code with existing systems may lead to reduced productivity. Such tensions are perhaps one reason why the literature cites conflicting evidence of MDE benefits – productivity gains ranging from -27% to +1000%, for example [5-7].

To unpick these conflicting factors affecting MDSD success, our questionnaire included a set of paired questions that asked about practitioners' experiences of positive and negative influences.

Although the questionnaire was not specific to MDSD education, and indeed covered a wide range of issues, one of the set of paired questions was designed to understand whether MDSD overall leads to an increase or decrease in training costs when companies adopt MDSD. The reason for asking such questions was anecdotal evidence about the impact of MDSD on training. Some assume, for example, that MDSD allows companies to make use of less experienced software engineers. This is because model-based code generators can build in design decisions and low-level programming decisions which, in turn, means that new employees do not necessarily need to fully understand such decisions. This phenomenon was, for example, one of the major findings in a Middleware Research study on MDSD productivity [8]. On the other hand, one could clearly argue that MDSD has the potential to increase training costs because of the need to train new employees in modeling tools and approaches. Our paired questions were therefore designed to ask about both sides of this debate.

Questionnaire respondents were asked the following two questions:

1. Training: Does using MDSD allow you to employ developers with less software engineering experience (e.g. new graduates)?[1]
2. Training: Does using MDSD require you to carry out significant extra training in modeling?

The responses to questions 1 and 2 are presented in Figures 1 and 2 respectively.

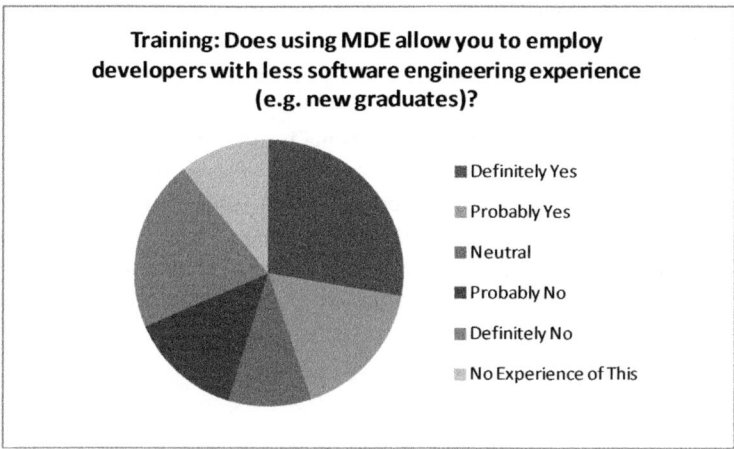

Fig. 1. Responses to question 1

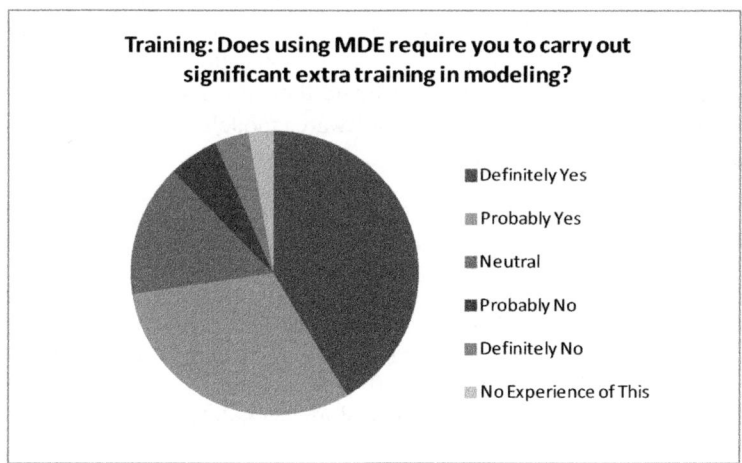

Fig. 2. Responses to question 2

---

[1] MDE was the term used in the questionnaire, rather than MDSD.

Figure 1 provides convincing evidence that some companies are indeed able to apply MDSD with less experienced software engineers, with almost 45% saying that they can definitely or probably do so. However, a further 10% were neutral and almost 35% said that they definitely or probably couldn't. Figure 2 shows that over 70% of respondents say they are definitely or probably required to carry out significant extra training in modeling. This means that a relatively small number (<10%) believe that the necessary skills already exist – in turn, this suggests that any new graduates being used to apply MDSD are probably not already equipped with the skills necessary to use MDSD in industry.

Although care must be taken in comparing the results of these two questions, a comparison does provide some insights into whether overall training costs are higher or lower. Since a healthy majority claim that MDSD allows their company to hire less experience software engineers, yet a *strong* majority say that significant extra training is required due to MDSD, it does seem that, on balance, MDSD probably increases overall training costs.

Clearly, there may be many nuanced reasons for this in practice, and simple yes-no questions in a survey cannot uncover these. However, when comparing these results with interview data, it is possible to conclude that one of the reasons that training costs increase may be due to insufficient education in MDSD in universities. Arguably, if the mismatches between university education and industry practice highlighted in this paper were to be addressed, then industry training costs for MDSD could be lowered.

6   Conclusion

This paper has presented some insights from a large scale study on industry adoption of MDSD, concentrating on those findings relevant to MDSD education. The paper has suggested three ways to reconsider the way MDSD is taught, to better align it with industry practice. At this point, these suggestions are untested so further educational research is required to investigate their potential benefits and understand their drawbacks. We encourage the software modeling research community to investigate these hypotheses further.

References

[1] Hutchinson, J., Whittle, J., Rouncefield, M., Kristoffersen, S.: Empirical assessment of MDE in industry. In: ICSE 2011, pp. 471–480 (2011)
[2] Hutchinson, J., Rouncefield, M., Whittle, J.: Model-driven engineering practices in industry. In: ICSE 2011, pp. 633–642 (2011)
[3] Clark, T., Sammut, P., Willans, J.: Applied Metamodelling, A Foundation for Language Development, 2nd edn., Ceteva (2008)
[4] Kramer, J.: Is abstraction the key to computing? Commun. ACM 50(4), 36–42 (2007)
[5] Mohagheghi, P., Dehlen, V.: Where Is the Proof? - A Review of Experiences from Applying MDE in Industry. In: Schieferdecker, I., Hartman, A. (eds.) ECMDA-FA 2008. LNCS, vol. 5095, pp. 432–443. Springer, Heidelberg (2008)

[6] Kelly, S., Pohjonen, R.: Worst Practices for Domain-Specific Modeling. IEEE Software 26(4), 22–29 (2009)

[7] Kelly, S., Tolvanen, J.-P.: Domain-Specific Modeling: Enabling Full Code Generation. John Wiley & Sons (2008)

[8] The Middleware Company, Model Driven Development for J2EE Utilizing a Model Driven Architecture (MDA) Approach: Productivity Analysis, http://www.omg.org/mda/mda_files/MDA_Comparison-TMC_final.pdf (accessed September 2011)

VARY – Variability for You

Øystein Haugen

SINTEF
oystein.haugen@sintef.no

Abstract. The VARY workshop took place on the first day of the MODELS conference week and brought together researchers and practitioners in the field of variability modeling. The workshop contained invited talks on empirics of MDD and reuse, and on the Common Variability Language standardization. The example session showed how variability modeling could be useful in e-commerce and multiple country business software. The generic result session showed a survey on variability modeling approaches and how to evolve variability definition when base model is changed. Finally the analysis session handled techniques for optimizing product validity checking and product line metrics. The ample time for discussions was easily filled and engaged many in the stable audience throughout the day.

1   Overview of VARY Workshop

The VARY workshop was initiated as a consequence of the ongoing work to standardize a language for describing variability within the OMG (Object Management Group). The academic partners in the standardization effort decided to try and organize a workshop during the MODELS conference week to solicit opinions on the ongoing standardization as well as providing a more comprehensive view on variability modeling.

The format of our workshop reflected this since the workshop papers were presented in 20 minutes followed by another 20 minutes of discussion for each paper. There were three paper sessions: Examples, Generic results and Analysis. Each session had two papers and we had given the authors the extra assignment to provide questions and comments to the other paper in their session. This turned out to be very successful as all the authors had done their homework well and had detailed inquiries into the other paper. This got the discussion going and others in the audience would join in with supplementing questions and comments which again would trigger more discussion. The twenty minutes discussion time went without any awkward moments of silence. The pair papers in a session meant that the authors were familiar with the topic of the other paper in the session and could therefore easily find questions and compare it with their adjacent contribution. Furthermore, it supported the MODELS flexible approach to participation in the satellite events where people can move from one event to the other freely. The pair paper sessions were perfect for this mobility since it minimized the dependency between the sessions.

J. Kienzle (Ed.): MODELS 2011 Workshops, LNCS 7167, pp. 48–52, 2012.

In addition to the paper sessions we started the workshop with a session of two invited talks. Jon Whittle first gave a talk on software modeling and reuse with results from comprehensive studies that they had made into the empirics of software modeling. This was a fine start which brought variability modeling together with reuse and gave some general vision onto the area to which variability modeling intends to improve software design. Then the author of this summary (Øystein Haugen) gave a talk on the ongoing standardization of a common variability language informing the modeling community about what had happened, what kind of technology was being standardized and the prospects for the near future on this.

We accepted only six papers out of a dozen original submissions. The acceptance number followed from our strategy for sessions and seemed to fit the evaluation of the set of contributions. The program also featured one poster presentation.

We were happy to observe that our audience was appropriate for the room that was assigned to us and that our participants were quite loyal to us throughout the day. The VARY workshop had normally 20-25 participants through the day. The papers of the workshop were made available as a technical report from the IT University of Copenhagen and can be obtained from the web-site of the workshop hosted by INRIA, http://vary2011.irisa.fr/

2   Invited Presentations

The first session consisted of two invited talks. The initial audience present at the invited talk by Jon Whittle. It was clear that the topic was attractive and that the presenter was well known to the audience for his enthusiastic presentations.

2.1   Software Modeling and Reuse: The Good, the Bad and the Ugly (Whittle)

Jon Whittle gave a very inspired presentation of the results of project EAMDE of Lancaster University where they have tried to study the actual effects of applying Model-driven engineering. Through questionnaires and in-depth interviews of experienced practitioners he had some surprising results:

— Domain specific languages are often preferred over general purpose ones
— The positive effect of code generation from models is overrated.
— The real success of MDD is holistic and MDD works best in companies that are not in the software business.

2.2   Standardizing the Common Variability Language (Haugen)

Øystein Haugen (the author of this summary and the organizer chair of the workshop) informed about the ongoing standardization efforts within OMG (Object Management Group) where the Common Variability Language (CVL) is emerging. A global consortium with academic as well as industry partners has been working towards submissions against a Request for Proposals that were published in the end of 2009.

CVL will become a generic language that can work seamlessly with any other domain specific or general modeling language. CVL defines how a base model is transformed into product models such that this can be automated. Furthermore, CVL contains the concepts of traditional feature modeling and means to handle variability on several abstraction levels. For the publicly available news about CVL please refer to http://variabilitymodeling.org .

3   Paper Session on Examples

Following the invited presentations we decided it was time to get a glimpse into some examples of what this area of variability modeling was through a couple of papers that had combined some ideas with use case studies. The audience got a clear impression that variability modeling and product lines are important in reality and that improving our methods in this area had potentials for significant business gains.

3.1   A Model-Driven Approach for Specifying and Configuring Variability in Business Applications (Barat, Roychoudhury, Kulkarni)

Kulkarni presented the experiences from Tata in modeling variability of business applications. He pointed out that often there is customization based on differences in countries even when the core of the application is the same. The differences may be trivial or intricate and that therefore there is a need for advanced ways to define the transformation of the base model. While CVL proposes a few general transformation constructs, Tata also makes use of general transformations expressed in QVT bound to the feature models. As Tata has input this to the CVL standardization process, this possibility will be found as "opaque variation points" in CVL.

3.2   Service Variability Meta-modeling for Service-Oriented Architectures (Abu-Matar, Gomaa)

Gomaa presented an approach for variability modeling of services based on profiling UML and the standard UML profile SoaML. By adding more stereotypes and even a new diagram type similar to traditional feature diagrams variability of the services was expressed. The approach has been explored with a prototype implementation in the e-Commerce domain.

This submission was selected as one of the two best papers and has been evolved into [1].

4   Paper Session on Generic Results

After a healthy lunch we were ready for a session with generic results. We started by a metamodel-based classification of variability modeling approaches followed by a generic approach to evolving a product line when the base model is changed.

4.1 A Metamodel-Based Classification of Variability Modeling Approaches (Istoan, Klein, Perrouin, Jezequel)

Istoan presented a classification of approaches to describing product lines. The main distinction is between those that apply a single model to represent the product line and its assets, and those that apply a pair of separate models, one base model to define the assets and another model for the variability.

The single model approach again subdivides in two where the most common one is the use of profiles or stereotypes to extend the base language. The other approach is to combine the base language metamodel with a variability metamodel into a new combined language for that single description.

The separate approach with two descriptions comes in several variants of which the upcoming CVL standard is one. In this category is also the orthogonal variability model (OVM) and several techniques based on decision trees as the variability model.

4.2 Towards Evolution of Generic Variability Models (Svendsen, Zhang, Haugen, Møller-Pedersen)

Svendsen presented on result of applying an early version of CVL on evolving product lines. The challenge is when there are two separate descriptions that together define the product line and the base model evolves. Is it possible to support this evolution by ensuring that the variability model is expressing the intended product line on the evolved base model? The approach applies CVL both to describe the product line and the difference between the old and the new base models. Careful analysis of the combination of the two CVL descriptions results in differentiated advice. Some evolution of the product line CVL model can be automatically decided while other base model changes must trigger a manual consideration. This paper was the other one selected for this LNCS volume [2].

5 Poster Session

In the afternoon coffee break we performed a poster session. The poster had been placed inside the workshop room and during the last coffee break people could gather around the poster and get an oral introduction to the topic by Gomaa of the poster: Modeling Executable Architectural Design Patterns for Software Product Lines (Fant, Gomaa, Pettitt).

6 Paper Session on Analysis

Following the sessions on examples and on generic results it was natural to have a session on analysis of product lines and of variability models.

6.1   Towards a Family-Based Analysis of Applicability Conditions in Architectural Delta Models (Haber, Kutz, Rendel, Rumpe, Schaefer)

Rumpe presented Δ-MontiArc which is a textual research language for delta modeling and architectural modeling. The focus of their paper was on providing an efficient way to analyze a Δ-MontiArc description to determine if all products of the product line were valid. They introduced the concept of inverse-deltas such that traversing the choice tree could be more effectively computed when there was industry size variety in the product line.

6.2   Complexity Metrics for Software Product Lines (Zhang, Haugen, Møller-Pedersen)

Zhang presented several suggested metrics to estimate the complexity of the product line. Since the foundation for her complexity metrics was CVL the metrics suggested are totally generic and can in principle be applied to product lines in any domain provided it is defined by CVL. An example on a product line of train station signaling was shown.

7   Conclusions

After the last paper session we summarized the workshop with the final audience. It was general consent that the workshop format had been very good and that the long discussion sessions had worked constructively partly because the other author had been instructed to provide questions and comments. This did get the discussion going for every paper.

The final audience was approximately as numerous as the first paper session and this indicated that the topic and the quality of the workshop had been rather successful. Naturally the audience was not entirely the same throughout the day, but quite a few of the participants stayed for the better part of the day.

The introductory session of invited talks was in particular well attended which was perhaps not surprising, but nevertheless encouraging considering that also other workshops had invited speakers in the beginning of the day.

The poster session was rather ad-hoc, but we believe that giving the rejected authors a chance to provide a poster with their idea could be something to consider also in eventual future workshops.

The final audience consented to a suggestion to apply for a similar workshop during the MODELS 2012 conference week.

References

1. Abu-Matar, M., Gomaa, H.: Feature-Based Variability Meta-modeling for Service-Oriented Product Lines. In: Kienzle, J. (ed.) MODELS 2011 Workshops. LNCS, vol. 7167, pp. 68–82. Springer, Heidelberg (2012)
2. Svendsen, A., Zhang, X., Haugen, Ø., Møller-Pedersen, B.: Towards Evolution of Generic Variability Models. In: Kienzle, J. (ed.) MODELS 2011 Workshops. LNCS, vol. 7167, pp. 53–67. Springer, Heidelberg (2012)

Towards Evolution of Generic Variability Models

Andreas Svendsen[1,2], Xiaorui Zhang[1,2],
Øystein Haugen[1], and Birger Møller-Pedersen[2]

[1] SINTEF, Pb. 124 Blindern, 0314 Oslo, Norway
[2] Department of Informatics, University of Oslo, Pb. 1080 Blindern, 0316 Oslo, Norway
{andreas.svendsen,xiaorui.zhang,oystein.haugen}@sintef.no,
birger@ifi.uio.no

Abstract. We present an approach for evolving separate variability models when the associated base model is altered. The Common Variability Language (CVL) is a generic language for modeling variability in base models. The base models are oblivious to the associated variability models, causing additional challenges to this association when the base models are maintained. Assuming that a base model has been changed, we suggest using CVL to record this change. Further analysis of this CVL model reveals the impact of the change, an may in some cases result in automatic evolution of the variability model corresponding to the changed base model. We illustrate and discuss the approach using an example from the train domain.

Keywords: Variability modeling, variability model evolution, coupled evolution, Common Variability Language.

1 Introduction

Model-Driven Development (MDD) has in the recent years increased in popularity, since it allows the developer to solve problems at a higher level of abstraction. Techniques, such as software product line modeling, are increasingly adopted by the industry to produce software more efficiently. Thus, the development of methods for creating software product line models is important. One such method is to use separate variability models to describe how a base model, representing a software system, can be changed to form other (product) models, representing variations of the original software system.

The Common Variability Language (CVL) is a generic language for modeling variability in base models [7, 8, 10]. CVL consists of a variability model, specifying the possible variations on the base model, and a resolution model, resolving the variability in the variability model to form new product models. Thus, CVL models the variants of a base model without adding annotations or variability concepts to the base model (and base language).

The importance of a standardized and generic variability language has been recognized, and a standardization process has been initiated to create such a language [8]. However, keeping the variability concepts separate from the base model adds

J. Kienzle (Ed.): MODELS 2011 Workshops, LNCS 7167, pp. 53–67, 2012.
© Springer-Verlag Berlin Heidelberg 2012

certain challenges which should be addressed. One of these challenges, which will be the focus of this paper, is the maintenance of a variability model when the associated base model is altered. Assume that a product line consists of a base model and several variability models associated to this base model. If the base model is maintained, how can we ensure that the variability models are still valid? Updating the variability models according to the changed base model can be a tedious task.

In this paper we suggest an approach for automating the maintenance of variability models when their associated base model is changed. We apply CVL to record the changes in the base model, and perform analysis of these CVL models to reveal the impact of the change on the variability models. Based on the results of the analysis, we give feedback on all changes that invalidate the variability model, and if possible, we update the variability model to correspond correctly to the changed base model.

More specifically, the contribution of this paper is an approach for evolving separate variability models when the associated base model is changed. The approach originates and uses concepts from CVL, and can be a useful contribution to the CVL standardization process. We perform preliminary evaluation and exemplify the approach using a prototype implementation based on CVL in Eclipse and an example from the train domain.

The outline for the rest of the paper is as follows: In Section 2 we give some background information necessary for the rest of the paper. Section 3 further elaborates and exemplifies the challenge raised when the base model is changed. Section 4 explains the approach of using CVL to evolve CVL models and illustrates the approach using an example from the train domain. Section 5 evaluates and illustrates the generality of the approach by applying it to another domain. In Section 6 we give a discussion about the approach. Section 7 gives some related work, before Section 8 gives some concluding remarks and future work.

2   Background

2.1   Common Variability Language

CVL is a generic language for modeling variability in any models in any MOF-based[1] modeling language. In other words, CVL can be applied to both models in Domain-Specific Languages (DSL) and models in more general languages like UML. One key feature of CVL is that it is separate from the base model and applies one-way associations to the base model. Since CVL is separate, no annotations or variability concepts is added into the base model or base language.

The core part of CVL consists of substitutions, which replace model elements and model element attributes to produce new variants of the base model. In addition to the substitutions, CVL also includes concepts for abstractions, such as using features as part of the concrete syntax, as known from feature models. A prototype implementation of CVL, as an Eclipse plug-in, has been developed and a case study has been conducted for evaluation (see [17]).

---

[1] http://www.omg.org/mof/

In this paper we focus on the most expressive substitution in CVL, namely the *fragment substitution*. A fragment substitution replaces a *placement fragment* in the base model, which is a set of model elements, with a *replacement fragment*, which is another set of model elements. Since the model elements in the replacement fragment are copied, the only change performed in the base model is to the placement fragment. This substitution is illustrated in Fig. 1. Both the placement fragment and replacement fragment are represented by *boundary elements*, recording all references to and from the model elements inside the fragments. A fragment substitution binds these boundary elements (*ToBinding* and *FromBinding*) such that executing the substitution will replace the references according to the binding (i.e. the reference from *A* to *B* will be redirected to *F*). Note that these references must follow the type rules from the metamodel, so that the substitution is type safe.

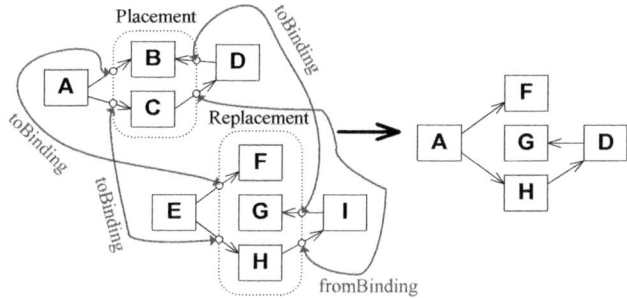

Fig. 1. Fragment substitution replaces a placement fragment with a replacement fragment

2.2   CVL Compare

CVL Compare is a generic approach with tool support for synthesizing a Software Product Line (SPL) from a set of existing product models using model comparison techniques [18]. The approach answers to the need that often in practice the SPL developer intends to synthesize an SPL from a set of existing products instead of building from scratch. The CVL Compare tool automates the variability identification phase of the SPL development, by automatically suggesting a preliminary product line model for further manual enhancement.

For model difference detection, the CVL Compare tool utilizes EMF Compare [4], a generic model differencing tool that is meta-model independent. For specifying variability of the product line, CVL Compare applies the Common Variability Language (CVL). Thus, the resulting product line model is in the form of a CVL model and can be further enhanced using the CVL tool support. Benefiting from the generic nature of both the CVL language and EMF Compare, the CVL Compare tool can be applied to any product model specified in any language that has been defined based on Meta Object Facility (MOF).

With CVL Compare, the SPL developer first prepares a set of product models, choosing one of them as the base model for the target product line, and then running the CVL Compare tool. The tool detects the differences between the product models and performs further comparisons to explore the commonality and variability of the product line. A preliminary product line model (a CVL model) is induced automatically based on the comparison results. The SPL developer can further enhance the product line model manually using CVL tool support.

The capability of producing CVL models automatically, based on a set of models, is very useful for this approach, as we will see later in the paper.

2.3   Train Control Language

The Train Control Language (TCL) is a DSL for modeling signaling systems on train stations [5, 16]. The intention of TCL is to automate the development of interlocking source code which ensures safe train movement on a train station. TCL has been developed in cooperation with ABB, Norway[2].

TCL is defined by a metamodel and has been developed as an Eclipse plug-in with an editor, model analyzer and code generator. The concrete syntax of TCL is illustrated in Fig. 2, with the most significant concepts annotated: *TrainRoute*, *TrackCircuit*, *LineSegment*, *Switch*, *Endpoint* and *Signal*. A TrainRoute is a path between two signals that must be allocated before a train can move into or out of the station. A TrainRoute is divided into TrackCircuits, which are segments where a train can be located. A TrackCircuit is further divided into LineSegments and Switches, which are connected by Endpoints.

We will use a TCL model as a base model to illustrate how we can evolve the CVL model when the base model changes.

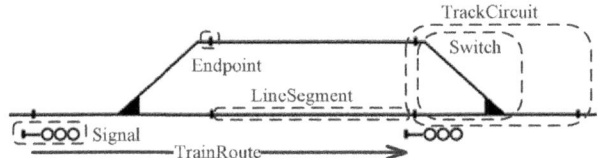

Fig. 2. TCL concrete syntax (with annotations)

3   Problem Description

Since CVL models are kept separate from the base model, changes can be conducted to the base model that may invalidate the CVL models associated with this base model. This is extra challenging since CVL models, to be truly separate, only contains one-way references to the base model. The CVL model can be invalidated either syntactically, e.g. null-pointer references, or semantically, resulting in meaningless product models. In this paper we focus on the syntactic changes in the base model and the evolution of the CVL model according to these kinds of changes.

---

[2] http://www.abb.no

The most expressive construct of CVL is the fragment substitution, allowing a set of model elements to be replaced by another set of model elements. In other words, the fragment substitution is flexible, and can express any kind of structural changes, where base model elements are added, deleted or modified. If the placement or replacement fragments refers base model elements that are changed in this way, these fragments are invalidated. We limit the analysis presented in this paper to placement fragments, since replacement fragments easily can be saved and maintained as library models, which are kept separate from the base model (see [17]).

Fig. 3 illustrates the challenge of evolving CVL models and shows an overview of the approach (see Section 4). Step 1 describes the original product line by specifying a CVL model to transform a base model to a product model, i.e. inserting a *side track* into a two-track station model. However, assume that the base model is modified, ending up with an evolved base model, i.e. a three-track station model (top right). The original CVL model does not apply to the evolved base model. Our approach is concerned with evolving the original CVL model according to the evolved base model (step 3). Step 4 involves executing the evolved CVL model to obtain an evolved product model. We explain step 2 and give further details about step 3 in Section 4.

4   Using CVL to Evolve CVL Models

4.1   The Approach

We suggest using CVL and fragment substitution to record the evolution of the base model (see Fig. 3, step 2). CVL Compare is used to determine the evolution CVL model. This CVL model is then combined with the original CVL model, and the combination is analyzed for inconsistencies. We let the user decide whether to obtain this CVL model manually or automatically (using CVL Compare on the base model and the evolved base model).

Recall that a fragment in CVL is defined by boundary elements, which record the references to and from the base model elements in the fragment. Furthermore, note that the base model elements in a placement fragment are replaced by the model elements in a replacement fragment. Thus, two placement fragments cannot overlap, meaning that two changes cannot be performed to the same base model element.

Fig. 4 gives an overview of possible inconsistencies between the two CVL models. A *border inconsistency* indicates that two model elements that are replaced in two different substitutions are directly connected. Since the substitutions are independent, the association between them cannot be set in either of the substitutions. An *element inconsistency* indicates that a base model element is being replaced by two different substitutions. The base model element cannot be replaced twice. Note that the purpose of the figure is for illustrating the kinds of inconsistencies and not all possible situations where inconsistencies can occur. For instance, there will still be inconsistencies if the associations are inverted.

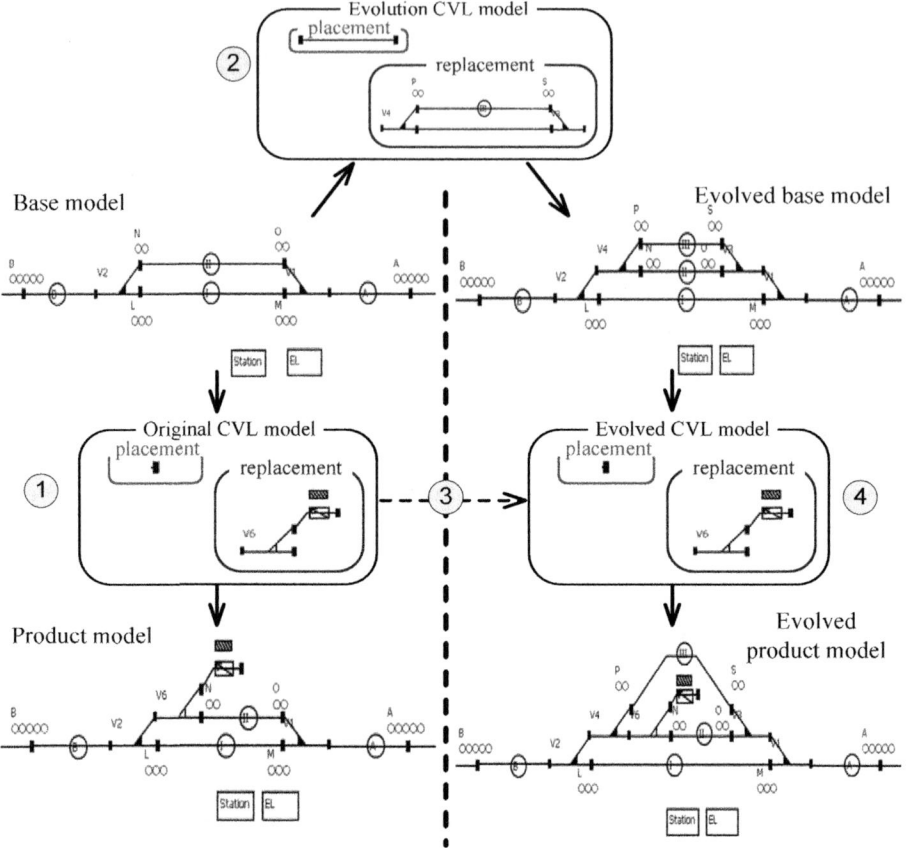

Fig. 3. Overview of the approach

We have developed an algorithm to deal with the inconsistencies between CVL models. Intuitively, when an inconsistency is found, the algorithm makes an attempt to solve the inconsistency by using the model elements in the replacement fragment. For instance, for the border inconsistency in Fig. 4 the base model element *A* is replaced by the evolution CVL model while base model element *B* is replaced by the original CVL model. In this case, the algorithm transforms the original CVL model such that it refers the replacement of *A* (from the evolution CVL model) instead of *A* as the context of the fragment *P2*. For the element inconsistency in Fig. 4 the base model element *B* is being replaced by both CVL models. Thus, the algorithm transforms the original CVL model such that the replacement of base model element *A* (from the evolution CVL model) is referred instead of *A* as the context of fragment *P2*. In addition, the replacement of *B* (from the evolution CVL model) is recorded as a contained element instead of *B*. Note that in some cases, with too little context information, the algorithm may not be able to find a unique base model element from the replacement fragment (evolution CVL model). The user is then prompted to make a decision for which one to use.

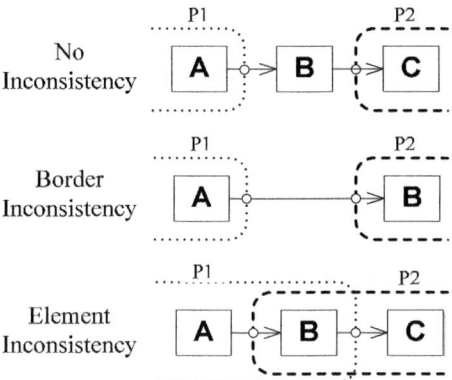

P1: Placement fragment in evolution CVL model
P2: Placement fragment in original CVL model

Fig. 4. Types of inconsistencies between two CVL models

As a summary, our approach involves creating a CVL evolution model to record the evolution of the base model (Fig. 3, step 2). By comparing and analyzing the differences between this CVL model and the original CVL model, we reveal and solve inconsistencies between them, and transform the original CVL model to an evolved CVL model (Fig. 3, step 3), which applies to the evolved base model.

4.2   Evolving CVL Models

To illustrate the approach, we briefly walk through an example where we apply CVL to a TCL model, evolve this TCL model and finally evolve the original CVL model according to the evolved TCL model. The example is illustrated in Fig. 3, where the base model is a two-track station, which is evolved to a three-track station, and the original CVL model adds a side track to the base model.

We first develop (either manually or automatically) the evolution CVL model, which applies to the base model. This CVL model is then compared to the original CVL model to reveal any inconsistencies between them. The algorithm discovers an element inconsistency, since both CVL models contain a placement fragment that spans over a common TCL endpoint. The inconsistency is illustrated in Fig. 5 (middle), where the placement fragment *P1* (original CVL model) replaces the endpoint with a side track, and the placement fragment *P2* (evolution CVL model) replaces the endpoint, together with a line segment and another endpoint, with a double-track. The replacement fragments are illustrated on the left and right side of the figure, where *R1* is bound to *P1* and *R2* is bound to *P2*.

To solve the inconsistency, the algorithm fetches the model element from the replacement fragment (in the evolution CVL model) that is bound to the common endpoint in Fig. 5. Note that in this replacement fragment there are several TCL endpoints that can potentially match the common endpoint. E.g. the side track can be placed on top of the third track. However, the context of the placements include among others a reference to signal *N*, which is unique and located at the second track in the evolved base model. This is illustrated in Fig. 5 with circles around the endpoints (in *R1* and *R2*) which have references (context) to signal *N*. Thus, the matching is unique and the inconsistency can be solved automatically by the algorithm. The solution to the inconsistency is stored in a mapping table for use when transforming the original CVL model. For this example, a mapping is created between the endpoint in *P1* and the endpoint in the circle in *R2*.

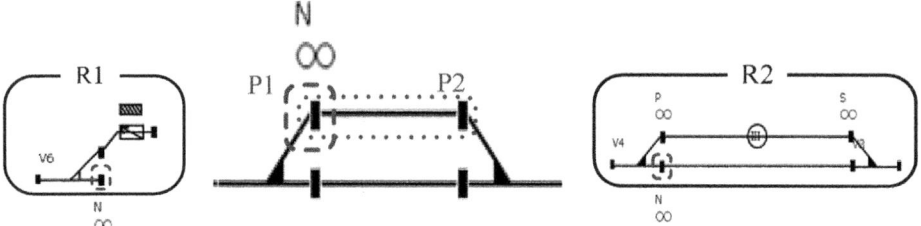

Fig. 5. Element inconsistency between two CVL placement fragments on a TCL model

When the strategy for how to solve the inconsistency is known, the algorithm transforms the original CVL model to the evolved CVL model (Fig. 3, step 3). This is a one-to-one mapping where the references to the two-track station model are replaced with references to the three-track station model. For any inconsistency, the mapping table is used to obtain how to associate the evolved CVL model to the evolved base model. For this example, the placement in the evolved CVL model contains the model element in the circle in *R2*, with the appropriate context, instead of the endpoint in *P1*.

When the evolved CVL model is created, it can be executed to obtain the evolved product model, which yields a three track station with a side track on the second track (see Fig. 3, step 4). Note that the procedure of evolving the CVL model and executing it is automatic, and do not require any user interaction, unless the inconsistencies cannot be solved automatically.

5   Exploratory Evaluation

We have extended the CVL editor with functionality to perform the algorithm described in the previous sections. In order to evaluate the feasibility of the approach, we form the following questions: (1) How well does our tool prototype apply to other CVL-based SPLs in other domains? (2) With a new SPL, how much manual effort is required to set up our tool? (3) How correct is the resulting evolved product line that is automatically generated? Does the correctness correlate with the language characteristic of the DSL behind the SPL, or the complexity of the domain?

In order to answer the questions, we perform a case study on the application of our approach to a specific SPL. This is performed by exploratory means, based on the following considerations: (1) CVL, as the currently proposed approach, has limited popularity in Software Product Line Engineering (SPLE). Thus we may have insufficient subjects for quantitative methods; (2) The case study method excels at providing an understanding of complexity issues, especially when the boundaries between phenomenon and context are not clearly evident [14]. It emphasizes detailed analysis of a limited number of events and conditions and their relationships [14]. This fulfills our need to evaluate the generality, the tool usability, the correctness of the result and the influencing factors.

The SPL we use in the case study is a product line of arithmetic expressions. The base language of this SPL is ARI, which is a DSL for specifying arithmetic expressions, defined by a metamodel [1] (see Fig. 6). An ARI model consists of a set of *expressions* and a set of *variables*. An expression can either be a *variable term*, referring to a variable, an *integer literal*, representing a constant integer, or a *binary expression*, with five possible operators (*Plus*, *Minus*, *Multiplicity*, *Division* and *Power*).

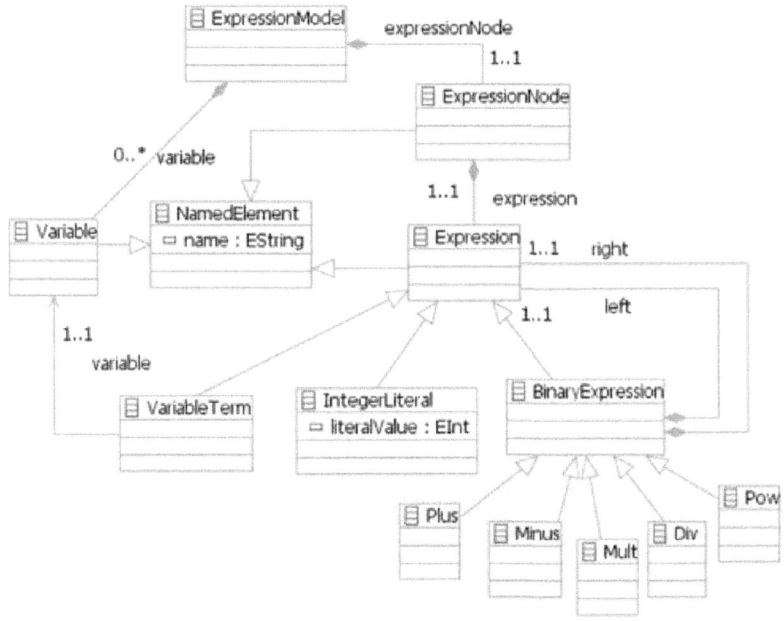

Fig. 6. The ARI metamodel

ARI is used for specifying expressions (polynomials) by concatenating variables with integers using the traditional operations of addition, subtraction, multiplication, division and power. The ARI tool support comes in terms of an Eclipse plug-in, which includes a tree editor, a graphical editor and an expression evaluator. The ARI tool has also been integrated with the original CVL tool prior to the exploratory evaluation in this section. With the ARI evaluator, values can be assigned to the variables, and the expression will be evaluated based on that. Fig. 7 shows an ARI model in the ARI graphical editor. This model specifies the polynomial "11 − x * 9". By assigning value to the variable "x", the ARI evaluator is able to evaluate the expression accordingly.

We demonstrate the generic nature of our approach by illustrating its application to evolve an ARI product line. The original base model of this product line is an ARI model defining the arithmetic expression "11 − x / 3" (see Fig. 8). A product model of this product line is the expression "11 − x / (4 + x)", which can be obtained by substituting "3" with "(4 + x)" (see Fig. 8).

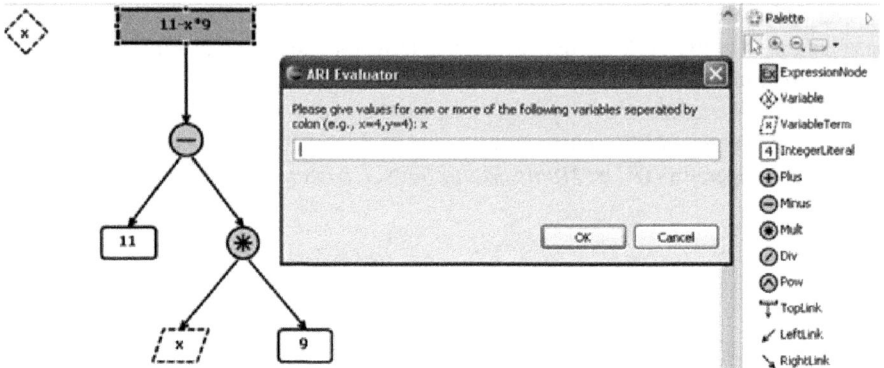

Fig. 7. Arithmetic expression in the ARI graphical editor

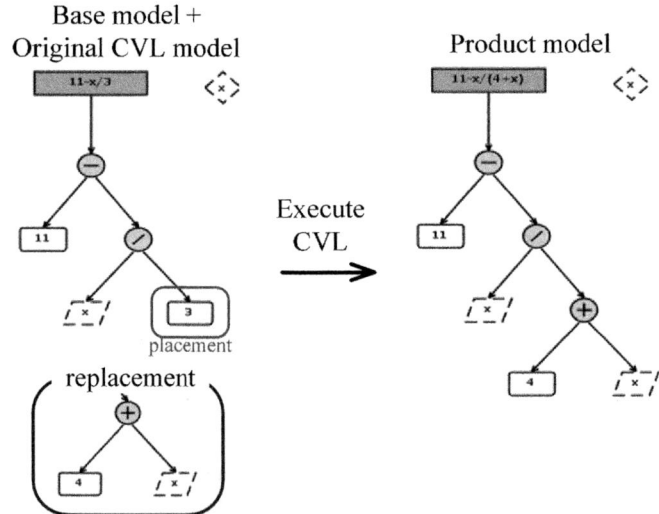

Fig. 8. Transformation from base model to product model using original CVL model

We further assume that we have discovered a bug in this product line, and that the product models should never have more than one "x". Note that the purpose of this example is solely for illustrating the approach, and the semantics of the arithmetic expressions are not of importance. We modify the base model by switching the children of the division from "x / 3" to "3 / x" to obtain an evolved base model with the following expression "11 – 3 / x" (see Fig. 9). In order to evolve the product line (CVL model) we follow the procedure from our approach, which is described in the following.

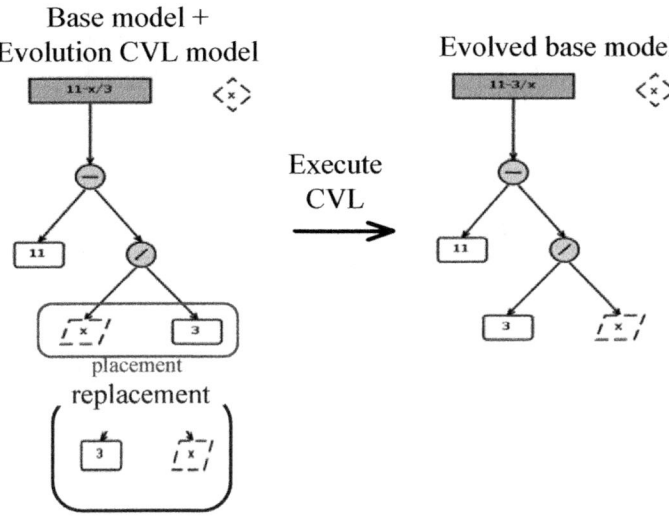

Fig. 9. Evolving the ARI base model using evolution CVL model

First we use the CVL Compare tool, with the original base model and the evolved base model as inputs, to obtain an evolution CVL model, which is applied to the original base model (see Fig. 9). This evolution CVL model specifies a fragment substitution replacing "x" on the left side and "3" on the right side with "3" on the left side and "x" on the right side.

Then we use the original base model, the original CVL model and the evolution CVL model as inputs to our prototype tool in order to produce an evolved CVL model that is applied to the evolved base model (see Fig. 10). First our algorithm searches for any possible inconsistencies that may occur between the original CVL model and the evolution CVL model. In this case it detects an element inconsistency at the integer literal "3", since it is to be replaced in both models. The algorithm continues the execution by searching for a match for the "3" in the replacement fragment (based on the binding). The matching process accounts for two considerations: Whether the base model element is of the kind *Expression*, which means that it can be *Variable*, *TermIntegerLiteral* or *BinaryExpression*; and whether the base model element has the same context as the "3", in terms of the number and types of the references associated to it. Based on these considerations, the algorithm only discovers one possible match in the replacement fragment, namely *VariableTerm* "x", based on the context (the operand on the right side of the operator "/"). This match is then stored in a map with "3" as the key and "x" as the value for later use.

Furthermore, to resolve the inconsistencies, the algorithm looks into the original CVL model, where it traverses every model element within the placement fragment, looking for a match with the model elements in the map, which was obtained earlier. For each match, the algorithm substitutes the key (i.e. "3") with the value (i.e. "x"), resulting in an evolved CVL model, which replaces "x" with "4+x" (see Fig. 10).

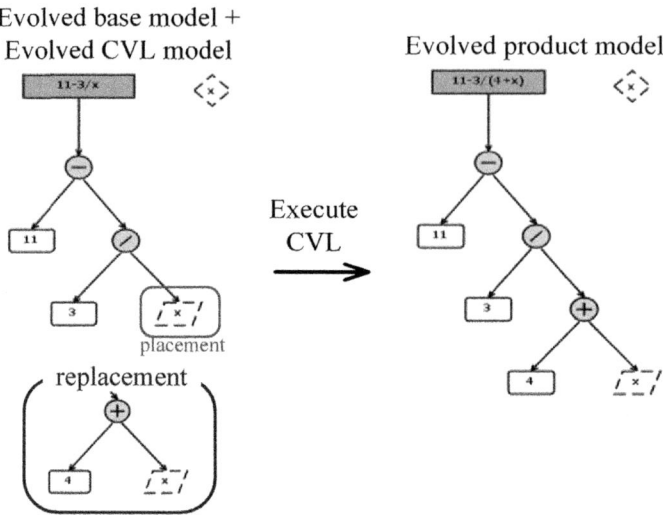

Fig. 10. From evolved base model to evolved product model using evolved CVL model

Here we summarize our observations during the case study: (1) No additional manual effort was required for setting up our tool prototype, which is an extension to the original CVL tool; (2) ARI has a relatively simple domain and language definition; (3) The automatically evolved product line is considered to still correctly serve the original purpose of the product line. Based on those observations, we make the following hypothesis: (1) Our approach is generic and feasible for any CVL-based product line with MOF-based domain language; (2) Complexity of the domain and the DSL definition may affect the performance of our approach, which requires further evaluation.

Internal Validity. The TCL product line was developed with domain experts from industry. However, the ARI product line was initially developed for educational and demonstrational purposes. Therefore the difference of complexity of the domains and of expertise of the SPL developers poses threats to the internal validity.

External Validity. The fact that we only use TCL and ARI as cases, which are small examples, is at the cost of external validity. Can we generalize our findings and hypothesis to other product lines?

We propose a further evaluation plan, including: (1) applying our approach to a number of real-life representative SPLs in various domains of different sizes; (2) trying out different strategies in the trade-off between the construction of internal and external validity.

6   Discussion

Even though our approach is specific for CVL and fragment substitution, CVL and fragment substitution are generic and can describe variability in any model in any DSL. The approach takes advantage of the nature of CVL, which specifies specifically where and how the variability is applied to the base model, to perform the analysis. Thus, the approach fits well with the intentions of the upcoming CVL standard.

Since the approach is performed automatically, it has its strength when more than one substitution and/or more than one original CVL model is associated with the base model. Then manual work of evolving the CVL models or the product models without tool support can be huge. Furthermore, since base models most often is updated based on bug-fixes or other small changes, the amount of inconsistencies, and their impact, remains small. Thus, our approach can in particular be useful in these situations.

Even though a stronger association between the CVL model and the base model can avoid some of the issues discussed in this paper, e.g. by using two-way references, having a clear separation has its advantages. For instance, having several variability models associated with a single base model is possible, for describing different kinds of product lines. Furthermore, CVL can model variability in a base model without the need to change the base language to add variability concepts or associations. This results in the possibility of applying CVL and creating product lines more rapidly.

Only using simpler kinds of substitutions, limiting the type of replacement to attributes or single base mode elements, would simplify the possible inconsistencies when performing the evolution of the CVL model. However, we believe that the fragment substitution plays an important role in making CVL flexible and generic for expressing all kinds of variability. On the other hand, note that this approach can easily be modified to support these kinds of substitutions instead or in addition to the fragment substitution.

7   Related Work

Much research effort has been put forward in the area of model coupled-evolution in the recent years. Existing work mainly fall into two categories: (1) when the metamodel evolves, how to update the existing instance models in order to conform to the evolved metamodel [9, 11, 12]; (2) when a model changes, how to update its existing related models in order to eliminate all the possible inconsistencies caused by the model changes. The latter is similar to the coupled-evolution we deal with in this paper.

Approaches for bidirectional model transformation have been proposed to keep two models consistent by updating one model in accordance with the other [15]. Chivers and Paige [2] propose a reversible template language that supports round-trip transformations between UML models and predicate logic, such that new information encoded in logic can be seamlessly integrated with information encoded in the model. Mu et al. [13] present an algebraic approach to bidirectional updating, where a formal model of the bidirectional transformations is proposed. The developer writes the transformations as a functional program, such that the synchronization behavior is automatically derived by algebraic reasoning. The approach is able to deal with duplication and structural changes.

Finkelstein et al. [6] propose an approach for inconsistency handling in multi-perspective specifications by combining their *ViewPoints* framework for perspective development with a logic-based approach for inconsistency handling.

Deng et al. [3] present techniques for addressing domain evolution challenges in software product lines. They show how to minimize the inconsistencies caused by the evolution of MDD-based product line architectures for large-scale distributed real-time and embedded systems by adopting a layered architecture and model-to-model transformation tool support.

8   Conclusion and Future Work

This paper has presented an approach for evolving a CVL model when the associated base model is changed. We applied CVL to record the change (evolution step) in the base model and presented an algorithm for transforming the original CVL model accordingly. We presented the kinds of inconsistencies that can occur in this process, and gave suggestions for how to solve them. The approach was illustrated on a concrete example using a CVL model applied on a two-track station model from the Train Control Language. We also applied the approach to an ARI example to illustrate the generality of the approach. Furthermore, we indicated how the approach has been implemented and discussed advantages and challenges with the approach.

We see further evaluation of the approach using additional examples and other domains as important future work. Furthermore, the current approach only considers the syntax of the base models when performing the evolution step. In other words, the evolved product models are syntactically correct, but can be semantically invalid according to the base language semantics. Hence, extensions of the approach to take the semantics of the base language into account will be investigated. Another extension to the approach to also consider language evolution is significant and should be investigated. We can then be able to handle not only changes to base models, but also changes to the base language definitions.

Acknowledgements. The work presented here has been developed within the MoSiS project ITEA 2 – ip06035 part of the Eureka framework and the CESAR project funded by ARTEMIS Joint Undertaking grant agreement No 100016.

References

1. ARI, Ari Tool, http://www.omgwiki.org/variability/ doku.php?id=cvl_tool_from_sintef
2. Chivers, H., Paige, R.: Xround: Bidirectional Transformations and Unifications Via a Reversible Template Language. In: Hartman, A., Kreische, D. (eds.) ECMDA-FA 2005. LNCS, vol. 3748, pp. 205–219. Springer, Heidelberg (2005)

3. Deng, G., Lenz, G., Schmidt, D.C.: Addressing Domain Evolution Challenges in Software Product Lines. In: Bruel, J.-M. (ed.) MoDELS 2005. LNCS, vol. 3844, pp. 247–261. Springer, Heidelberg (2006)
4. EMF, Emf Compare Project, http://www.eclipse.org/emf/compare/
5. Endresen, J., Carlson, E., Moen, T., Alme, K.-J., Haugen, Ø., Olsen, G.K., Svendsen, A.: Train Control Language - Teaching Computers Interlocking. In: Computers in Railways XI (COMPRAIL 2008), Toledo, Spain (2008)
6. Finkelstein, A.C.W., Gabbay, D., Hunter, A., Kramer, J., Nuseibeh, B.: Inconsistency Handling in Multiperspective Specifications. IEEE Trans. Softw. Eng. 20, 569–578 (1994)
7. Fleurey, F., Haugen, Ø., Møller-Pedersen, B., Olsen, G.K., Svendsen, A., Zhang, X.: A Generic Language and Tool for Variability Modeling. SINTEF, Oslo (2009)
8. Fleurey, F., Haugen, Ø., Møller-Pedersen, B., Svendsen, A., Zhang, X.: Standardizing Variability – Challenges and Solutions. In: Ober, I., Ober, I. (eds.) SDL 2011. LNCS, vol. 7083, pp. 233–246. Springer, Heidelberg (2011)
9. Gruschko, B.: Towards Synchronizing Models with Evolving Metamodels. In: Int. Workshop on Model-Driven Software Evolution held with the ECSMR (2007)
10. Haugen, Ø., Møller-Pedersen, B., Oldevik, J., Olsen, G., Svendsen, A.: Adding Standardized Variability to Domain Specific Languages. In: Proceedings of the 2008 12th International Software Product Line Conference. IEEE Computer Society (2008)
11. Herrmannsdoerfer, M.: COPE – A Workbench for the Coupled Evolution of Metamodels and Models. In: Malloy, B., Staab, S., van den Brand, M. (eds.) SLE 2010. LNCS, vol. 6563, pp. 286–295. Springer, Heidelberg (2011)
12. Herrmannsdoerfer, M., Benz, S., Juergens, E.: Automatability of Coupled Evolution of Metamodels and Models in Practice. In: Czarnecki, K., Ober, I., Bruel, J.-M., Uhl, A., Völter, M. (eds.) MODELS 2008. LNCS, vol. 5301, pp. 645–659. Springer, Heidelberg (2008)
13. Mu, S.-C., Hu, Z., Takeichi, M.: An Algebraic Approach to Bi-directional Updating. In: Chin, W.-N. (ed.) APLAS 2004. LNCS, vol. 3302, pp. 2–20. Springer, Heidelberg (2004)
14. Soy, S.K.: The Case Study as a Research Method. University of Texas, Austin (1997)
15. Stevens, P.: A Landscape of Bidirectional Model Transformations. In: Lämmel, R., Visser, J., Saraiva, J. (eds.) GTTSE 2007. LNCS, vol. 5235, pp. 408–424. Springer, Heidelberg (2008)
16. Svendsen, A., Olsen, G.K., Endresen, J., Moen, T., Carlson, E.J., Alme, K.-J., Haugen, Ø.: The Future of Train Signaling. In: Czarnecki, K., Ober, I., Bruel, J.-M., Uhl, A., Völter, M. (eds.) MODELS 2008. LNCS, vol. 5301, pp. 128–142. Springer, Heidelberg (2008)
17. Svendsen, A., Zhang, X., Lind-Tviberg, R., Fleurey, F., Haugen, Ø., Møller-Pedersen, B., Olsen, G.K.: Developing a Software Product Line for Train Control: A Case Study of CVL. In: Bosch, J., Lee, J. (eds.) SPLC 2010. LNCS, vol. 6287, pp. 106–120. Springer, Heidelberg (2010)
18. Zhang, X., Haugen, Ø., Møller-Pedersen, B.: Model Comparison to Synthesize a Model-Driven Software Product Line. In: 15th International Software Product Line Conference, Munich, Germany (2011)

Feature-Based Variability Meta-modeling
for Service-Oriented Product Lines

Mohammad Abu-Matar and Hassan Gomaa

Department of Computer Science
George Mason University,
Fairfax, Virginia, USA
{mabumata,hgomaa}@gmu.edu

Abstract. Service Oriented Architecture (SOA) has emerged as a paradigm for distributed computing that promotes flexible deployment and reuse. However, SOA systems currently lack a systematic approach for managing variability in service requirements and design. Our paper addresses this problem by applying software product line (SPL) concepts to model SOA systems as service families. We introduce an approach to model SOA variability with a multiple-view SOA variability model and a corresponding meta-model. The approach integrates SPL concepts of feature modeling and commonality/variability analysis with different service views using UML and SoaML. This paper describes a multiple-view meta-model that maps features to variable service models as well as model consistency checking rules. We describe how to derive family member applications and also present a validation of the approach.

Keywords: Meta-Modeling, Software Product Lines, Service-Oriented Architecture (SOA), Feature Modeling, Multiple-view modeling.

1 Introduction

Service Oriented Architecture (SOA) has emerged as an architectural style for distributed computing that promotes flexible deployment and reuse [1]. However, SOA systems currently lack a systematic approach for managing variability and are typically platform-dependent. Since services in SOA could be used by different clients with varying functionality, we believe that SOA variability modeling can benefit from software product lines (SPL) variability modeling techniques.

This paper describes a meta-modeling approach that integrates SPL concepts of feature modeling and commonality/variability analysis to model SOA variability. The main goal of SPL is the reuse-driven development of SPL member applications by using reusable assets from all phases of the development life cycle. This goal is similar to the goal of SOA where flexible application development is a common theme.

Our approach integrates feature meta-modeling [2], [3] with service views using UML and SoaML the newly released SOA standardized modeling language. Such an approach facilitates variability modeling of service family architectures in a systematic and platform independent way.

J. Kienzle (Ed.): MODELS 2011 Workshops, LNCS 7167, pp. 68–82, 2012.

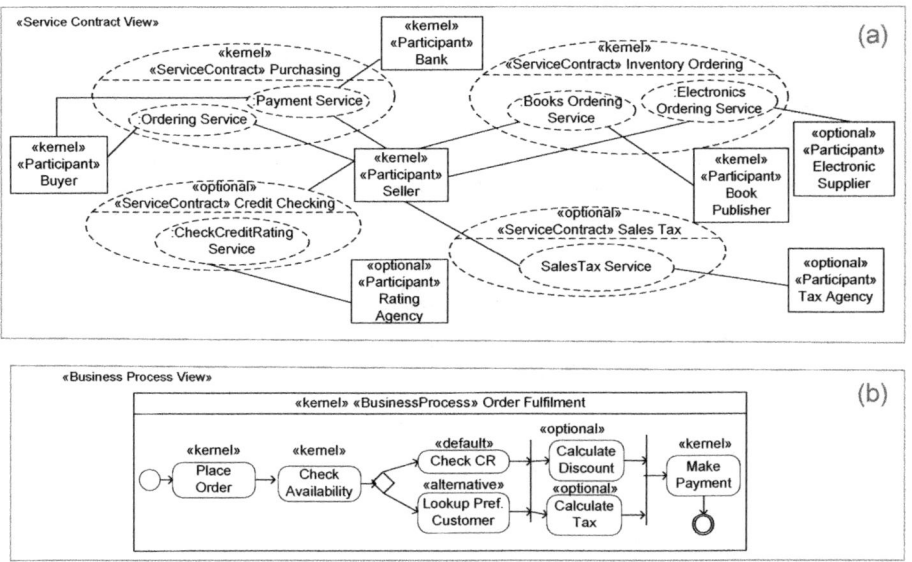

Fig. 1. E-Commerce Requirements Service Variability Views

At the heart of the approach is a meta-model that describes requirements and architectural views of service oriented systems. In addition, the meta-model describes variability in the service views and adds a feature view that addresses the variability in the SOA system. The meta-model also describes relationships among the services views and among the feature and services views. Our approach builds on previous research as follows: feature modeling and multiple-view modeling of software product lines engineering [2], meta-modeling of SPL phases [4], software coordination and adaptation patterns for SOA systems [5], an early version of our meta-model [6], and SoaML.

The rest of the paper is structured as follows. Section 2 briefly presents our multiple view service variability model, section 3 describes the multiple view variability meta-model while section 4 describes feature to service relationships and constraints, section 5 describes feature-based service application derivation, section 6 outlines the validation of the approach, section 7 presents related work, and section 8 concludes the paper.

2   Multiple View Service Variability Model

Erl [1] describes service-oriented systems as having multiple perspectives where these perspectives depend on each other. In essence, each perspective describes a distinct view of the whole SOA system. In this paper, the different SOA perspectives are formalized into multiple Requirements and Architectural views. In this section, we briefly describe our multiple-view service model which is formalized by our meta-model. Each view of the multiple view model is depicted by a UML diagram that is extended by using stereotypes. In particular, each modeling meta-class is depicted using two stereotypes, one to represent an SOA concept and the other to represent a commonality/variability concept.

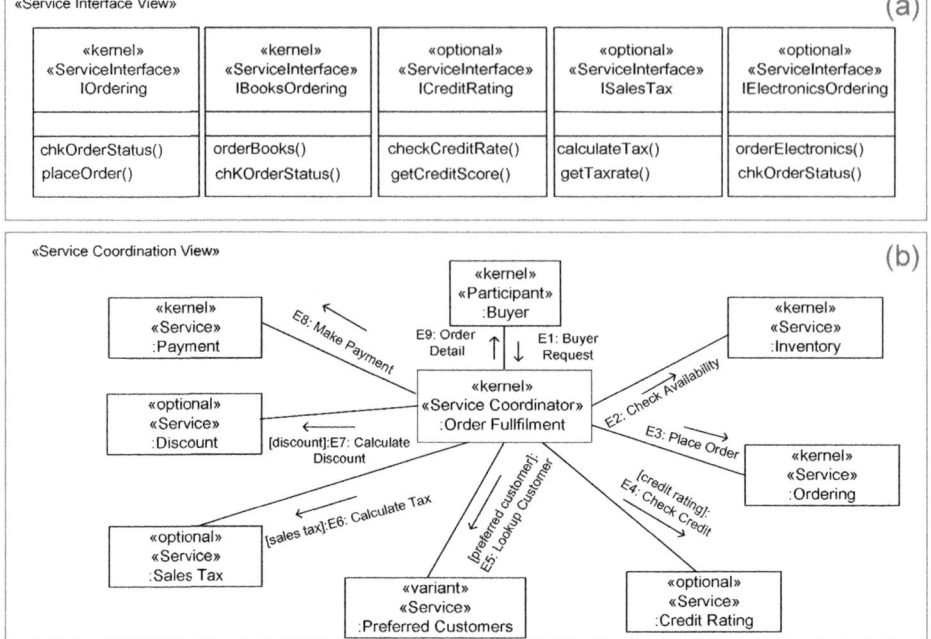

Fig. 2. E-Commerce Architectural Service Variability Views

Kruchten [14] introduced the 4+1 view model of software architecture, in which he advocated a multiple view modeling approach for software architectures, in which the use case view is the unifying view (the 1 view of the 4+1 views). FODA introduced feature modeling as the key concept for modeling commonality and variability [3] in SPLE. RSEB [15] advocated both use case modeling and feature modeling for SPLE, use cases to determine the functional requirements of the SPL and feature modeling to concentrate on modeling SPL variability. PLUS [2] integrated feature modeling into a UML based multiple view modeling approach, which included use case modeling, static and dynamic analysis modeling, and architectural design modeling.

Our research describes a multiple view modeling approach for service oriented software product lines in which the unifying view is the feature model. Thus, feature modeling provides the added dimension of modeling variability in service-oriented SPL. The approach uses the SPL multi-view modeling approach advocated by the PLUS method [2] but defines three new views which are needed for service-oriented product lines, namely the service contract view and business process view for SOA requirements modeling, and the service coordination view for SOA design modeling.

A service modeling example is introduced in this section (Fig. 1, 2, and 3) and used throughout the paper to explain our approach. This example depicts the different service modeling views and describes variability in each view using SPL concepts.

The Service Contract Variability View is a Requirements view that describes service contracts, which are prescribed by collaborating organizations in order to govern and regulate their interactions. Service contracts (Fig. 1a) are modeled by SoaML's ServiceContract element. This view also contains SoaML's Participant elements that model providers or consumers of services. An example of the Service Contract View is given in Fig. 1a which models an E-Commerce SPL. We categorize Service Contracts and Participants as kernel, optional, or alternative. Kernel elements are required by all members of an SPL, whereas optional elements are required by only some members. Alternative elements are required by different SPL members.

The Business Process Variability View is a Requirements view that models the workflow of business processes. We use UML Activity diagrams to model this view with variability stereotypes (Fig. 1b). An example of the Business Process View is given in Fig. 1b. The Seller Participant could have its own internal business process such as the Order Fulfillment business process. Note that this business process is modeled as an SPL service activity model consisting of a sequence of service activities (kernel, optional, default, and alternative), which can be tailored into a member service business process in the SPL application derivation phase.

Services expose their capabilities through interfaces. The Service Interface Variability View is an architectural view that models service interfaces by using SoaML's ServiceInterface class. ServiceInterfaces are categorized as kernel, optional, and variant. An example of the Service Interface View is given in Fig. 2a. An organization that plays the Seller role in the Purchasing **ServiceContract** implements the Ordering service and Buyer **Participants** order goods from the Seller **Participant**. The Ordering service is exposed via the Ordering **ServiceInterface**.

The Service Coordination Variability View is an architectural view that models the sequencing of service invocations. Services should be self-contained and loosely coupled in order to have a high degree of reuse; dependencies between services should be kept to a minimum [5]. Hence, coordinators are used in situations where access to multiple services needs to be coordinated and sequenced. The Service Coordination View consists of coordinators which are modeled as classes with a <<Service Coordinator>> stereotype (Fig. 2b). Service coordinators are categorized as kernel, optional, and variant. An example of the Service Coordination View is shown in Fig. 2b where the Order Fulfillment coordinator coordinates service invocations for the Order Fulfillment business process (Fig. 1b). Note how the Order Fulfillment service coordinator encapsulates all sequencing logic and only sends and receives messages to and from services thus minimizing coupling among services.

With the above service modeling views, it is possible to define the variability in each view and how it relates to other views. However, it is difficult to get a complete picture of the variability in the service architecture because it is dispersed among the multiple views. The Feature View is a unifying view that focuses on service family variability and relates this to the other service views. Feature models are used to manage similarities and differences among family members in a SPL. Features are analyzed and categorized as kernel, optional, or alternative. Related features can be grouped into feature groups, which constrain how features are used by a SPL member. Fig. 3 depicts the feature model for the E-Commerce product line. More information on multiple view service variability modeling is given in [7, 19].

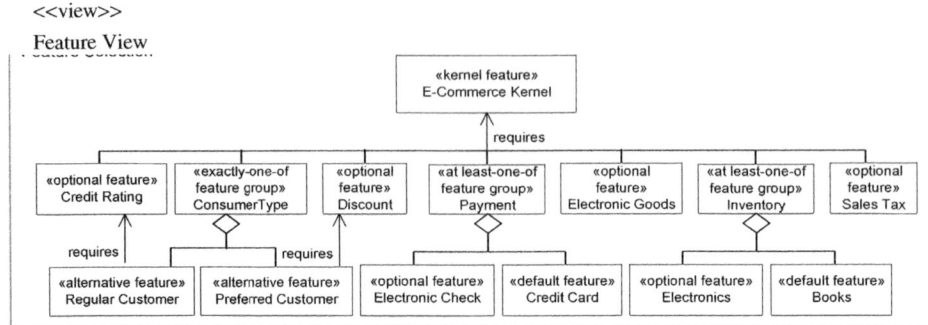

Fig. 3. E-Commerce Feature View

3   Multiple View Service Variability Meta-modeling

The multiple-view variability modeling approach is based on a meta-model that precisely describes all views and views relationships. Each view in the multiple-view model (Fig. 1, 2) is described by a corresponding meta-view in the meta-model (Fig. 4). There are two Requirements meta-views, Service Contract and Business Process, and two Architecture meta-views, Service Interface and Service Coordination. To get a full understanding of the variability in service architectures, it is necessary to have one view that focuses entirely on variability and defines dependencies in this variability, which is the purpose of the feature meta-modeling view described in Section 3.5. Our meta-modeling approach builds on previous work in SPL multiple-view modeling and meta-modeling [4].

3.1   Service Contract Meta-view

We use SoaML's ServiceContract meta-class to specify the agreement between providers and consumers, by using the <<ServiceContract>> stereotype. To model SOA variability, we categorize a ServiceContract as kernel, optional, or alternative.

Each service contract (Fig. 4b) prescribes roles for the organizations participating in it. This view also models contract participants, which are entities that abide by service contracts. We use SoaML's Participant meta-class which specifies providers or consumers of services. This meta-class extends the UML Class meta-class by using the <<Participant>> stereotype.

3.2   Business Process Meta-view

Neither SoaML nor UML explicitly model business process workflow. Since a business process is composed of a sequence of activities, we use UML Activity meta-classes (Fig, 4c), as part of an activity diagram for each business process.

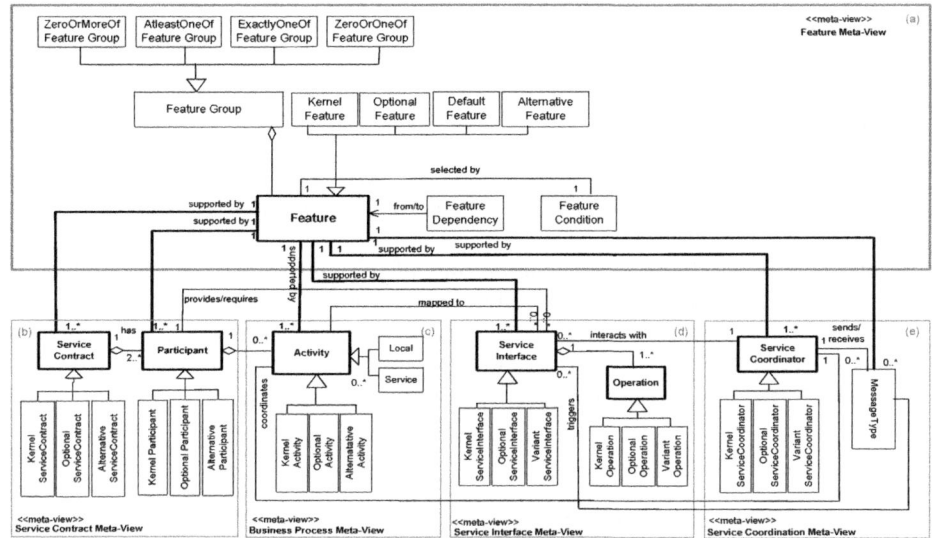

Fig. 4. Service Variability Meta-Model

3.3   Service Interface Meta-view

We model service interfaces by SoaML's ServiceInterface meta-classes (Fig. 4d). ServiceInterface meta-classes specify provided and required service interfaces. A ServiceInterface is categorized as kernel, optional, or variant. To manage variability, we restrict variability modeling for service interfaces to the whole interface and the operation.

3.4   Service Coordination Meta-view

The service coordination view consists of coordinators which are modeled as classes with a <<Service Coordinator>> stereotype (Fig, 4e). Service coordinators, depicted on UML communication diagrams, interact with clients and services. The sequencing of service invocations is encapsulated within the Coordinator. Service coordination is categorized by type of coordination (independent, distributed, or hierarchical) and degree of concurrency (sequential or concurrent) [5].

3.5   Feature Meta-view

Since UML has no native support for feature modeling, we use a UML based feature meta-model based on our previous work [2], [4]. Fig. 4a depicts a feature meta-model. Features are specialized into kernel, optional, alternative, and default depending on the characteristic of the requirements as described in section 2.

Kernel features are requirements common to all members of the SPL. Optional features are required by only some members of a SPL. An alternative feature is an alternative of a kernel or optional feature to meet a specific requirement of some members. A default feature is the default choice among the features in a feature group. Feature groups define constraints on feature selection from a group of features (e.g., preventing selection of mutually exclusive features) during application derivation. Feature dependencies represent relationships between features where one feature requires the presence of another feature.

4   Service Variability Meta-model Relationships

In this section, we describe the relationships of the unified service variability meta-model (Fig. 4) that integrates all the aforementioned views. The meta-model consists of 5 meta-views (4+1 feature view) that correspond to each view in the multiple-view model (section 2). The Feature View (Fig. 3) unifies the service views as explained in Section 2.5. The meta-model describes the following relationships:

4.1   Intra-view Relationships

The associations and dependencies within each view are described. A **ServiceContract** meta-class, in the Service Contract view (Fig. 4b), is associated with two or more **Participant** meta-classes, because a **ServiceContract** meta-class defines the rules for participating entities in the SOA system. For example, in Fig. 1a, the Purchasing ServiceContract is associated with the Buyer and Seller Participants. The **ServiceCoordinator** meta-class in the Service Coordination view (Fig, 4e) is associated with a **Message** meta-class as it sends/receives messages to/from services.

4.2   Inter-view Relationships

The associations and dependencies between the different service views are described in this section. The relationship between the Feature View and the other views are described in section 4.3. A **ServiceContract** meta-class (Fig. 4b) includes one or more **ServiceInterface** meta-classes (Fig. 4d). For example, in Fig. 1a, the Purchasing ServiceContract contains the Ordering Service ServiceInterface which is part of the Service Interface View (Fig. 2a).

Participant meta-classes (Fig. 4b) provide or require **ServiceInterface** meta-classes (Fig. 4d), because participating entities only interact through interfaces to minimize coupling among services. For example, in Fig. 1a, the Tax Agency **Participant** provides the SalesTax **ServiceInterface** (Fig. 2a), while the Seller **Participant** (Fig. 1a) requires the same service **ServiceInterface**.

Participant meta-classes (Fig. 4b) may define their own internal business processes, which are comprised of activities (Fig. 4c). For example, in Fig. 1b, the Seller **Participant** has an Order Fulfillment business process which is comprised of a sequence of activities.

Activity meta-classes (Fig. 4c) can be either *local* or *service* meta-classes. Local activities are executed within the **Participant** execution environment. Service activities require **ServiceInterfaces** (Fig. 4d). For example, in Fig. 1b, the Calculate Tax **Activity** is mapped to a SalesTax **ServiceInterface** (Fig. 2a).

ServiceCoordinator meta-classes (Fig. 4e), in the Service Coordination View coordinate service invocations based on the workflow of **Activity** meta-classes in the Business Process view (Fig 4c). For example, the Order Fulfillment **ServiceCoordinator** (Fig. 2b) coordinates service invocations to correspond to the **Activities** of the Order Fulfillment business process (Fig. 1b).

Message meta-classes in the Service Coordination View (Fig. 4e) trigger operation invocations on the **ServiceInterfaces** in the Service Interface View (Fig. 4d). For example, the 'Calculate Tax' **Message** in Fig. 2b triggers the invocation of an operation, which is part of the Sales Tax **ServiceInterface** (Fig. 2a).

Meta-classes in one view of the service model affect meta-classes in other views. For example, in Fig. 1b, when the Calculate Tax **Activity** is added to the Order Fulfillment Business Process View, a Sales Tax **ServiceContract** is introduced into the E-Commerce SPL in the Service Contract View (Fig. 1a). Consequently, a Tax Agency **Participant** is also added which provides a SalesTax **ServiceInterface** in the Service Interface View (Fig. 2a).

4.3 Feature to Service Meta-view Relationship

This section describes the meta-model relationships describe the Feature meta-view and the Service meta-views. This section also describes consistency checking rules, written in OCL, which add explicit constraints on relationships between the meta-classes of the multiple-view service variability meta-model (Fig. 4). For each inter-view relationship, a representative consistency checking rule is described.

4.3.1 Feature to Service Contract Meta-view Relationship

A **Feature** (Fig. 4a) is associated with one or more ServiceContract meta-classes in the Service Contract View (Fig. 4b). For example, when feature Credit Rating (Fig. 3) is selected, the Credit Checking ServiceContract will be activated and enforced in the SOA system (Fig. 1a). The variability stereotype on a ServiceContract dictates the type of feature it may map to. For instance, an optional feature (e.g., Credit Rating) can only map to optional service contracts (e.g., Credit Checking service contract). Similarly, an alternative feature may map to alternative service contracts only.

> *A Kernel ServiceContract can only support a kernel Feature*
> **context** Feature **inv:** reuseStereotype = 'kernel' **implies**
> servicecontract->size() >= 1 and servicecontract.reuseStereotype = 'kernel'

A **Feature** (Fig. 4a) is associated with one or more **Participants** (Fig. 4b). For example, if the *Electronic Goods* optional feature (Fig. 3) is selected, the *Seller* will sell electronic items in addition to books and the *ElectronicSupplier* **Participant** will participate in the *InventoryOrdering* **ServiceContract** (Fig. 1a). Consequently, the *ElectronicsOrdering* **ServiceInterface** will be introduced into the *InventoryOrdering* **ServiceContract** (Fig. 1a). Hence, the selection of one feature meta-class in the feature meta-view was mapped to two service meta-classes (contract and interface) in the contract and interface meta-views.

An optional Participant can only support an optional Feature
context Feature **inv:** reuseStereoType = 'optional' **implies**
participant->size() >=1 and participant.reuseStereoType = 'optional'

4.3.2   Feature to Business Process Meta-view Relationship

A **Feature** (Fig. 4a) is associated with one or more **Activities** in the Participant's
BusinessProcess (Fig. 4c). For example, when the Discount optional feature is
selected (Fig. 3), which means that the system changes to provide the 'Discount'
capability, the Calculate Discount Activity is added to the Order Fulfillment business
process (Fig. 1b). Thus, the Discount <<optional feature>> is mapped to
<<optional>> Calculate Discount Activity in the business process view.

An optional Activity can only support an optional Feature
context Feature **inv:** reuseStereoType = 'optional' **implies**
activity->size() >=1 and activity.reuseStereoType = 'optional'

4.3.3   Feature to Service Interface Meta-view Relationship

A **Feature** is associated with one or more **ServiceInterfaces**. For example, if the
Credit Rating optional feature is selected (Fig. 3), the Seller Participant has to provide
a new service Interface that can interact with a credit rating agency. Thus, the Credit
Rating <<optional feature>> is mapped to <<optional>> Credit Rating service
Interface in the Service Interface View (Fig. 2a).

A variant ServiceInterface can only support an alternative Feature
context Feature **inv:** reuseStereoType = 'alternative' **implies**
serviceinterface->size() >= 1 and serviceinterface.reuseStereoType =
'variant'

It should be noted that we use the term 'variant' for architectural meta-classes, while
we use the term 'alternative' for requirements meta-classes [4].

4.3.4   Feature to Service Coordination Meta-view Relationship

A **Feature** (Fig. 4a) is associated with one or more **ServiceCoordinator** meta-classes
(Fig. 4e) in the Service Coordination View. For example, since the Order Fulfillment
feature (Fig. 3) is supported by the Order Fulfillment Activities in the business
process view (Fig. 1b), the same feature is supported by the Order Fulfillment
ServiceCoordinator in the Service Coordination view (Fig. 2b). It should be noted
that each business process is associated with a unique **ServiceCoordinator**.

A **Feature** is associated with one or more **Message** meta-classes (Fig. 4e). For
example, the Preferred Customer optional feature (Fig. 3) is supported in part, by the
'Lookup Customer' **Message** in Fig. 2b.

4.4   Service Variability Meta-model Relationships and Consistency Checking Rules

In this sub-section, we provide representative consistency checking rules to precisely
describe the relationships among the variable service meta-model meta-classes in Fig. 4.

We are inspired by our previous work [4] where we used OCL to describe consistency checking rules to describe the relationships among the various meta-modeling views of the SPL phases.

The following are typical meta-modeling consistency checking rules, which are expressed in both English and OCL.

1. *A kernel ServiceContract must have at least 2 kernel Participants*
    context servicecontract **inv:** reuseStereotype ='kernel' **implies** (**select** participant.reuseStereotype = 'kernel')->size() >= 2
2. *A kernel ServiceContract must be supported by at least one kernel ServiceInterface*
    context servicecontract **inv:** reuseStereotype ='kernel' **implies** serviceinterface->**exists**(si | si.reuseStereotype = 'kernel')
3. *A Participant must provide or require at least one ServiceInterface*
    context participant **inv:** reuseStereotype ='kernel' **implies** serviceinterface->**exists**(si | si.reuseStereotype = 'kernel')
4. *If kernel Activity is a Service Activity, it must call a kernel ServiceInterface.*
    context activity **inv:** self.**oclIsKindOf**(Service) **implies** activity.serviceinterface.reuseStereotype = 'kernel'

5 Feature-Based Service Application Derivation

Many SPL application derivation approaches are based on feature selection [2,3,18]. In this section, we describe how SOA based member applications can be derived from an E-Commerce product line multiple view model by using feature selection to derive an application multiple view model.

Member application derivation is based on feature selection from the feature model. It should be noted that the derived model is an application multiple-view model that is based on the multiple-view service variability model and meta-model described in sections 2 and 3.

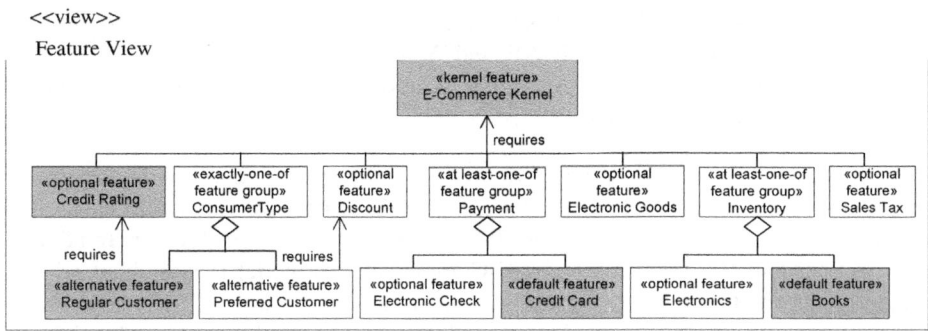

Fig. 5. Basic E-Commerce Application Feature Selection

To derive a basic member application, feature selection (Fig. 5) from the feature model (Fig. 3) is performed. Based on the relationships and consistency checking rules embedded in the service variability meta-model, a multiple-view service member application is derived as shown in Figs. 6 and 7. Fig. 5 depicts the features selected for the member application. This results in feature-based selections of related SOA elements in each of the four service views, as shown in Figs. 6 and 7. Notice how the selection of one feature drives the selection of several SOA elements that span multiple views. Application derivation is described in more detail in [7, 19].

6   Validation of the Approach

To validate our approach, we created a proof-of-concept prototype for service oriented SPL. The prototype allows users to specify feature models, build service models, relate features to service views, and create SPL member applications. The purpose of the validation is to evaluate our approach with regard to:

1.   The multiple views of the service oriented product line are <u>consistent with each other</u>.
2.   The multiple-view service variability model is <u>compliant</u> with the underlying multiple-view service variability meta-model
3.   Derived service oriented member applications are <u>consistent</u> with the service oriented SPL requirements and architectural models.

The prototype is based on the open-source Eclipse Modeling Framework (EMF). The prototype relies on Eclipse's plug-in mechanisms to provide integrated functionality for users. The prototype consists of the following components:

- EMF core modeling facilities.
- Apache ODE – ODE is an open source BPEL engine. The generated BPEL code is compiled and deployed to ODE. The BPEL code invokes services based on WSDL files.
- Apache CXF – CXF is an open-source web-services framework which supports standard APIs such as JAX-WS and JAX-RS as well as WS standards including SOAP, and WSDL.
- Eclipse Swordfish – Swordfish is an open-source extensible Enterprise Service Bus (ESB).

By building the E-Commerce SPL feature and multiple view service models correctly, i.e. without errors detected by the underlying OCL rules, we validated that multiple views of the service oriented product line are consistent with each other. In addition, we validated that the multiple-view E-Commerce SPL model is compliant with the underlying multiple view variability meta-model, because EMF ensures the compliance of models by applying the underlying meta-model syntax rules. We also validated the automated derivation of the E-Commerce SPL member applications.

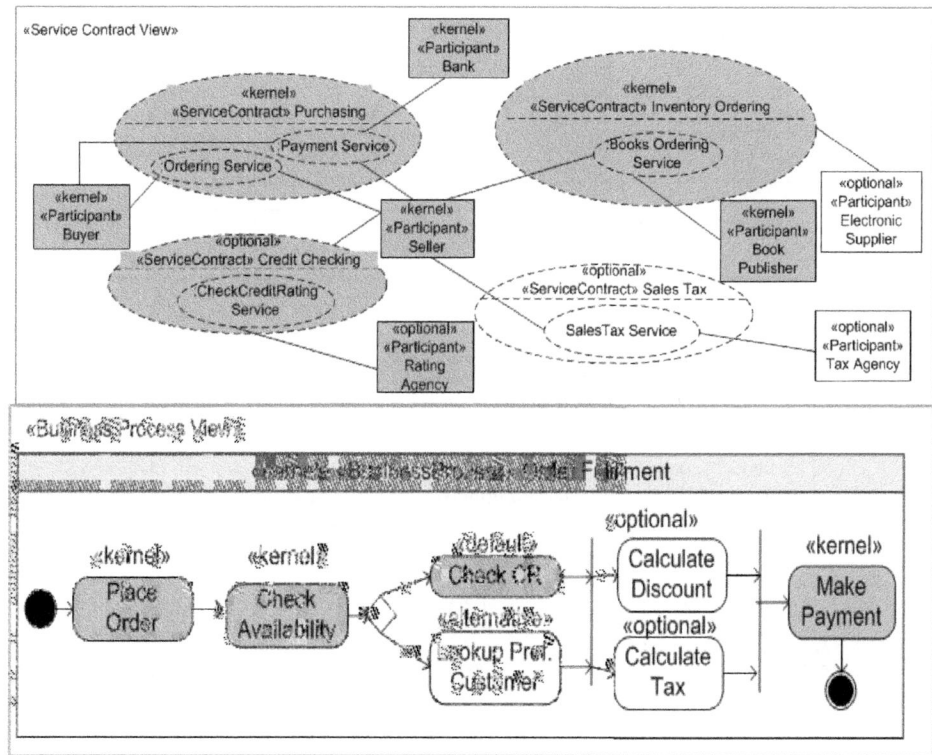

Fig. 6. Service Requirements Views of the Basic E-Commerce Member Application

7   Related Work

There have been several approaches for modeling variability in SOA. This section discusses related work and examines them in light of our work.

Chang and Kim in [8] add variability analysis techniques to an existing service oriented analysis and design method (SOAD). Decision tables, rather than feature models, are used to record variability types in each phase of the SOAD process.

Topaloglu and Capilla [9] present architectural pattern approaches to model variation points in Web Services. Capilla and Topaloglu [11] advocate an SPL engineering approach that has a specific phase for service composition in the SPL architecture. Variation points are used to customize the SPL during service selection. However, service selection is not tied to SPL features.

Gomaa and Saleh [10] present an SPL engineering approach based on Web Services. Feature selection is used to determine the selection of Web Services for a business application. This paper builds on this research to address several additional SOA views.

In [12], the authors used the concept of features to solve variability problems for SOA. However, the authors' approach assumes the availability of service implementation code, which is not the norm in most SOA scenarios.

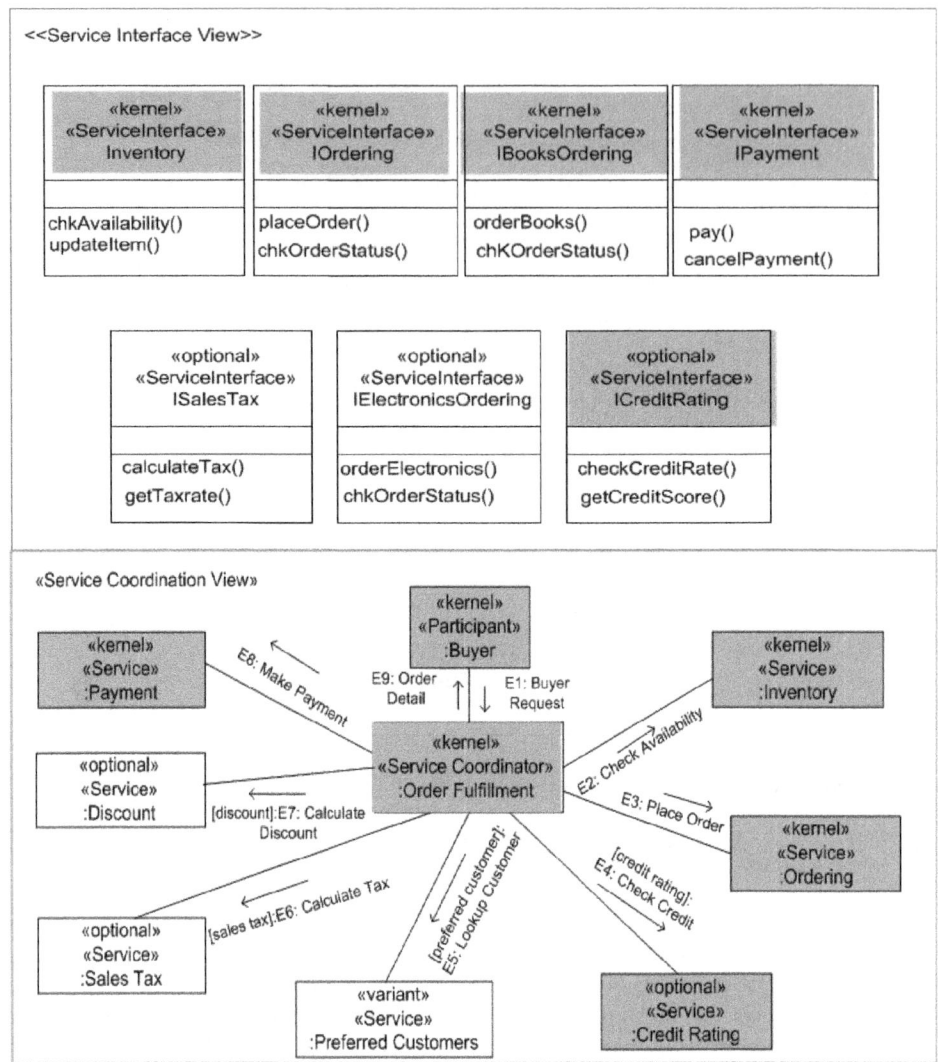

Fig. 7. Service Architectural Views of the Basic E-Commerce Member Application

Park et al. [13] suggest a feature-based reusable domain service development approach to create reusable domain services. However, the approach in [13] above does not consider the relationships between features and services.

The authors in [16] propose a top down approach for service oriented SPL architectures which systematically identifies and documents reusable service core assets. The approach in this paper is similar to our approach in that it uses multiple views to represent the architecture of the SPL. However, the approach does not provide a rigorous description of the relationships between the views and how feature selection affects all views. Our modeling approach also relies on an underlying meta-model that formalizes the relationships within and among the views.

The authors in [17] combine SPL and SOA principles to design a service-oriented SPL, which uses feature models. Selected features are mapped to Web Services represented in WSDL files. Each WSDL file is tied to a specific step in a predefined business process flow. Unlike our approach, the authors assume that the business process flow does not change with different member applications of the SPL. Additionally, their research is concerned only with the service interface (one of our multiple views) represented in WSDL, which make it platform specific. The authors do not employ a meta-model for their approach.

It should be noted that our research addresses design-time variability and not runtime SOA variability issues. Our previous work on dynamic adaptation has addressed some issues of runtime adaptation in SOA [5, 20].

8   Conclusions

In this paper, we have described a multiple-view meta-modeling approach that addresses service oriented variability concerns in a unified and platform independent manner. In particular, we described the integration of SPL concepts of feature modeling and commonality/variability analysis with service views using UML and SoaML. We validated our approach by developing a proof-of-concept prototype, which we used to build a multiple view E-Commerce service oriented product line.

The contributions of this paper are:

- Modeling of SOA variability concerns in a unified, systematic, multiple-view variability meta-model.
- Provide a multiple view meta-model for service oriented product lines.
- Define OCL consistency checking rules for the multiple view meta-model.
- Facilitate variability modeling of service families in a platform independent way.
- Integrate SPL concepts of feature modeling techniques and commonality/variability analysis with service modeling approaches to manage variability in SOA.
- Extend SoaML with variability modeling notation.
- Provide a proof-of-concept prototype to validate our approach.

In our ongoing research, we are building on our existing research to introduce a service variability mediation layer to further decouple service providers and consumers. In addition, we are investigating evolution and dynamic run-time adaptation of service-oriented SPLs.

Acknowledgment. This research is partially supported by grant CCF-0820060 from the National Science Foundation.

References

[1] Erl, T.: Service-Oriented Architecture (SOA): Concepts, Technology, and Design. Prentice Hall (2005)
[2] Gomaa, H.: Designing Software Product Lines with UML: From Use Cases to Pattern-Based Software Architectures. Addison-Wesley Professional (2004)
[3] Kang, K., Cohen, S., Hess, J., Nowak, W., Peterson, S.: Feature-Oriented Domain Analysis (FODA) Feasibility Study (1990)

[4] Gomaa, H., Shin, M.E.: Multiple-view modelling and meta-modelling of software product lines. IET Software 2(2), 94–122 (2008)

[5] Gomaa, H., Hashimoto, K., Kim, M., Malek, S., Menascé, D.A.: Software adaptation patterns for service-oriented architectures. In: Proceedings of the 2010 ACM Symposium on Applied Computing, New York, NY, USA, pp. 462–469 (2010)

[6] Abu-Matar, M., Gomaa, H., Kim, M., Elkhodary, A.M.: Feature Modeling for Service Variability Management in Service-Oriented Architectures. In: SEKE 2010, pp. 468–473 (2010)

[7] Abu-Matar, M., Gomaa, H.: Feature Based Variability for Service Oriented Architectures. In: The 9th Working IEEE/IFIP Conference on Software Architecture, Boulder, Colorado, USA (2011)

[8] Chang, S.H., Kim, S.D.: A Service-Oriented Analysis and Design Approach to Developing Adaptable Services. In: IEEE International Conference on Services Computing, Los Alamitos, CA, USA, pp. 204–211 (2007)

[9] Topaloglu, N.Y., Capilla, R.: Modeling the Variability of Web Services from a Pattern Point of View. In: Zhang, L.-J., Jeckle, M. (eds.) ECOWS 2004. LNCS, vol. 3250, pp. 128–138. Springer, Heidelberg (2004)

[10] Gomaa, H., Saleh, M.: Software product line engineering for Web services and UML. In: Proceedings of the ACS/IEEE 2005 International Conference on Computer Systems and Applications, Washington, DC, USA, p. 110–vii (2005)

[11] Capilla, R., Topaloglu, N.Y.: Product Lines for Supporting the Composition and Evolution of Service Oriented Applications. In: International Workshop on Principles of Software Evolution, Los Alamitos, CA, USA, pp. 53–56 (2005)

[12] Apel, S., Kaestner, C., Lengauer, C.: Research challenges in the tension between features and services. In: Proceedings of the 2nd International Workshop on Systems Development in SOA Environments, New York, NY, USA, pp. 53–58 (2008)

[13] Park, J.: An approach to developing reusable domain services for service oriented applications, New York, NY, USA, pp. 2252–2256 (2010)

[14] Kruchten, P.: The 4+1 View Model of Architecture. IEEE Software 12(6), 42–50 (1995)

[15] Griss, M., Favaro, J., d'Alessandro, M.: Integrating Feature Modeling with the RSEB. In: Devanbu, P., Poulin, J. (eds.) Proceedings of Fifth International Conference on Software Reuse, Victoria, British Columbia, Canada, June 2-5, pp. 1–10. IEEE Computer Society Press, Los Alamitos (1998)

[16] Medeiros, F.M., de Almeida, E.S., de Lemos Meira, S.R.: Towards an Approach for Service-Oriented Product Line Architectures. In: Proceedings of the Workshop on Service-oriented Architectures and Software Product Lines, San Francisco, CA (2009)

[17] Gunther, S., Berger, T.: Service-oriented product lines: Towards a development process and feature management model for web services. In: Proc. 12th International Software Product Line Conf., pp. 131–136 (2008)

[18] Perrouin, G., Klein, J., Guelfi, N., Jezequel, J.-M.: Reconciling Automation and Flexibility in Product Derivation. In: Proc. 12th International Software Product Line Conference, pp. 339–348 (2008)

[19] Abu-Matar, M., Gomaa, H.: Variability Modeling for Service Oriented Product Line Architectures. In: Proc. 15th International Software Product Line Conference, Munich, Germany (August 2011)

[20] Gomaa, H., Hashimoto, K.: Dynamic Software Adaptation for Service-Oriented Product Lines. In: Proc. Fifth International Workshop on Dynamic Software Product Lines, Munich, Germany (August 2011)

Summary of the Workshop on Multi-Paradigm Modelling: Concepts and Tools

Vasco Amaral[1], Cécile Hardebolle[2], Hans Vangheluwe[3,4],
László Lengyel[5], and Peter Bunus[6]

[1] Universidade Nova de Lisboa, Portugal
vasco.amaral@di.fct.unl.pt
[2] Supélec, France
cecile.hardebolle@supelec.fr
[3] University of Antwerp, Belgium
Hans.Vangheluwe@ua.ac.be
[4] McGill University, Canada
hv@cs.mcgill.ca
[5] BME, Budapest
Lengyel.Laszlo@aut.bme.hu
[6] Linkoping University, Sweden
peter.bunus@liu.se

Abstract. Following the trend of other editions, it was held this year (2011) in Wellington, New Zealand, the 5th International Workshop on Multi-Paradigm Modelling: Concepts and Tools (MPM). Once again has been a satellite event of the International Conference on Model-Driven Engineering Languages and Systems (MoDELS). It aims at further the state-of-the-art as well as to define future directions of this emerging research area by bringing together world experts in the field for an intense one-day workshop. This paper summarizes the results of this year's event.

1 Introduction

Multi-Paradigm Modelling (MPM) is a research field focused on solving the challenge of combining, coupling, and integrating rigorous models of some reality, at different levels of abstraction and views, using adequate modelling formalisms and semantic domains, with the goal to simulate (for optimization) or realize systems that may be physical, software or a combination of both. This field promotes that modeling by means of different modeling formalisms, with different perspectives of the system, it can be avoided the tendency to over-design, the modeler works with more manageable models and the system's integration is better supported. The identified key challenges are on finding adequate Model Abstractions, Multi-formalism modelling, Model Transformation and the application of MPM techniques and tools to Complex Systems.

MPM is a series of annual events [1] that has experienced a steady growth in participation, having this year, stabilized around the figure of 25 participants.

---

[1] The MoDELS MPM workshop was first held in 2006 in Genova, Italy, then in 2007 in Nashville, USA, and 2009 in Denver, USA and the last one in Oslo, Norway, 2010 and finally this year 2011 in Wellington, New Zealand.

J. Kienzle (Ed.): MODELS 2011 Workshops, LNCS 7167, pp. 83–88, 2012.

After a review process that counted with 4 reviewers per paper, 6 high quality contributions out of 13 were selected for oral communications (grouped in two sessions), and 3 papers were accepted for a poster session. This time, a session was dedicated for discussion groups.

2   Communications

1) Session: Multiple Models and Model Composition-MoC

Paper [1] presents a framework called Cometa for heterogeneous modeling based on the concept of MoC. The central element of Cometa is a meta-model for representing models in which components are connected to each other through ports and connectors. Different "domains", i.e. different semantics can be attached to different elements of a model (components, ports, connectors) depending on the Model of Computation according to which they should be executed.

The focus of paper [2] is specifically on the notion of "adaptation" between models interpreted according to different Models of Computation. In this approach, based on a framework called ModHel'X, different MoC can only be used in different hierarchical levels of a heterogeneous model. The authors argue that the adaptation between the different semantics of two hierarchical levels involving different MoCs must be modeled explicitly and separately from the models to adapt. To this end, they propose to use a language for specifying clocks and constraints between clocks called CCSL (Clock Constraint Specification Language), defined in the specification of the MARTE UML profile (Modeling and Analysis of Real Time and Embedded Systems). The example of a power window, modeled using two different models of computation, Discrete Events (DE) and Timed Finite State Machine (TFSM), is taken as a case study.

In [3], it is presented a methodology in which concern-specific meta-models for describing views can be derived from an initial overall meta-model (projective aspect of the methodology). Each view meta-model comes with automatically generated mechanisms for synchronizing and for preserving the consistency among all the views (synthetic aspect of the methodology). An implementation in Eclipse of the methodology using EMF, Ecore and ATL model transformations is presented, showing how editors can be generated to allow multiple designers to concurrently create and edit views which conform to different view meta-models, which is interesting for heterogeneous multi-view modeling.

2) Session: Model Transformations

Paper[4] investigates techniques to prove that model transformations are correct. Even though it is now possible to explicitly build the set of syntactic correspondences from a given transformation, it is still not clear how to reason about the correctness of these syntactic correspondences w.r.t. to both the source and target language's underlying semantics. In the paper, correctness of a model-to-model transformation is analyzed by establishing a semantic relation between the respective operational semantics. The approach is demonstrated through a concrete translation between two languages: State Machines and Petri Nets.

Paper [5] addresses the problem of model transformation re-use in different context. Their work is inspired by generic programming and proposes *generic model transformations*. Such generic transformations are defined over meta-model *concepts* which are later bound to specific meta-models. Current binding mechanisms lack automated resolution support for recurring structural heterogeneity between meta-models. Therefore, based on a systematic classification of meta-model heterogeneity, the paper proposes a flexible binding mechanism able to automatically resolve recurring structural heterogeneity between metamodels. For this, the binding model is analyzed and required adapters are automatically added to the transformation.

Finally, paper [6] addresses the complexities of deployment-space exploration, by means of refinement (model) transformations. In particular, a high-level architecture description provides the basis for the choice of a low-level implementation. It focuses on real-time systems. All possible solutions of a deployment step are generated using a refinement transformation while the non-conforming results are pruned as early as possible using a simulation model or analytical method. The feasibility of the approach was demonstrated by deploying part of an automotive power window.

3) Session: Posters

Poster [7] presents on-going work on an approach for querying, selection and pruning models. Under the assumption that models are often treated wholly or in part as trees, the authors propose a novel approach to model querying-by-example, treating models as trees. It exploits tree-based patterns in expressing queries, where the results of the queries are also trees. Thus, it provides means to compose (conjoin) queries without requiring intermediate manipulations.

Poster [8] concentrates on the issue of Languages Usability. Departing from the statement that usability evaluation of new languages is often skipped or relaxed, although being a key factor for its successful adoption, the authors argue that a systematic approach based on User Interface experimental validation techniques should be used to assess the impact of those same languages. The poster goes a little bit further discussed the quality criteria, proposes a development and evaluation process that could be used to achieve usable languages.

Finally, poster [9] presents work on verifying access control policies in statecharts. The approach is based on the transformation of a statechart into an Algebraic Petri net to enable checking access control policies and identifying potential inconsistencies with an OrBAC set of access control policies.

4) Discussion Group: Modular Design of Modelling Languages

The working group on modular design of modelling languages recognized that there is a growing need for the principled and modular design, not only of models, but also of modelling languages.

In software-intensive systems for example, the need is increasingly felt for rigorously designed modelling languages to describe, analyze, simulate, optimize, and where appropriate synthesize their physical, control, and software components, as well as the often intricate interplay of those components. In addition, requirements/property languages for these highly diverse formalisms should be carefully engineered to match the design languages and to form the basis for automated analyzes. The need for combining modelling languages to form new ones goes beyond Domain-Specific Modelling Languages. Even simple State Machines are in practice already combined languages as their use requires not only the basic automata with states and transitions, but also an action language to describe what the effects of transitions are on the values of variables.

The starting point for the modular design of modelling languages is the realization that to define a language, its abstract syntax (AS), concrete syntax (CS), and semantics (SEM), including both semantic domain and semantic mapping, need to be explicitly modelled. In the working group, the different combinations of modelling languages were discussed. At the level of abstract syntax (modelled in the form of meta-models), this led to the insight that meta-models may need to be Reduced (when only part of a language is needed), Augmented (when new notions need to be incorporated) and Combined. The latter can be through the introduction of Associations, through merging, inheritance, and embedding.

The working group explored practical examples and took initial steps towards a classification of techniques for the modular design of modelling languages.

5) Discussion Group: Modeling Model Compositions - MoCs

A major challenge in MoCs is to obtain a meaningful result from models with heterogeneous semantics implying that the semantics of the modeling languages must be explicitly and formally described in order to enable model composition. One approach for representing semantics is the concept of Model of Computation. The working group tackled the definitions of the main concepts to use in the methodology to describe Models of Computation. For that, the group focused the discussion on models which describe the behavior of systems and two hypothesis were made: i) the abstract syntax of the modeling language used to describe a model is described by a *meta-model*(i.e. there is a conformance relation between a model and the meta-model of its language) ii) the semantics of the language must enable the *execution* of the model (executing a model means computing one of the possible behaviors described by the model, and the result of its execution is a series of observation, i.e. a trace which represents of the computed behavior).

In this context, the discussion group has agreed on the following definition: *Model of Computation:* A Model of Computation is a constructive definition of the behavior of a model obtained by composition of the behavior of its elements.

The concepts defined by the discussion group is an attempt to lay the foundations for a methodology to represent models of computation. The group has discussed how to explicit the notion of state of a model and to define means to model it. In spite of the enthusiastic discussion held by this discussion group, much work remains to obtain a complete framework for describing models of computation, i.e. for describing execution semantics for models.

6) Discussion Group: Evaluating Usability in the Context of MPM

Departing from a perspective that MPM, as a methodology, thrives for removing the accidental complexity in software development, by choosing adequate formalisms at the right level of abstraction, the working group raised the following questions: Once decided the modeling formalisms how do we know that they are adequate? What is a good formalism adequate for a given problem?an finally, how do we measure that same adequacy to the problem?

It was generally accepted, by the discussion group, that to answer those questions we have to define Quality criteria. In addition, we need to proceed with empirical studies with real users and have a sound process for evaluation. The discussion proceeded by highlighting that an evaluation process can be (from a loose approximation to a more serious and strong one): a toy example, industrial case study, or properly conceived empirical studies. For the last one, the Quality criteria, supporting the evaluation process, implies metrics and measurement.

From this general vision, several questions arose as being still open for discussion: Does the composition of demonstrated usable Languages implies to be still usable?and, what is the difference between usability and Re-usability? Is MPM itself a good solution for Usability purposes?

The rest of the working group discussion was focused on sketching the road-map for a sound methodology and tool support to determine Usability in MPM.

3   Conclusion

The workshop was deemed very successful by the participants, and we plan to continue organizing future workshops. It is a vibrant forum for research and industry experts to join together and discuss fundamental concepts and tools for Multi-Paradigm Modelling. At the end of the event the attendants voted for papers [2] and [3] for the best two papers award.

This workshop would not been possible without the help of many people besides the authors. We wish to acknowledge our Programme Committee[2].

---

[2] Antonio Vallecillo (Universidad de Málaga), Arnaud Cuccuru (CEA LIST), Bruno Barroca (UNL), Bernhard Westfechtel (U. Bayreuth), Cécile Hardebolle (Supélec), Chris Paredis (Georgia Tech), Christophe Jacquet (Supélec), Didier Buchs (U. Geneva), Dirk Deridder (Free U. Brussels), Esther Guerra (U. Carlos III de Madrid), Eugene Syriani (U. Alabama), Franck Fleurey (SINTEF), Frédéric Boulanger (Supélec), Gergely Mezei (Budapest University of Technology and Economics), Hessam Sarjoughian (U. Arizona State), Hans Vangheluwe (U. McGill and U. Antwerp), Holger Giese (Hasso-Plattner-Institut), Jeff Gray (U. Alabama), Jeroen Voeten (Eindhoven University of Technology), Jonathan Sprinkle (U. Arizona), Laurent Safa (Silver Egg Technology),László Lengyel (Budapest University of Technology and Economics), Luís Pedro (D'Auriol Assets), Mamadou K. Traoré (FR Sciences et Technologies), Manuel Wimmer (Vienna University of Technology), Mark Minas (U. Federal Armed Forces), Martin Törngren (KTH Royal Institute of Technology), Matteo Risoldi (U. Geneva), Peter Bunus (Linkoping University), Pieter van Gorp (Eindhoven University of Technology), Stefan Van Baelen (K.U. Leuven), Steve Hostettler (U. Geneva), Thomas Feng (Oracle), Thomas Kühne (Victoria University of Wellington), Vasco Amaral (UNL).

References

1. Diallo, P.I., Champeau, J., Leilde, V.: Model based engineering for the support of models of computation: The cometa approach. In: MPM 2011. ECEASST (2011)
2. Boulanger, F., Dogui, A., Hardebolle, C., Jacquet, C., Marcadet, D., Prodan, I.: Semantic adaptation using ccsl clock constraints. In: MPM 2011. ECEASST (2011)
3. Cicchetti, A., Ciccozzi, F., Leveque, T.: A hybrid approach for multi-view modeling. In: MPM 2011. ECEASST (2011)
4. Barroca, B., Amaral, V.: Asserting the correctness of translations. In: MPM 2011. ECEASST (2011)
5. Wimmer, M., Kusel, A., Retschitzegger, W., Schoenboeck, J., Schwinger, W., Cuadrado, J.S., Guerra, E., Lara, J.D.: Reusing model transformations across heterogeneous metamodels. In: MPM 2011. ECEASST (2011)
6. Denil, J., Cicchetti, A., Biehl, M., Meulenaere, P.D., Eramo, R., Demeyer, S., Vangheluwe, H.: Automatic deployment space exploration using refinement transformations. In: MPM 2011. ECEASST (2011)
7. Radjenovic, A., Paige, R.: An approach for model querying-by-example applied to multi-paradigm models. In: MPM 2011. ECEASST (2011)
8. Barisic, A., Amaral, V., Goulão, M., Barroca, B.: How to reach a usable dsl? moving toward a systematic evaluation. In: MPM 2011. ECEASST (2011)
9. Lucio, L., Zhang, Q., Sousa, V., Traon, Y.L.: Verifying access control in statecharts. In: MPM 2011. ECEASST (2011)

Supporting Incremental Synchronization in Hybrid Multi-view Modelling

Antonio Cicchetti, Federico Ciccozzi, and Thomas Leveque

School of Innovation, Design and Engineering - MRTC
Mälardalen University, Västerås, Sweden
`firstname.lastname@mdh.se`

Abstract. Multi-view modelling is a widely accepted technique to reduce the complexity in the development of modern software systems. It allows developers to focus on a narrowed portion of the specification dealing with a selected aspect of the problem. However, multi-view modelling support discloses a number of issues mainly due to consistency management, expressiveness, and customization needs. A possible solution to alleviate those problems is to adopt a hybrid solution for multi-view modelling based on an arbitrary number of custom views defined on top of an underlying modelling language. In this way it is possible to benefit from the consistency by-construction granted by well-formed views while at the same time providing malleable perspectives through which the system under development can be specified. In this respect, this paper presents an approach for supporting synchronization mechanism based on model differences in hybrid multi-view modelling. Model differences allow to focus only on the manipulations operated by the user in a particular view, and to propagate them to the other views in a incremental way thus reducing the overhead of a complete recomputation of modified models.

Keywords: Multi-view modelling, separation of concerns, model-driven engineering, model synchronization, higher-order model transformation.

1 Introduction

Nowadays software systems are employed in any kind of applicative domain, ranging from a tiny music player to the management of nuclear plants or air traffic control. The growth of their complexity is never ceasing demanding adequate techniques to face their development. Model-driven engineering (MDE) [16] has been conceived as a way to face such difficulties by means of models, that is precise abstractions of real-world phenomena highlighting the salient details with respect to the system under study [1]. Moreover, models are no more considered as mere documentation but exploited as the specification of the application itself.

Because of the aforementioned complexity of software systems, that also tend to mix heterogeneous domains, a problem is typically decomposed into different viewpoints, each of which approaches the solution from a domain-specific perspective. Multi-view modelling mechanisms are usually distinguished between [11]:

J. Kienzle (Ed.): MODELS 2011 Workshops, LNCS 7167, pp. 89–103, 2012.

- **synthetic:** each view is implemented as a distinct meta-model and the overall system is obtained as *synthesis* of the information carried by the different views;
- **projective:** end-users are provided with *virtual* views made up of selected concepts coming from a single base meta-model by hiding details not relevant for the particular viewpoint taken into account.

The former is a powerful solution to multi-view modelling as it can exploit the expressive power of disparate meta-models, each of which dealing with a particular aspect of the system under study [1]. However, the use of a constellation of domain-specific meta-models opens up a number of problems, mainly related to consistency management [13]. The projective approach technically relies on a single underlying meta-model to ease the consistency management; even if end-users[1] work virtually on multiple views changes are operated on the same shared model. This often amounts to being too restrictive because either the meta-model is too generic (i.e., with scarcely specified semantics) or the views are too specific to be reused in several development contexts [4].

To alleviate the issues discussed so far, in [6] we elicited a set of desirable features a multi-view modelling environment should support, and then provided a solution in order to satisfy such demands. In particular, we introduced an automated mechanism representing a hybrid technique for multi-view modelling based on the definition of multiple views on top of a meta-model, each of which entails a corresponding sub-portion of the overall meta-model. In this way, it is possible to obtain a good trade-off between synthetic and projective techniques for multi-view modelling implementation.

In this paper, it is presented the synchronization mechanism on which the hybrid approach in [6] relies. Model differencing techniques are exploited to detect end-users' manipulations in a given view, represent them both for the view and the overall model, and propagate them to the remaining views. The aim is to realize an incremental synchronization approach able to punctually update changes, hence without requiring to deal with complete artefacts. This characteristic is very useful, e.g., whenever dealing with large models, since in general the amount of changes is much smaller than the involved models considered as a whole. As a consequence, the portion of changes that has to be first propagated to the overall model and then to the other views is remarkably reduced.

The structure of the paper is as follows: the next section discusses related solutions available for both the synthetic and the projective implementations of multi-view modelling. Then, Section 3 illustrates the overall proposal for providing a hybrid approach for multi-view and summarizes the properties it is intended to support, while Section 4 provides the technical insights of the incremental synchronization mechanism which is the aim of this work. Section 5 and 6 discuss the current status of the work and limitations, future investigation directions, and draw some conclusions.

2   Background and Related Works

Separation of concerns is not a novel concept; it is, in fact, the basic principle prescribing to reduce problem complexity by tackling it from different perspectives. The IEEE 1471

---

[1] *Developer* represents the person creating the views, while *end-user* the one using them.

standardized a set of recommended practices for the description of software-intensive systems' architectures that have been adopted as standard by ISO in 2007 [11]. In particular, architectural descriptions are conceived as inherently multi-view, since an exhaustive specification of a system can only be provided by means of different viewpoints. In particular, a *viewpoint* is a set of concerns and modelling techniques to define the system from a certain perspective, and a *view* is the corresponding instance of the viewpoint taken into account for the system under development. As distinguished in the ISO specification and in other works [13,2], multi-view approaches can be categorized in synthetic and projective. Depending on the kind of approach, different techniques have been developed to support development and maintenance of the system specification.

For the synthetic approach, a constellation of (typically) distinct meta-models is used to describe different features of the system depending on the domain the system is studied in. For instance, a web modelling language based on the Model-View-Controller pattern [8] allows to specify a web application by considering the data underlying the application, the business logic, and the user presentation as three different concerns that are modelled on their own. Then, in order to obtain the blended application, those concerns have to be synthesized (or woven) toward a resulting system [9,10]. Analogously it happens with, for example, embedded systems, whose development is made by separating hardware from software characteristics, and in turn functional from extra-functional features, and so forth [2]. In these and similar cases, interplays between the different viewpoints have to be explicitly defined in order to allow the synthesis of the resulting system. In other words, it must be clarified how the different viewpoints can be merged (the matches between entities in different models), and the semantics of overlaps. In general such relationships can be defined by means of transformations that embed the semantics behind views interplays [15]. Alternatively, all the views can be reduced to a *common denominator* through which it is possible to synthesize the information carried by the different viewpoints and derive the resulting system specification [17].

The main issue related to synthetic approaches is consistency management: since semantics is involved in the relationships across models, interconnections have to be carefully defined, a task that grows with the number of exploited views. Moreover, adding or updating views, especially if not orthogonal to the existing ones, demands a revision of the current consistency rules as well as synthesis mechanisms [13].

In order to partially overcome the problems mentioned above, a possible solution is to build up views on top of a single base meta-model. In this way, end-users can be provided with a set of views allowing the specification of the system from different perspectives. At the same time, consistency management can be obtained for free by-construction, since all the changes boil down to manipulations of the same model, even if virtually operated from different viewpoints [13]. Despite an easier consistency management, such projective approaches demand a well defined semantics of the base language. For instance, synchronization of UML diagrams [3] poses several issues, even if developers are operating on the same model, because of ambiguities in the formalization of such language. Moreover, projective solutions suffer a limited customizability because of the fixed base language and the predefined set of views. It is worth noting that in general the base language has no knowledge of the concept of view, therefore implementing cross-checks between user operations or providing editing rights within each view to drive the application design either require language extensions [14] or have to be hard-coded in the supporting tool [4].

The work in [6] presents a hybrid technique aiming to reach a good trade-off between synthetic and projective approaches. The main idea is to start from a base meta-model (referred to as overall meta-model in the paper) and to allow the developer to create views through an extensive set of customization opportunities. Compared to projective approaches, such methodology creates proper meta-models, one for each view, instead of simply hiding elements that do not matter a particular viewpoint. Moreover, the principal distinction with synthetic solutions is the consistency and synthesis management: interdependencies between views are directly derived when a view is built, as well as synthesis mechanisms, that can be automatically generated to keep the different perspectives up-to-date. Moreover, views are not predetermined and can be introduced at any time of the development together with manipulation rights. A similar approach is provided by the Obeo Designer[2]: it allows to create views on top of a meta-model, to select the elements to show for each view, and even to customize the graphical rendering of model elements and operations on them. However, the implementation mechanism does not rely on the creation of a proper meta-model for each view, and view creation is a preliminary step operated before the system development begins. Furthermore, editing rights granted on elements pertaining to each view cannot be controlled.

This paper extends the work in [6] by providing support for incremental synchronization of views: *i)* changes in a given view are detected by means of model differencing techniques; *ii)* a proper model-based difference representation approach is used to store modifications and propagate them to interconnected artefacts through appositely generated in-place model transformations. In this way, it is possible to focus on the manipulations that happened in a certain view, thus allowing a more efficient propagation of changes to the other views, especially in the case of large models. The methodology in [5] has been selected to support the proposal illustrated in this paper due to its generative fashion which permits, based on the meta-model given as input, to generate the corresponding difference representation. Based on such representation, this work also provides higher-order transformations able to derive in-place application transformations in terms of the Operational Query/View/Transformation language QVTo[3]. In this respect, this paper enhances the application mechanism in [5] by avoiding the regeneration of elements left untouched by the changes.

In the reminder of the paper, basic requirements for views are described and they underpin creation and management features illustrated in detail in the following sections.

3   Creating a Hybrid Multi-view Modelling Environment

The aim of this work is to provide a support for incremental synchronization of design models in a hybrid multi-view modelling environment based on a trade-off between synthetic and projective solutions [6]. In such sense, this section gives an overview on: *i)* the set of features we considered as basic needs for views in a multi-view modelling

---

[2] http://www.obeodesigner.com/
[3] http://wiki.eclipse.org/M2M/Operational_QVT_Language_(QVTO)

environment, *ii)* the rules for views and overall meta-models to be consistent and their respective models to be incrementally synchronizable; moreover, an overall description of the proposed approach is given.

3.1   View Editing Support and Consistency Requirements

In order to provide a support for the generation of multi-view modelling environment, a set of basic features for supporting such environment have to be specified and can be grouped in three main categories: *i)* view definition, tailored to guarantee high customization opportunities during view creation, *ii)* editing facilities, devoted to make the view as much "domain-specific" as possible, both by allowing only narrowed manipulation features and through the definition of appropriate concrete syntaxes, and *iii)* synchronization management, needed to make the end-users able to operate on separate views independently of one another. A detailed description of these features can be found in [6].

A new view is generated by selecting model elements from the overall meta-model; such selection must follow a set of rules in order for the views and the overall meta-model to be consistent and their respective models to be synchronizable. The rules identified for such purposes can be grouped in two categories: *i)* consistency rules, needed for allowing the manipulation of selected meta-classes; those rules are automatically applied and require elements to be automatically included for consistency reasons in order for the view to achieve well-formedness, and *ii)* synchronization rules, for the generation of synchronization mechanisms. The detailed list and description of the aforementioned rules is given in [6].

3.2   Generating Customized Views and Synchronization Mechanisms

The approach we propose is based on the creation of customized views starting from an initial meta-model defined in Ecore (under the EMF development environment available in Eclipse). Such views are meant to be consistent sub-portions (i.e., meta-models) of the overall initial meta-model that isolate the manipulation of a certain set of interesting aspects. In this section we describe the proposed solution in order to achieve the followings: *i)* creation of customized views, from an initial Ecore meta-model, for achieving a consistent concern-specific meta-model still conforming to the overall meta-model, *ii)* provision of automatically generated synchronization mechanisms for maintaining consistency among the customized views and the overall meta-model, and *iii)* provision of an automatically generated ad-hoc Eclipse environment for managing such views.

The core artefacts of the proposed approach are shown in Fig. 1. A set of customized views are generated as sub-portions of the overall meta-model (Fig. 1a) together with the synchronization engine which is composed by: mechanisms for calculating differences between view model versions (Fig. 1b) and routines for propagating the operated changes to the models pertaining to the remaining views (Fig. 1c).

Views Generation. Each view is independently generated by a wizard, described in [6], that drives the developer through the generation process which consists of the following steps: *i)* view properties selection, for the definition of *View Name, NameSpace*

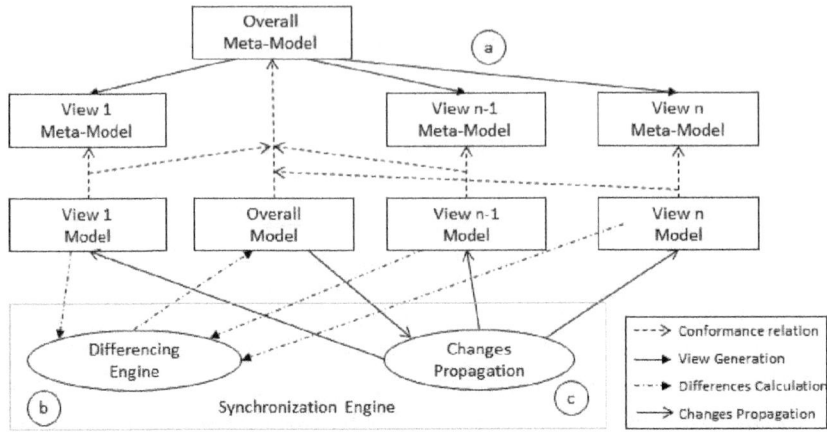

Fig. 1. Support for incremental synchronization by multi-view Modelling

Prefix, and *NameSpace URI* for the view meta-model, *ii)* view elements selection, for the selection of the elements constituting the overall meta-model to be part of the new view, *iii)* unique identifiers selection, in order to allow synchronization, *iv)* editing rights selection, for assigning customized editing rights to the view elements among two possibilities: read only or editable (e.g. read/write), *v)* selected view final check. The developer can decide to get the wizard itself to automatically select model elements in order to maintain consistency between the selected view and the overall meta-model. Such elements are selected according to the manually selected elements and the rules specified in Section 3.1 and applied to them. In case the developer decides not to use this facility, the wizard will anyhow inform the developer about the missing elements needed to create a consistent view in a dedicated page after the selection phase.

In Fig. 2 an example of generation of customized views from an overall meta-model is depicted. Starting from the *School* meta-model representing basic information about an education institution (Fig. 2A), the view creation wizard is applied for the generation of two new views in terms of separated meta-models (as sub-portions of the overall *School* meta-model):

1. *Teacher View*: with read rights on most of the *School* meta-model elements excluding the *FinancialRecord* elements while editing rights on *Program*, *Teacher* and *Student* meta-classes as well as their related meta-attributes and meta-references (Fig. 2B);
2. *Student View*: with no read rights on both *Employment* elements and *Program*'s *attendedBy* reference representing other students attending the program; editing rights are also restricted, giving the possibility to act only on the information related to *Student* meta-class (Fig. 2C).

The described overall meta-model and generated views are used in the remainder of the paper as running example for describing the other tasks of the proposed approach.

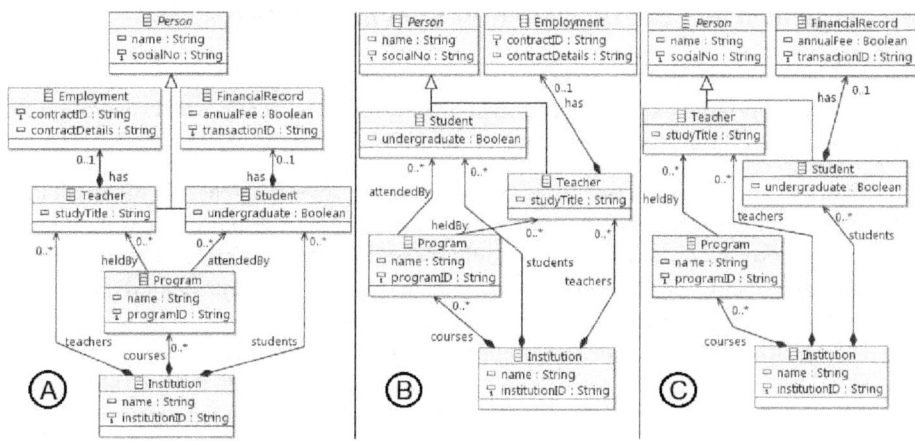

Fig. 2. Overall meta-model and generated views

Generating Synchronization Mechanisms. During the generation of the customized views, synchronization mechanisms are generated as follows:

- An ATL model-to-model transformation [5] generates the difference meta-models, which represent model modifications, starting from original and view meta-models;
- Corresponding differences computation and representation transformations are generated for each difference meta-model through higher-order transformations;
- At this point, a bidirectional patch for differences application, by means of in-place model-to-model transformations (from overall model to view model and vice versa), should be produced in order to be able to propagate model differences among views and overall models; also in this case higher-order transformations are used. Moreover, thanks to the properties carried by the difference representation mechanism it is possible to exploit the same difference model pertaining to a view to update the overall model and also the other views, whenever overlapping elements would exist.

A detailed description of such steps and involved artefacts is given in Section 4.

Customization of the Modelling Environment. The view creation process provides also a customized editing environment for the created view. This is achieved through a model-to-text transformation that takes as input a specific model generated during the view creation process and generates an Eclipse plug-in implementing the Eclipse model editor associated with the created view as described in [6]. The editor model is automatically generated by a QVTo model-to-model transformation that takes as input the created view meta-model and other needed information inserted by the developer in the wizard. The editor is similar to the default EMF generated tree editor except that *i)* model element creation opens a wizard which contains editing pages and *ii)* fields in property views can be not editable depending on the specified editing rights. In addition, a filter is used to hide details on the meta-classes that have been added to the view meta-model only for consistency purposes and a resource listener is generated in order to call the synchronization mechanism when required.

4   Implementing the Incremental Synchronization

Fig. 1 shows how the various artefacts are interconnected through the synchronization engine. We propose to exploit a generic approach for incremental synchronization that coordinates these artefacts as described in the following:

1. First, model changes detection is triggered by a resource listener on the model file;
2. Then, a model differencing algorithm is applied between the old and new model versions producing a difference model representing the performed modifications;
3. Hereafter, the difference model is mapped into another difference model representing the corresponding modifications on the overall model;
4. The resulting difference model is applied to the overall model;
5. Then, for each view, the difference model exploited to update the overall model in the previous step is transformed into appropriate difference models, each of which representing the corresponding modifications on a certain view model;
6. Eventually, the difference models are applied to the corresponding view models.

It may be worth noting that, when modifications come from the original model, steps 3 and 4 are skipped. However, our solution relies on the assumption that view models and overall model can not be changed concurrently in the workspace, and on the fact that every evolution action is first applied to the overall model and then propagated to the other views; thus, direct evolutions propagation among views is never performed.

The synchronization between customized views and overall model is heavily based on model transformations and model differencing techniques: the former allow to automate the intermediate coordination steps, as mapping difference formats between original model and views; the latter disclose the opportunity to efficiently propagate the changes occurred in one view to the others by punctually updating the involved models by means of model differences propagation. In the following, details are provided on how modifications are represented, detected, and applied. Moreover, it is illustrated how such mechanisms can be abstracted from the specific meta-model in order to provide a generic support for the incremental synchronization of views.

4.1   Model Differences Representation

The model difference representation is based on an existing work [5] which introduces a generic technique to derive a difference meta-model (MMD) from an original one (MM). It relies on the partitioning of the manipulations into three basic operations: *additions*, *deletions*, and *updates* of model elements. Then, MMD can be automatically obtained from MM by extending each meta-class (MC) with three specializations, AddedMC, DeletedMC, ChangedMC, respectively. Difference meta-models for both the overall meta-model and the view meta-model are generated during the view creation process through an adapted version of the ATL transformation described in [5]. The transformation takes as input a meta-model and enriches it with the constructs able to express the modifications that are performed on the initial version of a given model in order to obtain the modified version. For instance, in Fig. 3 it is shown an excerpt of the difference meta-model (*AddedTeacher*, *ChangedTeacher* and *DeletedTeacher* for representing differences concerning the Teacher meta-class, and *AddedProgram*,

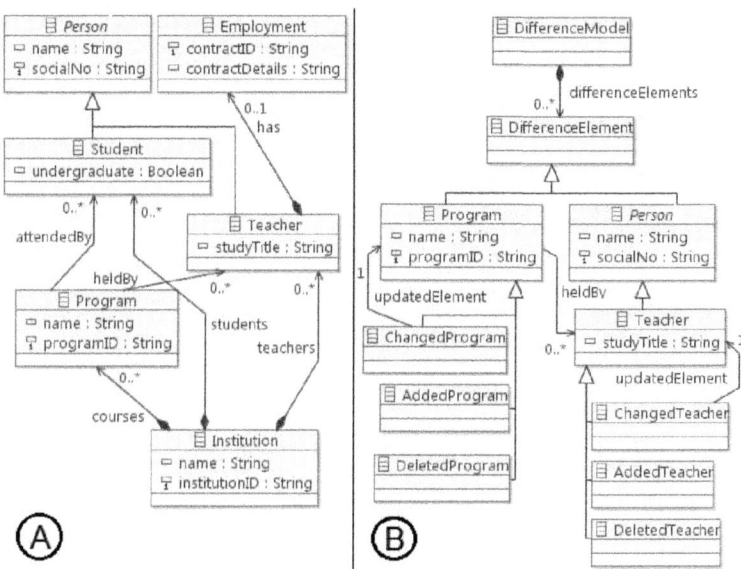

Fig. 3. Teacher View meta-model (A) and excerpt of the generated difference meta-model (B)

ChangedProgram and *DeletedProgram* for differences for the Program meta-class) for the *Teacher View* meta-model. Since view meta-models are proper sub-portions of the original meta-model, also difference meta-models automatically derived from the former ones are well-formed sub-portions of the overall difference meta-model by-construction. This makes the representation of modifications happened on view models to conform also to the overall difference meta-model, that is valid to be applied on the overall model too. As a consequence, the propagation of modifications from views to the overall model and vice versa can be remarkably simplified. Furthermore, difference models are minimal in the sense that they contain only the amount of operations needed to obtain the new version of a model from the old one, no extra information is added [5]. In this way, it is possible to have an optimal set of synchronization updates.

4.2 Detection of Model Changes

The computation of the differences between model versions is based on transformations specified in terms of the Epsilon comparison, merge and transformation languages [4] in a similar way as used in [7].

First, a set of rules defined using the Epsilon Comparison Language (ECL) is applied to original and modified version of the model. These rules aim at identifying matching elements between the two models by comparing the elements unique identifiers defined at view creation phase as well as identifying and storing possible changes. Using identifiers allows to correctly find the two corresponding elements between initial and modified version of the model and explore their properties to detect possible changes. At this

---

[4] http://eclipse.org/gmt/epsilon/

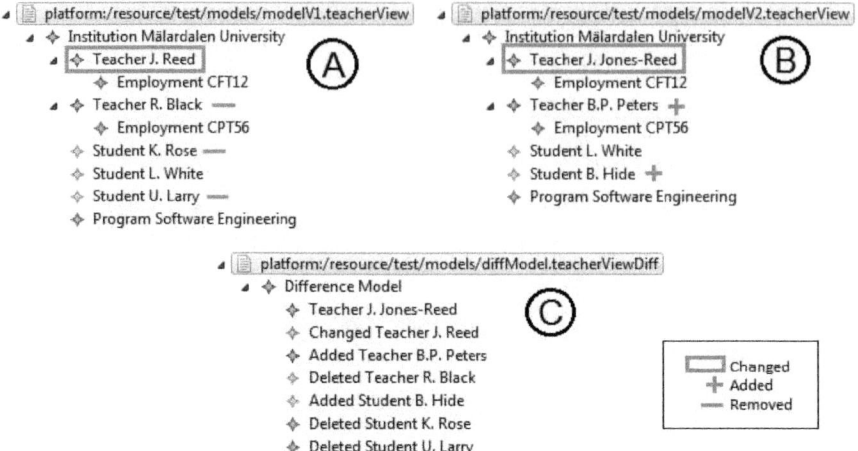

Fig. 4. Teacher View model versions (A-B) and difference model (C)

point a set of rules defined using the Epsilon Merge Language (EML) are in charge of transparently taking the ECL transformation results and thereby generate the difference model in terms of changed/original element pairs. If the ECL result structure contains information about a modification which affected the element, the changed element is created and linked to the original within the rule's body by using EOL expressions. As well as modified elements, deleted and added elements have to be identified too in order to produce a complete difference model; this step is performed through apposite rules defined using the Epsilon Transformation Language (ETL).

When the differences computation is completed, the difference model will show the results in a structured manner, ready to be used for the differences application to the overall model. In Fig. 4 original (Fig. 4A) and modified (Fig. 4B) of the *Teacher View* model are depicted together with the computed difference model (Fig. 4C). Regarding the operated changes, the element *Teacher J. Reed* is modified while elements *Teacher R. Black*, *Student K. Rose* and *Student U. Larry* are deleted. Furthermore, elements *Teacher B.P. Peters* and *Student B. Hide* are added.

The Epsilon transformations for differences calculation and difference model creation are generated by higher-order transformations, defined in the Acceleo model-to-text transformation language [5], which are able to create the needed difference transformations starting from any meta-model defined in Ecore and in which each meta-class has a specified meta-attribute acting as unique identifier. In Fig. 5 an excerpt of such higher-order transformations is given (left-hand side) as well as the ETL rules for detecting added and removed elements that result from their execution (right-hand side).

4.3   Synchronization of Views

Once changes operated in a certain view have been properly detected and represented, they have to be propagated. As introduced above, this is done by first updating the

---

[5] http://www.acceleo.org

```
[file (root.name+'_added_removed.etl', false, 'UTF-8')]    //Added Program Element
[for (econtent : EClass | root.eAllContents(EClass))]      rule AddProgram
//Added [econtent.name/] Element                             transform s : right!Program
rule Add[econtent.name/]                                     to t : diffModel!AddedProgram {
 transform s : right![econtent.name/]                         guard : not left.allInstances().
 to t : diffModel!Added[econtent.name/] {                     select(type|type.isTypeOf(left!Program)).
 guard : not left.allInstances().                                  exists(iter|iter.programID==
 select(type|type.isTypeOf(left![econtent.name/])).                        s.programID)
       exists(iter|iter.[econtent.eIDAttribute.name/]==      and not diffModel.allInstances().
                   s.[econtent.eIDAttribute.name/])          select(type|type.isTypeOf(diffModel!Program)).
 and not diffModel.allInstances().                                 exists(iter|iter.programID==
 select(type|type.isTypeOf(diffModel![econtent.name/]                       s.programID)
       exists(iter|iter.[econtent.eIDAttribute.name/]==      t.name := s.name;
                   s.[econtent.eIDAttribute.name/]))         t.programID := s.programID;
 [for (attr : EAttribute | econtent.eAllAttributes)]         diffModel!DifferenceModel.allInstances().first()
 t.[attr.name/] := s.[attr.name/];                                            .differenceElements.add(t);
 [/for]                                                     }
 diffModel!DifferenceModel.allInstances().first()
                       .differenceElements.add(t);
 }

//Removed [econtent.name/] Element                          //Removed Program Element
rule Delete[econtent.name/]                                 rule DeleteProgram
 transform s : left![econtent.name/]                          transform s : left!Program
 to t : diffModel!Deleted[econtent.name/] {                   to t : diffModel!DeletedProgram {
 guard : not right.allInstances().                           guard : not right.allInstances().
 select(type|type.isTypeOf(right![econtent.name/])).         select(type|type.isTypeOf(right!Program)).
       exists(iter|iter.[econtent.eIDAttribute.name/]==            exists(iter|iter.programID==
                   s.[econtent.eIDAttribute.name/])                         s.programID)
 and not diffModel.allInstances().                           and not diffModel.allInstances().
 select(type|type.isTypeOf(diffModel![econtent.name/]        select(type|type.isTypeOf(diffModel!Program)).
       exists(iter|iter.[econtent.eIDAttribute.name/]==            exists(iter|iter.programID==
                   s.[econtent.eIDAttribute.name/]))                        s.programID)
 [for (attr : EAttribute | econtent.eAllAttributes)]         t.name := s.name;
 t.[attr.name/] := s.[attr.name/];                           t.programID := s.programID;
 [/for]                                                      diffModel!DifferenceModel.allInstances().first().
 diffModel!DifferenceModel.allInstances().first().                   differenceElements.add(t);
                     differenceElements.add(t);             }
 }
[/for]
[/file]
```

Fig. 5. Higher-order transformation for model differencing and resulting transformation

overall model, as depicted in Fig. 6 where the *Teacher View* difference model shown previously is applied to the overall *School* model, and then by propagating the changes to the other views in a similar way. In particular, we rely on higher-order transformations that take as input a difference meta-model and derives in output a set of two QVTo transformations able to interpret the changes represented in difference models and apply them *i)* from view to overall model, for propagating changes performed on the particular view to the overall model, and *ii)* from overall to view model, for propagating the changes to the remaining views.

Considering our running example, in Fig. 7 it is shown an excerpt of both the higher-order transformation (left-hand side) and the resulting QVTo transformation (right-hand side) generated for the *Teacher View* meta-model for propagating differences to the overall *School* meta-model. In the example, the generated QVTo transformation is able to apply the changes represented in a *Teacher View* difference model, given in input, to an overall *School* model by means of in-place modifications.

At this point, some important clarifications have to be made about the hypotheses and background mechanisms the synchronization is based on. First of all, in order to avoid cyclic cascading of model changes, we associate a time-stamp with the difference model and ensure that modifications are only applied if the time-stamp is more recent than the one related to the current model file. However, that expedient does not avoid the appearance of conflicts, as modifications made concurrently on overlapping views

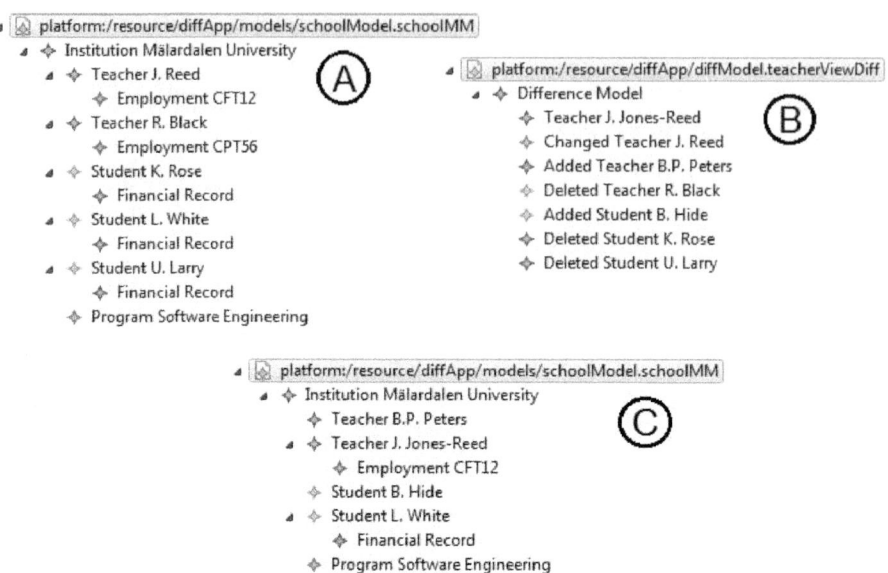

Fig. 6. Teacher View difference model (B) and School model before (A) and after (C) the differences application

could be inconsistent with one another. Therefore, in the current implementation we adopt a basic conflict resolution strategy such that updates are ordered by time-stamp and applied in the order they were operated. In this way, overlaps can be fixed by making the more recent changes to prevail; moreover, thanks to the application mechanism if a change does no longer make sense for a given input model (e.g., because the referred element has been deleted elsewhere) it is simply not applied. Nevertheless, more refined strategies for conflicts resolution, included partial automation of such resolution by means of suggested quick fixes and manual intervention by end-user is left for future work.

5   Discussion and Future Works

So far, the theoretical approach and the adopted implementation solutions of the incremental synchronization methods have been illustrated; for each step of the coordination procedure described in Section 4 corresponding resolving techniques have been described as relying on three main activities, namely difference representation, calculation, and application. Difference calculation poses a number of problems mainly related to element matching [12], therefore a more efficient solution could have been the exploitation of a tracking system (technically called a change listener) embedded in the model editor able to capture modifications in the meanwhile they were operated. In this way, element matching could have been solved. However, such solution could prevent the usage of other tools to edit models since a modifications tracker would be required to be embedded in the selected tool and trace the changes accordingly [5]. Nevertheless, the approach described in this work tries to alleviate element matching issues by

```
modeltype [root.name/] uses "[root.nsURI/]";
modeltype School uses "http://se.mdh.school";
transformation [root.name/]App(in diffModel : [root.name/],
                                inout input : School);
main() {
  diffModel.rootObjects()->asOrderedSet()->first().
  oclAsType([root.name/]::DifferenceModel).applyDiff();}
helper [root.name/]::DifferenceModel::applyDiff(){
  self.differenceElements.apply();
  return;}
helper [root.name/]::DifferenceElement::apply(){
[for(econtent : EClass |
  root.eAllContents(EClass)->select(name.startsWith('Changed')))]
[if(econtent.abstract <> true)]
if(self.oclIsTypeOf([root.name/]::[econtent.name/]))then{
  self.oclAsType([root.name/]::[econtent.name/])
                 .change[econtent.name.substring(8)/]();}endif;
[/if][/for]
[for(econtent : EClass |
  root.eAllContents(EClass)->select(name.startsWith('Added')))]
[if(econtent.abstract <> true)]
if(self.oclIsTypeOf([root.name/]::[econtent.name/]))then{
  self.oclAsType([root.name/]::[econtent.name/]).
                 .add[econtent.name.substring(6)/]();}endif;
[/if][/for]
[for(econtent : EClass |
  root.eAllContents(EClass)->select(name.startsWith('Deleted')))]
[if(econtent.abstract <> true)]
if(self.oclIsTypeOf([root.name/]::[econtent.name/]))then{
  self.oclAsType([root.name/]::[econtent.name/]).
                 del[econtent.name.substring(8)/]();}endif;
[/if][/for]
[for(econtent : EClass |
  root.eAllContents(EClass)->select(name.startsWith('Changed')))]
[if(econtent.abstract <> true)]
helper [root.name/]::[econtent.name/]::change[econtent.name.substring(8)/](){
  var temp[econtent.name/] : School::[econtent.name.substring(8)/];
  var tempChanged : [root.name/]::[econtent.name.substring(8)/];
  tempChanged := self.updatedElement;
  temp[econtent.name/] := input.
  objectsOfType(School::[econtent.name.substring(8)/])->
  select([econtent.eIDAttribute.name/] = self.[econtent.eIDAttribute.name/])
  ->asOrderedSet()->first();
  [for(attr : EAttribute | econtent.eAllAttributes)]
  if(tempChanged.[attr.name/] <> null)then{
    temp[econtent.name/].[attr.name/]:=tempChanged.[attr.name/]; }endif;
  [/for]
  return;}
[/if][/for]
```

```
modeltype teacherViewDiff uses
        "http://se.mdh.school teacherViewDiff";
modeltype School uses "http://se.mdh.school";
transformation teacherViewDiffApp(
                    in diffModel : teacherViewDiff,
                    inout input : School);
main() {
  diffModel.rootObjects()->asOrderedSet()->first().
  oclAsType(teacherViewDiff::DifferenceModel).applyDiff();}
helper teacherViewDiff::DifferenceModel::applyDiff(){
  self.differenceElements.apply();
  return;}
helper teacherViewDiff::DifferenceElement::apply(){
  if(self.oclIsTypeOf(teacherViewDiff::ChangedTeacher))then{
    self.oclAsType(teacherViewDiff::ChangedTeacher)
                   .changeTeacher();}endif;
  if(self.oclIsTypeOf(teacherViewDiff::AddedTeacher))then{
    self.oclAsType(teacherViewDiff::AddedTeacher)
                   .addTeacher();}endif;
  if(self.oclIsTypeOf(teacherViewDiff::DeletedTeacher))then{
    self.oclAsType(teacherViewDiff::DeletedTeacher).
                   delTeacher();}endif;
}

helper teacherViewDiff::ChangedTeacher::changeTeacher(){
  var tempChangedTeacher : School::Teacher;
  var tempChanged : teacherViewDiff::Teacher;
  tempChanged := self.updatedElement;
  tempChangedTeacher := input.
  objectsOfType(School::Teacher)->
  select(socialNo = self.socialNo)->
  asOrderedSet()->first();
  if(tempChanged.name <> null)then{
    tempChangedTeacher.name:=tempChanged.name;
    }endif;
  if(tempChanged.socialNo <> null)then{
    tempChangedTeacher.socialNo:=tempChanged.socialNo;
    }endif;
  if(tempChanged.studyTitle <> null)then{
    tempChangedTeacher.studyTitle:=tempChanged.studyTitle;
    }endif;
  return;}
```

Fig. 7. Higher-order transformation for differences application and resulting transformation

providing an automated identification mechanisms based on the unique identifiers selected at view creation time. As future enhancement of the differencing procedure, will be investigated the opportunity of automated customization of the matching heuristics based on the elements included in a particular view, possibly making the developer able to define accurate comparison metrics at view definition time.

Once modifications have been detected for a particular view, they have to be propagated for synchronization purposes. In this respect, the properties enjoyed by the difference representation and application mechanisms allow us to avoid the definition of mapping procedures from view manipulations to corresponding overall model changes and vice versa, as clarified in Section 3. In fact, what is correctly modelled in the views conforms also to the overall meta-model, and by-construction, each difference model pertaining to a view is also a model conforming to the difference meta-model for the overall. Therefore, it is possible to use the same propagation strategies from both overall model to views modes and vice versa. In this way, matching attempts will be avoided for those elements outside the view, thus enhancing performances especially in the case of large models.

The usage of views typically promotes distributed development, meaning that experts in different domains can concurrently work on their respective views and then update the overall model for consistency purposes. Since in general the intersection of views can not be supposed as empty, it could happen that modifications are operated on the same entity such that they diverge from each other. As described in Section 4 the adopted strategy is to serialize the changes applying the concurrent sequence from the older to the newer manipulations. A more complete support for those cases would entail features like conflict detection and resolution mechanisms, able to warn the user whenever conflicts would arise and provide support for (semi-)automated fixes. Once again, the view definition wizard may be potentially exploited to define by-default reconciliation strategies, as giving highest priority to changes operated in a certain view, more recent updates, and so forth.

In the current prototypical version of the approach implementation, the presented technologies have to be manually coordinated, that is in views creation phase appropriate meta-models are derived devoted to both modelling in each view and storage of modifications through the difference representation mechanism described before. Moreover, apposite QVTo transformations are generated to apply changes contained in the difference models. Then, when manipulations are operated on a certain view, the user has to manually invoke first the differencing procedure, then the application of changes to the overall model, and eventually the propagation of the current updates toward the other views. Such sequence of steps could be automated by creating a workflow by means of available tools in the Eclipse platform. Since the workflow is dependent on the overall meta-model and the set of custom views, we believe that the most appropriate way to provide it is by means of a transformation able to generate the workflow accordingly. This topic is currently under investigation and is left for future improvement of our proposal.

6   Conclusions

This paper presented an approach for incremental synchronization in hybrid multi-view modelling. The hybrid solution aims at alleviating those issues arising when dealing with synthetic and projective approaches, namely consistency management and view expressiveness/customization. The incremental propagation of changes allows to keep views update in an efficient way by punctually applying modifications coming from the other views instead of regenerating new ones at each change. Despite the implementation being technology specific (i.e., based on EMF), the approach presented for incremental synchronization can be considered as general and applicable in different technology contexts. Nonetheless, additional work will be required to cope with the validation of the proposed technique in industrial settings in order to verify feasibility and analyse possible scalability issues related to the proposed mechanism. Especially, we will have to survey the reliability of the element identification mechanism; the current version allows us an efficient element identification for difference calculation and view synchronization, but still leaves place to possible undesired duplications. Finally, investigation efforts will be devoted toward the application of our approach in the reverse direction, i.e., as a method to create a common denominator as proposed in [17].

References

1. Bézivin, J.: On the Unification Power of Models. Jour. on Software and Systems Modeling (SoSyM) 4(2), 171–188 (2005)
2. Boulanger, F., Jacquet, C., Hardebolle, C., Rouis, E.: Modeling Heterogeneous Points of View with ModHel'X. In: Ghosh, S. (ed.) MODELS 2009. LNCS, vol. 6002, pp. 310–324. Springer, Heidelberg (2010)
3. Chechik, M., Lai, W., Nejati, S., Cabot, J., Diskin, Z., Easterbrook, S., Sabetzadeh, M., Salay, R.: Relationship-based change propagation: A case study. In: MISE 2009, pp. 7–12. IEEE CS, Washington, DC (2009)
4. Cicchetti, A., Ciccozzi, F., Krekola, M., Mazzini, S., Panunzio, M., Puri, S., Santamaria, C., Vardanega, T., Zovi, A.: CHESS Tool presentation. In: 1st TOPCASED Days, Toulouse (2011)
5. Cicchetti, A., Di Ruscio, D., Pierantonio, A.: A Metamodel Independent Approach to Difference Representation. Journal of Object Technology 6, 165–185 (2007)
6. Cicchetti, A., Ciccozzi, F., Leveque, T.: A hybrid approach for multi-view modeling. Electronic Communications of the EASST 10 (2011), to appear in the Proceedings of the 5th International Workshop on Multi-Paradigm Modeling (MPM)
7. Cicchetti, A., Ciccozzi, F., Leveque, T., Sentilles, S.: Evolution management of extra-functional properties in component-based embedded systems. In: The 14th Int'l ACM SIGSOFT Symposium on Component Based Software Engineering (2011)
8. Conallen, J.: Modeling Web Application Architectures with UML. Comm. ACM 42(10), 63–71 (1999)
9. Del Fabro, M.D., Bézivin, J., Jouault, F., Breton, E., Gueltas, G.: AMW: a Generic Model Weaver. In: Procs. of IDM 2005 (2005)
10. Elrad, T., Aldawud, O., Bader, A.: Aspect-Oriented Modeling: Bridging the Gap between Implementation and Design. In: Batory, D., Blum, A., Taha, W. (eds.) GPCE 2002. LNCS, vol. 2487, pp. 189–201. Springer, Heidelberg (2002)
11. ISO/IEC/(IEEE): ISO/IEC 42010 (IEEE Std) 1471-2000 : Systems and Software engineering - Recommended practice for architectural description of software-intensive systems (2007)
12. Kolovos, D.S., Di Ruscio, D., Pierantonio, A., Paige, R.F.: Different models for model matching: An analysis of approaches to support model differencing. In: Procs. of the ICSE Workshop on Comparison and Versioning of Software Models (CVSM 2009), pp. 1–6. IEEE Computer Society, Washington, DC (2009)
13. Miotto, E., Vardanega, T.: On the integration of domain-specific and scientific bodies of knowledge in model driven engineering. In: Procs. of STANDRTS 2009, Dublin, Ireland (2009)
14. Nassar, M.: VUML : a Viewpoint oriented UML Extension. In: Procs. of ASE 2003, pp. 373–376. IEEE Computer Society (2003)
15. Romero, J.R., Jaen, J.I., Vallecillo, A.: Realizing correspondences in multi-viewpoint specifications. In: Procs. of the 13th IEEE EDOC, Auckland, New Zealand, September 1-4, pp. 163–172. IEEE CS (2009)
16. Schmidt, D.C.: Guest Editor's Introduction: Model-Driven Engineering. Computer 39(2), 25–31 (2006)
17. Vangheluwe, H.L.M.: DEVS as a Common Denominator for Multi-formalism Hybrid Systems Modelling, pp. 129–134 (2000)

Semantic Adaptation
Using CCSL Clock Constraints

Frédéric Boulanger, Ayman Dogui, Cécile Hardebolle,
Christophe Jacquet, Dominique Marcadet, and Iuliana Prodan

Supelec Systems Sciences (E3S)
Computer Science Department
Gif-sur-Yvette, France
firstname.lastname@supelec.fr

Abstract. When different parts of a system depend on different technical domains, the best suitable paradigm for modeling each part may differ.
In this paper, we focus on the semantic adaptation between parts of a
model which use different modeling paradigms in the context of model
composition. We show how CCSL, a language for defining constraints
and relations on clocks, can be used to define this semantic adaptation
in a formal and modular way.

Keywords: Multi-Paradigm Modeling, Clock Calculus.

1   Introduction

Models are the primary way of handling complexity by providing abstract representations of a system, in which only the details that are useful for a given
task are kept. When different parts of a system depend on different technical domains (e.g. signal processing, automatic control, power management, etc.), the
best suitable modeling paradigm may differ for each part. A global model of such
a system is a heterogeneous model. Heterogeneous modeling, or multi-paradigm
modeling, is the research domain which aims at handling heterogeneous models.

This paper focuses on *model composition*, one of the existing multi-paradigm
techniques [8]. The main principle of model composition is the "gluing" of model
parts which are described using different modeling languages. In model composition, the main difficulty is to define accurately the *semantic adaptation*, i.e. the
mechanism to "glue" together model parts that may have very different semantics, in order to obtain a global heterogeneous model which is meaningful and
can therefore be used for early verification and validation in the design process.

We have developed a framework called ModHel'X for heterogeneous model
composition. ModHel'X is mainly aimed at model execution, i.e. techniques such
as simulation or code generation. We compose models in a hierarchical way. In [4],
we have presented in detail how hierarchical semantic adaptation between two
models is handled in ModHel'X. One drawback of our current approach is the lack
of conciseness and the rather low level of abstraction of the semantic adaptation
descriptions. Inspired by the work by André et al. [9] on the description of the

J. Kienzle (Ed.): MODELS 2011 Workshops, LNCS 7167, pp. 104–118, 2012.
© Springer-Verlag Berlin Heidelberg 2012

semantics of dataflow models using MARTE's Clock Constraint Specification Language (CCSL), we propose an approach in which CCSL is used to model semantic adaptation.

The paper is organized as follows. We first present the concept of model of computation in Sect. 2, together with an example that we use throughout the paper to illustrate the underlying concepts of our approach. After presenting ModHel'X in Sect. 3, we focus on semantic adaptation in Sect. 4. Then, Section 5 briefly introduces the basic concepts of CCSL needed in Sect. 6 to describe the semantic adaptation between heterogeneous models. We discuss the results in Sect. 7 and, after a comparison of our approach with related work in Sect. 8, we conclude in Sect. 9.

2   Models of Computation

There are two main tasks to achieve in order to obtain a meaningful heterogeneous model using model composition: (1) the precise definition of the semantics of each modeling paradigm; (2) the precise definition of the semantic adaptation between parts of a model which use different modeling paradigms. One method for defining the semantics of different modeling paradigms is to use a common syntax or meta-model to describe the structure of models, and to attach semantics to this structure using so-called *models of computation (MoC)*. A model of computation is a set of rules which define the nature of the components of a model and how their behaviors are combined to produce the behavior of the model. It can be seen as a way to interpret the structure of a model. For instance, Figure 1 shows that two models can share the same structure (two components linked by two arrows) with different semantics, depending on the model of computation: here a finite state machine or two communicating sequential processes.

We use this concept of model of computation to achieve hierarchical model composition. To illustrate our approach, let us introduce the example of a power window system that we will use throughout the paper. The system, shown on Fig. 2, is composed of a control switch, a controller board and an electro-mechanical subsystem. These components communicate through a bus.

Since the communications on the bus can be modeled by events which carry some data and occur at a given time, a "Discrete Events" (DE) [5] model of computation is suitable for the top level of the hierarchical model of this system. The control switch is considered as an atomic component which produces an event each time its position (neutral, up or down) changes.

The controller board is in charge of interpreting both the actions of the user on the switch and the information from the electro-mechanical subsystem in order to drive the motor which makes the window move. It also implements advanced features such as the *"one touch"* mode, i.e. the automatic raising or lowering of the window after a *brief* pull or push of the control switch. The behavior of this controller can be described naturally using a finite state machine. However, the one touch mode feature implies *timed behavior*: it is activated only when the control switch has been pulled or pushed during less than a given delay, 10 ms for

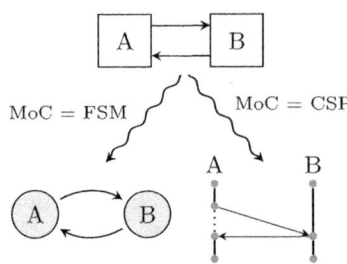

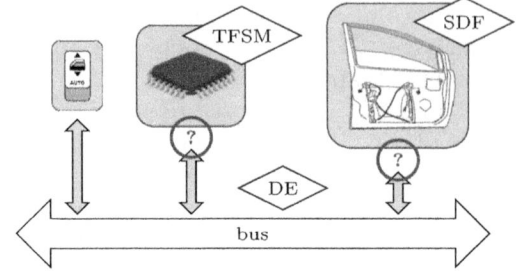

Fig. 1. Models of computation   **Fig. 2.** Structure of the power window model

instance. Therefore the state machine describing the behavior of the controller board includes *timed transitions*, so the "Timed Finite State Machine" (TFSM) model of computation is used.

Finally, the electro-mechanical part is described as a periodically sampled system, represented by a "Synchronous Data Flow" (SDF) [5] MoC. In this model of computation, blocks are data flow operators which consume and produce a fixed number of data samples on their pins each time they are activated.

Once these choices are made, it is necessary to define how these three models, involving three different models of computation, can be composed. In the following, we present how the power window system is modeled in ModHel'X.

3   ModHel'X, a Framework for Heterogeneous Modeling

ModHel'X [4] is an experimental framework developed at Supélec. It allows one to describe the structure of heterogeneous models, to define models of computation for interpreting such structures, and to define the semantic adaptation between heterogeneous parts of a model. For this, ModHel'X relies on a meta-model which is the common syntax for all models, whatever their semantics.

Figure 3 shows how the power window system is modeled using ModHel'X. ModHel'X uses *Blocks* as the basic unit of behavior. For instance, the Switch, Position and EndStop elements on the figure are blocks. Blocks are considered as black boxes, meaning that their behavior can only be observed at their interface which is composed of *Pins* (black circles on the figure). The structure of a model is defined by setting relations between pins, shown as solid arrows on the example.

A structure (set of blocks and relations) has a meaning only when it is associated with a model of computation that allows its *interpretation*. Therefore, a ModHel'X model is a ⟨structure, MoC⟩ *pair*. MoCs are depicted by diamonds on Fig. 3. In ModHel'X, interpreting a model means executing the behavior described by that model according to the semantics of the MoC. An execution is a series of observations of the model, each observation being computed through the sequential observation of the blocks of the model using a fixed-point algorithm. The observation of one block is called an *update*. Each MoC dictates the rules for scheduling the update of the blocks of a model, for propagating values

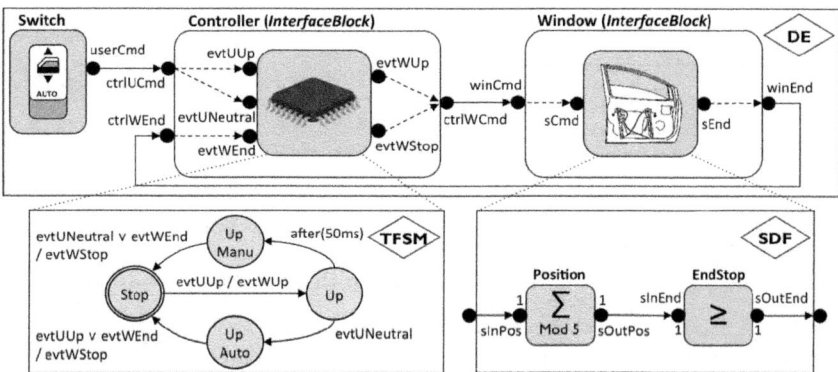

Fig. 3. Simplified ModHel'X model of the power window system

between blocks, and for determining when the computation of the observation of the model is complete.

Note that like all other models, the TFSM model is a set of interconnected blocks. However, a more traditional depiction is used on Fig. 3. Also for simplicity's sake, only the upward movement of the window is taken into account, including the one touch mode. The other part of its behavior is symmetric.

In ModHel'X, heterogeneity is handled through hierarchy: the behavior of some blocks can be defined by another model. Such blocks are called *InterfaceBlocks*. The model of computation used in the model of the block (the inner MoC) can differ from the model of computation of the model in which the interface block is used (the outer MoC). The Controller and Window elements on Fig. 3 are examples of InterfaceBlocks. The dashed arrows between the pins of an interface block and the pins of its internal model represent the *semantic adaptation* between the two MoCs, which is performed by the interface block. As we have shown in [4], semantic adaptation must consider three aspects: the adaptation of data (data may not have the same form in the inner and outer models), the adaptation of time (the notions of time and the time scales may differ in the inner and outer models) and the adaptation of control (control meaning the instants at which it is possible or necessary to communicate with a block through its interface). In the next section, we illustrate these three aspects on the power window example.

4   Semantic Adaptation

The most obvious form of adaptation between models of computation is **adaptation of data**. For instance, in the DE model of computation, blocks communicate by posting events which are composed of a value and a timestamp. In the finite state machine, data appears as symbols which can trigger transitions. In the data flow model of the electro-mechanical part, data appears as periodic samples. The adaptation of data between DE and TFSM can be performed by mapping symbols (processed by the TFSM) to event values. The adaptation of data between DE and SDF is more complex because SDF expects periodic samples while DE

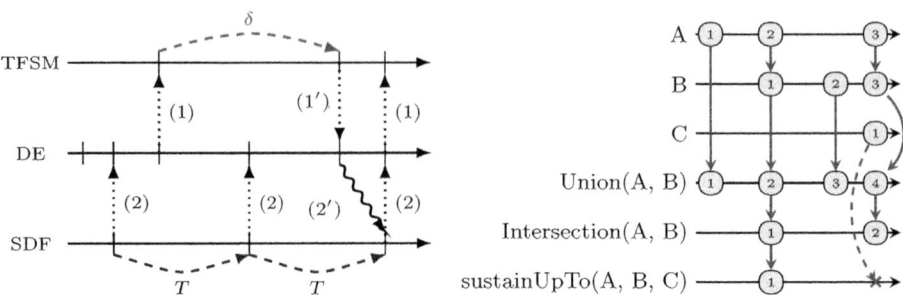

Fig. 4. Adaptation of control   **Fig. 5.** Example of clock expressions

has only sporadic events. A usual way to handle this it to interpret a DE event as a new value for the next samples of a SDF signal, until a further event is received. Similarly, a *change* in a sequence of SDF samples is converted into a DE event. The value carried by this event is easy to determine: it is the new value of the SDF signal. However, it is also necessary to choose a timestamp for this event because there is no explicit notion of time in SDF: *time* needs to be adapted too.

When we generate a DE event to reflect a change of an SDF signal, a possible timestamp for this event is the value of the current time in the DE model when the SDF signal changes (the DE MoC maintains a *current time* at each instant of the model execution [5]). **Adaptation of time** must also be performed between the DE model and the timed finite state machine. We can assume that the state machine reacts instantaneously to input symbols, and also uses the current time in DE as a timestamp for the events it produces. However, time can also trigger transitions in the TFSM model. Such a transition is based on a duration expressed on a time scale that is local to the TFSM model. The transition may produce an event that will have to be adapted to the DE model, so the duration must have a correspondence in DE time. The adaptation of time between DE and TFSM consists in resetting a timer each time a new state is entered, and therefore measuring the time elapsed in DE since entering the state in the automaton.

Control is the set of instants at which a block should be able to take inputs into account and to produce outputs. Figure 4 illustrates the **adaptation of control** between DE, TFSM and SDF. On this figure, the "ticks" on each timeline represent the instants at which each model is given control. The arrows represent the adaptation of control performed between the models by the interface blocks. Let us have a look at a few examples.

Between DE and TFSM. When the DE model produces an input for the state machine, control should be given to the TFSM model so that it can process the symbol and take a transition. This is illustrated by arrows labelled (1) on the figure. Conversely, control is created in DE when the state machine produces an output (arrow (1′)). If the state machine enters a state with an outgoing timed transition, the state machine should receive control when the delay δ expires so that the transition fires (arrow labelled δ on the figure).

Between DE and SDF. The sampled nature of SDF signals induces periodic control for the model of the electro-mechanical part of the system (arrows labelled

T at the bottom of the figure). Since this model is embedded in the DE model, control in DE has a periodic part induced by SDF. This is shown by arrows labelled (2) on Fig. 4. When data is made available by DE to the SDF model, this data must not create control directly in SDF but must be processed at the next periodic control point, as shown by the wavy arrow labelled $(2')$ on Fig. 4.

As we see in this example, adaption of control not only depends on data and time, but it must also obey rules that depend on the models of computation. It is therefore cumbersome to define this adaptation in an operational way as we did until now in ModHel'X. In this paper, we present an approach in which we *declare* all the constraints that apply on the control points of the different parts of a model. This work has been inspired by the work by André et al. [9] in which the Clock Constraints Specification Language (CCSL) is used to define the SDF model of computation. Our goal is to use CCSL to model the semantic adaptation between models involving different models of computation. Section 5 introduces the basics of the CCSL language, as a prerequisite to Sect. 6 that describes our methodology for semantic adaptation using CCSL.

5   The Clock Constraint Specification Language (CCSL)

CCSL (Clock Constraint Specification Language) is a declarative language annexed to the specification of the MARTE UML Profile (Modeling and Analysis of Real Time and Embedded systems). CCSL is based on the notion of *clock* which represents a set of discrete event occurrences, called *instants*. A clock can be either *chronometric* or *logical*. Chronometric clocks are a means to model "physical time" and to measure durations between two instants. Logical clocks represent discrete time composed of abstract instants called *ticks*. The number of ticks between two instants may have no relation to any "physical duration".

The concrete syntax of CCSL is quite verbose and requires to prefix actual parameters with the name of the formal parameter in operator calls. For the sake of simplicity and conciseness, we will omit such prefixes and use generalized n-ary versions of the binary operators. For instance, we will write

Expression E = **Union**(C1, C2, ..., Cn) instead of:

Expression U1 = **Union**(Clock1->C1, Clock2->C2)
Expression U2 = **Union**(Clock1->U1, Clock2->C3)
   . . .
Expression E = **Union**(Clock1->Un-1, Clock2->Cn)

CCSL has a series of operators to define new clocks. The operators **Union** and **Intersection** build clocks which consist of respectively the union and the intersection of the ticks of two clocks (see Fig. 5). We also use **sustainUpTo**(A, B, C), which defines a clock that starts ticking each time A ticks at the first tick of B, and stops ticking at the first tick of C. **Discretize** defines a chronometric clock from *physicalTime*, a dense clock defined by MARTE. For instance, **Discretize**(physicalTime, 0.001) specifies a discrete chronometric clock with

a period of 0.001 second = 1 ms. **DelayFor**(A, B, n) specifies a clock which
ticks at the nth instant of B that follows an instant of A.

CCSL also offers means to specify constraints between clocks, namely sub-
clocking and coincidence. **Relation[SubClock]**(A, B) means that the set of
ticks of A is a subset of the set of ticks of B. **Relation[Coincides]**(A, B)
means that A and B share the same set of ticks.

The TimeSquare environment, an Eclipse plug-in, may be used to solve a set
of CCSL constraints. A graphical interface displays waveforms for the solution
clocks and shows the constraints between their instants.

6   Semantic Adaptation Using CCSL

This section presents our general methodology for describing semantic adaptation between models involving different MoCs using CCSL. The methodology is
illustrated on the power window example introduced in Sect. 2.

The switch (see Fig. 3) is an elementary DE block that models the user's
actions. The user pulling and releasing the button is represented by DE events
on the switch's *userCmd* pin with values "1" and "0" respectively. These events
are provided to the controller, which, in turn, sends *ctrlWCmd* DE events to the
window to turn the motor on (value "1") or off (value "0"). The controller knows
when the window is fully closed when it receives an event with value "1" from
the window on its *ctrlWEnd* pin.

The controller is described using a timed finite state machine, with initial state
Stop. When the automaton receives the *evtUUp* event indicating that the user
wants to raise the window, it produces the *evtWUp* event to start the window
motor and goes to the *Up* state. If the automaton receives the *evtUNeutral*
event before 10 units of time, thereby indicating that the user has released the
button to activate the one touch mode, it goes to the *UpAuto* state. Else, and
after 10 units of time, it goes to the *UpManu* state. The controller produces
the *evtWStop* when the user releases the button in manual mode, when the user
pulls the button in one touch mode, or when the window is fully closed (*evtWEnd*
events represent end-stops). As introduced in Sect. 4, the notions of data, control
and time have to be adapted between the DE top level model and the internal
TFSM model of the controller. In particular, a correspondence has to be defined
between DE events carrying given values and TFSM events.

The window is described using a synchronous data-flow model. In this simplified example, we suppose that the window has 5 vertical positions, where 0 is the
lowest and 4 is the highest. The *Position* block is a modulo-5 accumulator which
computes the position of the window from the input command signal. The role
of the *EndStop* block is to detect when the window reaches its highest possible
position. It produces a signal with value "1" when the window is at its highest
position and "0" otherwise. Again, the notions of data, control and time have to
be adapted between the DE top-level model and the internal SDF model of the
window. In particular, a correspondence has to be defined between DE events
(carrying values) and SDF samples (carrying values).

In order to be able to describe the semantic adaptation between models using CCSL and to simulate the global heterogeneous model using ModHel'X, we have to integrate TimeSquare, the CCSL solver, with ModHel'X. However, given the fundamental differences between the tools, we have preferred to first experiment our approach using CCSL only, as a proof of concept. For this reason, the following sections explain how models governed by the TFSM, SDF and DE MoCs may be described using CCSL, before focusing on semantic adaptation between them. Then we present the simulations obtained with TimeSquare.

6.1   Describing TFSM Using CCSL

This section describes our methodology for translating a TFSM model into a CCSL specification. In CCSL, all clocks must be subclocks of a root clock. We choose to explicitly define a chronometric clock called *chronoTFSM*. This clock serves several purposes: it measures the durations of the timed transitions, the input events occur at instants of this clock (they are subclocks of it), and therefore the state machine reacts at instants of this clock.

For simulating the behavior of a state machine, we need to memorize its current state. For each state S, we use an *enterS* clock which ticks when a transition leading to S fires, and an *inS* clock which ticks at each instant when S is the current state. *enterS* is the *condition* for entering S, and *inS* is a *memory* of the current state.

To define the *enterS* family of clocks, let us describe first *when* transitions are followed. A *non-timed* transition T that leaves S upon receipt of E is fired when the current state is S, and E occurs. Therefore, the clock which ticks each time T fires can be defined as:

Expression T = **Intersection**(E, inS)

For a *timed* transition T that leaves state S after d units of time, the firing event is derived from *enterS*:

Expression T = **Intersection**(**DelayFor**(enterS,chronoTFSM,d), inS)

We are now able to define the *enterS* clock of a state S with incoming transitions $T_1, \ldots, T_n$. If S is not the initial state, S is entered when one of the transition fires, thus:

Expression enterS = **Union**(T1, T2, ... , Tn)

For any state S, the state machine is in state S the instant just after the firing of a transition leading to S, so:

Expression enteredS = **DelayFor**(enterS, chronoTFSM, one)
Expression inS = **sustainUpTo**(chronoTFSM, enteredS,
                                    Union(inS', inS'', ...))

where S', S'', ... is the list of successor states of S.

If S is the initial state, then the state machine S is also in S at the first instant. For this, we define a clock that ticks only once, on the first tick of *chronoTFSM*:

Expression initial = **FilterBy**(chronoTFSM, 1(0))

and we add *initial* to the conditions for being in S:

Expression enteredS = **Union**(initial, **DelayFor**(enterS, ...))

The events produced by the state machine are modeled by clocks too. A given output event E is emitted when one of the transitions that may produce it is fired. Let us call $T_1, \ldots, T_n$ the family of such transitions. Then we can define a clock E which ticks each time E is present as:

Expression E = **Union**(T1, T2, ..., Tn)

Based on those generic patterns, we have created a script that generates automatically the constraints needed for any instance of a TFSM model. For the TFSM model of the power window system example described previously, we obtain the following constraints (using the simplified CCSL syntax):

```
Clock physicalTime:Dense
Expression chronoTFSM = Discretize(physicalTime, 0.001)
Expression initial = FilterBy(chronoTFSM, 1(0))
// state S [Stop] and incoming transitions
Expression transition1 = Intersection(Union(evtUNeutral, evtWEnd), inM)
Expression transition2 = Intersection(Union(evtUUp, evtWEnd), inA)
Expression enterS = Union(transition1, transition2)
Expression enteredS = Union(initial, DelayFor(enterS, chronoTFSM, one))
Relation[SubClock](enterS, chronoTFSM)
Expression inS = sustainUpTo(chronoTFSM, enterS, inU)
Relation[SubClock](inS , chronoTFSM)
// state M [Up Manu] and incoming transitions
Expression transition3 = Intersection(DelayFor(enterU, chronoTFSM, 10), inU)
Expression enterM = transition3
Expression enteredM = DelayFor(enterM, chronoTFSM, one)
Expression inM = sustainUpTo(chronoTFSM, enteredM, inS)
Relation[SubClock](inM, chronoTFSM)
[...] // same thing for states U [Up] and A [Up Auto]
// output events
Expression evtWStop=Union(transition1, transition2)
[...]
```

Figure 6 shows the causal relationships between the ticks upon which the automaton changes its state.

6.2   Describing DE Using CCSL

We now describe our methodology for translating a DE model into a set of CCSL constraints. As for TFSM, we define a chronometric clock *chronoDE* to measure time. All the other clocks are subclocks of *chronoDE*. Each block B is associated with a clock *updateB* that ticks at each update of B. As the updates themselves depend on events sent and received by the blocks, we need to associate a clock to each pin (with the same name), which ticks each time an event is sent or received. DE semantics imply the following constraints on these clocks: (a) the clock of an output pin must coincide with all the clocks of the connected input pins and (b) the *update* clock of a block is the union of all the clocks of its input and output pins. Again, based on these rules, a script can generate automatically the constraints needed for any specific DE model. On the power window system example, we obtain the following constraints:

```
Clock physicalTime:Dense
Expression chronoDE=Discretize(physicalTime, 0.001)
// "Switch" block
Clock updateSwitch
Clock userCmd
Relation[Coincides](updateSwitch, userCmd)
Relation[SubClock](updateSwitch, chronoDE)
// "Controller" block
Clock updateController
Clock ctrlUCmd
Clock ctrlWEnd
Clock ctrlWCmd
Relation[Coincides](updateController, Union(ctrlUCmd, ctrlWEnd, ctrlWCmd))
Relation[SubClock](updateController, chronoDE)
// Relations between blocks
Relation[Coincides](userCmd, ctrlUCmd)
[...]
```

To fully simulate our model in TimeSquare, we have to take into account the values of the DE events. However, CCSL has no mechanism for representing data. Therefore, we represent data values by clocks. For instance, since the *Switch* block produces DE events with values "0" or "1" on its *userCmd* pin, we use a *userCmd0* (resp. *userCmd1*) clock which ticks each time the value of the produced event is 0 (resp. 1). This mechanism is applied to all the clocks representing the emission or reception of events in the DE model. Figure 6 shows traces obtained when a *userCmd* event is sent by the switch (upon update) with value "1". It is received by the controller as a *ctrlUCmd* event with value "1", which sends out a *ctrlWCmd* event to the window with value "1" to start the window motor.

6.3   Describing SDF Using CCSL

This section explains how an SDF model can be translated into a CCSL specification. First, we define a *superSDF* clock to represent the instants at which blocks are updated in the SDF model. For each block B we associate a clock *updateB* that ticks at each update of B. The *updateB* clock is necessarily a subclock of *superSDF*. For each input/output pin of a block B, we define a clock *sInBi*/*sOutBj* that ticks each time it receives/produces a token. Block B is updated when each of its input pins has received at least one token. Therefore, the *updateB* clock must coincide with the slowest clock among all the *sInBi* clocks in order to tick upon the receipt of the last required token. This gives:

Relation[Coincides](updateB, **Sup**(sInB1, ..., sInBn))

When B is updated, each of its output pins produces a token. Therefore, the *updateB* clock coincides with all the *sOutBj* clocks. This gives, for each j:

Relation[Coincides](updateB, sOutBj)

The semantics of SDF implies that, for two blocks A and B connected through relations, each token produced by each output pin $sOutA_j$ of block A is received instantaneously by the input pin $sInB_i$ of block B connected at the other end of a relation. Therefore the clocks $sOutAj$ and $sInBi$ must coincide:

Relation[Coincides](sOutAj, sInBi)

Based on these rules, a script generates automatically the constraints needed for any SDF model. On the window system, we obtain the following constraints:

```
Clock physicalTime:Dense
Clock superSDF
// "Position" block
Clock updatePosition
Relation[SubClock](updatePosition, superSDF)
Clock sInPos
Clock sOutPos
Relation[Coincides](updatePosition, Sup(sInPos))
Relation[Coincides](updatePosition, sOutPos)
[...] // same thing for the "EndStop" block
// Relation: sOutPos ==> sInEnd
Relation[Coincides](sOutPos, sInEnd)
```

As for DE, we also need to represent data in SDF to be able to simulate the behavior of the model. In the window system example, two clocks are associated with the two possible values of tokens produced by the *sInPos* input pin: *sInPos0* for value "0" and *sInPos1* for value "1". We do the same for the possible values at the *sOutPos*, *sInEnd* and the *sOutEnd* pins.

Figure 6 shows the evolution of *sOutPos* and *sOutEnd* with respect to *sInPos*.

6.4   Semantic Adaptation between DE and TFSM

Semantic adaptation between the DE and TFSM models boils down to a set of relations between clocks of the outer and inner models. More specifically: (a) an equality is written for each pair of related input and output pins of the inner/outer models, and (b) there must be a relation between the two chronometric clocks *chronoTFSM* and *chronoDE*.

```
// Adaptation of inputs
Relation[Coincides](ctrlUCmd1, evtUUp)
Relation[Coincides](ctrlUCmd0, evtUNeutral)
Relation[Coincides](ctrlWEnd, evtWEnd)
// Adaptation of outputs
Relation[Coincides](evtWUp, ctrlWCmd1)
Relation[Coincides](evtWStop, ctrlWCmd0)
// chronoDE is periodic on chronoTFSM with period 2 and offset 0
Expression chronoDE = Periodic(chronoTFSM, 2, 0)
```

Figure 6 shows an example of adaptation between the DE signal *ctrlUCmd* with value "1" and the TFSM event *evtUUp* (dashed arrow).

6.5   Semantic Adaptation between DE and SDF

Since the SDF model of the window is periodic, the semantic adaptation between DE and SDF must enforce the fact that the SDF model is updated every T ticks of *chronoDE*, and not at other instants. This also implies that if an event is present on the *winCmd* pin at an instant when the model should not be updated, the event must be memorized until the next update of the SDF model.

The first relation in the listing below states that *superSDF* is periodic on *chronoDE* with period 2. The next two lines specify that the *sCmd* pin receives a new value (*sCmd0* or *sCmd1*) only on ticks of *superSDF*, and keeps the last value until a different one is produced. The initial value of *sCmd* is set to 0.

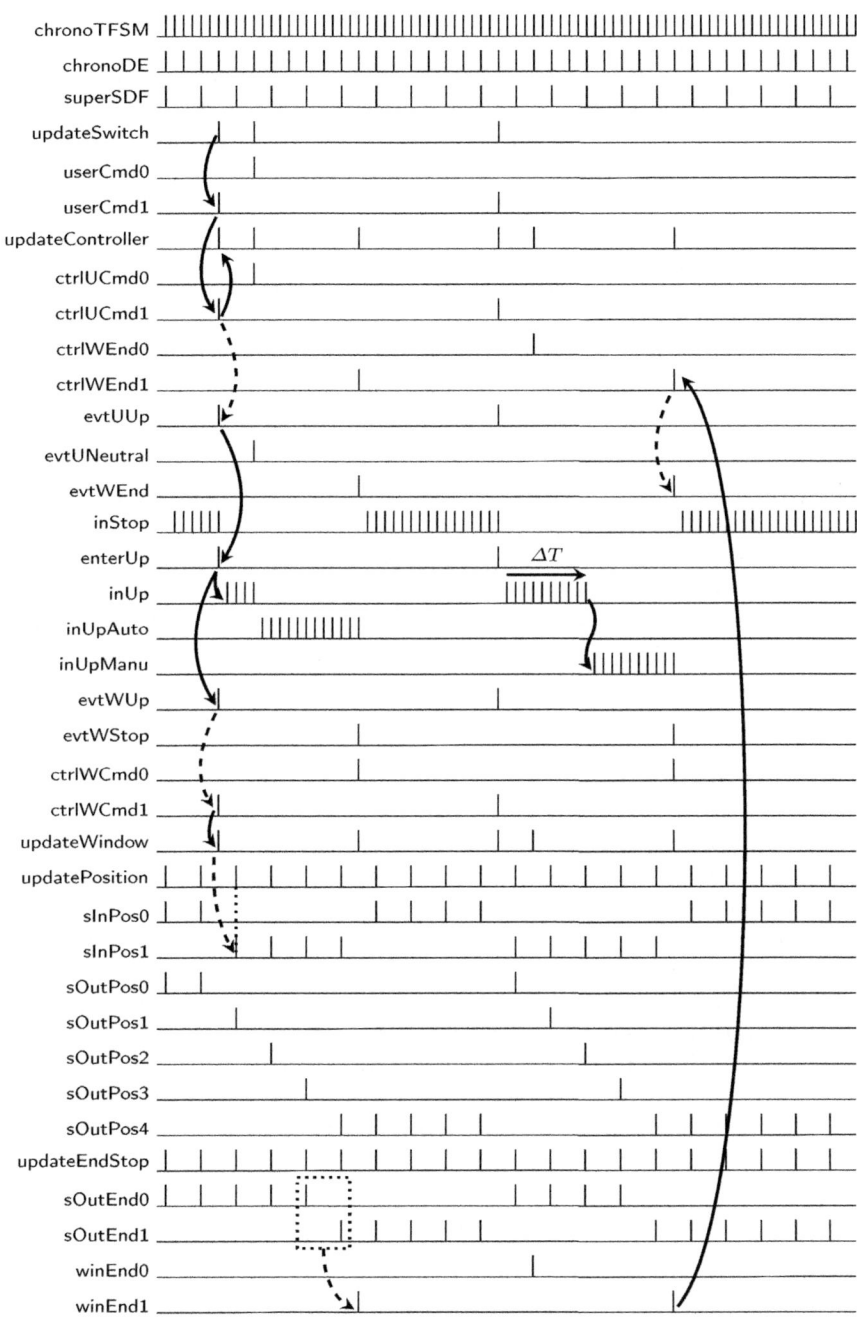

Fig. 6. Simulation of the overall model. Solid lines represent causal relationships within a given model; dashed lines represent *adaptation* between MoCs. Some clocks are omitted to make the figure clearer.

The adaptation of the output is described by the last two lines. In order to detect when *sOutEnd* goes from 0 to 1, and to generate an "on" *winEnd* DE event, we compute the intersection of *sOutEnd1* with *sOutEnd0* delayed by one sample. A similar calculus on *sOutEnd1* allows us to generate "off" *winEnd* events each time the window leaves the end stop position. Notice the delay on the output events to avoid an instantaneous dependency loop in the DE model.

```
// The activation of the SDF model is periodic
Relation[Coincides](superSDF, Periodic(chronoDE, 2, 0))
// The value of the input signal is the value of the last DE event
Relation[Coincides](sCmd0, sustainUpTo(superSDF, Union(initial, winCmd0), winCmd1))
Relation[Coincides(sCmd1, sustainUpTo(superSDF, winCmd1, winCmd0))
// A DE event is generated only when the output of the model changes
Relation[Coincides](winEnd0, DelayFor(Intersection(sOutEnd0,
                              DelayFor(sOutEnd1, superSDF, 1)), chronoDE, 1))
Relation[Coincides](winEnd1, DelayFor(Intersection(sOutEnd1,
                              DelayFor(sOutEnd0, superSDF, 1)), chronoDE, 1))
```

Figure 6 shows how the *ctrlWCmd* event induces a change of the value of *sInPos*, only on the next tick of *superSDF*. The dotted square shows how a change in the value of *sOutEnd* translates into a *winEnd* event. Globally, Figure 6 shows that the overall model is correctly simulated using CCSL: we see the controller change state, and command the window to go up, as well as the window model calculate the successive positions of the window until the end stop is reached, causing the controller to finally rest in the *Stop* state. Some clocks have been omitted for clarity.

7   Discussion

The above results show some benefits and drawbacks of our approach. We were able to obtain concise CCSL specifications for MoCs, which is an improvement over the lengthy descriptions of MoCs in ModHel'X. However, we consider as a drawback the fact that the CCSL specifications are model instances instead of independent descriptions of MoCs. To enforce genericity, we had to write scripts that generate model instances according to the semantics of the MoC.

Another positive point is that semantic adaptation of control and time is quite easy to define using CCSL. In addition, we were able to check the consistency of the CCSL specifications of the whole heterogeneous model of the power window. For instance, if the adaptation constraints specify that the DE clock is of higher frequency than the TFSM clock, the global specification is inconsistent: the delay of timed transitions in TFSM cannot be mapped on DE time. The solver actually detects a deadlock. Analysis features are of utmost interest for an approach dedicated to the specification of MoCs (and of semantic adaptation), which by nature are very difficult to verify and validate.

One limitation of this clock-based approach is that CCSL lacks primitives for manipulating data. Therefore, we had to define an ad-hoc methodology for it, which is not satisfactory. Another issue is the integration of this approach in ModHel'X. TimeSquare's solver is a static solver, which computes solutions over the whole timespan. It is not possible to compute the ticks *at runtime*. Therefore, we cannot use TimeSquare directly in ModHel'X. For the time being we cannot use the mechanisms that exist in ModHel'X to handle the adaptation of data together with CCSL specifications for the adaptation of control and time.

The following section compares this paper's proposal with existing approaches.

8   Related Work

As stated earlier, this paper is inspired by the work by André et al. [9]. First we have adapted their approach to the ModHel'X framework. We use CCSL clocks to model the control points of the execution algorithm of ModHel'X on the different elements of a model (conforming to the meta-model of ModHel'X). Then we have applied this approach to additional MoCs. But our main contribution is the use of CCSL specifications not only to model MoCs but also to model the semantic adaptation between two models involving different MoCs. We have shown on an example that this approach is particularly suitable for describing the semantic adaptation of control and of time, and that using CCSL specifications is significantly simpler than using an imperative method. Although not integrated in ModHel'X yet (as exposed in Sect. 7), this preliminary work seems promising since it allowed us to detect inconsistencies in the specifications.

To our knowledge, no other approach uses clocks and clock constraints to model semantic adaptation in the context of model composition. However, the issue of handling different notions of time and multiple control clocks has been extensively studied, in particular in the domain of hardware synthesis. Synchronous languages (see [2,1]) like Lustre, Esterel and Signal use abstract logical time and introduce the notion of multiform time. Other approaches, like Lucid Synchrone [3], have explicit support for specifying multi-clock systems.

Regarding model composition itself, ModHel'X can be compared to other approaches such as Ptolemy II or Simulink/Stateflow. Ptolemy II [7] is one of the first approaches to model composition. It supports a wide range of MoCs that may be combined with each other to form heterogeneous models. In ModHel'X, we propose an extension and a generalization of the solutions introduced by Ptolemy. Adaptation rules at the boundary between two heterogeneous models is one of our main contributions. In Ptolemy, those rules are hardcoded in the kernel. The modeler has either to rely on default adaption and design his system accordingly, or to add adaptation blocks explicitly into the models themselves, which makes models less reusable and more difficult to understand. In ModHel'X, adaptation is explicit, insulated from the models and encapsulated into interface blocks. This work on the modeling of semantic adaptation using CCSL is another step towards an easier way to "glue" together heterogeneous parts of a model.

A case study about a similar power window, available on The MathWorks' website[1]., illustrates heterogeneous model composition for Simulink (SDF-like) and Stateflow (TFSM-like). Semantic adaptation between Simulink and Stateflow is specified explicitly using functions and truth tables. However, all MoCs

---

[1] http://www.mathworks.com/products/demos/simulink/PowerWindow/
html/PowerWindow1.html

cannot be composed like this. For instance, using a Simulink (SDF-like) model into a SimEvents (DE-like) model requires different adaptation artifacts such as event translation blocks [6]. Not only are the interactions of SimEvents with Simulink hardcoded: SimEvents is actually executed *on top of* Simulink, thus constraining their interactions. The abstract syntax and semantics at the core of ModHel'X allow MoCs to be described independently from each other, and interface blocks allow the description of adaptation patterns for any pair of MoCs.

9   Conclusion

In this paper, we propose to use CCSL, a language for defining clocks and clock constraints, to specify the semantic adaptation at the border between two heterogeneous models composed in a hierarchical way. We have adapted to ModHel'X, our framework for model composition, an approach proposed in [9]. This paper contains three examples of models of computation described using CCSL and we show how semantic adaptation of control and of time can be specified between two models using these MoCs. Although preliminary, this work shows interesting results regarding the conciseness and the readability of the descriptions of both MoCs and adapters. Moreover, the TimeSquare solver allowed us to check the consistency of the semantic adaptation between pairs of models. This work will be integrated into ModHel'X so that CCSL-like specifications for the semantic adaptation of control and of time can be used. In parallel, we are working on a methodology for modeling the semantic adaptation of data.

References

1. Benveniste, A., Caspi, P., Edwards, S., Halbwachs, N., Le Guernic, P., de Simone, R.: The synchronous languages 12 years later. Proc. of the IEEE 91(1), 64–83 (2003)
2. Berry, G., Gonthier, G.: The Esterel synchronous programming language: Design, semantics, implementation. Science of Computer Programming 19(2), 87–152 (1992)
3. Biernacki, D., Colaco, J.L., Hamon, G., Pouzet, M.: Clock-directed Modular Code Generation of Synchronous Data-flow Languages. In: Proceedings of LCTES (2008)
4. Boulanger, F., Hardebolle, C., Jacquet, C., Marcadet, D.: Semantic Adaptation for Models of Computation. In: Proceedings of ACSD 2011, pp. 153–162 (2011)
5. Brooks, C., Lee, E.A., Liu, X., Neuendorffer, S., Zhao, Y., Zheng, H.: Heterogeneous Concurrent Modeling and Design in Java (Volume 3: Ptolemy II Domains). Tech. Rep. UCB/EECS-2008-30, University of California, Berkeley (2008)
6. Cassandras, C.G., Clune, M.I., Mosterman, P.J.: Hybrid system simulation with SimEvents. In: Proceedings of ADHS, pp. 267–269 (2006)
7. Eker, J., Janneck, J.W., Lee, E.A., Liu, J., Liu, X., Ludvig, J., Neuendorffer, S., Sachs, S., Xiong, Y.: Taming heterogeneity – the Ptolemy approach. Proc. of the IEEE 91(1), 127–144 (2003)
8. Hardebolle, C., Boulanger, F.: Exploring multi-paradigm modeling techniques. Simulation 85, 688–708 (2009)
9. Mallet, F., DeAntoni, J., André, C., de Simone, R.: The clock constraint specification language for building timed causality models. Innovations in Systems and Software Engineering 6, 99–106 (2010)

Summary of the First International Workshop on Experiences and Empirical Studies in Software Modelling

Michel R.V. Chaudron[1], Marcela Genero[2], Silvia Abrahão[3],
Parastoo Mohagheghi[4], and Lars Pareto[5]

[1] LIACS – Leiden University
Niels Bohrweg 1, 2333 CA Leiden, The Netherlands
chaudron@liacs.nl
[2] ALARCOS Research Group, University of Castilla-La Mancha
Paseo de la Universidad 4, 13071, Ciudad Real, Spain
Marcela.Genero@uclm.es
[3] ISSI Research Group, Department of Information Systems and Computation,
Universitat Politècnica de València
Camino de Vera, s/n, 46022, Valencia, Spain
sabrahao@dsic.upv.es
[4] SINTEF and Norwegian University of Science and Technology
Forskningsveien 1, 0373 Oslo, Norway
parastoo.mohagheghi@sintef.no
[5] Chalmers – University of Gothenburg
Gothenburg, Sweden
pareto@chalmers.se

1 Introduction

Most software development projects apply modelling in some stages of development and to various degrees in order to take advantage of the many and varied benefits of it. Modelling is, for example, applied for facilitating communication by hiding technical details, analysing a system from different perspectives, specifying its structure and behaviour in an understandable way, or even for enabling simulations and generating test cases in a mode-driven engineering approach. Thus, the evaluation of modelling techniques, languages and tools is needed in order to assess their advantages and disadvantages, to ensure their applicability to different contexts, their ease of use, and other issues such as required skills and costs; either isolated or in comparison with other methods.

The need to reflect and advance on empirical methods and techniques that help improving the adoption of software modelling in industry led us to organize the first edition of the International Workshop on Experiences and Empirical Studies in Software Modelling (EESSMod 2011) that was held in conjunction with the ACM/IEEE 14th International Conference on Model Driven Engineering Languages and Systems (MoDELS 2011) in Wellington, New Zealand. The main purpose of the workshop was to bring together professionals and researchers interested in software modelling to discuss in which way software modelling techniques may be evaluated, share experiences of performing such evaluations and discuss ideas for further

J. Kienzle (Ed.): MODELS 2011 Workshops, LNCS 7167, pp. 119–122, 2012.

research in this area. The workshop accepted both experience reports of applying software modelling in industry and research papers that describe more rigorous empirical studies performed in industry or academia.

2   Workshop Format and Session Summaries

The workshop was held as a one-day workshop in MODELS. The activities were structured into a keynote speech session, paper presentations and discussion sessions.

The workshop opened with a very interesting keynote presentation entitled *"What do 449 MDE Practitioners Think About MDE?"*. The keynote was given by Prof. Jon Whittle from Lancaster University, UK. Jon presented the results of an in-depth survey of model-driven engineering (MDE) industrial practice. The study focused on six key criteria related to productivity and maintainability for evaluating MDE success. Jon concluded his presentation with a discussion of future directions, such as identifying how the positive impacts of MDE outweigh the negative ones.

In the paper sessions five papers were presented. All the submitted papers were peer-reviewed by three independent reviewers. The accepted papers discuss theoretical and practical issues related to experimentation in software modelling or the use of modelling techniques in industry. Authors presented their papers in a twenty-minute-time slot, and five minutes were allowed for questions and discussion.

Paper presentations were done during the morning to allow enough time for discussion during the second part of the day. In the afternoon, we presented the findings of an on-going survey on the *Challenges and Hurdles in Empirical Modeling Research* (http://www.eesmod.org/survey.html). The workshop participants were organized in four groups in order to discuss possible actions to facilitate empirical research in software modeling. Each group took care of discussing specific questions suggested by the workshop organizers. At the end of the workshop, each group selected a delegate who presented the conclusions and research questions raised by the group. The following papers were presented at the workshop:

Session 1: Empirical Research at MODELS Conference
- Assessing the Frequency of Empirical Evaluation in Software Modeling Research by Jeffrey Carver, Eugene Syriani and Jeff Gray

The authors analyse the frequency with which empirical evaluation has been reported in the software modelling community. The results of an analysis of papers published in the MoDELS conference (from 2006-2010) showed that, of 266 papers, 195 of them (73%) performed no empirical evaluation.

Session 2: Empirical Studies
- Assessing Does the Level of Detail of UML Models Affect the Maintainability of Source Code? by Ana M. Fernández-Sáez, Marcela Genero and Michel R. V. Chaudron *(best paper)*

The authors present a controlled experiment for analysing the influence of the level of detail of UML models on the maintenance of the corresponding source code. The results obtained indicate a slight tendency towards obtaining better results when using low level of detail UML models, which contradicts previous research found in literature.

- Assessing the Impact of Hierarchy on Model Understandability: A Cognitive Perspective by Stefan Zugal, Jakob Pinggera, Barbara Weber, Jan Mendling and Hajo Reijers *(best paper)*

The authors propose a framework for assessing the impact of hierarchy on model understandability and discuss the implications for experiments investigating the impact of modularization on conceptual models.

- Empirical evaluation of the conjunct use of MOF and OCL by Juan Cadavid, Benoît Combemale and Benoit Baudry

The authors proposes a process for analysing meta-models expressed using MOF and OCL and reports on the pre-processing of 52 meta-models in order to get them ready for automatic empirical analysis.

- Building VECM-based Systems with a Model Driven Approach: an Experience Report by Maurizio Leotta, Gianna Reggio, Filippo Ricca and Egidio Astesiano

The authors present an experience report on the use of a model-driven method for developing VECM-based systems in the context of two Italian companies.

The papers by Ana M. Fernández-Sáez, Marcela Genero and Michel R. V. Chaudron and Stefan Zugal, Jakob Pinggera, Barbara Weber, Jan Mendling and Hajo Reijers were rated as the best 2 papers of this workshop. The discussion during the afternoon was oriented to analyse the results of the survey on the Challenges and Hurdles in Empirical Modeling Research gathered so far. Workshop participants suggested a list of actions aimed at increasing the volume of empirical research on software modelling. The presentations and slides associated with the discussions are available at the workshop webpage.

We would like to thank the authors for submitting their papers to the Workshop. Also thanks to Prof. Jon Whittle from University of Lancaster in England, who gave a very interesting keynote speech. We are also grateful to the members of the Program Committee for their efforts in the reviewing process, and to the MoDELS 2011 organizers for their support and assistance during the workshop organization.

The members of the Program Committee were Bente Anda (University of Oslo), Teresa Baldasarre (Universita' Degli Studi di Bari), Narasimha Bolloju (University of Hong Kong), Lionel Briand (Simula Research Laboratory), Danilo Caivano (Universita' Degli Studi di Bari), Karl Cox (University of Brighton), Jose Antonio Cruz-Lemus (University of Castilla-La Mancha), H. Eichelberger (Universität

Hildesheim), Felix Garcia (University of Castilla-La Mancha), Carmine Gravino (University of Salerno), Torchiano Marco (Politecnico di Torino), Jan Mendling (Humboldt-University Berlin), James Nelson (Southern Illinois University), Ariadi Nugroho (LIACS, Leiden University), Jeffrey Parson (Memorial University of Newfoundland), Keith Phalp (Bournemouth University), Geert Poels (University of Ghent), Jan Recker (Queensland University of Technology), Giuseppe Scaniello (Universita' Degli Studi della Basilicata), Samira Si-Said Cherfi (CEDRIC-CENAM), Keng Siau (University of Nebraska-Lincoln), Dag Sjøberg (University of Oslo), Sara Sprenkle (Washington & Lee University), Miroslaw Staron (University of Gothenburg). More details on the Workshop are available at http://www.eesmod.org.

Assessing the Impact of Hierarchy on Model Understandability – A Cognitive Perspective*

Stefan Zugal[1], Jakob Pinggera[1], Barbara Weber[1],
Jan Mendling[2], and Hajo A. Reijers[3]

[1] University of Innsbruck, Austria
{stefan.zugal,jakob.pinggera,barbara.weber}@uibk.ac.at
[2] Humboldt-Universität zu Berlin, Germany
jan.mendling@wiwi.hu-berlin.de
[3] Eindhoven University of Technology, The Netherlands
h.a.reijers@tue.nl

Abstract. Modularity is a widely advocated strategy for handling complexity in conceptual models. Nevertheless, a systematic literature review revealed that it is not yet entirely clear under which circumstances modularity is most beneficial. Quite the contrary, empirical findings are contradictory, some authors even show that modularity can lead to decreased model understandability. In this work, we draw on insights from cognitive psychology to develop a framework for assessing the impact of hierarchy on model understandability. In particular, we identify abstraction and the split-attention effect as two opposing forces that presumably mediate the influence of modularity. Based on our framework, we describe an approach to estimate the impact of modularization on understandability and discuss implications for experiments investigating the impact of modularization on conceptual models.

1 Introduction

The use of modularization to hierarchically structure information has for decades been identified as a viable approach to deal with complexity [1]. Not surprisingly, many conceptual modeling languages provide support for hierarchical structures, such as sub-processes in business process modeling languages like BPMN and YAWL [2] or composite states in UML statecharts. While hierarchical structures have been recognized as an important factor influencing model understandability [3,4], there are no definitive guidelines on their use yet. For instance, for business process models, recommendations for the size of a sub-process, i.e., sub-model, range from 5–7 model elements [5] over 5–15 model elements [6] to up to 50 model elements [7]. Also in empirical research into conceptual models (e.g., ER diagrams or UML statecharts) the question of *whether and when* hierarchical structures are beneficial for model understandability seems not to be entirely clear. While it is common belief that hierarchy has a positive influence

---

* This research is supported by Austrian Science Fund (FWF): P23699-N23.

J. Kienzle (Ed.): MODELS 2011 Workshops, LNCS 7167, pp. 123–133, 2012.

on the understandability of a model, reported data seems often inconclusive or even contradictory, cf. [8,9].

As suggested by existing empirical evidence, hierarchy is not beneficial by default [10] and can even lead to performance decrease [8]. The goal of this paper is to have a detailed look at which factors cause such discrepancies between the common belief in positive effects of hierarchy and reported data. In particular, we draw on concepts from cognitive psychology to develop a framework that describes how the impact of hierarchy on model understandability can be assessed. The contribution of this theoretical discussion is a perspective to disentangle the diverse findings from prior experiments.

The remainder of this paper is structured as follows. In Sect. 2 a systematic literature review about empirical investigations into hierarchical structuring is described. Afterwards, concepts from cognitive psychology are introduced and put in the context of conceptual models. Then, in Sect. 3 the introduced concepts are used as basis for our framework for assessing the impact of hierarchy on understandability, before Sect. 4 concludes with a summary and an outlook.

2   The Impact of Hierarchy on Model Understandability

In this section we revisit results from prior experiments on the influence of hierarchy on model understandability, and analyze them from a cognitive perspective. Sect. 2.1 summarizes literature reporting experimental results. Sect. 2.2 describes cognitive foundations of working with hierarchical models.

2.1   Existing Empirical Research into Hierarchical Models

The concept of hierarchical structuring is not only applied to various domains, but also known under several synonyms. In particular, we identified synonyms *hierarchy, hierarchical, modularity, decomposition, refinement, sub-model, sub-process, fragment and module*. Similarly, model understandability is referred to as *understandability* or *comprehensibility*. To systematically identify existing *empirical investigations* into the *impact of hierarchy on understandability* within the domain of conceptual modeling, we conducted a systematic literature review [11]. More specifically, we derived the following key-word pattern for our search: (synonym modularity) X (synonym understandability) X experiment X model. Subsequently, we utilized the cross-product of all key-words for a full-text search in the online portals of Springer[1], Elsevier[2], ACM[3] and IEEE [4] to cover the most important publishers in computer science, leading to 9,778 hits. We did not use any restriction with respect to publication date, still we are aware that online portals might provide only publications of a certain time period. In the next step, we removed all publications that were not related, i.e., did not

---

[1] http://www.springerlink.com
[2] http://www.sciencedirect.com
[3] http://portal.acm.org
[4] http://ieeexplore.ieee.org

consider the impact of hierarchy on model understandability or did not report empirical data. All in all, 10 relevant publications passed the manual check, resulting in the list summarized in Table 1. Having collected the data, all papers were systematically checked for the influence of hierarchy. As Table 1 shows, reported data ranges from negative influence [12] over no influence [12,13,14] to mostly positive influence [15]. These experiments have been conducted with a wide spectrum of modeling languages. It is interesting to note though that diverse effects have been observed for a specific notation such as statecharts or ER-models. In general, most experiments are able to show an effect of hierarchy either in a positive *or* a negative direction. However, it remains unclear *under which circumstances* positive or negative influences can be expected. To approach this issue, in the following, we will employ concepts from cognitive psychology to provide a systematic view on which factors influence understandability.

Table 1. Empirical studies into hierarchical structuring

Work	Findings
Moody [15] Domain: ER-Models	Positive influence on accuracy, no influence / negative influence on time
Reijers et al. [16,17] Domain: Business Process Models	Positive influence on understandability for one out of two models
Cruz-Lemus et al. [9,18] Domain: UML Statecharts	Series of experiments, positive influence on understandability in last experiment
Cruz-Lemus et al. [13] Domain: UML Statecharts	Hierarchy depth of statecharts has no influence
Shoval et al. [14] Domain: ER-Models	Hierarchy has no influence
Cruz-Lemus et al. [8] Domain: UML Statecharts	Positive influence on understandability for first experiment, negative influence in replication
Cruz-Lemus et al. [12,19] Domain: UML Statecharts	Hierarchy depth has a negative influence

2.2 Inference: A General-Purpose Problem Solving Process

As discussed in Sect. 2.1, the impact of hierarchy on understandability can range from negative over neutral to positive. To provide explanations for these diverse findings, we turn to insights from cognitive psychology. In experiments, the understandability of a conceptual model is usually estimated by the difficulty of answering questions about the model. From the viewpoint of cognitive psychology, answering a question refers to a *problem solving task*. Thereby, three different problem-solving *"programs"* or *"processes"* are known: search, recognition and inference [20]. Search and recognition allow for the identification of information of low complexity, i.e., locating an object or the recognition of patterns. Most conceptual models, however, go well beyond complexity that can be handled by search and recognition. Here, the human brain as a *"truly generic problem solver"* [21] comes into play. Any task that can not be solved by search or recognition, has to be solved by deliberate thinking, i.e., inference, making *inference* the *most important cognitive process* for understanding conceptual models. Thereby, it is widely acknowledged that the human mind is limited by the capacity of its working memory, usually quantified to as 7 ± 2 slots [22]. As soon as a mental task, e.g., answering a question about a model, overstrains this capacity, errors are likely to occur [23]. Consequently, mental tasks should always be designed such that they can be processed within this limit; the amount of working memory a certain task thereby utilizes is referred to as *mental effort* [24].

In the context of this work and similar to [25], we take the view that the impact of modularization on understandability, i.e., the influence on inference, ranges from negative over neutral to positive. Seen from the viewpoint of cognitive psychology, we can identify two *opposing forces* influencing the understandability of a hierarchically structured model. Positively, hierarchical structuring can help to reduce the mental effort through *abstraction* by reducing the number of model elements to be considered at the same time [15]. Negatively, the introduction of sub-models may force the reader to *switch her attention* between the sub-models, leading to the so-called *split-attention effect* [26]. Subsequently, we will discuss how these two forces presumably influence understandability.

Abstraction. Through the introduction of hierarchy it is possible to group a part of a model into a sub-model. When referring to such a sub-model, its content is hidden by providing an abstract description, such as a complex activity in a business process model or a composite state in an UML statechart. The concept of abstraction is far from new and known since the 1970s as *"information hiding"* [1]. In the context of our work, it is of interest in how far abstraction influences model understandability. From a theoretical point of view, abstraction should show a positive influence, as abstraction reduces the amount of elements that have to be considered simultaneously, i.e., abstraction can hide irrelevant information, cf. [15]. However, if positive effects depend on whether information can be hidden, the way how hierarchy is displayed apparently plays an important role. Here, we assume, similar to [15,17], that each sub-model is presented separately. In other words, each sub-model is displayed in a separate window if viewed on a computer, or printed on a single sheet of paper. The reader may arrange the sub-models according to her preferences and may close a window or put away a paper to hide information. To illustrate the impact of abstraction, consider the BPMN model shown in Fig. 1. Assume the reader wants to determine whether the model allows for the execution of sequence A, B, C. Through the abstraction introduced by sub-processes A and C, the reader can answer this question by looking at the top-level process only (i.e., activities A, B and C); the model allows to hide the content of sub-processes A and C for answering this specific question, hence reducing the number of elements to be considered.

Split-Attention Effect. So far we have illustrated that abstraction through hierarchical structuring can help to reduce mental effort. However, the introduction of sub-models also has its downsides. When extracting information from the model, the reader has to take into account several sub-models, thereby switching attention between sub-models. The resulting *split-attention effect* [26] then leads to increased mental effort, nullifying beneficial effects from abstraction. In fact, too many sub-models impede understandability, as pointed out in [4]. Again, as for abstraction, we assume that sub-models are viewed separately. To illustrate this, consider the BPMN model shown in Fig. 1. To assess whether activity J can be executed after activity E, the reader has to switch between the top-process as well as sub-processes A and C, causing her attention to split between these models, thus increasing mental effort.

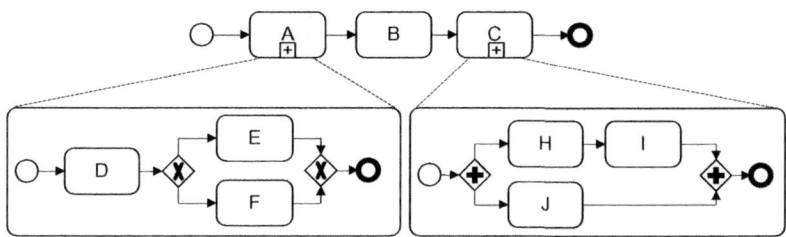

Fig. 1. Example of hierarchical structuring

While the example is certainly artificial and small, it illustrates that it is not always obvious in how far hierarchical structuring impacts a model's understandability.[5]

3   Assessing the Impact of Hierarchy

Up to now we discussed how the cognitive process of inferencing is influenced by different degrees of hierarchical structuring. In Sect. 3.1, we define a theoretical framework that draws on cognitive psychology to explain and integrate these observations. We also discuss the measurement of the impact of hierarchy on understanding in Sect. 3.2 along with its sensitivity to model size in Sect. 3.3 and experience in Sect. 3.4. Furthermore, we discuss the implications of this framework in Sect. 3.5 and potential limitations in Sect. 3.6.

3.1   Towards a Cognitive Framework

The typical research setup of experiments investigating the impact of hierarchy, e.g., as used in [8,9,15,17,18], is shown in Fig. 2. The posed research question thereby is how the *hierarchy* of a model influences *understandability*. In order to operationalize and measure model understandability, a common approach is to use the performance of answering questions about a model, e.g., accuracy or time, to *estimate* model understandability [9,17,18]. In this sense, a *subject* is

---

[5] At this point we would like to remark that we do not take into account class diagrams hierarchy metrics, e.g. [27], since such hierarchies *do not* provide abstraction in the sense we define it. Hence, they fall outside our framework.

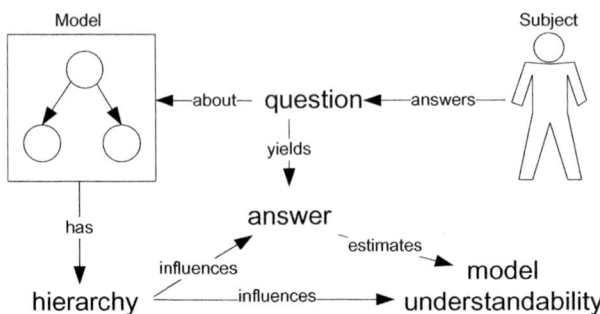

Fig. 2. Research model

asked to *answer questions* about a model; whether the model is hierarchically structured or not serves as treatment.

When taking into account the interplay of abstraction and split-attention effect, as discussed in Sect. 2.2, it becomes apparent that the impact of hierarchy on the performance of answering a question might not be uniform. Rather, each individual question may benefit from or be impaired by hierarchy. As the estimate of understandability is the average answering performance, it is essential to understand how *a single question* is influenced by hierarchy. To approach this influence, we propose a framework that is centered around the concept of mental effort, i.e., the load imposed on the working memory [24], as shown in Fig. 3. In contrast to most existing works, where hierarchy is considered as a dichotomous variable, i.e., hierarchy is present or not, we propose to view the impact of hierarchy as the result of two opposing forces. In particular, every *question* induces a certain *mental effort* on the reader caused by the question's complexity, also referred to as *intrinsic cognitive load* [23]. This value *depends* on model-specific factors, e.g., model size, question type or layout, and person-specific factors, e.g., experience, but is *independent* of the model's hierarchical structure. If hierarchy is present, the resulting mental effort is decreased by *abstraction*, but increased by the *split-attention effect*. Based on the resulting mental effort, a certain answering performance, e.g., accuracy or time, can be expected. In the following, we discuss the implications of this framework. In particular, we discuss how to measure the impact of hierarchy, then we use our framework to explain why model size is important and why experience affects reliable measurements.

3.2   Measuring the Impact on Model Understandability

As indicated [9,8,15,17,18] it is unclear whether and under which circumstances hierarchy is beneficial. As argued in Sect. 2.2, hierarchical structuring can affect answering performance positively by abstraction and negatively by the split-attention effect. To make this trade-off measurable *for a single question*, we provide an operationalization in the following. We propose to estimate the gains of abstraction by counting the number of model elements that can be "hidden" for

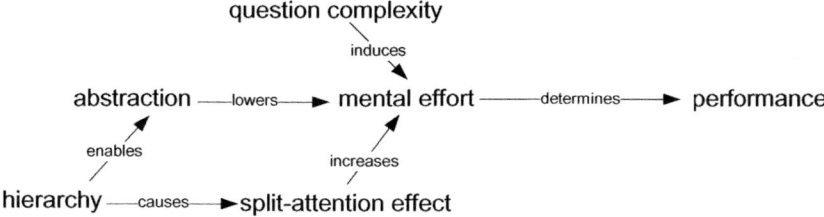

Fig. 3. Theoretical framework for assessing understandability

answering a specific question. Contrariwise, the loss through the split-attention effect can be estimated by the number of context switches, i.e., switches between sub-models, that are required to answer a specific question. To illustrate the suggested operationalization, consider the UML statechart in Fig. 4. When answering the question whether sequence A, B is possible, the reader presumably benefits from the abstraction of state C, i.e., states D, E and F are hidden—leading to a gain of three (hidden model elements). On the contrary, when answering the question, whether the sequence A, D, E, F is possible, the reader does not benefit from abstraction, but has to switch between the top-level state and composite state C. In terms of our operationalisation, no gains are to be expected, since no model element is hidden. However, two context switches when following sequence A, D, E, F, namely from the top-level state to C and back, are required. Overall, it can be expected hierarchy *compromises* this question.

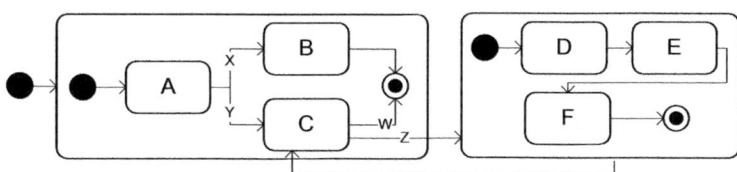

Fig. 4. Abstraction versus split-attention effect

Regarding the use of this operationalization we have two primary purposes in mind. First, it shall help experimenters to design experiments that are not biased toward/against hierarchy by selecting appropriate questions. Second, on the long run, the operationalization could help to estimate the impact of hierarchy on a conceptual model. Please note that these applications are to be viewed under some limitations as discussed in Sect. 3.6.

3.3   Model Size

Our framework defines two major forces that influence the impact of hierarchy on understandability: abstraction (positively) and the split-attention effect (negatively). In order that hierarchy is able to provide benefits, the model must be large enough to benefit from abstraction. Empirical evidence for this theory can be found in [9]. The authors conducted a series of experiments to assess the understandability of UML statecharts with composite states. For the first four experiments no significant differences between flattened models and hierarchical ones could be found. Finally, the last experiment showed significantly better results for the hierarchical model—the authors identified increased complexity, i.e., model size, as one of the main factors for this result. While it seems very likely that there is a certain complexity threshold that must be exceeded, so that desired effects can be observed, it is not yet clear where exactly this threshold lies. To illustrate how difficult it is to define this threshold, we would like to provide an example from the domain of business process modeling, where estimations range from 5–7 model elements [5] over 5–15 elements [6] to 50 elements [7]. In order to investigate whether such a threshold indeed exists and how it can be computed, we envision a series of controlled experiments. Therein, we will systematically combine different model sizes with degrees of abstraction and measure the impact on the subject's answering performance.

3.4 Experience

Besides the size of the model, the reader's experience is an important subject-related factor that should be taken into account [28]. To systematically answer why this is the case, we would like to refer to Cognitive Load Theory [23]. As introduced, it is known that the human working memory has a certain capacity, if it is overstrained by some mental task, errors are likely. As learning causes additional load on the working memory, novices are more likely to make mistakes, as their working memory is more likely to be overloaded by the complexity of the problem solving task in combination with learning. Similarly, less capacity is free for carrying out the problem solving task, i.e, answering the question, hence lower performance with respect to time is to be expected. Hence, experimental settings should ensure that most mental effort is used for problem solving instead of learning. In other words, subjects are not required to be experts, but *must be* familiar with hierarchical structures. Otherwise, it is very likely that results are influenced by the effort needed for learning. To strengthen this case, we would like to refer to [8], where the authors investigated composite states in UML statecharts. The first experiment showed *significant benefits* for composite states, i.e., hierarchy, whereas the *replication* showed *significant disadvantages* for composite states. The authors state that the *"skill of the subjects using UML for modeling, especially UML statechart diagrams, was much lower in this replication"*, indicating that experience plays an important role.

3.5 Discussion

The implications of our work are threefold. First, hierarchy presumably does not impact answering performance uniformly. Hence, when estimating model understandability, results depend on *which* questions are asked. For instance, when only questions are asked that do not benefit from abstraction, but suffer from the split-attention effect, a bias adversely affecting hierarchy can be expected. None of the experiments presented in Sect. 2.1 describes a procedure for defining questions, hence inconclusive results may be attributed to unbalanced questions. Second, for positive effects of hierarchy to appear, presumably a certain model size is required [9]. Third, a certain level of expertise is required that the impact of hierarchy instead of learning is measured, as to be observed in [8].

3.6 Limitations

While the proposed framework is based on established concepts from cognitive psychology and our findings coincide with existing empirical research, there are some limitations. First, our proposed framework is currently based on theory only, an empirical evaluation is yet missing. To counteract this problem, we are currently planning a thorough empirical validation, cf. Sect. 4. In this vein, also the operationalization of abstraction and split-attention effect needs to be investigated. For instance, we do not know yet whether a linear increase in context switches also results in a linearly decreased understandability, or the correlation can be described by, e.g., a quadratic or logarithmic behavior. Second, our proposal focuses on the effects on a single question, i.e., we can not yet assess the impact on the understandability of the entire model. Still, we think that the proposed framework is a first step towards assessing the impact on model understandability, as it is assumed that the overall understandability can be computed by averaging the understandability of all possible individual questions [29].

4   Summary and Outlook

We first had a look at studies on the understandability of hierarchically structured conceptual models. Hierarchy is widely recognized as viable approach to handle complexity—still, reported empirical data seems contradictory. We draw from cognitive psychology to define a framework for assessing the impact of hierarchy on model understandability. In particular, we identify abstraction and the split-attention effect as opposing forces that can be used to estimate the impact of hierarchy with respect to the performance of answering a question about a model. In addition, we use our framework to explain why model size is a prerequisite for a positive influence of modularization and why insufficient experience can bias measurement in experiments. We acknowledge that this work is just the first step towards assessing the impact of hierarchy on model understandability. Hence, future work clearly focuses on empirical investigation. First, the proposed framework is based on well-established theory, still, a thorough empirical validation is needed. We are currently preparing an experiment for verifying that the interplay of abstraction and split-attention effect can actually be observed in hierarchies. In this vein, we also pursue the validation and further refinement of the operationalization for abstraction and split-attention effect.

References

1. Parnas, D.L.: On the Criteria to be Used in Decomposing Systems into Modules. Communications of the ACM 15, 1053–1058 (1972)
2. van der Aalst, W., ter Hofstede, A.H.M.: YAWL: Yet Another Workflow Language. Information Systems 30, 245–275 (2005)
3. Davies, R.: Business Process Modelling With Aris: A Practical Guide. Springer (2001)
4. Damij, N.: Business process modelling using diagrammatic and tabular techniques. Business Process Management Journal 13, 70–90 (2007)
5. Sharp, A., McDermott, P.: Workflow Modeling: Tools for Process Improvement and Application Development. Artech House (2011)
6. Kock, N.F.: Product flow, breadth and complexity of business processes: An empirical study of 15 business processes in three organizations. Business Process Reengineering & Management Journal 2, 8–22 (1996)
7. Mendling, J., Reijers, H.A., van der Aalst, W.M.P.: Seven process modeling guidelines (7pmg). Information & Software Technology 52, 127–136 (2010)
8. Cruz-Lemus, J.A., Genero, M., Manso, M.E., Piattini, M.: Evaluating the Effect of Composite States on the Understandability of UML Statechart Diagrams. In: Briand, L.C., Williams, C. (eds.) MoDELS 2005. LNCS, vol. 3713, pp. 113–125. Springer, Heidelberg (2005)
9. Cruz-Lemus, J.A., Genero, M., Manso, M.E., Morasca, S., Piattini, M.: Assessing the understandability of UML statechart diagrams with composite states—A family of empirical studies. Empir. Software Eng. 25, 685–719 (2009)
10. Burton-Jones, A., Meso, P.N.: Conceptualizing systems for understanding: An empirical test of decomposition principles in object-oriented analysis. ISR 17, 38–60 (2006)
11. Brereton, P., Kitchenham, B.A., Budgen, D., Turner, M., Khalil, M.: Lessons from applying the systematic literature review process within the software engineering domain. JSS 80, 571–583 (2007)
12. Cruz-Lemus, J., Genero, M., Piattini, M.: Using Controlled Experiments for Validating UML Statechart Diagrams Measures. In: Cuadrado-Gallego, J.J., Braungarten, R., Dumke, R.R., Abran, A. (eds.) IWSM-Mensura 2007. LNCS, vol. 4895, pp. 129–138. Springer, Heidelberg (2008)
13. Cruz-Lemus, J., Genero, M., Piattini, M., Toval, A.: Investigating the nesting level of composite states in uml statechart diagrams. In: Proc. QAOOSE 2005, pp. 97–108 (2005)
14. Shoval, P., Danoch, R., Balabam, M.: Hierarchical entity-relationship diagrams: the model, method of creation and experimental evaluation. Requirements Engineering 9, 217–228 (2004)
15. Moody, D.L.: Cognitive Load Effects on End User Understanding of Conceptual Models: An Experimental Analysis. In: Benczúr, A.A., Demetrovics, J., Gottlob, G. (eds.) ADBIS 2004. LNCS, vol. 3255, pp. 129–143. Springer, Heidelberg (2004)
16. Reijers, H., Mendling, J., Dijkman, R.: Human and automatic modularizations of process models to enhance their comprehension. Inf. Systems 36, 881–897 (2011)
17. Reijers, H., Mendling, J.: Modularity in Process Models: Review and Effects. In: Dumas, M., Reichert, M., Shan, M.-C. (eds.) BPM 2008. LNCS, vol. 5240, pp. 20–35. Springer, Heidelberg (2008)

18. Cruz-Lemus, J.A., Genero, M., Morasca, S., Piattini, M.: Using Practitioners for Assessing the Understandability of UML Statechart Diagrams with Composite States. In: Hainaut, J.-L., Rundensteiner, E.A., Kirchberg, M., Bertolotto, M., Brochhausen, M., Chen, Y.-P.P., Cherfi, S.S.-S., Doerr, M., Han, H., Hartmann, S., Parsons, J., Poels, G., Rolland, C., Trujillo, J., Yu, E., Zimányie, E. (eds.) ER Workshops 2007. LNCS, vol. 4802, pp. 213–222. Springer, Heidelberg (2007)

19. Cruz-Lemus, J.A., Genero, M., Piattini, M., Toval, A.: An Empirical Study of the Nesting Level of Composite States Within UML Statechart Diagrams. In: Akoka, J., Liddle, S.W., Song, I.-Y., Bertolotto, M., Comyn-Wattiau, I., van den Heuvel, W.-J., Kolp, M., Trujillo, J., Kop, C., Mayr, H.C. (eds.) ER Workshops 2005. LNCS, vol. 3770, pp. 12–22. Springer, Heidelberg (2005)

20. Larkin, J.H., Simon, H.A.: Why a Diagram is (Sometimes) Worth Ten Thousand Words. Cognitive Science 11, 65–100 (1987)

21. Tracz, W.J.: Computer programming and the human thought process. Software: Practice and Experience 9, 127–137 (1979)

22. Miller, G.: The Magical Number Seven, Plus or Minus Two: Some Limits on Our Capacity for Processing Information. The Psychological Review 63, 81–97 (1956)

23. Sweller, J.: Cognitive load during problem solving: Effects on learning. Cognitive Science 12, 257–285 (1988)

24. Paas, F., Tuovinen, J.E., Tabbers, H., Gerven, P.W.M.V.: Cognitive Load Measurement as a Means to Advance Cognitive Load Theory. Educational Psychologist 38, 63–71 (2003)

25. Wand, Y., Weber, R.: An ontological model of an information system. IEEE TSE 16, 1282–1292 (1990)

26. Sweller, J., Chandler, P.: Why Some Material Is Difficult to Learn. Cognition and Instruction 12, 185–233 (1994)

27. Chidamber, S.R., Kemerer, C.F.: A metrics suite for object oriented design. IEEE Trans. Softw. Eng. 20, 476–493 (1994)

28. Reijers, H.A., Mendling, J.: A Study into the Factors that Influence the Understandability of Business Process Models. SMCA 41, 449–462 (2011)

29. Melcher, J., Mendling, J., Reijers, H.A., Seese, D.: On Measuring the Understandability of Process Models. In: Rinderle-Ma, S., Sadiq, S., Leymann, F. (eds.) BPM 2009. LNBIP, vol. 43, pp. 465–476. Springer, Heidelberg (2010)

Does the Level of Detail of UML Models Affect the Maintainability of Source Code?

Ana M. Fernández-Sáez[1], Marcela Genero[2], and Michel R.V. Chaudron[3]

[1] Alarcos Quality Center, S.L., Department of Technologies and Information Systems,
University of Castilla-La Mancha
Paseo de la Universidad 4, 13071, Ciudad Real, Spain
ana.fernandez@alarcosqualitycenter.com
[2] ALARCOS Research Group, Department of Technologies and Information Systems,
University of Castilla-La Mancha
Paseo de la Universidad 4, 13071, Ciudad Real, Spain
Marcela.Genero@uclm.es
[3] LIACS - Leiden University
Niels Bohrweg 1, 2333 CA Leiden, The Netherlands
chaudron@liacs.nl

Abstract. This paper presents an experiment carried out as a pilot study to obtain a first insight into the influence of the quality of UML models on the maintenance of the corresponding source code. The quality of the UML models is assessed by studying the amount of information they contain as measured through a level of detail metric. The experiment was carried out with 11 Computer Science students from the University of Leiden. The results obtained indicate a slight tendency towards obtaining better results when using low level of detail UML models, which contradicts our expectations based on previous research found in literature. Nevertheless, we are conscious that the results should be considered as preliminary results given the low number of subjects that participated in the experiment. Further replications of this experiment are planned with students and professionals in order to obtain more conclusive results.

Keywords: UML, maintenance, empirical studies, controlled experiment.

1   Introduction

The current increasing complexity of software projects [1] has led to the emergence of UML [2] as a tool with which to increase the understanding between customer and developer and to improve communication among team members [3]. Despite this, not all UML diagrams have the same complexity, layout, level of abstraction, etc. Previous studies have shown that the style and rigor used in the diagrams may vary considerably throughout software projects [4], in addition to affecting the source code of the system in a different way.

On the one hand, the different purposes for which a model may be intended (for example: architecting solutions, communicating design decisions, detailed specification

J. Kienzle (Ed.): MODELS 2011 Workshops, LNCS 7167, pp. 134–148, 2012.

for implementation, or automatically generating implementation code) signifies that the same system can be represented with different styles. On the other hand, the development diagrams are sometimes available for maintainers, but this is not always the case, and the diagrams must be generated with a reverse engineering process. The difference in the origin of the models and the different techniques that can be used to generate a reverse engineering model result in different styles of models. Some of the most notable differences between these models may be the level of detail shown. In this work we therefore analyze whether the different levels of detail (LoD) affect the work that must be carried out by a maintainer.

This document is organized as follows. Section 2 presents the related work. Section 3 presents the description of the experiment. The results obtained in the experiment are presented in Section 4, whilst the threats to validity are summarized in Section 5. Finally, Section 6 outlines our main conclusions and future work.

2   Related Work

We performed an SLR [5] to discover all the empirical studies performed as regards the use of UML in maintenance, and found only the following two works related to the maintenance of source code:

— In [6] an experiment was performed to investigate whether the use of UML influences maintenance in comparison to the use of only source code. The results of this work show a positive influence of the presence of UML for maintainers.
— In the work presented in [7], the experiment performed is focused on the comprehension and the difficulties involved in maintaining object-oriented systems. UML models were also presented to the subjects of the experiment, but they were only focused on exploring the participant's strategies and problems while they were conducting maintenance tasks on an object-oriented application.

We therefore decided to perform an experiment related to the influence of different levels of detail on UML diagrams when assisting in maintenance tasks. We found a paper [8] focused on the understandability of models with different LoD in the development phase. The results show a better understanding of models when they have a high LoD. We would like to discover whether high LoD diagrams help workers to perform the changes that need to be made to the source code during the maintenance phase.

3   Experiment Description

The experiment was carried out at the University of Leiden (The Netherlands) in March 2011. In order to run and report this experiment, we followed the recommendations provided in several works [9-11]. The experiment was presented by following the guidelines for reporting empirical research in software engineering [11] as closely as possible. The experimental material is available for downloading at: http://alarcos.esi.uclm.es/experimentUMLmaintenance/

In the following subsections we shall describe the main characteristics of the experiment, including goal, context, variables, subjects, design, hypotheses, material, tasks, experiment procedure and analysis procedure.

3.1   Goal

The principal goal of this experiment was to investigate whether the LoD in UML models influences the maintenance of source code. The GQM template for goal definition [12, 13] was used to define the goal of our experiment as follows: *"Analyze the level of detail in UML models with the purpose of evaluating it with respect to the maintainability of source code from the point of view of researchers, in the context of Computer Science students at the University of Leiden.*

As in [3], we considered that the LoD in UML models should be defined as the amount of information that is used to represent a modeling element. LoD is a 'continuous' metric, but for the experiment we have taken two "extremes" - high and low LoD.

Table 1. Levels of detail in UML models

Diagram	Element	Low LoD	High LoD
Class diagram	Classes (box and name)	✓	✓
	Attributes	✗	✓
	Types in attributes	✗	✓
	Operations	✗	✓
	Parameters in operations	✗	✓
	Associations	✓	✓
	Association directionalities	✗	✓
	Association multiplicities	✗	✓
	Aggregations	✓	✓
	Compositions	✓	✓
Sequence diagram	Actors	✓	✓
	Objects	✓	✓
	Messages in informal language	✓	✗
	Messages with formal language (name of a method)	✗	✓
	Parameters in messages	✗	✓
	Labels in return messages	✗	✓

We decided to use 3 different types of diagrams (use case, sequence and class diagrams) since they are those most frequently used. When the LoD used in a UML model is low, it typically employs only a few syntactical features, such as class-name and associations, without specifying any further facts about the class. When it is high, the model also includes class attributes and operations, association names, association directionality, and multiplicity. In sequence diagrams, in which there is a low LoD, the messages among objects have an informal label, and when the LoD is high the label is a method name plus the parameter list. We consider that it is not possible to distinguish between low and high LoD in use case diagrams because they are very simple diagrams. The elements that fit each level of detail are shown in Table 1.

3.2 Context Selection

The experimental objects consisted of use case, class and sequence diagrams and the JAVA code of two software systems, which are summarized below:

- A-H: high LoD diagrams and JAVA code of system A.
- A-L: low LoD diagrams and JAVA code of system A.
- B-H: high LoD diagrams and JAVA code of system B.
- B-L: low LoD diagrams and JAVA code of system B.

Diagrams A-x described a library domain from which a user can borrow books. Diagrams B-x described a sport centre domain from which users can rent services (tennis courts, etc.). System A is a Library extracted from [14]. We decided to use it because it was a representative system, it was complete (source code and models were available) and it gave us a starting point from which to compare our results (it was only possible to compare the results obtained from the subjects who received System A with high LoD with [7]). System B is a Sport centre application created as part of the Master's degree Thesis of a student from the University of Castilla-La Mancha, and we therefore consider it to be a real system. Both systems are desktop applications and have more or less the same complexity. These experimental objects were presented in English.

The subjects students on a Software Engineering course from which they had acquired training in UML diagrams. Their knowledge was sufficient for them to understand the given systems, and they had roughly the same background. They had knowledge about the use of UML diagrams in general, but they were taught about UML diagrams and JAVA in a training session organized to take place the day before the experiment was carried out.

The experiment was carried out by 11 Computer Science students from the University of Leiden (The Netherlands) who were taking the Software Engineering course in the second-year of their B.Sc.

Working with students also implies various advantages, such as the fact that their prior knowledge is fairly homogeneous, there is the possible availability of a large number of subjects [15], and there is the chance to test experimental design and initial hypotheses [16]. An additional advantage of using novices as subjects in experiments on comprehensibility and modifiability is that the cognitive complexity of the objects under study is not hidden by the subjects' experience. Nonetheless, we also wish to test the findings with practitioners in order to strengthen the external validity of the results obtained.

The students who participated in the experiment were volunteers selected for convenience (the students available in the corresponding course). Social threats caused by evaluation apprehension were avoided by not grading the students on their performance.

3.3   Variables Selection

The independent variable (also called "main factor") is the LoD, which is a nominal variable with two values (low LoD and high LoD). We combined each level of the independent variable with the two different systems used to obtain four treatments (see Table 2).

The dependent variables are modifiability and understandability. These two variables were considered because understandability and modifiability directly influence maintainability [17]. In order to measure these dependant variables, we defined the following measures:

— **Understandability Effectiveness (U_{Effec}):** This measure reflects the ability to correctly understand the system presented. It is calculated with the following formula: number of correct answers / number of questions. A higher value of this measure reflects a better understandability.
— **Modifiability Effectiveness (U_{Effic}):** This measure reflects the ability to correctly modify the system presented. It is calculated with the following formula: number of correctly performed modification tasks / number of modification tasks. A higher value of this measure reflects a better modifiability.
— **Understandability Efficiency (M_{Effec}):** This measure also reflects the ability to correctly understand the system presented. It is calculated with the following formula: time spent / number of correctly answered questions. A lower value of this measure reflects a better understandability.
— **Modifiability Efficiency (M_{Effic}):** This measure also reflects the ability to correctly modify the system presented. It is calculated with the following formula: time spent / number of correctly performed tasks. A lower value of this measure reflects a better modifiability.

Additional independent variables (called "co-factors") were considered according to the experimental design of the replication, and their effect has been controlled and analyzed:

— **Order.** The selected design (see Table 2), i.e., the variation in the order of application of each method (low LoD, high LoD), was intended to alleviate learning effects. Nonetheless, we analyzed whether the order in which the LoD were used by the subjects biased the results.
— **System.** This factor indicates the systems (i.e., A and B) used as experimental objects. The design selected for the experiment (see Table 2) forced us to

choose two application domains in order to avoid learning effects. Our intention was that the system factor would not be a confounding factor that might also influence the subjects' performances. We therefore selected well-known domains and experimental objects of a similar complexity.

3.4   Hypotheses Formulation

Based on the assumption that the more information a model contains, the more is known about the concepts/knowledge described in the model, the hypothesis are:

1. $H_{1,0}$: There is no significant difference in the subjects' understandability effectiveness when working with UML diagrams modeled using high or low levels of detail.
   $H_{1,1}:\neg H_{1,0}$
2. $H_{2,0}$: There is no significant difference in the subjects' understandability efficiency when working with UML diagrams modeled using high or low levels of detail.
   $H_{2,1}:\neg H_{2,0}$
3. $H_{3,0}$: There is no significant difference in the subjects' modifiability effectiveness when working with UML diagrams modeled using high or low levels of detail.
   $H_{3,1}:\neg H_{3,0}$
4. $H_{4,0}$: There is no significant difference in the subjects' modifiability efficiency when working with UML diagrams modeled using high or low levels of detail.
   $H_{4,1}: \neg H_{4,0}$

The goal of the statistical analysis will be to reject these null hypotheses and possibly to accept the alternative ones (e.g., $H_{n1}=\neg H_{n0}$).

3.5   Experimental Design

We selected a balanced factorial design in which the group-interaction acted as a confounding factor [18] which permits the lessening of the effects of learning and fatigue. The experiment's execution consisted of two runs. In each round, each of the groups was given a different treatment. The corresponding system (source code + UML models) was assigned to each group at random, but was given out in a different order in each case. Table 2 presents the outline of the experimental design.

Table 2. Experimental design

RUN 1		LoD		RUN 2		LoD	
		Low	High			Low	High
System	A	Group 1	Group 2	System	A	Group 3	Group 4
	B	Group 3	Group 4		B	Group 2	Group 1

Before carrying out the experiment, we provided the subjects with a background questionnaire and assigned them to the 4 groups randomly, based on the marks obtained in the aforementioned questionnaire (blocked design by experience) in an attempt to alleviate experience effects. To avoid a possible learning effect, the diagrams came from different application domains (A-a Library and B-a Sport centre).

When designing the experiment we attempted to alleviate several issues that might threaten the validity of the research done by considering the suggestions provided in [19].

3.6   Experimental Tasks

The tasks to be performed did not require high levels of industrial experience, so we believed that the use of students could be considered appropriate, as suggested in literature [20, 21]. The material used was written in English.

There were three kinds of tasks:

— **Understandability Task:** This contained 3 questions concerning the semantics of the system, i.e. the semantics of diagrams and the semantics of code. These questions were multiple choice questions and were used to obtain U_{Effec} and U_{Effic}.
— **Modifiability Task:** The subjects received a list of requirements in order to modify the code of the system in order to add/change certain functionalities. This part of the experiment contained 3 modifiability tasks and allowed us to calculate M_{Effec} and M_{Effic}. The subjects were provided with answer sheets to allow them to structure their responses related to maintenance tasks. They had to fill in a different form depending on the element that they wished to maintain. The answer sheets can be found at:

    http://alarcos.esi.uclm.es/experimentUMLmaintenance/

— **Post-questionnaire Task:** At the end of the execution of each run, the subjects were asked to fill in a post-experiment questionnaire, whose goal was to obtain feedback about the subjects' perception of the experiment execution, which could be used to explain the results obtained. The answers to the questions were based on a five-point Likert scale [22].

3.7   Experimental Procedure

The experiment took place in two sessions of two hours each. The subjects first attended a training session in which detailed instructions on the experiment were presented and the main concepts of UML and JAVA were revised. In this session, the subjects carried out an exercise similar to those in the experimental tasks in collaboration with the instructor. During the training session, the subjects were required to fill in a background questionnaire. Based on the marks obtained in this questionnaire, the subjects were randomly assigned to the 4 groups shown in Table 2, thus obtaining balanced groups in accordance with the marks obtained in the background questionnaire.

The experiment then took place in a second session, consisting of two runs. In each run, each of the groups was given a different treatment, as is shown in Table 2.

The experiment was conducted in a classroom, where the students were supervised by the instructor and no communication among them was allowed.

After the experiment execution, the data collected from the experiment were placed on an excel sheet.

3.8   Analysis Procedure

The data analysis was carried out by considering the following steps:

1. We first carried out a descriptive study of the measures of the dependent variables, i.e., understandability and modifiability.
2. We then tested the formulated hypotheses using the non-parametric Kruskal-Wallis test [23] for the data collected in the experiment. The use of this test was possible because, according the design of the controlled experiment, we obtained paired samples. In addition, Kruskal-Wallis is the most appropriate test with which to explore the results of a factorial design with confounded interaction [18, 24], i.e., the design used in our experiment, when there is non-normal distribution of the data.
3. We next used the Kruskal-Wallis test to analyze the influence of the co-factors (i.e., System and Order).
4. The data collected from the post-experiment questionnaire was finally analyzed using bar graphs.

4   Results

The following subsections show the results of the data analysis of the experiment performed using SPSS [25].

4.1   Descriptive Statistics and Exploratory Analysis

Table 3 and Table 4 show the descriptive statistics of the Understandability and Modifiability measures, respectively (i.e., mean ($\overline{X}$), standard error (SE), and standard deviation (SD)), grouped by LoD.

Table 3. Descriptive statistics for U_{Effec} and U_{Effic}

LoD	Subjects	U_{effec}			U_{Effic}		
		$\overline{X}$	SE	SD	$\overline{X}$	SE	SD
Low	N = 10 (1 outlier)	**0.767**	0.051	0.161	**334.500**	36.308	114.816
High	N = 11	0.758	0.650	0.215	363.924	82.602	273.960

Table 4. Descriptive statistics for M_{effec} and M_{Effic}

LoD	Subjects	M_{effec}			M_{Effic}		
		$\overline{X}$	SE	SD	$\overline{X}$	SE	SD
Low	N = 11	**0.437**	0.066	**0.221**	**240.121**	41.008	136.007
High	N = 11	0.402	0.050	0.169	294.637	47.198	156.539

At a glance, we can observe that when the subjects used low LoD diagrams they obtained better values in all variables. This indicates that low LoD diagrams may, to some extent, improve the comprehension and modification of the source code.

4.2   Influence of LoD

In order to test the formulated hypotheses we analyzed the effect of the main factor (i.e. LoD) on the dependent variables considered (i.e., UEffec, UEffic, MEffec and MEffic) using the Kruskal-Wallis test (see Table 5).

Table 5. Kruskal-Wallis test results for U_{effec}, U_{effic}, M_{effec} and M_{effic}

	U_{effec}	U_{Effic}	M_{effec}	M_{Effic}
LoD	1	0.439	0.792	0.491

Testing $H_{1,0}$ (U_{Effec})
The results in Table 5 suggest that the null hypothesis cannot be rejected since the p-value is greater than 0.05. This means that there is no significant difference in U_{Effec} in either group.

We decided to investigate this result in greater depth by calculating the number of subjects who achieved better values when using the low LoD models (i.e. a low LoD value is higher than a high LoD value):

Table 6. Comparison of subjects' results for each measure

	low LoD = high LoD	low LoD < high LoD	low LoD > high LoD
U_{Effec}	6	3	2
U_{Effic}	0	7	4
M_{Effec}	0	7	4
M_{Effic}	0	5	6

As Table 6 shows, the number of subjects who obtained the same results for both treatments (high and low LoD) is relatively high. There were more subjects who performed better with a high LoD than with a low LoD, but the differences in comparison to the opposite group is very small (only one subject).

Testing $H_{2,0}$ (U_{Effic})
The results in Table 5 suggest that the null hypothesis cannot be rejected since the p-value is greater than 0.05. This means that there is no significant difference in U_{Effic} in either group.

We decided to investigate this result in greater depth by calculating the number of subjects who achieved better values when using the low LoD models (i.e. a low LoD value is smaller than a high LoD value):

As Table 6 shows, no subjects obtained the same U_{Effic} for both treatments (high and low LoD). More subjects performed better with a low LoD than with a high LoD.

Testing $H_{3,0}$ (M_{Effec})
The results in Table 5 suggest that the null hypothesis cannot be rejected since the p-value is greater than 0.05. This means that there is no significant difference in M_{Effec} in either group.

We decided to investigate this result in greater depth by calculating the number of subjects who achieved better values when using the low LoD models (i.e. a low LoD value is higher than a high LoD value):

As Table 6 shows, no subjects obtained the same M_{Effec} for both treatments (high and low LoD). More subjects performed better with a high LoD than with a low LoD.

Testing $H_{4,0}$ (M_{Effic})
The results in Table 5 suggest that the null hypothesis cannot be rejected since the p-value is greater than 0.05. This means that there is no significant difference in M_{Effic} in either group.

We decided to investigate this result in greater depth by calculating the number of subjects who achieved better values when using the low LoD models (i.e. a low LoD value is smaller than a high LoD value):

As Table 6 shows, no subjects obtained the same M_{Effic} for both treatments (high and low LoD). More subjects performed better with a high LoD than with a low LoD, but the differences in comparison to the opposite group are also small.

4.3   Influence of System

In order to test the effect of the co-factor System, we performed a Kruskal-Wallis test whose results are shown in Table 7. As all the p-values were higher than 0.05, except in one case (U_{Effic}), we did not have sufficient evidence to reject the hypothesis, i.e. it seems that the system did not influence the subjects' performance (and this was therefore a controlled co-factor).

Table 7. Kruskal-Wallis test results for the influence of the System

	U_{effec}	U_{Effic}	M_{effec}	M_{Effic}
System	0.804	**0.035**	0.575	0.061

4.4   Influence of Order

In order to test the effect of Order, we performed a Kruskal-Wallis test (see Table 8). As all p-values were higher than 0.05, we did not have sufficient evidence to reject the hypothesis, i.e. the order did not influence the subjects' performance (and this was therefore a controlled co-factor).

Table 8. Kruskal-Wallis tests results

	U_{effec}	U_{Effic}	M_{effec}	M_{Effic}
Order	1	0.105	0.223	0.341

4.5   Post-experiment Survey Questionnaire Results

The analysis of the answers to the post-experiment survey questionnaire revealed that the time needed to carry out the comprehension and modification tasks was considered to be inappropriate (more time was needed), and that the subjects considered the tasks to be quite difficult (Fig. 1).

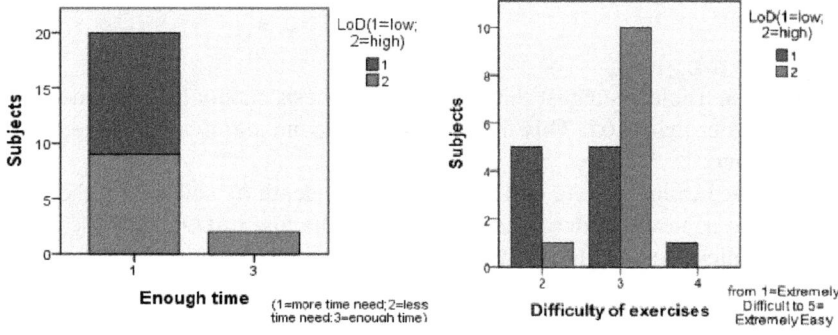

Fig. 1. Subjects' perception of the experiment

We also asked about the subjects' perception of some of the items that appeared in the high LoD diagrams but did not appear in the low LoD diagrams. Fig. 2 shows that high LoD elements seem to be appreciated by the subjects. With regard to the histograms in Fig. 2, if a subject responds 1 or 2, this indicates that s/he thinks that the element in the question was helpful, while a response of 4 or 5 indicates that the elements in the question are not helpful (3 is a neutral response). If we focus on the elements related to class diagrams (upper histograms) we can see that attributes are helpful for 9 subjects (versus 1 subject who does not believe them to be helpful). The same is true of operations (10 subjects vs. 1 subject). If we focus on the elements related to sequence diagrams (lower histograms) we can see that formal messages are more helpful (16 subjects) than natural language messages (0 subjects), and the same can also be said of the appearance of parameters in messages (13 subjects vs. 2 subjects).

4.6   Summary and Discussion of the Data Analysis

The null hypothesis cannot be rejected for any of the dependent variables. Although we cannot draw conclusive results on the main factor (LoD), we have found that co-factors (system, order) have not influenced the results.

Nevertheless, the descriptive statistics in general showed a slight tendency in favor of using low LoD diagrams in contrary to what we believed, as the diagrams with a high LoD helped developers in the software development stage [8]. This may result from the fact that the subjects did not have the expected amount of knowledge about UML (a mean of 8.8 correct answers out of 16 questions) and JAVA (a mean of 4.9 correct answers out of 9 questions) tested in the background questionnaire. The results of the experiment must be considered as preliminary results owing to the small size of the group of subjects who participated in the experiment.

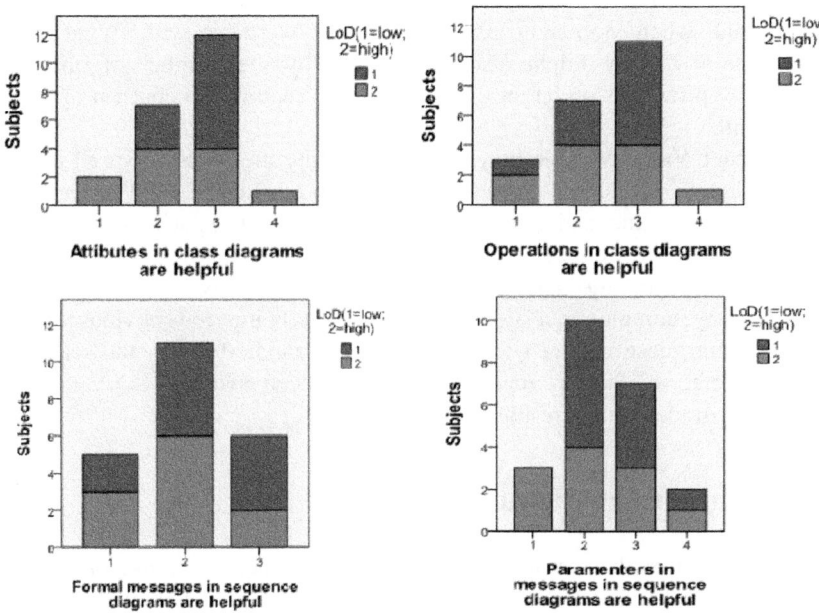

Fig. 2. Subjects' opinion of LoD (1=Complete Agreement 2=Partial Agreement 3=Neither agree/ nor disagree 4=Partial Disagreement 5=Total disagreement)

5   Threats to Validity

We must consider certain issues which may have threatened the validity of the experiment:

  — **External Validity:** External validity may be threatened when experiments are performed with students, and the representativeness of the subjects in comparison to software professionals may be doubtful. In spite of this, the tasks to be performed did not require high levels of industrial experience, so we believed that this experiment could be considered appropriate, as suggested in literature [13]. There are no threats related to the material used since the systems used were real ones.

— **Internal Validity:** Internal validity threats are mitigated by the design of the experiment. Each group of subjects worked on the same system in different orders. Nevertheless, there is still the risk that the subjects might have learned how to improve their performances from one performance to the other. Moreover, the instrumentation was tested in a pilot study in order to check its validity. In addition, mortality threats were mitigated by offering the subjects extra points in their final marks.

— **Conclusion Validity:** Conclusion validity concerns the data collection, the reliability of the measurement, and the validity of the statistical tests. Statistical tests were used to reject the null hypotheses. We have explicitly mentioned and discussed when non-significant differences were present. What is more, conclusion validity might also be affected by the number of observations. Further replications on larger datasets are thus required to confirm or contradict the results.

— **Construct Validity:** This may be influenced by the measures used to obtain a quantitative evaluation of the subjects' performance, the comprehension questionnaires, the maintenance tasks, and the post-experiment questionnaire. The metrics used were selected to achieve a balance between the correctness and completeness of the answers. The questionnaires were defined to obtain sufficiently complex questions without them being too obvious. The post-experiment questionnaire was designed using standard forms and scales. Social threats (e.g., evaluation apprehension) have been avoided, since the students were not graded on the results obtained.

6   Conclusions and Future Work

The main concern of the research presented in this paper is the use of a controlled experiment to investigate whether the use of low or high level of detail in UML diagrams influences the maintainer's performance when understanding and modifying source code. The experiment was carried out by 11 academic students from the University of Leiden in the Netherlands.

The results obtained are not significant owing to various factors such as the fact that the subjects selected had a low level of experience in using UML and JAVA code, and the small size of the group of subjects who participated in the experiment. It is only possible to observe a slight tendency towards obtaining better results with low LoD diagrams, contrary to the results obtained in [8].

Despite these drawbacks, we have ensured that the experimental results were not influenced by other co-factors such as the system used or the order in which the subjects received the experimental material.

We are planning to perform two replications with students from the University of Castilla-La Mancha (Spain) and students from the University of Bari (Italy). A third possible replication with professionals is also being planned. All the drawbacks found in the execution of this experiment will be taken into account in the replications.

Acknowledgment. This research has been funded by the following projects: MEDUSAS (CDTI-MICINN and FEDER IDI- 20090557), ORIGIN (CDTI-MICINN and FEDER IDI-2010043(1-5), PEGASO/MAGO (MICINN and FEDER, TIN2009-13718-C02-01), EECCOO (MICINN TRA2009-0074), MECCA (JCMM PII2I09-0075-8394) and IMPACTUM (PEII 11-0330-4414).

References

1. Van Vliet, H.: Software Engineering: Principles and Practices, 3rd edn. Wiley (2008)
2. OMG. The Unified Modeling Language. Documents associated with UML Version 2.3 (2010), http://www.omg.org/spec/UML/2.3
3. Nugroho, A., Chaudron, M.R.V.: Evaluating the Impact of UML Modeling on Software Quality: An Industrial Case Study. In: Schürr, A., Selic, B. (eds.) MODELS 2009. LNCS, vol. 5795, pp. 181–195. Springer, Heidelberg (2009)
4. Lange, C.F.J., Chaudron, M.R.V.: In practice: UML software architecture and design description. IEEE Software 23(2), 40–46 (2006)
5. Fernández-Sáez, A.M., Genero, M., Chaudron, M.R.V.: Empirical studies on the influence of UML in software maintenance tasks: A systematic literature review. Submitted to Science of Computer Programming - Special issue on Software Evolution, Adaptability and Maintenance. Elsevier
6. Dzidek, W.J., Arisholm, E., Briand, L.C.: A realistic empirical evaluation of the costs and benefits of UML in software maintenance. IEEE Transactions on Software Engineering 34(3), 407–432 (2008)
7. Karahasanovic, A., Thomas, R.: Difficulties Experienced by Students in Maintaining Object-Oriented Systems: an Empirical Study. In: Proceedings of the Australasian Computing Education Conference, ACE 2007 (2007)
8. Nugroho, A.: Level of detail in UML models and its impact on model comprehension: A controlled experiment. Information and Software Technology 51(12), 1670–1685 (2009)
9. Juristo, N., Moreno, A.: Basics of Software Engineering Experimentation. Kluwer Academic Publishers (2001)
10. Wohlin, C., et al.: Experimentation in Software Engineering: an Introduction. Kluwer Academic Publisher (2000)
11. Jedlitschka, A., Ciolkowoski, M., Pfahl, D.: Reporting Experiments in Software Engineering. In: Shull, F., Singer, J., Sjøberg, D.I.K. (eds.) Guide to Advanced Empirical Software Engineering. Springer, Heidelberg (2008)
12. Basili, V., Weiss, D.: A Methodology for Collecting Valid Software Engineering Data. IEEE Transactions on Software Engineering 10(6), 728–738 (1984)
13. Basili, V., Shull, F., Lanubile, F.: Building Knowledge through Families of Experiments. IEEE Transactions on Software Engineering 25, 456–473 (1999)
14. Eriksson, H.E., et al.: UML 2 Toolkit. Wiley (2004)
15. Verelst, J.: The Influence of Abstraction on the Evolvability of Conceptual Models of Information Systems. In: International Symposium on Empirical Software Engineering, ISESE 2004 (2004)

16. Sjøberg, D.I.K., et al.: A Survey of Controlled Experiments in Software Engineering. IEEE Transaction on Software Engineering 31(9), 733–753 (2005)
17. ISO/IEC, ISO/IEC 25000: Software Engineering, in Software product quality requirements and evaluation (SQuaRe), International Organization for Standarization (2008)
18. Kirk, R.E.: Experimental Design. Procedures for the Behavioural Sciences. Brooks/Cole Publishing Company (1995)
19. Wohlin, C., et al.: Experimentation in Software Engineering: An Introduction. Kluwer Academic Publishers, Norwell (2000)
20. Basili, V., Shull, F., Lanubile, F.: Building Knowledge through Families of Experiments. IEEE Transactions on Software Engineering 25(4), 456–473 (1999)
21. Höst, M., Regnell, B., Wholin, C.: Using students as subjects - a comparative study of students and professionals in lead-time impact assessment. In: 4th Conference on Empirical Assessment and Evaluation in Software Engineering (2000)
22. Oppenheim, A.N.: Questionnaire Design, Interviewing and Attitude Measurement. Pinter Publishers (1992)
23. Conover, W.J.: Practical Nonparametric Statistics, 3rd edn. Wiley (1998)
24. Winer, B.J., Brown, D.R., Michels, K.M.: Statistical Principles in Experimental Design, 3rd edn. Mc Graw Hill Series in Psychology (1991)
25. SPSS, SPSS 12.0, Syntax Reference Guide. SPSS Inc., Chicago, USA (2003)

Summary of the 6th International Workshop on Models@run.time

Nelly Bencomo[1], Gordon Blair[2], Robert France[3],
Betty H.C. Cheng[4], and Cédric Jeanneret[5]

[1] INRIA Paris-Rocquencourt, France
[2] Computing Dep., Lancaster University, UK
[3] Computer Science Dep., Colorado State University, USA
[4] Dep. of Computer Science and Engineering, Michigan State University, USA
[5] Department of Informatics, University of Zurich, Switzerland
nelly@acm.org, gordon@comp.lancs.ac.uk, france@CS.ColoState.EDU,
chengb@cse.msu.edu, jeanneret@ifi.uzh.ch

Abstract. The 6th edition of the workshop Models@run.time was held at the 14th International Conference MODELS. The workshop took place in the city of Wellington, New Zealand, on the 17th of October 2011. The workshop was organised by Nelly Bencomo, Gordon Blair, Robert France, Betty H.C. Cheng, and Cédric Jeanneret. We present a summary of the workshop and a synopsis of the papers presented during the workshop.

Keywords: runtime adaptation, MDE, reflection, run-time abstractions.

1 Introduction

The Models@run.time workshop series provides a forum for exchange of ideas on the use of run-time models. The main goal is to further promote cross-fertilization between researchers from different communities, including model-driven software engineering, software architectures, computational reflection, adaptive systems, autonomic and self-healing systems, and requirements engineering. This edition of the workshop successfully brought together researchers from different communities and, at least, twenty six (26) people attended the workshop.

This edition had six (6) papers presented. Two papers were selected as the best papers. Improved versions of these two papers are published in this post workshop proceedings with other selected papers from all the workshops at MODELS 2011.

2 Workshop Format and Session Summaries

The workshop was held as a one-day workshop in MODELS. The activities were structured into presentations and discussion sessions.

In the paper sessions six (6) papers were presented. Authors presented their papers in a twenty-minute-time slot, and five minutes were allowed for questions and discussion.

J. Kienzle (Ed.): MODELS 2011 Workshops, LNCS 7167, pp. 149–151, 2012.
© Springer-Verlag Berlin Heidelberg 2012

Paper presentations were done during the morning to allow enough time for discussion during the second part of the day. In the afternoon, the workshop participants formed three groups. Each group took care of discussing specific relevant topics. At the end of the workshop, each group selected a delegate who presented the conclusions and research questions raised by the group. The six (6) paper presentations:

Session 1

- Language and Framework Requirements for Adaptation Models by Thomas Vogel and Holger Giese (*best paper*):

The authors investigate requirements for Adaptation Models that specify the analysis, decision-making, and planning of adaptation as part of a feedback loop. In particular, they consider requirements for a modelling language of adaptation models. They also discuss patterns for using adaptation models within the feedback loop regarding the structuring of loop activities. The patterns and the requirements for adaptation models influence each other, which impacts at the same time the design of the feedback loop.

- Towards Autonomous Adaptive Systems through Requirements@Runtime   by Liliana Pasquale, Luciano Baresi and Bashar Nuseibeh

The authors address the problem of anticipation of requirements model in self-adaptive system. They argue, it is possible to trace requirements/adaptation changes and propagate them onto the application instances. The paper leverages the FLAGS methodology, which provides a goal model to represent adaptations and a runtime infrastructure to manage requirements@runtime. First, the paper explains how the FLAGS infrastructure can support requirements@runtime, by managing the interplay between the requirements and the executing applications. Finally, it describes how this infrastructure can be used to adapt the system, and, consequently, support the evolution of requirements.

- Model-based Situational Security Analysis by Jörn Eichler and Roland Rieke

The authors present an approach to support not only model-based evaluation of the current security status of business process instances, but also to allow for decision support by analyzing close-future process states. Their approach is based on operational formal models derived from development-time process and security models. This paper exemplifies the approach utilizing real world processes from the logistics domain and demonstrates the systematic development and application of runtime models for situational security analysis.

Session 2

- Runtime monitoring of functional component changes with behavior models by Carlo Ghezzi, Andrea Mocci and Mario Sangiorgio (*best paper*)

The authors consider the problem of run-time discovery and continuous monitoring of new components that live in an open environment. They focus on extracting a formal model - which may not be available - by observing the behavior of the running component. They show how the model built at run time can be enriched through new observations (dynamic model update). They also use the inferred model to perform run- time verification. That is, they try to identify if any changes are made to the component that modify its original behaviour, contradict the previous observations, and invalidate the inferred model.

- Using Model-to-Text Transformation for Dynamic Web-Based Model Navigation by Dimitrios Kolovos, Louis Rose and James Williams

The authors propose a model-to-text transformation approach for producing dynamic, web-based views of models - captured atop diferent modelling technologies and conforming to arbitrary metamodels - so that stakeholders can be provided with web-based, on-demand and up-to-date access to the models of the system using only their web browser. They demonstrate the practicality of this approach through case studies and identify a number of open challenges in the field of web-based model management.

- Runtime Variability Management for Energy-efficient Software by Contract Negotiation by Sebastian Götz, Claas Wilke, Sebastian Cech and Uwe Assmann

They authors tackle the question: which implementations should run on and utilize which resources in which performance mode to serve the user's demands? They argue that the question can only be answered at runtime, as it relies on the runtime state of the system. In the paper, they show how combined hard- and software models can be used at runtime to determine valid system configurations and to identify the optimal one.

The papers by Thomas Vogel and Holger Giese and Carlo Ghezzi, Andrea Mocci and Mario Sangiorgio were rated as the best 2 papers of this workshop. The discussion during the afternoon covered the role of runtime models during the development of adaptive software, reasoning at runtime, and self-adaptation in the cloud. The presentations and slides associated with discussions are in the web pages of the workshop.

Acknowledgments. *We would also* like to thank the members of the program committee who acted as anonymous reviewers and provided valuable feedback to the authors: *Uwe Assman, Franck Chauvel, Peter J. Clarke, Fabio Costa, Franck Fleury, Jeff Gray, Holger Giese, Gang Huang, Paola Inverardi, Jean-Marc Jezequel, Rui Silva Moreira, Brice Morin, Hausi Muller, Arnor Solberg, Mario Trapp, Thaís Vasconcelos Batista.*

Runtime Monitoring of Functional Component Changes with Behavior Models[*]

Carlo Ghezzi[1], Andrea Mocci[2], and Mario Sangiorgio[1]

[1] Politecnico di Milano, Dipartimento di Elettronica e Informazione
Piazza Leonardo da Vinci, 32, 20133 Milano (MI), Italy
{ghezzi,sangiorgio}@elet.polimi.it
[2] Computer Science and Artificial Intelligence Laboratory
Massachusetts Institute of Technology, Cambridge, MA 02139
am@csail.mit.edu

Abstract. We consider the problem of run-time discovery and continuous monitoring of new components that live in an open environment. We focus on extracting a formal model—which may not be available upfront—by observing the behavior of the running component. We show how the model built at run time can be enriched through new observations (dynamic model update). We also use the inferred model to perform run-time verification. That is, we try to identify if any changes are made to the component that modify its original behavior, contradict the previous observations, and invalidate the inferred model.

1 Introduction and Motivations

Modern software systems increasingly live in an open world [6]. In the context of this paper, we assume this to mean that the components that can be used to compose new application may be dynamically discovered and they may change over time. New components may appear or disappear; existing components that were already available may change without notice. Indeed, in an open world context, software components can be developed and made available by different stakeholders, who pursue their own objectives. In most cases, clients have no ways to control their development and evolution. Still, new applications may be developed in a way that they rely on third party components, often called *services*, that are composed to provide a specific new functionality[1].

In this setting, *models* play the role of formal specifications and have a crucial importance. In fact, to be able to compose components in applications and make sure they achieve ascertainable goals, one needs to have a model of the components being used. Unfortunately, such model, in practice, mays not exist. For example, in the case where components are Web services, suitable notations

---

[*] This research has been partially funded by the European Commission, Programme IDEAS-ERC, Project 227977-SMScom.

[1] Although the terms "component" and "service" can be (and should be) distinguished, in this paper the terms are used interchangeably.

J. Kienzle (Ed.): MODELS 2011 Workshops, LNCS 7167, pp. 152–166, 2012.
© Springer-Verlag Berlin Heidelberg 2012

(e.g., WSDL) exist to specify the syntax of service invocations, but no standard notation exists to specify the semantics (i.e., model the behavior) of the components. In this context, it becomes relevant to be able to infer a model for the component dynamically, at run time, by observing how the component behaves. We consider stateful components, hence the models we work with have to represent properly the state of the component and describe what happens when each operation is executed. Stateful components are harder to model because we cannot consider each operation in isolation: operation results depend on the state of the component.

In addition to the previous problems, one must consider the fact that the component may change at run time in an unannounced manner. In other words, even if a model were initially provided together with the exposed service, it may become unfaithful and inconsistent because the implementation may change at run time. For this reason, in open-world context the role of models is twofold. It may be necessary to infer it initially and it becomes then necessary to use the (inferred) model at run time to verify if changes to the component invalidate the assumptions we could make based on the initial observations.

In conclusion, in the case where the model is initially absent, we need techniques to infer a formal model (a formal specification) for the components we wish to combine. We then need to keep the (inferred) model alive to analyze the run-time behavior of the component and detect whether the new observed behaviors indicate that a change has occurred in the component, which invalidates the model.

In this paper, we propose a technique for run-time monitoring of component changes that relies on the use of a particular class of formal models, *behavior models*. The proposed approach requires a *setup phase*, in which the component to be monitored must be in a sort of *trial phase* in which it can be safely tested to extract an initial specification. This phase integrates techniques to infer formal specifications [7] with a new kind of behavior model, the *protocol behavior model*. This model enables the main phase of the approach — a *run-time validation activity* — which consists of monitoring the component behavior and detecting a particular class of component changes, which will be precisely described in the following sections. The approach is also able to distinguish likely new observations against component changes.

The paper is structured as follows. Section 2 presents the formalisms used in the approach, that is, the kind of behavior models we can infer and synthesize. Section 3 describes how these models are constructed to enable the setup step of our technique, while Section 4 describes their use at runtime to detect component changes. A simplified running example is used to give a practical hint on how the approach works. Finally, Section 5 discusses related approaches and Section 6 illustrates final considerations and future work. Space limitations only made it possible to explain the innovative approach and to provide basic examples. Additional details and more complex examples are available online [2].

2   Behavioral Equivalence and Protocol Models

We consider software components as *black boxes*, that is, their internals cannot be inspected and they are accessible only through their API, which consists of operations that may or may not modify the internal state. Furthermore, in this paper we focus on fine-grain components implemented as (Java) classes. Thus, each operation can be a *modifier* or an *observer*, or it can play both roles. As defined by Liskov in [8], observers are operations which can be used to inspect the state of an object while modifiers change it. An object can have both pure observers and modifiers, which respectively do not have side effects and which only change the state, and operations presenting both the behaviors. Operations may also have an exceptional result, which is considered as a special observable value. As a running example, we consider a simple component, called STORAGE-SERVICE, inspired by the ZIPOUTPUTSTREAM class of the *Java Development Kit* [1], which models a storage service where each stored entry is compressed. The component mixes container behaviors with a specific protocol of interaction. We consider the following operations: i) *putNextEntry*, which adds a new entry with a given name; ii) *write*, which adds data to the current entry; and iii) *close*, which disables any further interaction.

We now introduce the formal models used in our approach, which belong to the class of so-called *behavior models*. To accomplish the main task of the approach, that is, the runtime detection of component changes, we first need to define behavior models that they can "summarize" all the possible interactions with the software components, thus providing a description of the behaviors observed by its clients.

We start with *Behavioral equivalence models (*BEM [7]); i.e., finite state automata that provide a precise and detailed description of the behavior of a component in a limited *scope*. In a BEM, states represent *behaviorally equivalent* classes of component instances; that is, a set of instances that cannot be distinguished by any possible sequence of operations ending with an observer. Each state is labeled with observer return values and each transition models a specific modifier invocation with given actual parameter values. The *scope* of the model defines the set of possible actual parameters used in the model (called *instance pool*), and the number of states we restrict to. Intuitively, these models define the component behaviors within a limited scope. Figure 1 represents a possible BEM for the STORAGESERVICE component. We built it by limiting the scope to two entries (e_1 and e_2) which are used as parameters for operation *putNextEntry*. Each transition represents a specific operation invocation. The table in Figure 1 describes observer return values; in this specific case, they are only exceptional results.

To describe every possible component interaction outside the BEM scope, we introduce a second kind of behavior model that generalizes the BEM through an abstraction: the *protocol behavior models (*PBM). PBMs provide an abstracted, less precise but generalized description of the interaction protocol with the component, as opposed to the precise description in a limited scope provided by BEMs. The new model is still based on a finite state automaton, but now states

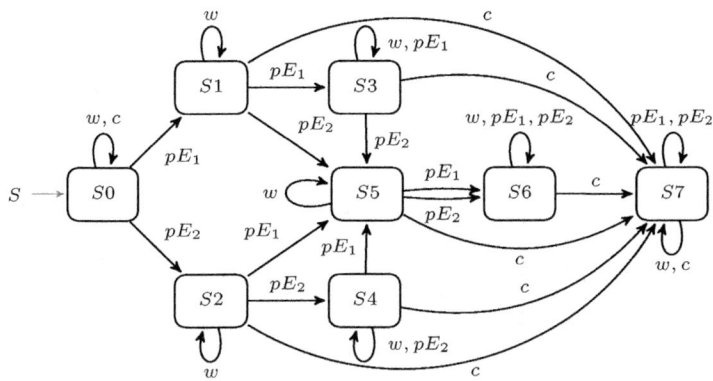

Legend:

$S:StorageService(),\ w:write(0),\ c:close()$
$pE_1:putNextEntry(e1),\ pE_2:\ putNextEntry(e2)$

State	close()	$putNextEntry(e_1)$	$putNextEntry(e_2)$	write(0)
S0	$\leadsto StorageEx_4$	—	—	$\leadsto StorageEx_3$
S1	—	$\leadsto StorageEx_1$	—	—
S2	—	—	$\leadsto StorageEx_2$	—
S3	—	$\leadsto StorageEx_1$	—	$\leadsto StorageEx_3$
S4	—	—	$\leadsto StorageEx_2$	$\leadsto StorageEx_3$
S5	—	$\leadsto StorageEx_1$	$\leadsto StorageEx_2$	—
S6	—	$\leadsto StorageEx_1$	$\leadsto StorageEx_2$	$\leadsto StorageEx_3$
S7	—	$\leadsto IOException_1$	$\leadsto IOException_1$	$\leadsto IOException_1$

$StorageEx_1.getMessage() = $ "duplicate entry: e1"
$StorageEx_2.getMessage() = $ "duplicate entry: e2"
$StorageEx_3.getMessage() = $ "no current entry"
$StorageEx_4.getMessage() = $ "File must have at least one entry"
$IOException_1.getMessage() = $ "Stream Closed"

Fig. 1. A BEM of the STORAGESERVICE component

encode whether the results of observers are normal or exceptional[2]. States also abstract the behavior of modifiers as *variant* or *invariant*. A modifier behavior is variant if there exists a possible invocation with specific actual parameters that brings the component in a different behavioral equivalence state. Otherwise, the modifier behavior is invariant. For example, the invocation of the remove operation on an empty set is invariant. This abstraction is usually (but not always) associated with an exceptional result of the operation: it is the typical behavior of a removal operation on an empty container or a add operation on a full bounded container.

PBM transitions are labelled by the name of the operation they represent, ignoring the values of the parameters. Thus, they model the behavior of every possible modifier invocation; they synthesize the behavior of possibly infinitely-many behavior changes induced by the possible operation invocation. In practice,

---

[2] If observers have parameters, then the abstraction can be i) always (i.e., for every parameter) normal; ii) always exceptional; iii) any intermediate situation, that is, for some parameters the result is normal and for others is exceptional.

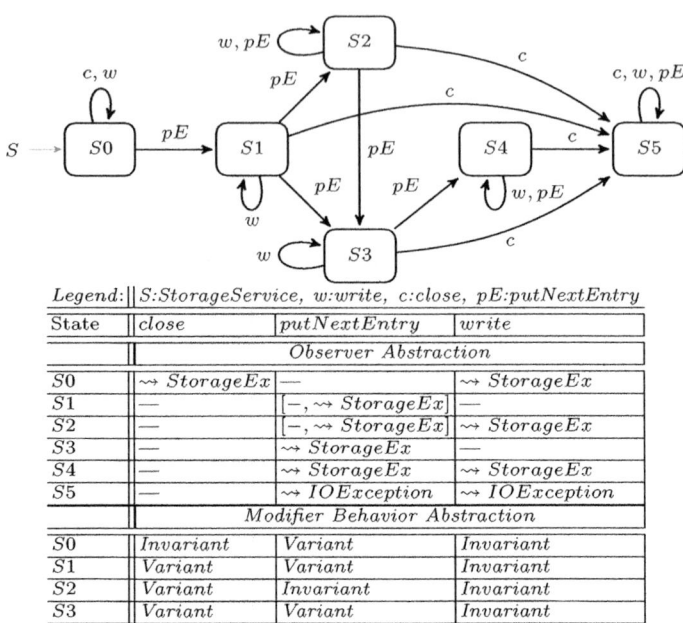

Legend:‖ S:StorageService, w:write, c:close, pE:putNextEntry

State	close	putNextEntry	write
		Observer Abstraction	
S0	↝ StorageEx	—	↝ StorageEx
S1	—	[—, ↝ StorageEx]	—
S2	—	[—, ↝ StorageEx]	↝ StorageEx
S3	—	↝ StorageEx	—
S4	—	↝ StorageEx	↝ StorageEx
S5	—	↝ IOException	↝ IOException
		Modifier Behavior Abstraction	
S0	Invariant	Variant	Invariant
S1	Variant	Variant	Invariant
S2	Variant	Invariant	Invariant
S3	Variant	Variant	Invariant
S4	Variant	Invariant	Invariant
S5	Invariant	Invariant	Invariant

The notation: [—, ↝ StorageEx] means that for some parameter the method returns correctly
(—), and for some other parameter throws StorageEx

Fig. 2. A PBM of the STORAGESERVICE component

they model the possibility that by performing an operation the set of operations enabled on the object may change.

By construction, BEMs are deterministic automata. This is not true for PBMs; in fact, the abstraction process used to build them may introduce non-determinism. For example, non-determinism can be introduced because we abstract away from the parameters when we define transitions, but also because abstract states in the PBM may represent a set of different behavioral equivalent states of the component. Non-determinism arises when the outcome of the execution of an operations is sometimes normal and sometimes exceptional, depending on input values. If invocations of a method with different parameters leads to different PBM states then the derived PBM contains non-deterministic transitions. Similarly, a non-deterministic transition appears if the same method, with the same parameters, lead to different PBM states when applied to two different BEM states that are abstracted to the same PBM state. Figure 2 represents the PBM derived by performing the abstraction described above to the BEM in Figure 1.

The main contribution of the proposed approach is the integration of PBMs and BEMs. Because the PBM is derived from the BEM through an abstraction process, its completeness and accuracy actually depends on the significance of the observations that produced the BEM during the setup phase. The setup phase is deeply rooted in the *small scope hypothesis*. In its original formulation [10], this hypothesis states that *most bugs have small counterexamples*, and that an exhaustive analysis of the component behavior within a limited scope is able to show most bugs. In our case, we cast it as follows: most of the significant behaviors of a component are present within a small scope. In our case, the term "significant behavior" refers to the abstracted version provided by a PBM. Thus, we expect that at setup time we can synthesize a likely complete PBM, which describes the protocol of all the possible interactions of clients with the component, while at runtime we can use the PBM to monitor compliance with the observed behaviors or possible mismatches that indicate component changes.

The two different models (BEMs and PBMs) can be used together at run time. The behavior of a component is monitored and checked with respect to the PBM. When violations are detected, a deeper analysis exploiting the more precise information contained in the BEM can be performed in order to discover whether the observation that is not described by the PBM is a new kind of behavior that was not observed before, and thus requires a change of both the BEM and the PBM to accommodate it, or instead it detects a component change that is inconsistent with the models. The BEM synthesizes the observations used to generate the PBM, and thus it can be used to distinguish between likely changes of the analyzed component from new observations that instead just enrich the PBM. In the following sections, we will discuss these aspects: the setup time construction of BEMs and PBMs, and the runtime use of both models to detect likely component changes.

It should be noted that the PBM is not a full specification of the component, thus it cannot be used to express complex functional behaviors, in particular the ones that are not expressible with a finite state machine, like complex container behaviors. Instead, the PBM models the protocol that clients can use to interact with the component, that is, the legal sequences of operations. This limitation is also the enabling factor for runtime detection of changes: violations can be checked and detected relatively easily and the model can be promptly updated when needed. Instead, a full fledged specification that supports infinite state behaviors, like the ones of containers, is definitely harder to synthesize, check and update at runtime.

3   Setup Phase: Model Inference

As we illustrated previously, the approach we propose prescribes two phases. The setup phase is performed on the component in a trial stage to infer an initial model. The other phase corresponds to runtime. In the former, the component is analyzed through dynamic analysis (a set of test cases) to infer a BEM for the component. A PBM abstraction is generated next to generalize the observed behaviors. In the latter phase, the two models are used at run time to detect component changes. In this section, we describe the first phase, with particular focus on the generation of models, so that designers can get a formal description of a component whose behavior must be validated.

3.1   Generation of the Initial Behavioral Equivalence Model

To generate a BEM during the setup phase, we adapt the algorithm and the tool described in [7], which extracts BEMs through dynamic analysis. The model is generated by incrementally and exhaustively exploring a finite subset of the component behavior, that is, by exploring a small scope. As illustrated previously, the scope is determined by a set of actual parameters for each component operation and a maximum number of states for the model. The exploration is performed by building a set of traces using the values in the instance pool and abstracting them to behavioral equivalence states. The exploration is incremental; that is, if a trace t is analyzed, then all its subtraces have been analyzed in the past. To build the BEM, the approach first uses observer return values: for a trace t and every possible observer o, with fixed actual parameters, we execute $t.o()$ and we build a state of the BEM labeled with observed return values. Unfortunately, such an abstraction does not always induce behavioral equivalence: for example, it can happen that for some operation m, and two traces t_1 and t_2 such that for every observer the return values are equal, $t_1.m()$ and $t_2.m()$ are not behaviorally equivalent. Operation m is called a behavioral discriminator. Thus, state abstraction is enriched with the information given by m as a behavioral discriminator. An example of behavioral discriminator is the *pop()* operation of a stack. Suppose that *size()* and *top()* are the only two observers; thus, for all the stacks with the same size and the same element in the top of the stack the observer return values are the same, despite some of them might not be behaviorally equivalent. To discriminate part of this difference, it is possible to iteratively call the *pop()* operation and further calling observers. By calling the discriminating operation we can inspect the *hidden state* of the object and thus we can take this information into account when we determine whether two states are behaviorally equivalent.

For space reasons, we cannot include the specific details of the inference algorithm, but the interested reader can refer to [7,12]. This approach guarantees the discovery of all the behaviors present in the class within the given scope. The way BEMs are generated implies a strong correlation between the quality of the model and the completeness of the instance pools used to build it. The more the instances are significant, the higher the coverage of the actual behavior of the class is.

Given the importance of the objects used to perform the BEM generation phase, we want to exploit as much as possible all the knowledge available to analyze the class behavior with the most significant set of instances. The original SPY tool relied entirely on instances provided by the user interested in obtaining the BEM of a component. While the assumption that the user is able to provide some significant instances is fair, it may be hard to achieve since it requires a lot of effort and a deep knowledge of the behaviors of the component. Fortunately, in practice the vast majority of the classes comes with a test suite containing exactly the operation calls with some significant instances as parameters.

The extraction of the significant instances is performed by collecting from the test suite all the objects passed as arguments in an operation call. Each value is then stored in an instance pool that collects all the values for each parameter. The values of the instances are stored directly in the instance pools, ready to be used in the exhaustive search. Instances collected from the test suite are very useful, but it happens that they may be redundant. To avoid the generation of models with a lot of states that do not unveil new behaviors, we should filter out the instances collected in order to keep a minimal subset able to exercise all the possible behaviors of the component without having to deal with a huge model. At this stage of the development, the tool is able to extract instances from a test suite but does not select the minimal subset of instances. This task is left to the user who has to find the best trade-off between the number of instances used for the analysis and the completeness of the generated BEM.

3.2 Synthesis of the Protocol Behavior Model

Once the BEM is generated we can go further with the analysis and generate the corresponding PBM. Generation is quite straightforward since the BEM already includes all the needed information about the outcome of each operation in each state of the model. PBM inference algorithm consists of the following steps: i) generalization of the BEM states through the PBM abstraction function; ii) mapping each BEM transition into a corresponding PBM transition. The generalization of the information contained in a BEM state is performed by applying to each state of the BEM the PBM abstraction function we discussed earlier. Then for each transition of the BEM we add a transition to the PBM starting from the representative of the equivalence class of the starting node in the BEM and ending in the representative of the destination node.

4   Runtime Phase: Monitoring and Change Detection

BEMs and PBMs are kept alive at run time for two main purposes. First, it may happen that new behaviors that were not exhibited in the set-up phase, and therefore are not reflected in in the current versions of BEM and PBM, actually manifest themselves at run time. In this case, the models must be updated and enriched so that the newly discovered behaviors are also modeled. However, it is also possible that the component undergoes modifications at run time that change its visible behavior. As mentioned, this is rather common in an open-world setting. For example, a Web service might undergo a change by the service provider, which alters the behavior as seen by clients. The method we describe here can automatically detect changes to the component that are inconsistent with the behaviors observed so far, and therefore are inconsistent with the models that were inferred. This is achieved by monitoring execution and analyzing it to detect possible model violations that lead either to a model update or to the detection of a behavioral change. These aspects are discussed in detail hereafter.

The boundary between model inference carried on at design time and at run time is blurred. The goal of both the phases is to generate the best representation possible of the behavior of a software component but each one has its own peculiarities. At design time we build models by exploring exhaustively the defined scope. At run time we complete them by covering also the residual behavior with a different technique specifically designed to complete the model by adding only the new information. However, one should strive for inferring the most complete possible model after the set-up phase so that developers can leverage precise and reliable information about the behavior of the component when they build their applications.

4.1   Monitoring

A monitor is introduced into the running system to support the comparison of the actual behavior of the component under analysis and the ones encoded by the models. Each time an instance of the scrutinized class is created, a monitoring process is associated with it to record the observed execution trace and analyze it to discover violations with respect to the previously inferred protocol model. Violation detection is performed by comparing the actual behavior with the one encoded in the model. The system reports a violation when it detects an exceptional outcome for an operation that, according to the model, should always terminate normally or, conversely, when an operation that the model describes as exceptional does not throw an exception.

In order to keep overhead as low as possible, the violation detector relies, when possible, exclusively on the observed trace. When the PBM has only deterministic transitions this process is straightforward and violations can be detected directly from the execution trace. Unfortunately, almost all components with a complex behavior are modeled by a non-deterministic PBM. Thus there is need for a deeper inspection by executing operations that could provide more information and thus reveal the state in which the component is. The solution proposed in this paper is an enhanced monitoring phase, which does not not rely exclusively on what it is observable from the current execution but also able to perform some more queries to the object under analysis. For any state having non-deterministic outgoing transitions, we must be able to uniquely select one of them. To do so, we need to determine which are the operations that make it possible to know which one has been taken. These operations, that we call *(PBM) state discriminators*, are the operations having different behaviors on the destination states. We do not require state discriminators to be pure observers. In fact, every method which can have both a normal and an exceptional result mode is a suitable state discriminator. Non-determinism can therefore be solved by invoking the state discriminators on the object under analysis. State characterization guarantees that we can always find a discriminator. Each pair of distinct PBM states has at least an operation producing different results. With these additional operations it is easy to find the compatible state among the different nondeterministic possibilities.

As an example, we may refer to the PBM of STORAGESERVICE reported in Figure 2. Consider a simple trace of the form *StorageService().putNextEntry(e_x). putNextEntry(e_y)*, where e_x, e_y are newly observed parameters, that is, they were not part of the instance pool used at setup phase to infer the model. The invocation of the last *putNextEntry* in state $S1$ is non-deterministic. Looking at the characterizations of states $S2$ and $S3$ we can find two possible state discriminators: a further *putNextEntry* or a *write*. The component is in state $S2$ if the test executions of *write* or *putNextEntry* give us respectively an always exceptional behavior or normal results for some parameter values and exceptional results for others. Conversely the component is in state $S3$, if the results of the state discriminators are always normal for *write* or always exceptional for *putNextEntry*, respectively. State discriminators have to be invoked on an newly generated instance of the object, which must be initialized exactly in the same state of the actual component. This new instance behaves as a *shadow component*, which provides the same functionality of the actual component and whose state can be safely modified and inspected without interfering with the currently running application. To initialize the state of the shadow component, the monitored execution trace is replayed to bring it into the state we are interested in. After the state is initialized, the shadow component can be used to resolve non-determinism by calling the state discriminator. Obviously, the scope of the running component is different from the scope used to build the models during the setup phase. In fact, at runtime, state discriminators must be called with parameter values coming from both the instance pool used during model inference, and the instances observed in the trace whose state must be discriminated.

In conclusion, the monitoring architecture requires: i) instrumenting the application using the external black-box services to collect execution traces; ii) enabling the possibility to call operations on a shadow component (i.e., a sandboxed instance of the service under scrutiny); iii) enabling the possibility to replay execution traces in order to put the shadow component in a suitable state. With such an infrastructure, the verification module can detect changes in the behavior of external services without interfering with the actual execution of the system.

4.2   Response to Violations

During the monitoring phase it may happen that an observation on the actual execution conflicts with what it is described by the model. There are two possible causes for the violation observed: the model could be incomplete, and therefore it needs to be updated, or the behavior of component has changed. The analysis phase has to be able to deal and react properly to both these situations. The detection of a component change is important because this is going to surprise the clients with an unexpected behavior, inconsistent with previous observations.

A shadow component comes into play also in this case. In fact it is possible to discover whether the violations is due to the incompleteness of the PBM or to a change in the behavior by replaying on a shadow component some significant executions encoded in the BEM. If all of them produce again the previously observed results, then the model needs to be completed and we can conclude that violations simply indicate behaviors never explored before. Otherwise the violation signals a change to the component that is unexpected and inconsistent with its previously observed behavior. This indicates that clients should plan suitable reactions to continue to satisfy their goal or reach some safe state.

In order to keep the approach feasible, we cannot just test that all previously observed behaviors encoded by the BEM are still valid. We should rather focus on the part of the model more closely related to the observed violation. The first step in the selection of the relevant execution traces is the identification of the set of BEM states corresponding to the state of the PBM in which the violation occurred. The prefixes of the test case traces can then be generated by looking for the shortest BEM paths that reach the selected BEM states. The prefixes have then to be completed with the operation that unveiled the violation. For any BEM state the operation has to be called with all the parameters present in the instance pool used to generate the model. If the result of execution of all traces on the shadow component coincide with the initially observed results we conclude that there is no evidence of behavioral change and therefore the model only needs to be updated.

Model Updates are first applied to the BEM and then to the corresponding PBM. Updating the BEM means enriching the scope it covers with the trace unveiling the new behavior. Keeping all the information in a single BEM would lead to an expensive update step. For example if the new behavior is caused by a certain value of a parameter that was not in the original instance pool, we would need to update the BEM by running on a shadow component a set of test cases that would complete the model with respect to the extended instance pool. Moreover this would lead to an increase of the BEM's size. We decided instead to place side by side the originally inferred BEM and a set of additional BEM fragments, each describing an additionally discovered behavior of the component. Doing that, we can easily keep track of all the relevant executions exposing the different behaviors. Although doing that we may miss some behavior due to the interaction of the behaviors described by different BEMs, this is not an issue: the model will describe them as soon as they appear at run time. From the set of BEMs it is easy to get the corresponding PBM. It is quite straightforward to extend the inference algorithm described in Section 3 to build a PBM starting from the information contained in more than one BEM so that the resulting PBM contains information about all the observed behaviors regardless of the BEM it comes form. To produce correct abstractions for the new PBM, all the BEMs must have a coherent set of observers. To ensure that, we must update the scope for the observer roles in the already existing BEMs to have them take into account all the significant values of the parameters discovered at run time.

As an example, a violation requiring to update the models of STORAGESERVICE reported in Figures 1 and 2 occurs after the execution of the following trace: *StorageService().putNextEntry(e_x).putNextEntry(e_x).putNextEntry(e_y).write(d)*. After the execution of the second *putNextEntry* the PBM prescribes the component to be in either state $S2$ or $S3$. By invoking *putNextEntry* as a state discriminator, we discover to be in $S2$, because for some entries (e_x) the operation is exceptional while for the entries e_1 and e_2, belonging to the scope used at inference time, the operation would terminate normally. The third *putNextEntry* is still non-deterministic and it is resolved in the same way. So according to the protocol described by the PBM, the component is in state $S2$ before the execution

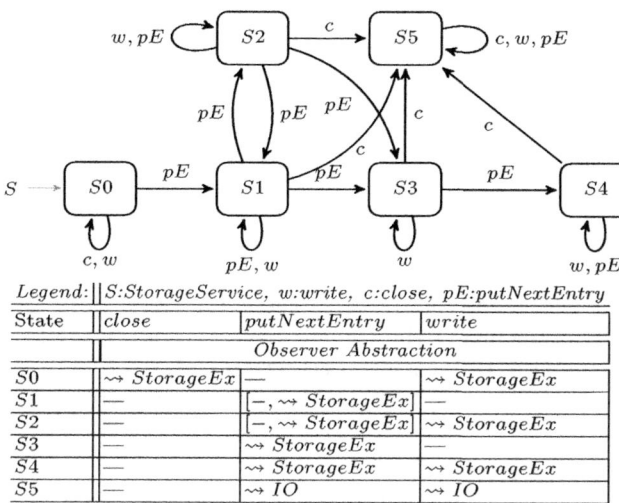

Fig. 3. An updated PBM of the STORAGESERVICE component

State	close	putNextEntry	write
		Observer Abstraction	
$S0$	$\rightsquigarrow StorageEx$	—	$\rightsquigarrow StorageEx$
$S1$	—	$[-, \rightsquigarrow StorageEx]$	—
$S2$	—	$[-, \rightsquigarrow StorageEx]$	$\rightsquigarrow StorageEx$
$S3$	—	$\rightsquigarrow StorageEx$	—
$S4$	—	$\rightsquigarrow StorageEx$	$\rightsquigarrow StorageEx$
$S5$	—	$\rightsquigarrow IO$	$\rightsquigarrow IO$

Legend: ‖ *S:StorageService, w:write, c:close, pE:putNextEntry*

of the *write* operation. However, the component now predicts the write to be exceptional for every possible parameter, while the component executes normally, because the last created entry is valid. The violation unveiled by the trace above is actually due to scope effects. While the initial PBM correctly describes the component behavior when only two entries are used as parameters for *putNextEntry*, this scope is not sufficient to describe all the component behaviors. During execution, when the scope of the analysis is enriched with other different entries, such previously unexplored behaviors emerge. Such a violation due to scope effects is a typical case that requires only model update.

In this case, BEM state characterization is enriched with results obtained with entries e_x and e_y for the *putNextEntry* operation and considering d as another possible parameter for *write*. In addition to that we also generated another BEM describing the execution trace which unveiled the violation. Figure 3 shows the PBM obtained at the end of the model update process. Scope effects are still there in states $S3$ and $S4$, but the updated version of the model takes into account properly the possibility to store infinitely-many different entries with the loops through states $S1$ and $S2$.

The detection of another interesting behavior missing in the initial models occurs when we try to write an empty string of data when no entry is available. In this case, the expected *StorageException* is not thrown because the *write* operation does not have to write anything and the component does not check for the availability of an entry. Therefore, we need to add a new BEM fragment describing the observed trace. Since the violating trace contained a previously unseen instance, we also have to update the existing BEM to have it consider the empty string as a parameter for the *write* operation. For space limitations the updated models are only available online at [2].

Change Detection takes place when there exists at least one test case behaving differently than what the PBM prescribes. Since the model encodes the behaviors observed in the past, any violation can be considered as an evidence of a change: at least in the case highlighted by the failing test, the same execution trace presented a different behavior than the one assumed by the model. The system has then to react in some way to the behavioral changes detected. A discussion of possible reaction strategies is outside the scope of this paper. Here we simply assume that the user of the system is in charge of reacting once he or she is notified that a change has been detected. Of course, in certain cases it is possible to continue to operate interacting with the component, despite its change. For example, it may happen that the change simply turns an operation call with an exceptional result into an invocation that terminates normally. In this case the existing application that uses the component under scrutiny may continue to operate. Probably, the detected change consists of adding new functionalities or interaction patterns that previously were not present or were disabled.

An example of change detection can be shown by referring again to the models reported in Figures 1 and 2 to monitor the behavior of a STORAGESERVICE. Consider a hypothetical change such that that the component always throws an exception when *putNextEntry* is invoked. In this scenario, any execution of *putNextEntry* would violate the PBM. The violation indicates a component change, not a new behavior that was not considered in the setup phase. To check this, we derive the simple test case *StorageService().putNextEntry(e_1)* from the BEM. Since this test case violates the BEM, it highlights the change of the behavior of the component.

A more comprehensive evaluation of the effectiveness of the change detection methodology has been performed injecting faults into the component under analysis and is available online at [2].

It is important to remark that this methodology is able to identify changes only when there is at least one failing test case in the ones that are synthesized by the BEM. In other words, our methodology identifies changes only if they manifest themselves as violations of previous observations synthesized by BEMs. Since BEMs describe the behavior of a component in a limited scope, and thus they do not contain information about every possible component execution, it is possible that what is an actual change is detected as a newly observed behavior. However, since the change is outside the knowledge inferred at setup phase, this different interpretation is safe.

5   Related Work

The protocol models discussed in this paper describe the behavior of a software component by making explicit which operations are enabled in different states. This underlying idea has been introduced quite some time ago through the concept of TYPESTATE in [15]. A similar abstraction has also been used in [5], which presents a technique to build an enabledness model from contracts and static analysis. The goal here is instead to validate software contracts. TAUTOKO [4] generates similar models starting from an existing test suite. Our tool does not infer the model directly from the test execution traces. It rather exploits the test suite to gather some domain knowledge to use with the SPY methodology.

Monitoring of both functional and non-functional properties of service-based systems are described in [3]. Our technique is based on PBMs and BEMs, therefore we are able to model and monitor very precisely functional properties of a software component.

INVITE [14] developed the idea of *runtime testing*, pointing out the requirements the running system has to satisfy in order to make it possible. In this work we also introduced a technique to encode test cases in BEMs and to select the ones that can highlight a behavioral change.

TRACER [11] builds runtime models from execution traces enabling richer and more detailed analysis at a higher abstraction level. In [9] models are used to monitor system executions and to detect deviation from the desired behavior of consumer electronic products. Our approach combines these two aspects providing a methodology able to both detect violations and build models according to the information gathered at run time.

DIVA [13] leverages the usage of models at runtime to support dynamic adaptation. The monitoring carried on by DIVA focuses on the parameters describing the execution environment of the application while we are concerned about functional correctness. Both these approaches are required in the development of reliable and dynamically adapting systems. The DIVA framework takes into account all the aspects of dynamic adaptation and it is based on a model driven engineering approach. In our work we target existing software that is not necessarily engineered with in a model driven fashion, therefore we had to introduce model inference methodologies and limit the application domain of our prototype to change detection.

6   Conclusions and Future Work

Behavior models can be useful throughout all the lifecycle of a software component. Like other software models, behavior models are traditionally used at design time to support system designers in their reasoning. However, they can also play a significant role after the application is deployed by monitoring its execution and checking system properties. This is particularly useful in the context of systems in which verification must extend to run time, because unexpected changes may occur dynamically.

This work focuses on the runtime aspects, extending the original scope of behavior models to running systems. The models and methodology proposed can maintain an updated representation of the behavior of the component considering observations made during the actual execution of a running system. Our approach is also able to detect and notify the system designer concerning behavioral changes in the monitored components. Preliminary experiments focusing on Java classes show that our approach is effective and can deal with non-trivial components. Further research is going to enhance the models removing current limitations and thus making it possible to monitor an even broader class of software components.

Other possible further directions concern reasoning at run time. Usually, runtime reasoning require a trade off between precision and the time required to perform the computation. Examples of these techniques are the ones providing exact solutions based on optimization algorithms and other, much faster, based for instance on heuristics or evolutionary techniques.

In this work, we relied on an exact reasoning technique which is more suitable for our application domain since we want to provide exact change detection information. Reasoning at the protocol level also provides relatively fast conformance checking against the PBM. However, to monitor more complex properties in a possible extension of the current work, we may take into account also an an hybrid approach to try to get the benefits from both exact and approximate reasoning approaches.

References

1. Oracle, java se 6.0 doc. (2011),
   http://download.oracle.com/javase/6/docs/index.html
2. Spy at runtime (2011), http://home.dei.polimi.it/mocci/spy/runtime/
3. Baresi, L., Guinea, S.: Self-supervising bpel processes. In: IEEE TSE (2011)
4. Dallmeier, V., Knopp, N., Mallon, C., Hack, S., Zeller, A.: Generating test cases for specification mining. In: ISSTA 2010, Trento, Italy (2010)
5. de Caso, G., Braberman, V., Garbervetsky, D., Uchitel, S.: Automated abstractions for contract validation. In: IEEE TSE (2010)
6. Di Nitto, E., Ghezzi, C., Metzger, A., Papazoglou, M., Pohl, K.: A journey to highly dynamic, self-adaptive service-based applications. In: ASE (2008)
7. Ghezzi, C., Mocci, A., Monga, M.: Synthesizing intensional behavior models by graph transformation. In: ICSE 2009, Vancouver, Canada (2009)
8. Guttag, J.V., Liskov, B.: Program Development in Java: Abstraction, Specification and Object-Oriented Design. Addison-Wesley (2001)
9. Hooman, J., Hendriks, T.: Model-based run-time error detection. In: Models@run.time 2007, Nashville, USA (2007)
10. Jackson, D.: Software Abstractions: Logic, Language, and Analysis. MIT Press (2006)
11. Maoz, S.: Using model-based traces as runtime models. Computer (2009)
12. Mocci, A.: Behavioral Modeling, Inference and Validation for Stateful Component Specifications. Ph.D. thesis, Politecnico di Milano, Milano, Italy (2010)
13. Morin, B., Barais, O., Jezequel, J.-M., Fleurey, F., Solberg, A.: Models@ run.time to support dynamic adaptation. Computer 42(10), 44–51 (2009)
14. Murphy, C., Kaiser, G., Vo, I., Chu, M.: Quality assurance of software applications using the in vivo testing approach. In: ICST 2009, Denver, Colorado (2009)
15. Strom, R.E., Yemini, S.: Typestate: A programming language concept for enhancing software reliability. In: IEEE TSE (1986)

Requirements and Assessment of Languages and Frameworks for Adaptation Models

Thomas Vogel and Holger Giese

Hasso Plattner Institute at the University of Potsdam, Germany
{thomas.vogel,holger.giese}@hpi.uni-potsdam.de

Abstract. Approaches to self-adaptive software systems use models at runtime to leverage benefits of model-driven engineering (MDE) for providing views on running systems and for engineering feedback loops. Most of these approaches focus on causally connecting runtime models and running systems, and just apply typical MDE techniques, like model transformation, or well-known techniques, like event-condition-action rules, from other fields than MDE to realize a feedback loop. However, elaborating requirements for feedback loop activities for the specific case of runtime models is rather neglected.

Therefore, we investigate requirements for *Adaptation Models* that specify the analysis, decision-making, and planning of adaptation as part of a feedback loop. In particular, we consider requirements for a modeling language of adaptation models and for a framework as the execution environment of adaptation models. Moreover, we discuss patterns for using adaptation models within the feedback loop regarding the structuring of loop activities and the implications on the requirements for adaptation models. Finally, we assess two existing approaches to adaptation models concerning their fitness for the requirements discussed in this paper.

1 Introduction

Self-adaptation capabilities are often required for modern software systems to dynamically change the configuration in response to changing environments or goals [4]. *Models@run.time* are a promising approach for self-adaptive software systems since models may provide appropriate abstractions of a running system and its environment, and benefits of model-driven engineering (MDE) are leveraged to the runtime phases of software systems [3].

Most models@run.time efforts to self-adaptive software systems focus on causally connecting models to running systems and just apply typical or well-known techniques from MDE or other fields on top of these models. These techniques are used for engineering a feedback loop that controls self-adaptation by means of *monitoring* and *analyzing* the running system and its environment, and the *planning* and *execution* of changes to the running system [12].

For example, the causal connection has been a topic for discussions at the last two workshops on models@run.time [1, 2], or the work of [15] particularly addresses the causal connection and it just applies MDE techniques, like

J. Kienzle (Ed.): MODELS 2011 Workshops, LNCS 7167, pp. 167–182, 2012.

model transformation, on top to show their technical feasibility. We proposed an approach to use incremental model synchronization techniques to maintain multiple, causally connected runtime models at different abstraction levels, and thereby, we support the monitoring and the execution of adaptations [16, 18].

While causal connections provide basic support for monitoring and for executing changes, they do not cover the analysis and planning steps of a feedback loop, which decide *if* and *how* the system should be adapted. For these steps, techniques originating from other fields than MDE are used. Most approaches, like [7, 10], employ rule-based mechanisms in some form of event-condition-action rules that exactly specify when and how adaptation should be performed, and thus, the designated target configuration is predefined. In contrast, search-based techniques just prescribe goals that the system should achieve. Triggered by conditions or events and guided by utility functions they try to find the best or at least a suitable target configuration fulfilling these goals (cf. [9, 13]).

All these approaches focus on applying such decision-making techniques for the analysis and planning steps, but they do not systematically investigate the requirements for such techniques in conjunction with models@run.time. Eliciting these requirements might help in engineering new or tailored decision-making techniques for the special case of models@run.time approaches to self-adaptive systems. Therefore, we elaborate requirements for such techniques by taking an MDE perspective. The techniques should be specified by models, which we named *Adaptation Models* in an attempt to categorize runtime models [19]. However, the categorization does not cover any requirements for runtime models.

In this paper, which is a revision of [17], we discuss requirements for adaptation models, in particular requirements for languages to create such models and for frameworks that employ and execute such models within a feedback loop. By language we mean a broad view on metamodels, constraints, and model operations, which are all used to create and apply adaptation models. Moreover, we discuss patterns for using adaptation models within the feedback loop. The patterns and the requirements for adaptation models influence each other, which impacts the design of the feedback loop by providing alternatives for structuring loop activities. Finally, we assess two existing approaches to adaptation models concerning their fitness for the language and framework requirements.

The paper is structured as follows. Section 2 reviews related work, and Section 3 sketches the role of adaptation models in self-adaptive systems. Section 4 discusses the requirements for adaptation models, while Section 5 presents different patterns of employing such models within a feedback loop. Section 6 discusses the assessment of existing approaches to adaptation models with respect to the requirements. The last section concludes the paper and outlines future work.

2   Related Work

As already mentioned, most models@run.time approaches to self-adaptive software systems focus on applying techniques for decision-making and do not systematically elaborate on the related requirements [7–10, 13]. A few approaches

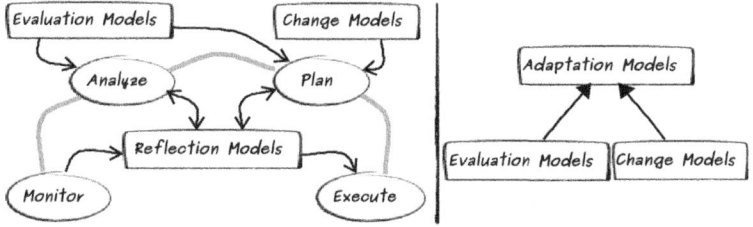

Fig. 1. Feedback Loop and Runtime Models (cf. [19])

merely consider the requirement of performance and efficiency for their adaptation mechanisms to evaluate the applicability at runtime [9, 13]. Likewise, in [14] several decision-making mechanisms are discussed in the context of ubiquitous computing applications by means of performance and scalability regarding the size of the managed system and its configuration space. In general, rule-based mechanisms are considered as efficient since they exactly prescribe the whole adaptation, while for search-based approaches performance is critical and often improved by applying heuristics or by reducing the configuration space.

This is also recognized by [8] that attests efficiency and support for early validation as benefits for rule-based approaches. However, they suffer from scalability issues regarding the management and validation of large sets of rules. In contrast, search-based approaches may cope with these scalability issues, but they are not as efficient as rule-based approaches and they provide less support for validation. As a consequence, a combination of rule-based and search-based techniques is proposed in [8] to balance their benefits and drawbacks.

To sum up, if requirements or characteristics of decision-making techniques are discussed, these discussions are limited to performance, scalability, and support for validation, and they are not done systematically. One exception is the work of Cheng [5] who discusses requirements for a self-adaptation language that is focused on specifying typical system administration tasks. However, the requirements do not generally consider self-adaptive software systems and they do not address specifics of models at runtime. Nevertheless, some of the requirements that are discussed in this paper are derived from this work.

3   Adaptation Models

Before discussing requirements for adaptation models, we sketch the role of these models based on a conceptual view on a feedback loop as depicted in Figure 1. The steps of monitoring and analyzing the system and its environment, and the planning and execution of changes are derived from autonomic computing [12], while we discussed the different models and their usage in a feedback loop in [19]. *Reflection Models* describe the running system and its environment, and they are causally connected to the system. According to observations of the system and environment, the monitor updates the reflection models. Reasoning on these models is done by the analyze step to decide whether the system fulfills its goals or not, and thus, whether adaptation is required or not. The reasoning is specified by *Evaluation Models*, which can be constraints that are checked on reflection models. If adaptation is required, the planning step devises a plan defining how the system should be adapted, which is guided by *Change Models* to explore the system's variability or configuration space. Deciding on the designated target configuration is guided by evaluation models to analyze different adaptation options, and the selected option is applied on reflection models. Finally, the execute step performs and effects the adaptations on the running system.

By *Adaptation Models* we generally consider evaluation and change models regardless of the concrete rule-based or search-based techniques that are employed for the analysis and planning steps, and thus, for the decision-making. This view on adaptation models is similar to [7], which just presents one adaptation model for the specific approach but no general discussion of such models.

4   Requirements for Adaptation Models

In this section, we describe requirements for adaptation models to be used in self-adaptive systems to analyze and decide on adaptation needs, and to plan and decide on how to adapt the running system. We assume that the self-adaptive system employs models at runtime, which influence the requirements. At first, we discuss requirements for a modeling language used to create adaptation models. Then, we elaborate the requirements for a framework as the execution environment for adaptation models. Being in the early requirements phase, we take a broad MDE view on the notion of language as combinations of metamodels, constraints, and model operations, which are all used to create and apply models.

Likewise to the common understanding that requirements for real-world applications cannot be completely and definitely specified at the beginning of a software project, we think that the same is true for the requirements discussed here. It is likely that some of these requirements may change, become irrelevant, or new ones emerge when engineering concrete adaptation models for a specific self-adaptive system and domain. Thus, we do not claim that the requirements are complete and finalized with respect to their enumeration and definitions.

4.1   Language Requirements for Adaptation Models

Language requirements (LR) for adaptation models can be divided into functional and non-functional ones. Functional requirements target the concepts that are either part of adaptation models or that are referenced by adaptation models. These concepts are needed for the analysis, decision-making, and planning. Thus, functional requirements determine the expressiveness of the language. In contrast, non-functional language requirements determine the quality of adaptation models. At first functional, then non-functional requirements are discussed.

Functional Language Requirements
LR-1 *Goals*: Enabling a self-adaptive system to continuously provide the desired functionality to users or other systems, adaptation models have to know about the current goals of the system. These goals as a functional specification define

what the system should do, and this information needs to be available in an operationalized form to relate it with the actual behavior of the running system. This is the foundation for adapting the functional behavior of the system.

LR-2 *Quality Dimensions*: While LR-1 considers *what* the system should do, quality dimensions address *how* the system should provide the functionality in terms of quality of service (QoS). To support QoS-aware adaptations, qualities, like performance or security, must be characterized by adaptation models (cf. [5]).

LR-3 *Preferences*: Since multiple quality dimensions (LR-2) may be relevant for the managed system, preferences across the dimensions must be expressed to trade-off and balance competing qualities (cf. [5]). Likewise, preferences for goals (LR-1) are necessary if several valid behavioral alternatives are feasible and not distinguished by the quality dimensions.

Thus, the language for adaptation models must incorporate the concepts of goals (LR-1), qualities (LR-2), and preferences (LR-3) in an operationalized form, such that they can be referenced or described and automatically processed by adaptation models. Goals, qualities, and preferences serve as references for the running system as they state what the system should do and how it should be.

LR-4 *Access to Reflection Models*: Adaptation models must reference and access reflection models to obtain information about the current situation of the running system and environment for analysis and to change the reflection models to effect adaptations. Thus, a language for adaptation models must be based on the languages of reflection models.

LR-5 *Events*: Adaptation models should reference information from events emitted by the monitor step when updating the reflection models due to runtime phenomena of the system. Besides serving as a trigger for starting the decision-making process, events support locating the phenomena in the reflection models (LR-4). Thus, evaluating the system and its environment (LR-6) may start right from the point in the reflection models where the phenomena have occurred.

LR-6 *Evaluation Conditions*: A language for adaptation models must support the specification of conditions to evaluate the running system and its environment (cf. [5]). These conditions relate the goals (LR-1), qualities (LR-2), and preferences (LR-3) to the actual running system represented by reflection models (LR-4). Therefore, conditions may refer to events notifying about runtime phenomena (LR-5) as a starting point for evaluation, and they should be able to capture complex structural patterns for evaluating architectural properties.

LR-7 *Evaluation Results*: Adaptation models must capture the results of computing the evaluation conditions (LR-6) because these results identify and decide on adaptation needs especially when the conditions are not met by the system. Adaptation models may annotate and reference the evaluation results in reflection models (LR-4) to locate adaptation needs in the running system.

LR-8 *Adaptation Options*: Adaptation models must capture the variability of the system to know the options for adaptation related to reflection models (LR-4). These options define the configuration space for the system.

LR-9 *Adaptation Conditions*: Adaptation models must consider adaptation conditions since not all adaptation options (LR-8) are feasible in every situation.

Thus, conditions should constrain all adaptation options to applicable ones for certain situations (cf. [5]). To characterize a situation for an adaptation option, conditions should refer to reflection models (LR-4), events (LR-5), evaluation results (LR-7), or other adaptation options. Likewise to such pre-conditions for adaptation options, post-conditions and invariants should be considered.

LR-10 *Adaptation Costs and Benefits*: Adaptation models should characterize costs and benefits of adaptation options (LR-8) as a basis to select among several possible options in certain situation (cf. [5]). Costs should indicate that adaptations are not for free, and benefits should describe the expected effects of adaptation options on the goals (LR-1) and qualities (LR-2) of the system. By relating costs and benefits to the preferences of the system (LR-3), suitable adaptation options should be selected and applied on the reflection models.

LR-11 *History of Decisions*: Adaptation models should capture a history of decisions, like evaluation results (LR-7) or applied adaptation options (LR-8), to enable learning mechanisms for improving future decisions.

Non-functional Language Requirements

LR-12 *Modularity, Abstractions and Scalability*: An adaptation model should be a composition of sub-models rather than a monolithic model to cover all concepts for decision-making. E.g., evaluation conditions (LR-6) and adaptation options (LR-8) need to be part of the same sub-model, and even different adaptation options can be specified in different sub-models. Thus, the language should support modular adaptation models. Moreover, the language should enable the modeling at different abstraction levels for two reasons. First, the level depends on the abstraction levels of the employed reflection models (LR-4), and second, lower level adaptation model concepts should be encapsulated and lifted to appropriate higher levels. E.g., several simple adaptation options (LR-8) should be composable to complex adaptation options. Language support for modularity and different abstractions promote scalability of adaptation models.

LR-13 *Side Effects*: The language should clearly distinguish between concepts that cause side effects on the running system and those that do not. E.g., computing an evaluation condition (LR-6) should not affect the running system, while applying an adaptation option (LR-8) finally should. Making the concepts causing side effects explicit is relevant for consistency issues (FR-1).

LR-14 *Parameters*: The language should provide constructs to parameterize adaptation models. Parameters can be used to adjust adaptation models at runtime, like changing the preferences (LR-3) according to varying user needs.

LR-15 *Formality*: The language should have a degree of formality that enables on-line and off-line validation or verification of adaptation models, e.g., to detect conflicts or thrashing effects in the adaptation mechanisms.

LR-16 *Reusability*: The core concepts of the language for adaptation models should be independent of the languages used for reflection models in an approach. This leverages the reusability of the language for adaptation models.

LR-17 *Ease of Use*: The design of the language should consider its ease of use because adaptation models are created by software engineers. This influences, among others, the modeling paradigm, the notation, and the tool support. Preferably the language should be based on a declarative modeling paradigm, which is often more convenient and less error-prone than an imperative one. Likewise, appropriate notations and tools are required to support an engineer in creating, validating, or verifying adaptation models.

4.2   Framework Requirements for Adaptation Models

In the following, we describe framework requirements (FR) for adaptation models. By framework we consider the execution environment of adaptation models, which determines how adaptation models are employed and executed in the feedback loop. Thus, only requirements specific for such a framework are discussed. Typical non-functional requirements for software systems, like reliability or security, are also relevant for adaptation mechanisms, but they are left here.

FR-1 *Consistency*: The execution of adaptation models should preserve the consistency of reflection models and of the running system. E.g., when adapting a causally connected reflection model, the corresponding set of model changes should be performed atomically and correctly. Thus, the framework should evaluate the invariants, pre- and post-conditions (LR-9) for adaptation options (LR-8) at the model level, before adaptations are executed to the running system.

FR-2 *Incrementality*: The framework should leverage incremental techniques to apply or execute adaptation models to promote efficiency. E.g., events (LR-5) or evaluation results (LR-7) annotated to reflection models should be used to directly locate starting points for evaluation or adaptation planning, respectively. Or, adaptation options (LR-8) should be incrementally applied on original reflection models rather than on copies. Incrementality could avoid costly operations, like copying or searching potentially large models.

FR-3 *Reversibility*: Supporting incremental operations on models (FR-2), the framework should provide the ability to incrementally reverse performed operations. E.g., the configuration space has to be explored for adaptation planning by creating a path of adaptation options (LR-8) applied on reflection models. Finding a suitable path might require to turn around and to try alternative directions without completely rejecting the whole path. Thus, *do* and *undo* of operations leverages, among others, incremental planning of adaptation.

FR-4 *Priorities*: The framework should utilize priorities to organize modular adaptation models (LR-12) to efficiently and easily identify first entry points for executing or applying adaptation models. E.g., priorities can be assigned to different evaluation conditions (LR-6) based on their criticality, and the framework should check the conditions in decreasing order of their criticality.

FR-5 *Time Scales*: The framework should simultaneously support different time scales of analysis and adaptation planning. For example, in known and mission-critical situations quick and precisely specified reactions might be necessary (cf. rule-based techniques), while in other situations comprehensive and sophisticated reasoning and planning are feasible (cf. search-based techniques).

FR-6 *Flexibility*: The framework should be flexible by allowing adaptation models to be added, removed, and modified at runtime. This supports including learning effects, and it considers the fact that all conceivable adaptation scenarios

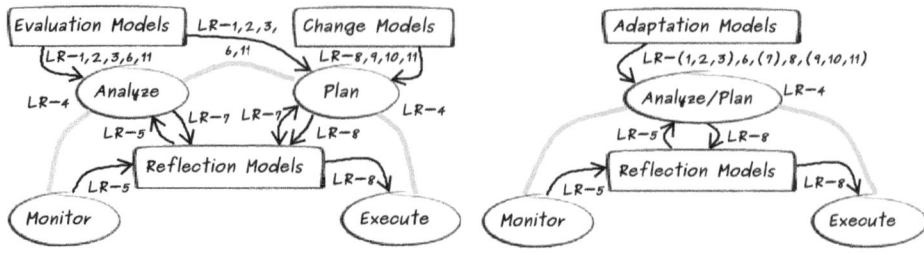

Fig. 2. Decoupled Analysis and Planning   **Fig. 3.** Coupled Analysis and Planning

cannot be anticipated at development-time. Moreover, it is a prerequisite of adaptive or hierarchical control using multiple feedback loops (cf. [12, 19]).

5   Feedback Loop Patterns for Adaptation Models

In the following, we discuss feedback loop patterns for adaptation models and how the functional language requirements (cf. Section 4.1) map to these patterns while considering the framework requirements (cf. Section 4.2). The non-functional language requirements are not further addressed here because they are primarily relevant for designing a language for adaptation models and not for actually applying such models. The patterns differ in the coupling of the analysis and planning steps of a feedback loop, which influences the requirements for adaptation models. Moreover, the adaptation model requirements likely impact the patterns and designs of the loop. Thus, this section provides a preliminary basis for investigating dependencies between requirements and loop patterns.

5.1   Analysis and Planning – Decoupled

The first pattern of a feedback loop depicted in Figure 2 decouples the analysis and planning steps as originally proposed (cf. Section 3). The figure highlights functional language requirements (LR) at points where the concepts of the corresponding requirements are relevant. This does not mean that adaptation models must cover all these points, but they must know about the concepts.

In response to events notifying about changes in the running system or environment, the monitor updates the reflection models and annotates the events (LR-5) to these models. The analyze step uses these events to locate the changes in the reflection models and to start reasoning at these locations. Reasoning is specified by *evaluation models* defining evaluation conditions (LR-6) that relate the goals (LR-1), qualities (LR-2), and preferences (LR-3) to the characteristics of the running system. These characteristics are obtained by accessing reflection models (LR-4). Analysis is performed by evaluating the conditions and probably enhanced by consulting past analyses (LR-11). This produces analysis results (LR-7) that are annotated to the reflection models to indicate adaptation needs.

The planning step uses these results (LR-7) attached to reflection models (LR-4) to devise a plan for adaptation. Planning is based on *change models* specifying adaptation options (LR-8) and their conditions (LR-9), costs, and benefits (LR-10). This information and probably plans devised in the past (LR-11) are used to find suitable adaptation options to create potential target configurations by applying these options on reflection models. These reflection models that prescribe alternative target configurations are analyzed with the help of evaluation models to select the best configuration among them. In contrast to the analyze step that uses evaluation models to reason about the current configuration (descriptive reflection models), the planning step uses them to analyze potential target configurations (prescriptive reflection models). Finally, the execute step enacts the selected adaptation options (LR-8) to the running system.

This pattern is similar to the generic idea of search-based approaches since planning is done by exploring adaptation options (LR-8, 9, 10) that are evaluated (LR-6, 7, 11) for their fitness for the preferenced system goals (LR-1, 2, 3) based on the current situation of the system and environment (LR-4). Explicitly covering all language requirements for adaptation models, this pattern rather targets comprehensive and sophisticated analysis and planning steps working at longer time scales (FR-5), while efficiency concerns could be tackled by incrementality.

This pattern leverages incrementality (FR-2) since the coordination between different steps of the loop is based on events, analysis results, and applied adaptation options, which directly point to location in reflection models for starting analysis, planning, or executing changes. Moreover, analysis and planning steps may incrementally interleave. Based on first analysis results that are produced by evaluation conditions with highest priorities (FR-4), a planning process might start before the whole system and environment have been completely analyzed. However, incrementality requires the reversibility of performed operations (FR-3) to ensure consistency of reflection models (FR-1), e.g., when alternative adaptation options are tested on-line on reflection models and finally discarded.

5.2   Analysis and Planning – Coupled

In contrast to decoupling the analyze and planning steps, they can be closely integrated into one step, which is sketched in Figure 3. Based on events (LR-5), the integrated analyze/plan step computes evaluation conditions (LR-6) that are directly mapped to adaptation options (LR-8). If a condition is met, the corresponding adaptation options are applied on the reflection models and finally executed to the running system. Access to reflection models (LR-4) is realized by the analyze/plan step as a link between adaptation and reflection models.

In Figure 3, the language requirements written in brackets are not explicitly covered by adaptation models because this pattern precisely specifies the adaptation by directly relating evaluation conditions to the application of adaptation options. This relation implicitly covers some of the requirements listed in brackets. E.g., it is assumed that the applied adaptation options effect the system in a way that fulfills the desired goals, qualities, and preferences (LR-1, 2, 3).

Considering the events and the mapping of evaluation conditions to adaptation options, this pattern is similar to rule-based approaches using event-conditions-action rules. Covering the whole decision-making process and integrating analysis and planning into one step, adaptation models as depicted in Figure 3 cannot be clearly differentiated into evaluation and change models.

Thus, this pattern targets adaptation mechanisms requiring quick reactions to runtime phenomena by enabling adaptation at rather short time scales (FR-5). Moreover, efficiency is improved by incrementality (FR-2) and priorities (FR-4). The steps may incrementally coordinate each other through locating events and applied adaptation options in reflection models for analysis/planning and executing changes to the system. Priorities may be used to order evaluation conditions for quickly identifying critical situations that need urgent reactions, while conditions for non-critical situations can be evaluated without strict time constraints.

The consistency requirement (FR-1) is not explicitly covered because it is assumed that the mapping of conditions to adaptation options preserves consistency by design of such rule-based mechanisms. Since these mechanisms strictly prescribe the adaptation, there need not to be any options left that have to be decided at runtime. This reduces the need for reversible operations (FR-3).

5.3   Discussion

Regarding the two different feedback loop patterns and their effects on adaptation models, we can make two observations. First, it might be necessary to combine both patterns in a self-adaptive system if simultaneous support for different time scales (FR-5) is required or if a specific self-adaptive system requires both flavors of rule-based and search-based decision-making mechanisms. Second, we think that these two patterns span a range of several other patterns. By explicitly covering more and more language requirements, the adaptation models get more elaborate, and we may move stepwise from the coupled pattern (cf. Section 5.2) toward the decoupled one (cf. Section 5.1). Which pattern and adaptation models suit best depends on the concrete self-adaptive system, especially on the system's domain requirements. Finally, the requirement of flexibility (FR-6) has not been discussed for the two patterns. However, it is relevant for both of them since it is usually not possible to anticipate all adaptation scenarios at development-time, which requires adjusting adaptation models at runtime.

6   Assessment of Approaches to Adaptation Models

In this section, we assess two approaches to adaptation models, namely *Stitch* [5] and *Story Diagrams* [11], concerning their support for the requirements presented in this paper. After sketching both approaches, the assessment is discussed.

Stitch is a self-adaptation language developed in the context of *Rainbow* [5], which is a framework for self-adaptive systems based on architecture description language (ADL) techniques, in particular the *Acme* ADL. The focus of Stitch is to capture routine system administration tasks as explicit adaptation strategies consisting of condition-action pairs. The conditions expressed in a first-order predicate logic are evaluated on an ADL-based reflection model (cf. Section 3) describing the running system. If a condition is met indicating a need for adaptation, the actions associated with this condition are analyzed based on utility preferences and the most promising action is directly executed to the system.

Story Diagrams [11], originally introduced in [6], are a general purpose graph transformation approach. They extend activity diagrams from the *Unified Modeling Language* (UML) by specifying each activity using a graph transformation rule, called *Story Pattern*. Thus, a Story Diagram defines the control flow between multiple Story Patterns. Story Diagrams and Patterns are specified on one or more user-defined metamodels and they work on corresponding instances of these metamodels. In the context of adaptation, they work on reflection models (cf. Section 3). A Story Pattern specifies a pattern that has to be matched in the reflection model. If a match has been found, the side effects of the rule – if any are specified – are executed by changing the model. Moreover, patterns can be extended with constraints specified in the *Object Constraint Language* (OCL) to allow more sophisticated conditions. Following MDE principles, Story Diagrams leverage the usage of MDE techniques, like OCL. Moreover, Story Diagrams themselves conform to a metamodel, which enables an interpreter to directly execute them and which in the end supports higher order transformations.

6.1   Assessment of Stitch and Story Diagrams

Having outlined both approaches to adaptation models, we analyze them with respect to their support for the requirements discussed in Section 4. Table 1 lists all requirements and shows the degree of support by both approaches. It has to be noted that both languages make use of other languages, primarily languages for reflection models, to specify an adaptation. E.g., an adaptation model may specify a condition, like *component.rt > MAX_RT*, to identify whether the response time of a running component exceeds a threshold. While the response times are provided by reflection models (*component.rt* is part of the reflection model language), the adaptation model just defines the threshold and references the reflection model. Thus, Stitch and Story Diagram models are not self-contained.

Concerning functional language requirements, Stitch focuses on QoS-aware adaptation and thus, it provides full support for quality dimensions (LR-2) and preferences across these dimensions (LR-3). Functional goals (LR-1) are not considered. Story Diagrams may provide full support for goals, qualities, and preferences (LR-1, 2, 3) as they work on reflection models and use OCL, which is similar to Stitch. To cover goals, Story Diagrams may even use an explicit goal model describing the designated functionality in addition to reflection models.

Access to reflection models (LR-4) is supported by both languages though Stitch strategies just have read access for analysis, but they do not perform changes on the model before executing them to the system. This might be helpful for model-based planning or testing of adaptation and thus, Stitch provides medium support. Story Diagrams and especially Story Patterns explicitly read and write (change) reflection models, such that we attest them full support here.

Table 1. Requirements (Req.), Stitch, and Story Diagrams (SD): '–' denotes no support, 'M' medium support, and 'F' full support for the requirements

Functional Language Requirements								
Req.	Stitch	SD	Req.	Stitch	SD	Req.	Stitch	SD
LR-1	–	F	LR-5	M	F	LR-9	F	F
LR-2	F	F	LR-6	F	F	LR-10	F	F
LR-3	F	F	LR-7	–	F	LR-11	M	F
LR-4	M	F	LR-8	F	F			
Non-functional Language Requirements								
Req.	Stitch	SD	Req.	Stitch	SD	Req.	Stitch	SD
LR-12	M	F	LR-14	M	F	LR-16	M	M
LR-13	–	M	LR-15	–	M	LR-17	M	F
Framework Requirements								
Req.	Stitch	SD	Req.	Stitch	SD	Req.	Stitch	SD
FR-1	M	F	FR-3	–	M	FR-5	–	F
FR-2	–	M	FR-4	–	F	FR-6	–	F

While Stitch uses events (LR-5) only as triggers for the adaptation process to compute all evaluation conditions, the Story Diagram interpreter uses as well the information contained in change events to locate points in reflection models where evaluation conditions as Story Patterns should be checked. Thus, event information is used to filter the conditions irrelevant for these locations, which improves efficiency. This motivates the medium resp. full support for events.

Evaluation conditions (LR-6) and adaptation conditions (LR-9) are supported by both approaches based on the integration of some form of first-order predicate logic (*Acme* predicates in case of Stitch, and OCL for Story Diagrams). However, Story Patterns provide additional means to specify structural conditions by means of patterns containing structured model elements to be checked.

Stitch does not explicitly capture evaluation results (LR-7) as they are used in a transient way to select adaptation strategies. In contrast, Story Diagrams may provide full support by employing Story Patterns just for analysis purposes. Thus, the pattern to be matched specifies the evaluation condition and the corresponding side effects compute results that are annotated to the reflection models.

Both approaches provide full support for adaptation options (LR-8) and adaptation costs and benefits (LR-10). Likewise to Stitch that uses multiple strategies and that defines cost-benefit attributes of each adaptation step, multiple Story Diagrams or multiple Story Patterns enriched with such attributes are feasible for specifying and selecting appropriate adaptations to be performed.

Finally, since Stitch does not clearly separate the analysis and planning steps, it just maintains a history (LR-11) for the applied adaptation strategies, but not for the analysis results as they are not explicitly captured. In contrast to this medium support, Story Diagrams or Patterns explicitly addressing evaluation results as well as the applied adaptation options may keep a history of both.

Concerning non-functional language requirements, Stitch partially supports modularity, abstractions, and scalability (LR-12) by the strategy, tactic, and operator concepts. Operators are system-level commands that are bundled in tactics to describe an adaptation step, and a strategy orchestrates multiple of these steps. Thus, Stitch is limited to these three levels of abstraction. In contrast, besides Story Diagrams and Story Patterns already provide an initial abstraction, Story Diagrams can be nested in other Story Diagrams without any restrictions.

Stitch does not distinguish between concepts causing side effects or not (LR-13) as the strategies are considered as inherently causing effects on the running system. In contrast, Story Patterns can be statically analyzed whether they potentially cause side effects as well as they can be annotated to make it explicit.

Parameters (LR-14) are supported by both. While Stitch seems to be restricted on parameters of basic data types, Story Diagrams and Patterns may have arbitrary parameters including references to objects of user-defined classes.

While the Stitch language is not based on a formal foundation (LR-15), Story Patterns built upon the graph transformation theory. This enables support for formal validation and verification, which is, however, impeded if OCL is used.

Regarding reusability (LR-16) both languages, Stitch and Story Diagrams, are similar as they are independent of the languages used for the reflection models. However, the concrete adaptation models created with Stitch or Story Diagrams use and reference concepts of the reflection model languages. Thus, the concrete adaptation models are coupled to the types of reflection models.

Stitch is basically an imperative scripting language and its tool support requires improvement [5]. For Story Diagrams and Patterns, the declarative notion of graph transformations and graphical editors assist an engineer in modeling and validating adaptation models. Therefore, checks for syntactical well-formedness, an interpreter, and a visual debugger are provided. This causes the different ratings of both approaches concerning the ease of use requirement (LR-17).

Finally, the support for the framework requirements is discussed. Since Stitch's adaptation strategies that have been selected to tackle the current adaptation need are directly executed to the running system, only limited support for consistency (FR-1) is provided. Consistency is only addressed by observing intermediate effects of the executed adaptation on the running system but not beforehand at the model level. The other framework requirements are not covered by Stitch.

Since Story Diagrams completely work on reflection models, consistency can be continuously checked at the model level. Incrementality (FR-2) is supported for single Story Patterns, and reversibility (FR-3) for typical model changes by tracking primitive operations performed on the model. Both requirements are hard to satisfy if OCL is used. Incremental evaluation of OCL statements is often not possible and for the case of side effects the inverse statements might not be detectable. Prioritizing (FR-4) Story Diagrams and Patterns to be executed is supported, and it is required for different time scales (FR-5). E.g., a Story Pattern defining the whole adaptation for urgent situations must have a higher priority to be executed than other Patterns that jointly define a sophisticated adaptation by separating analysis and planning steps. Since Story Diagrams and Patterns are interpreted at runtime, they can replaced or modified on-line, e.g., by higher order transformations. This satisfies the flexibility requirement (FR-6).

6.2 Discussion of the Assessment

The conducted assessment of Stitch and Story Diagrams concerning the requirements presented in this paper is constrained by two aspects. First, the analysis of Stitch is solely based on literature [5]. Second, the analysis of Story Diagrams for their fitness to specify adaptation models is based on our experience with Story Diagrams and thus, it has been done from a conceptual point of view.

The fact that Stitch does not support several requirements does not necessarily reveal design flaws, but it is rather motivated by the specific setting. On the one hand and as argued in [5], Stitch focuses on system administration tasks that could be tackled well by rule-based approaches and it limits runtime reasoning on computing utilities to select one among multiple applicable adaptation strategies. Thus, Stitch does not aim to support search-based mechanisms. On the other hand, Stitch is not based on MDE principles and it does not take into account specifics of models@run.time. However, using an ADL model at runtime, Stitch is still related to the research field for which the requirements are relevant.

Concerning the different feedback loop patterns discussed in Section 5, Stitch targets the pattern that couples the analysis and planning steps, which is similar to rule-based approaches. However, since Stitch supports utility-based analysis and selection of competing adaptation strategies (rules), it shares characteristics with the decoupled pattern. This motivates the need for explicitly capturing, e.g., qualities and preferences (LR-2, 3), which need not to be the case for pure rule-based approaches that do not allow competing or even conflicting rules.

Finally, Story Diagrams seem to be a promising language for adaptation models because they follow MDE principles, they are directly interpretable and flexible, and they seamlessly integrate with any user-defined metamodel for reflection models. However, Story Diagrams are a general-purpose language and not specifically tailored for adaptation models. This might be a drawback, but we think that concepts specific for adaptation models (like goals (LR-1)) can be covered by a different language (like for goal models), which can be integrated with Story Diagrams. Which of the different feedback loop patterns (cf. Section 5) can be covered by Story Diagrams requires further investigations or even experiences from employing Story Diagrams in a concrete self-adaptive system.

7 Conclusion and Future Work

In this paper, we have elaborated the requirements for adaptation models that specify the decision-making process in self-adaptive software systems using models@run.time. In particular, requirements for a modeling language incorporating metamodels, constraints, and model operations for creating and applying adaptation models have been discussed, as well as requirements for a framework that executes adaptation models. Moreover, we discussed patterns of a self-adaptive system's feedback loop with respect to the requirements for adaptation models. Additionally, we have assessed two existing languages and frameworks, namely Stitch and Story Diagrams, concerning their fitness for the requirements.

As future work, we want to elaborate the conducted assessment to confirm evidence for the relevance and completeness of the requirements. Moreover, we plan to use Story Diagrams for specifying adaptation models in our approach [16, 18] to close the feedback loop. Additionally, this can be seen as an evaluation of the promising results that Story Diagrams achieved in the assessment.

References

1. Bencomo, N., Blair, G., Fleurey, F., Jeanneret, C.: Summary of the 5th International Workshop on Models@run.time. In: Dingel, J., Solberg, A. (eds.) MODELS 2010. LNCS, vol. 6627, pp. 204–208. Springer, Heidelberg (2011)
2. Bencomo, N., Blair, G., France, R., Muñoz, F., Jeanneret, C.: 4th International Workshop on Models@run.time. In: Ghosh, S. (ed.) MODELS 2009. LNCS, vol. 6002, pp. 119–123. Springer, Heidelberg (2010)
3. Blair, G., Bencomo, N., France, R.B.: Models@run.time. Computer 42(10), 22–27 (2009)
4. Cheng, B.H.C., de Lemos, R., Giese, H., Inverardi, P., Magee, J., Andersson, J., Becker, B., Bencomo, N., Brun, Y., Cukic, B., Di Marzo Serugendo, G., Dustdar, S., Finkelstein, A., Gacek, C., Geihs, K., Grassi, V., Karsai, G., Kienle, H.M., Kramer, J., Litoiu, M., Malek, S., Mirandola, R., Müller, H.A., Park, S., Shaw, M., Tichy, M., Tivoli, M., Weyns, D., Whittle, J.: Software Engineering for Self-Adaptive Systems: A Research Roadmap. In: Cheng, B.H.C., de Lemos, R., Giese, H., Inverardi, P., Magee, J. (eds.) Self-Adaptive Systems. LNCS, vol. 5525, pp. 1–26. Springer, Heidelberg (2009)
5. Cheng, S.W.: Rainbow: Cost-Effective Software Architecture-Based Self-Adaptation. Ph.D. thesis, Carnegie Mellon University, Pittsburgh, USA (2008)
6. Fischer, T., Niere, J., Torunski, L., Zündorf, A.: Story Diagrams: A New Graph Rewrite Language Based on the Unified Modeling Language and Java. In: Ehrig, H., Engels, G., Kreowski, H.-J., Rozenberg, G. (eds.) TAGT 1998. LNCS, vol. 1764, pp. 296–309. Springer, Heidelberg (2000)
7. Fleurey, F., Dehlen, V., Bencomo, N., Morin, B., Jézéquel, J.-M.: Modeling and Validating Dynamic Adaptation. In: Chaudron, M.R.V. (ed.) MODELS 2008. LNCS, vol. 5421, pp. 97–108. Springer, Heidelberg (2009)
8. Fleurey, F., Solberg, A.: A Domain Specific Modeling Language Supporting Specification, Simulation and Execution of Dynamic Adaptive Systems. In: Schürr, A., Selic, B. (eds.) MODELS 2009. LNCS, vol. 5795, pp. 606–621. Springer, Heidelberg (2009)
9. Floch, J., Hallsteinsen, S., Stav, E., Eliassen, F., Lund, K., Gjorven, E.: Using Architecture Models for Runtime Adaptability. Software 23(2), 62–70 (2006)
10. Georgas, J.C., Hoek, A., Taylor, R.N.: Using Architectural Models to Manage and Visualize Runtime Adaptation. Computer 42(10), 52–60 (2009)
11. Giese, H., Hildebrandt, S., Seibel, A.: Improved Flexibility and Scalability by Interpreting Story Diagrams. In: GT-VMT 2009, vol. 18. ECEASST (2009)
12. Kephart, J.O., Chess, D.: The Vision of Autonomic Computing. Computer 36(1), 41–50 (2003)
13. Ramirez, A.J., Cheng, B.H.: Evolving Models at Run Time to Address Functional and Non-Functional Adaptation Requirements. In: Models@run.time 2009. CEUR-WS.org, vol. 509, pp. 31–40 (2009)

14. Rouvoy, R.: Requirements of mechanisms and planning algorithms for self-adaptation. Deliverable D1.1 of MUSIC (EU-FP6 project) (2007)
15. Song, H., Huang, G., Chauvel, F., Sun, Y.: Applying MDE Tools at Runtime: Experiments upon Runtime Models. In: Models@run.time 2010. CEUR-WS.org, vol. 641, pp. 25–36 (2010)
16. Vogel, T., Giese, H.: Adaptation and Abstract Runtime Models. In: SEAMS 2010, pp. 39–48. ACM (2010)
17. Vogel, T., Giese, H.: Language and Framework Requirements for Adaptation Models. In: Models@run.time 2011. CEUR-WS.org, vol. 794, pp. 1–12 (2011)
18. Vogel, T., Neumann, S., Hildebrandt, S., Giese, H., Becker, B.: Incremental Model Synchronization for Efficient Run-Time Monitoring. In: Ghosh, S. (ed.) MODELS 2009. LNCS, vol. 6002, pp. 124–139. Springer, Heidelberg (2010)
19. Vogel, T., Seibel, A., Giese, H.: The Role of Models and Megamodels at Runtime. In: Dingel, J., Solberg, A. (eds.) MODELS 2010. LNCS, vol. 6627, pp. 224–238. Springer, Heidelberg (2011)

MoDeVVa 2011 Workshop Summary

Levi Lúcio[1], Stephan Weißleder[2], Frédéric Fondement[3], and Harald Cichos[4]

[1] Université du Luxembourg, Luxembourg
levi.lucio@uni.lu
[2] Fraunhofer FIRST, Germany
stephan.weissleder@first.fraunhofer.de
[3] Université de Haute Alsace, France
frederic.fondement@uha.fr
[4] Technische Universität Darmstadt, Germany
harald.cichos@es.tu-darmstadt.de

1 Modeling, Verification, and Validation

All workshops of the MoDeVVa series are focused on Model-Driven Engineering, Verification, and Validation.

Models are purposeful abstractions. They are important elements in established life cycle management approaches, especially in model-driven approaches. Most importantly, they are very useful for communication of important aspects of the software being developed - they are used to support the focus on these important aspects and to make complex systems simple to understand. Furthermore, models are descriptions at an arbitrary level of detail and can, thus, be used to make traceability from requirements to any other object in development easier. If the models are not just sketches, but also have a formal foundation, they can also used for automatic transformation or code generation. Typical applications are the automatic generation of large parts of system source code, which results in a decrease of system engineering costs. One of the most important representatives for the application of models is the Model-Driven Engineering (MDE) approach. MDE is a development methodology that is based on models, meta models, and model transformations. There are many tools to support models, (domain-specific) modeling languages, model transformations, and code generation. The usage of models, model transformations, and code generation is becoming more and more important for industrial applications. The fact that development of MDE-related techniques still moves forward shows that MDE is quickly changing and that new approaches and corresponding issues arise frequently. The focus of the MoDeVVa series is on verification and validation (V&V) techniques in the context of MDE. V&V are currently very relevant in many safety-critical domains, with some of those domains being heavyweight representatives such automotive or avionics.

2 Objectives of the Workshop

The objective of the workshop on model-driven engineering, verification, and validation (MoDeVVa) in 2011 was to offer a forum for researchers and practitioners who are working on V&V and MDE. The main goals of the workshop

J. Kienzle (Ed.): MODELS 2011 Workshops, LNCS 7167, pp. 183–186, 2012.

were to identify the mutual impact of MDE and V&V: How can MDE improve V&V and how can V&V leverage the techniques around MDE? Thus, we asked for submissions that target the following areas:

- V&V techniques for MDE activities, e.g. V&V for model-to-model or model-to-text transformations;
- V&V at the level of the models: techniques for validating a model or generating test cases from models, including simulation, model-checking, model-based testing, etc.;
- V&V at the level of meta models: techniques for validating meta-models (languages) or for using meta-models to validate other artifacts;
- The application of MDE to validation, testing and verification;
- Impact analysis of (meta) model changes on validation, i.e. the result of a change in a (meta-)model on the previous results of validation;
- V&V techniques supporting refinement, abstraction and structuring;
- Difficulties and gains of applying V&V to MDE and vice versa;
- Case studies and experience reports;
- Tools and automation.

3   Submissions and Acceptance in 2011

In 2011, there were 21 submissions to MoDeVVa from 14 countries. This is the best submission rate of the previous 3 years. This clearly shows that MoDeVVa continues being an active workshop in the domain of MDD. In the review process, we chose 9 papers on mainly three topics: *verification, validation* and *model transformations* – also the topics of this year's MoDeVVa's three sessions.

The *verification* session was the longest, starting with new interesting topic of a usable definition partial models. During the verification session, two papers covered similar topics: how to understand and decrease the computational weight of formal verification. The two papers tackle the problem in different ways: one tries to provide an algorithm for finding an upper bound for the number of objects required to statically verify the consistency of UML class diagrams; the other one limits the number of scenarios of execution to be taken into consideration by a model checker by using environmental constraints for the system being modelled. In particular this last paper, called "Formal Extension of Use Cases for Context-Aware Verification" (by Amine Raji, Philippe Dhaussy and Benoit Baudry) is one of the two best papers of MoDeVVa in 2011.

In the *validation* session, the paper named "Specifying a Testing Oracle for Train Stations" (by Andreas Svendsen, Oystein Haugen, Birger Möller-Pedersen) stood out and is the second of the two best papers. The paper describes how to generate a test oracle for train stations. The fact that this paper won a best paper award is, in our opinion, an indicator that more case studies are necessary to prove the interest and validity of MDD techniques having been, or currently being proposed.

The verification and validation sessions are standard to MoDeVVa, but the continued submission of papers on model transformations (and their verification) show that this theme carries on gaining importance in the Model-Driven Development world.

4   Keynote

This year's keynote at MoDeVVa was kindly given by Hans Vangheluwe from the Universities of Antwerp and McGill. Hans has given a presentation with the name "What About Properties?", which points out the fact that properties are often left out of the equation when modeling – or at least tackled too late during the Model-Driven Development of a software system. This is so in spite of the fact that research on properties of models and their proofs has existed for some time and has gained serious attention recently with the advent of powerful model checkers. By basing his presentation on the MDD development of an electric power window for an automobile, Hans makes a case for the fact that the variety of modeling languages (and supporting transformations) in today's automotive software development makes it such that properties need to be taken into account across the whole development process. Since this is in general not currently the case, Hans' prospective solution for this problem is to consider a model as both a model in the typical sense, but also with a number of properties attached. These properties should then be maintained (at varying levels of abstraction) or transformed in an controller and understood fashion during an MDD process.

5   Discussion and Perspectives for the Workshop

In 2011, the attendees of MoDeVVa workshop series saw the 8th edition of MoDeVVa. In our opinion, this clearly shows that all kinds of verification and validation in combination with modeling is currently very interesting to people from both academia and industry. The workshop was well appreciated by participants who expressed very positive feedback. For this reason, and with the amount of submitted papers this year, we are convinced of the interest of the MDE community in MoDeVVa. We thus plan to continue the workshop series in the years to come. The tackled topics will continue to be in the area of modeling, validation, and verification. Stay tuned.

Acknowledgments. We would like to thank all the authors for their contributions and high quality presentations. A big thank you also to the Program Committee for their help and advice while selecting the best contributions: Paul Ammann, Bruno Barroca, Benoit Baudry, Fabrice Bouquet, Ruth Breu, John Derrick, Franck Fleurey, Mark Harman, Antti Huima, Bruno Legeard, Mercedes Merayo, Alexander Pretschner, Ina Schieferdecker, Holger Schlingloff, Dehla Sokenou, Yves Le Traon, Hans Vangheluwe and Manuel Wimmer.

Finally, we would like to especially thank Hans Vangheluwe for having helped us kicking off MoDeVVa with his keynote speech. His enthusiasm for "Modelling Everything" and his background in simulation have added value to this year's edition of MoDeVVa.

Specifying a Testing Oracle for Train Stations – Going beyond with Product Line Technology

Andreas Svendsen[1,2], Øystein Haugen[1], and Birger Møller-Pedersen[2]

[1] SINTEF, Pb. 124 Blindern, 0314 Oslo, Norway
[2] Department of Informatics, University of Oslo, Pb. 1080 Blindern, 0316 Oslo, Norway
{andreas.svendsen,oystein.haugen}@sintef.no, birger@ifi.uio.no

Abstract. This paper presents an approach for automatically generating a testing oracle for train stations. Based on a model of a train station and a formal definition of the behavior of the station, Alloy is used to generate all positive traces from a given situation. By specifying the precondition (test input), a simulation of the station model gives all legal train movement from this state, which defines the testing oracle. This oracle can be used for checking the result of testing the implementation of the station by comparing the train movement from the test with the legal train movement specified by the oracle. We suggest a prototype implementation based on the Train Control Language and give an example oracle for a typical test-case. Furthermore, we elaborate on the benefits of using product line technology, given by the Common Variability Language, to reduce the analysis effort necessary to obtain the oracle for product models.

Keywords: Model-based testing, testing oracle, traces, Train Control language, Alloy, product lines, variability modeling, Common Variability Language.

1   Introduction

Software testing is a practice in software engineering to discover and ensure that the implementation of a system behaves as intended. Thus, the intended behavior, from the specification, and the actual behavior, from the implementation, is compared to observe whether they differ in particular situations. Since software systems are complex and large in size, the number of situations necessary to test is usually huge. As a consequence, creating test-cases, specifying the verdict of these test-cases (specifying an oracle), and executing the test-cases require considerable (time) effort.

Model-based testing is a form of testing that uses models of the behavior of a system, System Under Test (SUT), and its environment to generate test-cases that can be executed to verify the implementation of the system. The behavior of the SUT and the environment are typically modeled using finite state machines (finite automata). These state machines specify the states of the system and the available transitions for each state. A test-case typically consists of a set of pre-conditions, a test step (path through the state machine) and a verdict. The pre-conditions specify the initial values of the model elements in the SUT that are relevant for the test-case, in other words the starting state. The test step defines the transition or set of transitions that are being tested. This is often realized as a path through the state machine starting from the state

J. Kienzle (Ed.): MODELS 2011 Workshops, LNCS 7167, pp. 187–201, 2012.

specified by the pre-conditions. The verdict specifies whether the outcome of the test step is as expected. In other words, whether the state following the test step is as expected. The verdict can usually have three values: *pass, fail* and *inconclusive*.

An oracle is a mechanism for deciding the verdict of a test-case. In other words, an oracle decides whether the outcome of the test-case has passed or failed. Automating the testing phase using model-based testing techniques requires not only the test-cases to be generated and executed, but also the oracle to be specified. Specifying such an oracle requires detailed knowledge about the execution of the SUT, involving the impact and cascading effects of executing the test-case. This is often a manual and tedious task that requires extensive domain knowledge.

In this paper we propose an approach for using traces for specifying the oracle of a set of test-cases. We define the operational semantics of the SUT in Alloy, we specify the test-cases as predicates and assertions in the Alloy model, and we use the Alloy Analyzer to generate and check traces to form the oracle. The operational semantics specify the positive behavior of the SUT, meaning only behavior that is intended. The predicates and assertions specify the pre-conditions and the test-step, and the oracle is defined as all positive traces or sub-traces obtained by the operational semantics starting from the test-step. Furthermore, we also give a discussion about how to use generic variability models to reduce the analysis and simulation effort necessary to obtain oracles for product models. This paper represents a modified and extended version of previous work [21].

The contribution of this paper is the description of an approach for using Alloy for generating and checking traces of an SUT to form a testing oracle. These traces can be compared to the outcome of executing the test-cases on the implementation of the SUT to decide whether they pass or fail. Furthermore, we propose an extension to this approach, using the Common Variability Language (CVL) to define a product line, to reduce the necessary effort of specifying the testing oracle for each product of the product line. We propose an implementation of the approach, and we illustrate the approach in detail on a typical test-case from the train domain.

The outline of the paper is as follows: In Section 2 we give some background information, before we introduce the concept of traces and relates it to the train domain in Section 3. Section 4 explains the approach of specifying a testing oracle and demonstrates it on an example. In Section 5 we extend the approach with product line techniques to reduce the effort of specifying oracles for several models. We discuss the approach in Section 6 and give related work in Section 7. Finally, concluding remarks and future work are given in Section 8.

2   Background

2.1   Train Control Language

The Train Control Language (TCL) is a Domain-Specific Modeling Language (DSML) for modeling train signaling systems [3, 24]. TCL has been developed in cooperation with ABB, Norway[1]. The purpose of TCL is to automate the production of interlocking source code, which ensures that only safe train movement is allowed.

TCL has been developed as an Eclipse plug-in based on the Eclipse Modeling Framework (EMF) [2] and the Eclipse Graphical Modeling Framework (GMF) [6]. The TCL tool suite includes a graphical editor, a code generator and a model analyzer. The concrete syntax of TCL is illustrated in Fig. 1. The main concepts of TCL are *TrainRoute, TrackCircuit, LineSegment, Switch, Endpoint* and *Signal*. A TrainRoute represents a path between two Signals which has to be allocated before a train can enter or depart the station. A TrainRoute is divided into one or more TrackCircuits, which are segments of the station consisting of LineSegments and Switches connected by Endpoints.

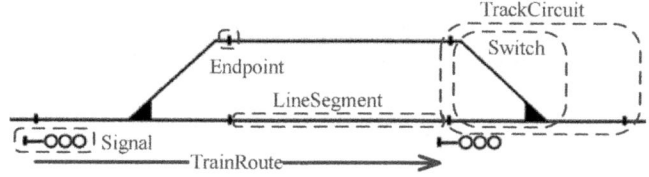

Fig. 1. TCL concrete syntax (with annotations)

The operational semantics of TCL has been defined in Alloy using the ordering utility to model a state machine by specifying the states of the station and the transitions [23]. The state machine specifies how the signaling system on a station behaves when trains are moving throughout the station. An executing of the state machine (executing Alloy) yields a trace capturing the train movement. Intuitively the TCL operational semantics is as follows: A train entering the station stops at a Signal giving a red light, until the TrainRoute following this Signal is considered safe and can be allocated. When the TrainRoute is allocated, the train moves one track (LineSegment or Switch) in each transition until the end of the TrainRoute. The train departs from the station using the same procedure. Several trains can move simultaneously as long as they can allocate TrainRoutes that are not in conflict.

2.2   Common Variability Language

The Common Variability Language (CVL) is a generic language for modeling variability in any model in any DSML [5, 7]. There are three models of importance in the CVL approach: The *base model* is a model defined by use of the base DSML (e.g. TCL). A *variability model* is a model that is applied to the base model, by the means of one-way references, specifying all the possible variability that can be applied to the base model for this product line. A *resolution model* binds the variability in the variability model to produce specific product models. A CVL model consists of the variability model and the resolution model.

---

[1] http://www.abb.no

In CVL variability is modeled in two layers: The *feature specification layer*, defining the high-level variability as choices, much like feature models, and the *product realization layer*, specifying how a feature is realized in the transformation of a copy of the base model to a product model. The features are realized in the transformation by the use of *substitutions*, which define how attributes or objects in the base model copy can be modified to obtain the product model. In this paper we will concentrate on this core part of CVL, and more specifically we will use the most flexible substitution available, namely the *fragment substitution*.

A fragment substitution replaces a placement fragment, defined as a set of base model elements, with a replacement fragment, defined as another set of base model elements (see Fig. 2). As illustrated in the figure, a fragment is specified by recording all references into and out of the fragment, as so-called *boundary elements*. A fragment substitution specifically binds the boundary elements in the placement fragment to the boundary elements in the replacement fragment. Thus, executing the substitution yields a modification of the references according to these bindings.

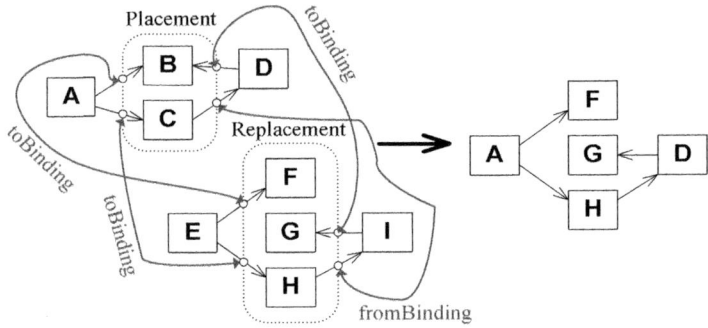

Fig. 2. A fragment substitution replaces a placement fragment with a replacement fragment

In this paper we investigate how we can use the information from such a substitution to predict whether the transformation to a product model has any impact on the oracle related to the base model. Furthermore, we will see how the effort of specifying an oracle can be reduced based on this kind of analysis.

2.3   Alloy

Alloy is a light-weight declarative language based on first-order logic for modeling a system formally using relational calculus [9]. Through its analyzer tool Alloy offers fully automated analysis over a finite set of cases, restricted by a user-defined scope. This scope limits the number of elements of each type in the model and it thus limits the solution space. When performing analysis of a model, the Alloy Analyzer only guarantees for the analysis within the scope. However, the small scope hypothesis ensures that if a solution or inconsistency exists, it is within a scope of small size [1].

An Alloy model typically consists of *signatures*, *fields*, *facts*, *predicates* and *assertions*. A signature represents a type in the model, and a signature can extend another signature to form a type hierarchy. Signatures contain fields, which refer other signatures. A fact consists of a set of global constraints that must always hold. A predicate consists of a set of local constraints that must hold if the predicate is processed. An assertion consists of a set of constraints that are claimed to hold if the assertion is processed.

Alloy offers two kinds of analysis: Find a solution model satisfying a predicate or find a model representing a counter-example to an assertion. When performing these kinds of analysis Alloy populates the signatures and fields up to the user-defined scope. All combinations are exhausted either until a solution satisfying the constraints in the predicate/assertion is found or until the search returns no solution.

3   Traces

A trace is defined by Haugen et al. [8] as "*a sequence of events ordered by time*". In other words, a trace determines the state of the system and its history. The behavior of a system is typically modeled with a finite state machine. A trace is then represented as the set of transitions through the state machine. In general, positive traces define intended behavior, while negative traces define unintended behavior of the system.

In TCL the operational semantics specify the legal train movement on a station model. More precisely, the operational semantics, defined by a state machine in Alloy, specify the set of all positive traces on the station model. The train movement can be captured by a tuple, consisting of the name of the train and the track the train is moving into. Fig. 3 illustrates a trace capturing the train movement of train *T1* entering a station from the left, moving through the main track of the station and departing the station to the right. The station model with track names annotated is illustrated in Fig. 4. Note that a trace can capture several trains moving simultaneously by ordering their track transitions, e.g. a train *T2* moving to *LS2* before train *T1* moves to *LS3*.

<{T1,LS1}, {T1,LS3}, {T1,V2}, {T1,LS5}, {T1,V1}, {T1, LS4}, {T1, LS2}, {T1, DEPARTED}>

Fig. 3. Trace capturing the movement of train T1

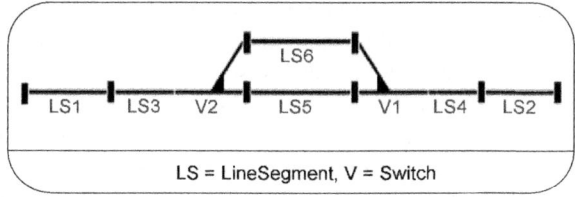

Fig. 4. Station annotated with Track names

Performing analysis on a particular TCL model involves processing a predicate or an assertion relative to the static or dynamic (operational) semantics of the TCL model in Alloy. In this paper we focus on verifying the train movement, and thus the operational semantics. Executing such predicates or assertions results in Alloy giving an ordered set of states as solution model (according to the *ordering* utility). This ordered set of states (in other words a sequence of states) defines the trace through the state machine giving the solution to the analysis.

Note that the analysis can be used both to generate traces based on a TCL model and to verify that a given trace conforms to the semantics for a TCL model. In the first case, a predicate or an assertion is processed and the solution model is interpreted to extract the generated trace. In the latter case, an assertion is specified such that the train movement given by the trace is claimed not to hold. Processing this assertion will then result in a counter-example if it holds or in no solution if the train movement is not as intended by the semantics.

4   Specify an Oracle Using Traces

4.1   The Approach

A testing oracle specifies whether the outcome of a test-case is as intended. In other words whether the test-case passes or fails for a particular model or program. To be able to predict the outcome of a test-case we use a formal specification of the operational semantics of the DSL. The operational semantics is defined as the set of all positive (legal) traces for a particular model or program.

These traces can be used to decide whether the execution of a test-case (on the implementation of the system) behaves as intended. In other words, the set of positive traces of the model or program compose the testing oracle. If the execution of a test-case results in the same set of transitions as the traces, or sub-traces of the traces, given by the oracle, the outcome of the test-case is as intended.

All test-cases define a set of pre-conditions, which defines the state of the system when starting the execution of the test-case. Thus, executing a test-case involves manipulating the system by specifying these pre-conditions. We use these pre-conditions to establish the starting state when executing the system according to the test-case. Since these pre-conditions can be different for each test-case, they result in a distinctive starting state for each test-case. From these starting states, all intended traces are calculated as part of the testing oracle, by having the execution of the simulation of the SUT constrained to begin at that starting state.

There are currently two possible methods to use the approach presented in this paper: (1) Generate all traces from a starting state, or (2) check whether a particular trace, or set of traces, conforms to the operational semantics of the DSL. In this paper we focus on the first method and how it can be extended to apply to product families. We refer to [21] for more information about how the second method can be applied.

The first method involves generating all traces and comparing the outcome from the test-case execution with the traces in this set. We use Alloy to specify the method by specifying a predicate which constrains the starting state to conform to the pre-conditions of the test-case, and execute this predicate (repeatedly) to gather all positive traces from the starting state. The two methods are illustrated in Fig. 5.

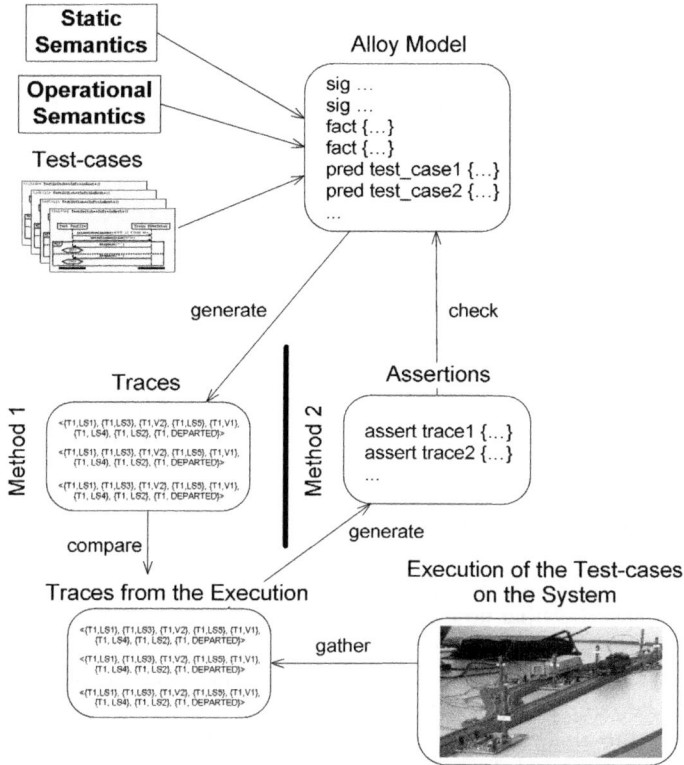

Fig. 5. Overview of the approach

The procedure, as illustrated in Fig. 5, is as follows: First the Alloy model is created based on the static and operational semantics of the DSL. Predicates for each test-case are also added to capture the pre-conditions for the starting states. For method 1, all traces from the starting state for each test-case are generated. This set of traces is then compared to the traces gathered from the execution of the test-cases on the implementation of the system. This comparison can either be performed manually or assisted by text-comparison techniques within our tool.

4.2   Reducing Verification Effort of TCL Models

To illustrate the approach, we apply it to a typical test-case for TCL models. The particular test-case example used in this paper is verifying the following safety property in a given situation: "No train can allocate a train route or enter the tracks within this route if any track within this route is occupied by another train". Intuitively, for a train to enter or depart the station, the tracks used by this train must be unoccupied. The test-case assumes that a train is already present on the main track of the station and that another train enters the station from the left side (see Fig. 6).

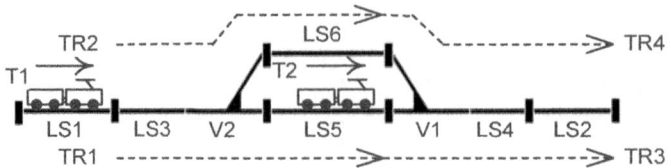

Fig. 6. Test-case example for TCL

As illustrated in the figure, a train *T1* is entering the station from the left and there is already a train *T2* present at the main track heading to the right. These are the pre-conditions for the test-case, and the outcome of executing the test-case should never result in a dangerous train movement. More specifically, train *T1* should not be allowed to allocate train route *TR1* before train *T2* has left *LS5* and the trains should not be allowed to allocate train route *TR3* and *TR4* simultaneously.

The pre-conditions (starting state) of the test-case are formalized to a predicate which is added to the Alloy model (see Fig. 5). In this case train *T1* is located on *LS1* heading to the right and train *T2* is located on *LS5* and also heading to the right. No train routes are allocated prior to the execution of the test-case. The predicate specifying the starting state of the test-case from Fig. 6 is illustrated in Fig. 7. The predicate first specifies that no train routes are allocated in the first state of the trace. Furthermore, it specifies the location of the two trains as the two relations *t1->t_LS1* and *t2->t_LS2*, the direction of the two trains, and their situation (*tsIdle*). The situation can be *tsInit* (prior to entering the station, *tsIdle* (waiting for a train route), *tsMoving* (moving along a train route) and *tsFinal* (departed from the station). In this test-case both trains are waiting for a train route, represented by the *tsIdle* situation.

```
pred test_case1 [trains: set Train]{
    no first.trainOnRoute
    some t1:trains, t2:trains - t1 {
        t1->t_LS1 in first.trainOnTrack
        t2->t_LS5 in first.trainOnTrack
        Right in t1.direction
        Right in t2.direction
        t1 in first.tsIdle
        t2 in first.tsIdle
    }
}
```

Fig. 7. Predicate specifying the starting state for a test-case

In this example test-case, train *T1* is not allowed to allocate train route *TR1* before train *T2* has left *LS5*, and train routes *TR3* and *TR4* cannot be allocated simultaneously. Following method 1, to generate all traces from this starting state, always yields all traces where this train movement is enforced. Two example traces generated by the Alloy model (using the predicate in Fig. 7) are illustrated in Fig. 8.

Following method 1, the set of traces generated from the Alloy model can be compared with the actual execution of the test-case on the implementation of the system. If a trace from the execution of the test-case is not within the oracle (set of traces generated by Alloy) then the test-case has failed. On the other hand, if it is part of the oracle, the test-case has passed.

<{T1,LS1}, {T2,LS5}, {T2,V1}, {T2,LS4}, {T1,LS3}, {T1, V2}, {T1, LS5},
{T2,LS2}, {T2, DEPARTED}, {T1,V1}, {T1,LS4}, {T1,LS2}, {T1, DEPARTED}>

<{T1,LS1}, {T2,LS5}, {T1,LS3}, {T1,V2}, {T1,LS6}, {T1, V1}, {T1, LS4},
{T1,LS2}, {T1, DEPARTED}, {T2,V1}, {T2,LS4}, {T2,LS2}, {T2, DEPARTED}>

Fig. 8. Two example traces generated from a test-case

5   Reducing Effort by Adding Product Line Capability

CVL is a generic variability language that specifies a product line precise enough for product models to be automatically generated from a base model. This is beneficial for both methods described in this paper, since a set of TCL models can be developed more efficiently. However, as discussed by our previous work [20, 22], CVL models can be analyzed to obtain the semantic impact of a CVL transformation from a base model to a product model. Recall that the semantics is defined as the set of all positive traces. Analysis of CVL models can then determine whether the traces given by the base model are preserved or affected (modified) for the product model. This can be of big advantage for method 1, which involves generating all positive traces to form the testing oracle, since we may be able to avoid re-generation of a set of these traces.

Assume that we use the two-track station described earlier in the paper (see Fig. 4 and Fig. 6) as our base model, and that we apply CVL to this model to form a product line of stations. A typical product model of this product line can be a three-track station where we have substituted the second track with a new two-track. This substitution is specified by a CVL model, meaning that the product model (three-track station) can be generated. The CVL transformation is illustrated in Fig. 9.

Based on this CVL model, we know precisely how and where the difference between the base model and the product model is. This information can be used for analyzing the impact of the modification on the already generated traces (for the base model). In this manner we may be able to avoid re-generating a subset of the traces for the product model. However, to be able to reason about the semantic impact of a CVL transformation, we need a formal description of not only the CVL model and the TCL model, but also of the combination of CVL and TCL. We have combined CVL and TCL in Alloy, which is further explained in [20].

This combination of CVL and TCL in Alloy allows us to do impact analysis of which traces that are different in the product model. Such impact analysis involves checking if the base model elements within or on the border of the placement fragment (set of base model elements that are replaced by CVL) can affect the execution of the operational semantics. An assertion claiming that there are no such overlapping TCL base model elements is illustrated in Fig. 10. If such base model elements exist, a counter-example is generated revealing these base model elements. Note that in an iteration of the assertion, one base model element is obtained. Subsequent iterations can then exclude this base model element before re-checking the assertion. The result of performing the analysis (checking the assertion) yields a list of affected model elements and the association that is affected (see Fig. 11). E.g. switches *V2* and *V1* are only affected on the *divert* association (related to the second/third track of the station).

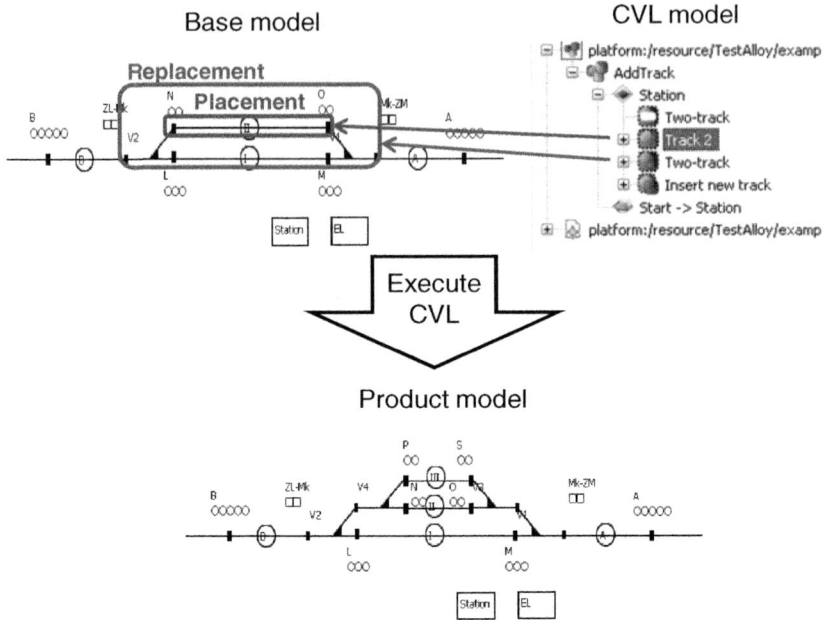

Fig. 9. CVL transformation

```
assert checkElements {
    all tp:ToPlacement, s:State,
        e: tp.insidePlacementBoundaryElement +
        tp.outsidePlacementBoundaryElement {
            no (s.occupiedTrack) & e
            no (s.allocatedRoute) & e
    }
}
```

Fig. 10. Check if the TCL traces are affected by the modified elements

Method 1 involves generating all positive traces from a starting state given by the pre-condition of a test-case. Based on the impact analysis of the CVL model, we add constraints to the original predicate (see Fig. 7) to restrict the analysis to only the traces that are different in the product model. To achieve this we add a constraint forcing all traces to include specific base model elements.

Interpretation of the analysis results shows that all of the train routes *BII1, N1, O1* and *AII1* are covered by at least one of the track elements *LS6, V2* and *V1*. In other words, restricting the train movement to cover only *LS6* and the *divert* positions of *V2* and *V1* would also cover the affected train routes. Such restrictions have the advantage of also covering other new train routes added by the transformation. Thus, we restrict the train movement to only cover the model elements that are replacing *LS6*, and thus are related to the property *divert* of *V2* and *V1* after the CVL transformation. The generated Alloy constraints, which ensure that only this kind of train movement is permitted, are illustrated in Fig. 12. Switches *V4* and *V3* are added by the CVL transformation. Note that these constraints are appended to the original predicate (see Fig. 7), and processing this combined predicate yields only traces that are new (i.e. that have been affected by the CVL transformation).

```
Analysis performed in 7 seconds.
The following elements are affected:

LS6 (inside PF) <------ Removed LineSegment
BII1 : end    ⌐
N1  : start   │       Affected TrainRoutes to/from
O1  : start   ├  <---     the second track
AII1 : end    ⌐
V2  : divert  ⌐       Affected Swiches in
V1  : divert  ⌐  <---    divert position
```

Fig. 11. Results of performing impact analysis of the CVL model

```
some s:State, t:trains {
        t->t_V4 in s.trainOnTrack or
        t->t_V3 in s.trainOnTrack
}
```

Fig. 12. Additional constraints restricting the train movement to avoid the main track

Processing the new combined predicate for the test-case yields traces where at least one of the trains *T1* and *T2* must be moving through at least one of the switches *V4* and *V3*. Fig. 13 illustrates the train movement traces that are generated for both the base model and the product model of our product line. According to this figure no traces where both trains are moving to the main track is generated. Note that all train movement on the main track is preserved in the product model and it is therefore not necessary to re-generate traces involving only such train movement. However, all traces where at least one of the trains are moving to the divert tracks are generated. For instance, the first trace in Fig. 8 involves only train movement on the main track, and is therefore not re-generated, but is rather re-used from the base model. However, the second trace in Fig. 8 involves train movement of the second track, which is affected by the transformation, and is therefore re-generated for the product model.

The reduction in the amount of generated traces depends, not only on the particular CVL transformation, but also on the given test-case. Our experience shows that by performing minor modifications to a base model, fewer of the traces are affected, and thus the number of traces that are re-generated is smaller. For our test-case given by the predicate in Fig. 7 applied to our product model, we reduced the number of generated traces by approximately 30%. This is also what we intuitively expected, due to the fact that train *T1* can choose between three tracks when entering the station, while train *T2* must exit the station from the main track. According to the analysis, only traces involving the second and the third track must be re-generated, yielding about 67% of the traces.

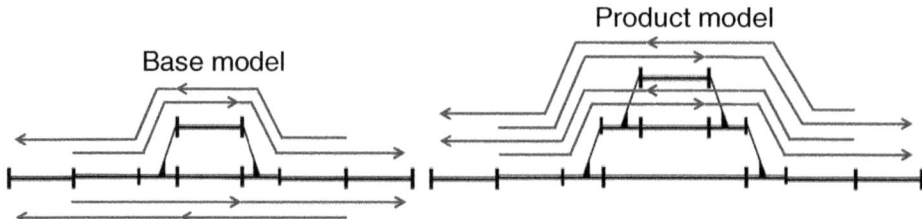

Fig. 13. Traces involving these train movements must be generated

During this work we have experienced that for some test-cases it can be an inconsistency between the pre-condition and the base model elements that are modified, such that it is not possible to determine the start state properly. Recall the test-case illustrated in Fig. 6. For this test-case, assume that train *T2* is positioned at *LS6* instead of *LS5*. Since *LS6* is replaced in the CVL transformation, the start position of train *T2* in the product model is not the same. For ensuring correctness, all traces representing the oracle for such a test-case must be re-generated. Note that it is possible to predict the new start position based on the base model elements that are replacing the original objects. We elaborate on a method for such prediction in [25].

When all the necessary new traces are generated for the product model, our algorithm picks all the traces from the base model that are still valid for the product model. All of these traces form the new testing oracle for a test-case valid for the product model. Note that the amount of time used to generate a trace is considerably higher than the time used to fetch it from a previous generated set of traces.

6   Discussion

The approach has been implemented and evaluated using various TCL models and CVL models. We have extended both the TCL and CVL editors with capability to invoke the Alloy Analyzer and perform the analysis automatically.

Since Alloy is based on SAT solving technology, it quickly runs into the *state-space explosion problem*. Thus, we have optimized the Alloy model using *partial instances* to avoid certain static calculations being performed on analysis time. Instead of using fields and facts to specify how the TCL model is connected, we use constant functions. Using this optimization, the Alloy Analyzer does not have to populate fields to calculate a relation, but can rather use a constant function to obtain it. Implementing this optimization results in a 1/10 reduction of analysis time.

Our experiences show that the specification of oracles can be even more productive using product line technology. By specifying a product line of stations, we optimize the development of the TCL models themselves, which benefits the whole process (including both methods). However, based on an impact analysis of the variability model in a product line, we further improve the specification of oracles by avoiding re-generation of traces.

For a user to be able to quickly grasp the train movement involved in a trace, or set of traces, the extension of the TCL editor also includes a tool for highlighting traces. This can give the user further confidence as traces can easily be checked manually using the concrete (graphical) syntax.

7   Related Work

Peter and Parnas [17] present an approach for generating testing oracles based on program documentation. They use formal documentation of the behavior of a program to generate an oracle deciding the outcome of the test-cases. This is similar to our approach, even though their comparison is not based on the use of traces. Since our approach is based on the use of Alloy, it offers automatic tool support for generating and checking the traces involved in the oracle.

Memon et al. [14, 15] generate testing oracles for graphical user interfaces (GUI). They use a formal model of the GUI and the test-case to calculate the expected states for every action in the test-case. They present a prototype implementation in C. Our approach is also based on a formal model of the behavior, but is, however, not limited to GUIs. Furthermore, we use automatic analysis offered by the Alloy Analyzer to perform the generation and checking of the outcome of test-cases.

Our approach is closely related to model-based testing and software product line testing, where a lot of work has been performed. Neto et al. [16] present a systematic review of model-based testing approaches. Out of 406 papers they selected 27, which were analyzed thoroughly. Utting et al. [26] give a taxonomy of model-based testing describing seven different approaches to model-based testing. They also classify several existing model-based testing tools. Furthermore, Shafique and Labiche [19] present a systematic review of model-based testing tool support.

For software product line testing Engström et al. [4] give a systematic survey of product line testing approaches. In their survey 64 papers are categorized into seven categories, ranging from test management to system and acceptance testing. Lamancha et al. [13] present another systematic review of approaches for software product line testing. They have obtained 23 studies that are categorized into seven different categories, similar to [4]. Pohl and Metzger [18] discuss issues in software product line testing, and suggests how they can be addressed. Uzuncaova et al. [27, 28] present an approach using incremental test generation to test product line models represented by feature models. Each feature of a program is defined as an Alloy formula, which is used to generate incremental tests.

Other related work includes the definition of operational semantics and the use of traces in Alloy. Kelsen and Ma [12] perform a comparison between using Alloy and using traditional techniques to formalize modeling languages. They discovered that Alloy enables automatic analysis and offers a uniform notation. Jacob [10] describes how to use Alloy to model trace specifications for verifying safety-properties. Similar to our approach, he also uses the *ordering* utility offered by Alloy to create traces.

Kanso et al. [11] present a small case-study of an approach for using SAT solver technology to perform automated verification of railway interlocking systems. They report on successful verification of smaller examples of railway interlocking systems. Our approach is based on Alloy, which also uses SAT solver technology.

8   Conclusion and Future Work

This paper has presented an approach for deciding the testing oracles for a set of test-cases based on a formal specification of the operational semantics of a DSL. We used

Alloy for specifying the semantics and the test-cases, and performed automatic analysis to generate traces, representing the expected outcome of executing the test-cases. Our experimentation with the approach shows that it works well for small and medium sized station models. Furthermore, we illustrated that the approach can take advantage of product line technology, and the application of variability models, to reduce the necessary analysis time by re-using preserved traces.

We see further development of the approach as important future work. This includes automatic generation of the predicates (in Alloy) representing the test-cases, stopping the cascading effects of a particular test-case, and automatic execution of the test-cases on the implementation of the system.

Acknowledgements. The work presented here has been developed within the MoSiS project ITEA 2 – ip06035 and the Verde project ITEA 2 – ip8020 parts of the Eureka framework.

References

1. Andoni, A., Daniliuc, D., Khurshid, S., Marinov, D.: Evaluating the Small Scope Hypothesis, MIT CSAIL MIT-LCS-TR-921 (2003)
2. EMF, Eclipse Modeling Framework,
   http://www.eclipse.org/modeling/emf/
3. Endresen, J., Carlson, E., Moen, T., Alme, K.-J., Haugen, Ø., Olsen, G.K., Svendsen, A.: Train Control Language - Teaching Computers Interlocking. In: Computers in Railways XI (COMPRAIL 2008), Toledo, Spain (2008)
4. Engström, E., Runeson, P.: Software Product Line Testing - a Systematic Mapping Study. Information and Software Technology 53, 2–13 (2011)
5. Fleurey, F., Haugen, Ø., Møller-Pedersen, B., Olsen, G.K., Svendsen, A., Zhang, X.: A Generic Language and Tool for Variability Modeling, SINTEF, Oslo, Norway, Technical Report SINTEF A13505 (2009)
6. GMF, Eclipse Graphical Modeling Framework,
   http://www.eclipse.org/modeling/gmf/
7. Haugen, O., Møller-Pedersen, B., Oldevik, J., Olsen, G.K., Svendsen, A.: Adding Standardized Variability to Domain Specific Languages. In: SPLC 2008, Limerick, Ireland (2008)
8. Haugen, Ø., Husa, K., Runde, R., Stølen, K.: Stairs Towards Formal Design with Sequence Diagrams. Software and Systems Modeling 4, 355–357 (2005)
9. Jackson, D.: Software Abstractions: Logic, Language, and Analysis. The MIT Press (2006)
10. Jacob, J.: Trace Specifications in Alloy. In: Frappier, M., Glässer, U., Khurshid, S., Laleau, R., Reeves, S. (eds.) ABZ 2010. LNCS, vol. 5977, pp. 105–117. Springer, Heidelberg (2010)
11. Kanso, K., Moller, F., Setzer, A.: Automated Verification of Signalling Principles in Railway Interlocking Systems. Electron. Notes Theor. Comput. Sci. 250, 19–31 (2009)
12. Kelsen, P., Ma, Q.: A Lightweight Approach for Defining the Formal Semantics of a Modeling Language. In: Czarnecki, K., Ober, I., Bruel, J.-M., Uhl, A., Völter, M. (eds.) MODELS 2008. LNCS, vol. 5301, pp. 690–704. Springer, Heidelberg (2008)
13. Lamancha, B.P., Usaola, M.P., Velthius, M.P.: Software Product Line Testing - a Systematic Review. In: Boris, S., José, C., Alpesh, R. (eds.) International Conference on Software and Data Technologies - ICSOFT, pp. 23–30. INSTICC Press (2009)

14. Memon, A.M., Pollack, M.E., Soffa, M.L.: Automated Test Oracles for Guis. In: Proceedings of the 8th ACM SIGSOFT International Symposium on Foundations of Software Engineering: Twenty-First Century Applications, pp. 30–39. ACM, San Diego (2000)
15. Memon, A.M., Pollack, M.E., Soffa, M.L.: Automated Test Oracles for Guis. SIGSOFT Softw. Eng. Notes 25, 30–39 (2000)
16. Neto, A.C.D., Subramanyan, R., Vieira, M., Travassos, G.H.: A Survey on Model-Based Testing Approaches: A Systematic Review. In: 1st ACM International Workshop on Empirical Assessment of Software Engineering Languages and Technologies: held in conjunction with the 22nd IEEE/ACM International Conference on Automated Software Engineering (ASE 2007), pp. 31–36. ACM, Atlanta (2007)
17. Peters, D., Parnas, D.L.: Generating a Test Oracle from Program Documentation: Work in Progress. In: 1994 ACM SIGSOFT International Symposium on Software Testing and Analysis, Seattle, Washington, United States (1994)
18. Pohl, K., Metzger, A.: Software Product Line Testing. Commun. ACM. 49, 78–81 (2006)
19. Shafique, M., Labiche, Y.: A Systematic Review of Model Based Testing Tool Support, Technical Report SCE-10-04, Department of Systems and Computer Engineering, Carleton University, Ottawa, Canada (2010)
20. Svendsen, A., Haugen, Ø., Møller-Pedersen, B.: Analyzing Variability: Capturing Semantic Ripple Effects. In: France, R.B., Kuester, J.M., Bordbar, B., Paige, R.F. (eds.) ECMFA 2011. LNCS, vol. 6698, pp. 253–269. Springer, Heidelberg (2011)
21. Svendsen, A., Haugen, Ø., Møller-Pedersen, B.: Specifying a Testing Oracle for Train Stations. In: Model-Driven Engineering, Verification, and Validation: Integrating Verification and Validation in MDE Workshop (MoDeVVa 2011). Co-located with MODELS 2011. ACM, Wellington (2011)
22. Svendsen, A., Haugen, Ø., Møller-Pedersen, B.: Using Variability Models to Reduce Verification Effort of Train Station Models. In: 18th Asia Pacific Software Engineering Conference (APSEC 2011). IEEE, Ho Chi Minh City (2011)
23. Svendsen, A., Møller-Pedersen, B., Haugen, Ø., Endresen, J., Carlson, E.: Formalizing Train Control Language: Automating Analysis of Train Stations. In: Ning, B., Brebbia, C.A. (eds.) Comprail 2010, pp. 245–256. WIT Press, Beijing (2010)
24. Svendsen, A., Olsen, G.K., Endresen, J., Moen, T., Carlson, E.J., Alme, K.-J., Haugen, Ø.: The Future of Train Signaling. In: Czarnecki, K., Ober, I., Bruel, J.-M., Uhl, A., Völter, M. (eds.) MODELS 2008. LNCS, vol. 5301, pp. 128–142. Springer, Heidelberg (2008)
25. Svendsen, A., Zhang, X., Haugen, Ø., Møller-Pedersen, B.: Towards Evolution of Generic Variability Models. In: Kienzle, J. (ed.) MODELS 2011 Workshops. LNCS, vol. 7167, pp. 53–67. Springer, Heidelberg (2012)
26. Utting, M., Pretschner, A., Legeard, B.: A Taxonomy of Model-Based Testing, Working paper series. Department of Computer Science, University of Waikato, Hamilton, New Zealand (2006)
27. Uzuncaova, E., Garcia, D., Khurshid, S., Batory, D.: Testing Software Product Lines Using Incremental Test Generation. In: Proceedings of the 19th International Symposium on Software Reliability Engineering, pp. 249–258. IEEE Computer Society (2008)
28. Uzuncaova, E., Khurshid, S., Batory, D.: Incremental Test Generation for Software Product Lines. IEEE Trans. Softw. Eng. 36, 309–322 (2010)

Use Cases for Context Aware Model-Checking

Amine Raji and Philippe Dhaussy

LISyC – ENSTA-Bretagne
Université Européenne de Bretagne
Rue François Verny 29806, Brest Cedex 9, France
{amine.raji,philippe.dhaussy}@ensta-bretagne.fr

Abstract. Despite technical improvements in current verification tools, the increasing size of developed systems makes the detection of design defects more difficult. Context-aware Model-Checking is an effective technique for automating software verifications considering specific environmental conditions. Unfortunately, few existing approaches provide support for this crucial task and mainly rely on significant effort and expertise of the engineer. We previously proposed a DSL (called CDL) to facilitate the formalization of requirements and contexts. Experiences has shown that manually writing CDL models is difficult and error prone task. In this paper, we propose a tool-supported framework to automatically generate CDL models using eXtended Use Cases (XUC). XUC models consistently link use cases with scenarios with respect to the domain specification vocabulary of the model to be checked. We also propose a requirements specification language to fill the gap between textual requirements and CDL properties. An industrial case study is presented to illustrate the effectiveness of XUCs to generate correct and complete CDL models for formal model analysis.

1 Introduction

Context aware verification techniques can reduce the complexity of the verification by limiting the scope of the verification to precise system modes related to some specific environmental conditions [1]. In the case of reactive embedded systems, the environment has an exceedingly powerful impact on a particular system component either because the latter needs to adapt in response to changing external conditions or because it relies on resources whose availability is subject to continuous change. Consequently, it is relevant to verify these systems in certain characteristic environmental conditions. In other words, checking some properties over specific system modes (use cases) is less complex since we are dealing with precise environmental behavior.

We previously presented a *Context description language* (CDL) [2] to precisely capture and formalize system contexts and properties to be checked. In [1], we evaluated CDL over six aeronautic and military industrial case studies. The conclusions of this evaluation is that the explicit consideration of contexts reduces considerably the size of the state space used for formal verifications. For instance, some properties, that led to state explosion without considering

J. Kienzle (Ed.): MODELS 2011 Workshops, LNCS 7167, pp. 202–216, 2012.

contexts, are verifiable within the CDL approach. However, due to the complexity of the System Under Verification (SUV), the number of CDL models required to precisely formalize contexts might be important (i.e. 15 CDL were required to verify 38 property on a 4 kloc[1] SDL model [1]). In addition, manually writing CDL models is a difficult and error prone task for engineers without formal methods background.

In this paper, we address these limitations to improve the scalability and the practicability of our context-aware model verification within industrial settings. Our approach bridges the gap between user specification models and CDL models by automating the generation of contexts. This is performed thanks to a generative process that consists of three phases. First, in the *context specification* phase, we have proposed an extension to the UML metamodel to capture important interactions between the system[2] and its environment. This extension, called *eXtended Use Case* (*XUC*), combines use cases and scenarios to model precise contexts. Scenarios are directly specified into the use case body using a constrained natural language which is close to user requirements. In the *activities derivation* phase, *XUCs* are used to automatically generate a UML activity diagram describing the complete behavior of each use case. Finally, in the *behavior synthesis* phase, behavioral models of environment actors are synthesized from obtained activities by means of the proposed synthesis algorithm.

In addition to the generation of CDL context models from XUCs, we propose to automatically generate CDL properties from an intermediate requirement specification language. This language, that we call URM (User Requirement Models) aims to fill the gap between natural language textual requirements and formal CDL properties. For this, we use a constrained natural language and property specification patterns to ease requirements formalization.

This paper is organized as follows. Section 2 presents a real world case study and summarizes background information on CDL language and describes the verification technology used. Then, it highlights the motivation for this paper. Section 3 details our approach. Section 4 illustrates the application of our proposal to the provided case study and reports on our experiments and results. Section 5 discusses how the approach relates to other applications in industrial engineering processes and presents related work. Section 6 provides a summary and some remarks about future work.

2   Motivation

2.1   The *S_CP* Case Study

To illustrate our approach, we present the *S_CP* case study. *S_CP* is the software part of an anti-aircraft system developed by our industrial partner. Figure 1 shows an excerpt of the *S_CP* use cases and an example of interactions.

---

[1] kloc = kilo line of code = 1000 x line of code.
[2] By system we mean the model to be validated.

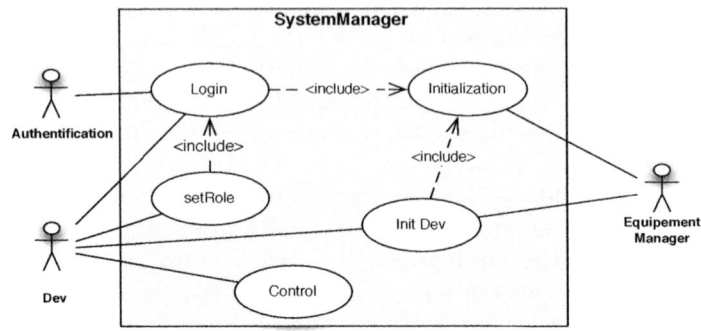

Fig. 1. S_CP use cases

S_CP controls the internal modes of the anti-aircraft system, its physical devices (radars, sensors, actuators...) and their actions in response to incoming signals from the environment. The operator can interact with the system through Devices (*Devs*). S_CP controls login operations and assigns roles (with specific permission) to each device. In this paper, we focus on the *Devs* behavior to ensure that the S_CP remains hacker-proof.

The objective of our study is to perform formal verification of timed and event ordering requirements. Below is an example of such requirements.

ReqS_CP_Init: *"If the SM is in state Standby, and the mission is not yet selected, upon reception of a valid EvtRequestLoginHmi message from the HMI, the SM shall send the following messages to the HMI in this order : (1) EvtAckHmi with result to TRUE, (2) EvtCurrentUserHmi with Username to currentUsername."*

2.2   Context-Aware Verification with CDL

Context-aware verification aims to reduce the complexity of the verification by explicitly identifying relevant contexts in which the property must hold. CDL [1] is a DSL proposed to capture and formalize contexts and properties of the SUV. Contexts correspond to well-defined operational phases, such as initialization, reconfiguration, degraded modes, etc. CDL contributes to overcome the combinatorial explosion by allowing partial verification on restricted scenarios specified by the context automata. When considering contexts, properties are verified only in relevant contexts.

CDL models have well grounded formal semantics described as a set of traces [3]. The property description language in CDL is based on property description patterns [4]. Patterns are textual templates that capture common logical and temporal properties and that can be instantiated in a specific context.

The purpose of linking properties to specific system configurations is to specify/restrict the context in which the property to verify is meaningful.

We have evaluated the use of the CDL approach over six aeronautic and military industrial case studies [1] and demonstrated its effectiveness. CDL contributes to overcome the combinatorial explosion by allowing partial verification on restricted scenarios specified by the context automata. However, CDL is a *low level* language that requires design details at early development phases to produce sufficiently precise specifications. For instance, scenarios described in CDL are expressed in the form of basic send/receive events which is difficult to precisely determine at early development process phases. Also, the number of CDL models required to precisely formalize contexts might be high according to the system complexity and the number of interacting actors. So, manually writing CDL models is a difficult and error prone task for non-expert users. For instance, when writing CDL models, engineers have to explicitly reference system *events* with corresponding arguments to form *interactions*. These interactions are then composed into *activities*. Thus, there are several error sources in this process (i.e. argument mismatch, typing error in events/interactions names).

In addition to the context specification, the transition from textual requirement found in requirements documents to CDL properties is not a straightforward activity. Despite the facilities offered by property patterns used in CDL, the gap between natural language requirements and CDL still important.

In the rest of this paper, we propose solutions to these drawbacks to improve the scalability of formal verification activities and effectively manage the complexity of industrial models.

3   Approach

We propose a use case based DSL called eXtended Use Cases with an algebraic framework for mapping XUC models to CDL models. We also proposed a textual requirements description language (called URM) to ease the transition from requirement documents and CDL properties. We then defined and implemented model transformations to derive CDL models from user defined XUC models and requirements. XUC scenarios are specified using sequences of simple English sentences. These sentences are expressed in a controlled natural language and describe both normal and erroneous scenarios to precisely formalize system/ environment interactions. Moreover, interaction scenarios and URM requirements rely on a knowledge base corresponding to the system domain specification to ensure the consistency of the XUC model with the models under validation.

3.1   From eXtended Use Cases to CDL Contexts

We propose to extend traditional UML use cases with the capability of describing interaction scenarios between the system and context entities (actors). Figure 2 shows the XUC metamodel. The main class is the *eXtendedUseCase* class which is a specialization of the *uml::UseCase* class [5].

An extended use cases is defined as follow:

Definition 1. (eXtended Use Cases.) *We assume that an XUC specification is denoted by a 8-tuple*

$(MS, E, H, Ac, St, Ps, T, \lambda)$ *where:*

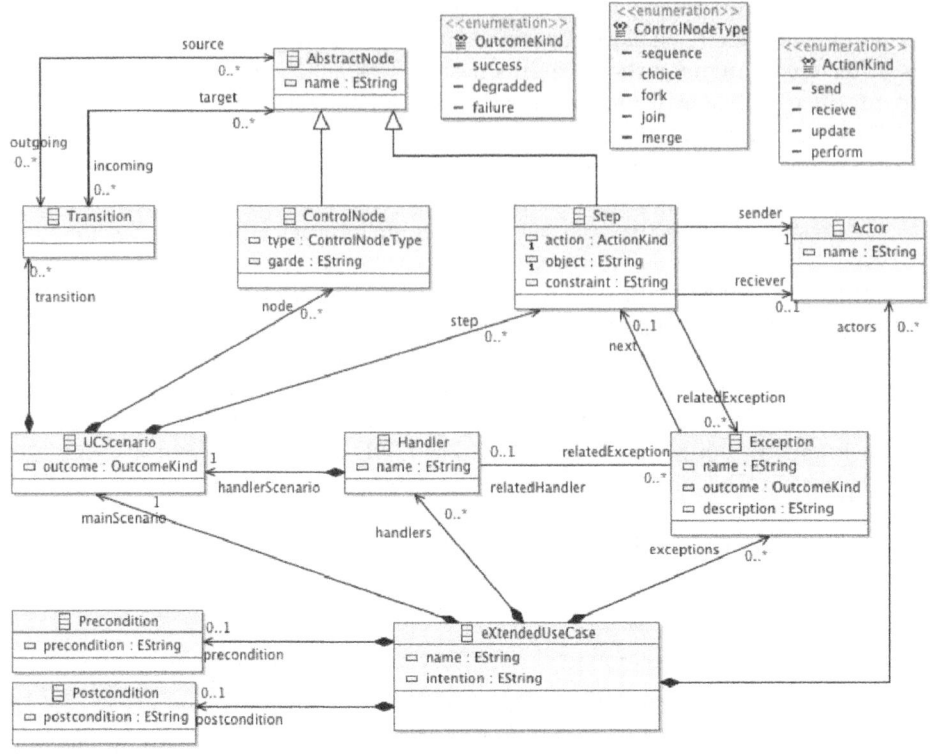

Fig. 2. eXtended Use Case metamodel

- $MS = S \cup T$ represents the main success scenario of an XUC which describes the standard way of achieving the use case. Where $S = St \cup Ps$ is the set of steps of the scenario.
- E is the set of exceptions that might occur during the main scenario steps.
- H is the set of handlers that describe the way the system might deal with identified exceptions.
- Ac is the set of actors involved in the XUC
- St is the set of steps. Each step $s \in S$ is a triple (tr, m, re) of a message $m \in M$, a transmitter tr and a receiver re. M denote the set of all messages. Let Ev denote the set of events such as an event is a pair of kind and message:$(k, m) \in \{!, ?\} \times M$.
- $Ps = SP \cup EP \cup Fk \cup Jn \cup Ch$ is the set of Pseudo Steps. Where SP denote the set of start points, EP, the set of end points, Fk the set of fork nodes, Jn the set of joint nodes and Ch the set of choice nodes.
- T is the set of edges connecting steps to each other.
- λ is a transition relation defined as: $\lambda = T \times S \cup Ps \times T$.

The idea behind this extension is to gather all useful information about the system behavior and its interactions with environment actors. In fact, many exceptional situations might appear during the execution of an application. The difficulties arising during the verification process are usually related to the lack of relevant information about system behavior, especially when an exception endangers the normal execution of a use case [6,7]. To prevent this problem, we propose the XUC language which foresees these exceptional situations and documents how the system should deal with them. This approach leads engineers to systematically investigate all possible exceptions arising in the environment to which the system may be exposed. Handlers are invoked when an exception occurs.

The steps defined in each scenario (main scenario or handler scenarios) are composed using pseudo steps as follow:

$$
\begin{aligned}
XUC ::= \quad & e \\
| \quad & S_0 \longrightarrow N \\
N ::= \quad & e \\
| \quad & l : S_f \\
| \quad & l : Merge(N) \\
| \quad & l : Fork(N_1, N_2) \\
| \quad & l : x.Join(N) \\
| \quad & l : Decision(\langle g \rangle N_1, \langle \neg g \rangle N_2)
\end{aligned}
$$

- $l : S_f$ represents final nodes
- $l : Merge(N)$ (resp. $l : x.Join(N)$) define the *merge* (resp. *join*) nodes. the node *join* represents a synchronization, i.e. the node N is traversed iff all transitions are active. The node N is then active. The x variable denotes the number of incoming transitions to the node *join*.
- $l : Fork(N_1, N_2)$ represents the node *fork* (or parallel). Parameters N_1 et N_2 represents target nodes of the outgoing transitions.
- $l : Decision(\langle g \rangle N_1, \langle \neg g \rangle N_2)$ represents decision node. The decision is performed between two nodes N_1 et N_2 considering a boolean expression g.

We also formalized the include relationship between XUC use cases (as shown by the figure 1). This formalization is inspired from the work of Stevens *et. al* [8]. Thus we defined inclusion points to include behaviors defined in other included use cases as follow:

Definition 2. (Inclusion Point.) *is, in a base use case (noted XUC_b), the point where the behavior of the included use case (noted XUC_i) starts. At the end of the execution of XUC_b behavior, the XUC_i continue its execution from this point.*

- *Each inclusion point is relative to one and only one XUC_i such as $XUC_i \neq Xuc_b$*
- *The inclusion point can be used as a step s in the scenarios of XUC_b*

– In the inclusion relation (noted $XUC_b \xrightarrow{I} XUC_i$), the transition targeting the inclusion point replace the transition leaving the initial point S_0 of XUC_i and the transition targeting the final node S_f of XUC_i is replaced by the transition targeting the node just after the inclusion point of XUC_b.

Figure 3 shows the use of the inclusion between XUCs, directly inside the interactions scenarios, of the use case diagram presented in figure 1.

```
XUC login

body {
    include Initialization
    step s1: HMI sends evtRequestLogin to SM
    step s2: SM sends checkRights to Authentification
    step s3: SM receives ackEvtRequestLogin from Authentification
    step s4: SM sends evtAvaliableMissions to HMI
}

exception badIdentifier{
    description 'The user enter wrong identifier/password three times'
    relatedStep s2
    relatedHandler badIdentifierHandler
    next s1
    outcome failure
}

handler badIdentifierHandler{
    step h1: SM sends ErrorFailedMessage to HMI
    step h2: SM sends LockAccount to Authentification
}
```

```
XUC Initialization

body{
    step s1: HMI sends login to SM
    step s2: SM sends check to Authentification
    step s3: Authentification sends ackCheckOK to SM
    step s4: SM sends ackLoginOK to HMI
    step s5: SM sends currentUserID to HMI
    step s6: SM sends currentUserMission to HMI
}

exception MessageLost{
    description 'In that case that the response to a message
                 is not received within d_max duration'
    relatedStep s3,s4
    relatedHandler MessageLostHandler
    next s2
}

handler MessageLostHandler{
    step h1: SM sends check to Authentification
}
```

```
XUC setRole

body {
    include login
    step s1: SM sends evtCurrentActivity to HMI
    step s2: SM receives ackevtCurrentActivity from HMI
    step s3: SM sends evtAvalibleMissions to HMI
    step s4: HMI sends evtSelectMission to SM
    step s5: SM sends setContextMode to Authentification
}
```

Fig. 3. XUC models

Figure 3 shows the XUC corresponding to the *login, setRole* and *Initialization* use cases. *Steps* are declared using the keyword *step* followed with the step identifier (S1, S2,...). Edges are not explicitly described in the concrete syntax to keep the XUC syntax as concise as possible. Our translation algorithm handle the appropriate instantiation of transitions based on the ordering of steps and control nodes.

3.2   Mapping XUC Scenarios to CDL

Figure 4 shows an overview of our verification approach. The shaded rectangle highlights the contribution of this paper that bridges the gap between user specification models and CDL models by automating the generation of contexts.

The entry point of our approach is the elaboration of an extended form of use cases (*XUC*). We generate activity diagrams from XUCs because CDL are special cases of UML activity diagrams[3]. Our model transformation is partially inspired by the work presented by Gutierrez *et al.* [9]. Authors in the cited article propose a method for representing functional requirements by automatically transforming use cases into activity diagrams. However, proposed use cases do not support the handling of identified exceptions. In this paper, we propose a model transformation of *XUCs* with handlers into UML2 activity diagrams.

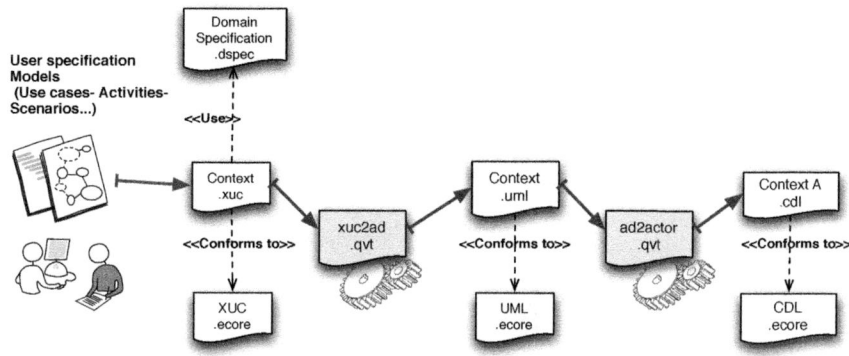

Fig. 4. Approach overview

Each exception identified in the use case is represented by a *decisionNode* in the activity diagram with a boolean condition. Additionally with the decision node, an *activity* representing the exception handler is generated. If no handler is defined for the considered exception, an *ActivityFinalNode* is generated and linked to the decision node using a new *controlFlow*. Generated *ActivityFinalNodes* are labeled with a stereotype corresponding to the *OutputKind* of the related exception.

Then we use the generated activity diagram of the considered use case to extract the behavior of each actor involved in it. For this extraction process, we propose an algorithmic approach to generate a separate activity diagram for each identified actor in the considered use case. The algorithm extracts nodes and edges related to the same actor (based on *activity Partitions*) then links them together using control flow. To preserve the semantics of the global behavior described in the source activity diagram, events triggering the flow between actions and coming from the system or other actors are added to the target activity diagram. These events are represented with instances of *AcceptEventAction* and *SendSignalAction* classes [5]. Thus, the flow between actions in the activity of a specific actor is conditioned with the reception of the corresponding event.

3.3   User Requirements Models

We propose a constrained natural language based on property description patterns to ease the formalization of CDL properties. We also use this language to describe the steps of XUC scenarios. The motivation behind the use of constrained natural language is the remain accessible for domain experts. Scenarios description is usually provided in requirements document as natural language sentences. We proposed a grammar to be able to parse such textual descriptions to automatically generate scenario models. Our grammar is inspired form the work of H. Zhu *et al.* [10,11] on human/machine interactions.

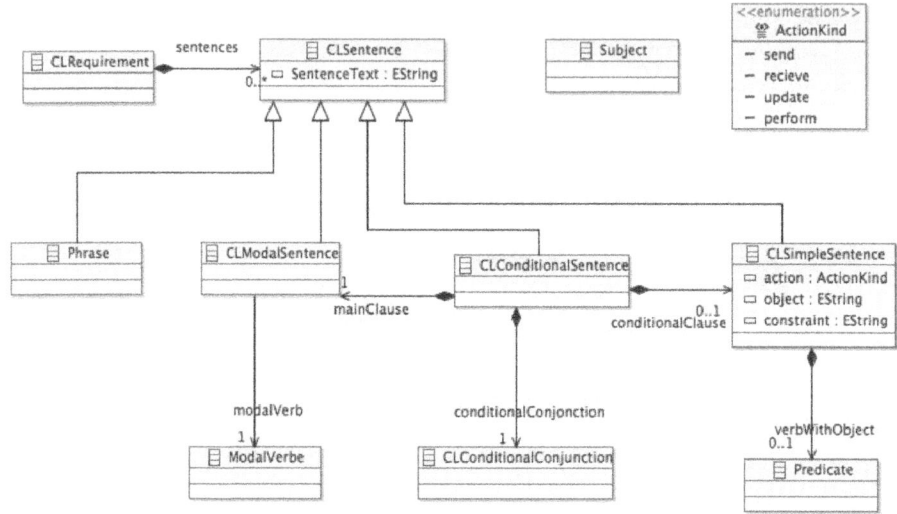

Fig. 5. URM metamodel

In URM, requirements are presented as a composition of Constrained Language Sentences (figure 5. Each sentence is one of the following:

- *CLSimpleSentence*: sentence can be defined using two phrases: a subject phrase and a predicate phrase. Subject can include any notion from a domain vocabulary.
- *Phrase*: simple natural language phrase used if the requirement is described using a non supported structure.
- *CLModalSentence*: represents a CLSimpleSentence extended with a ModalVerb.
- *CLConstrainedSentence*: is an ordered set of two structured sentences. First of the sentences, forming a conditional sentence describes state, possibility or in general, a condition in which the activity expressed in the second sentence can occur.

So the structure of the requirement **ReqS_CP_Init** presented in section 2.1 is as follow: | **if** *CLSimplePhrase*, **Then** *CLModalPhrase* |. The condition part is composed of the concatenation of three CLSimpleSentences : (1) "the SM is in standby", (2) "the mission is not selected", (3) "upon reception of...".

The modal part is composed of actions that the SM have to perform in a defined order : "the SM shall send the following messages to the HMI in this order...".

We parse such requirements based on the constrained natural language and property specification patterns in addition to the use of domain specification models (presented in the next section). After the application of our requirement formalization process[3] we get the following representation of the considered requirement.

In the context of *"the* SM *is in state Standby"*
and *"the mission is not yet selected"*
It is always the case that if *"a valid* EvtRequestLoginHmi *message from the* HMI*" **occurs***
then *the* SM ***shall send*** *the following messages to the HMI **in this order** :
(1)* EvtAckHmi ***with*** *result = TRUE, (2)* EvtCurrentUserHmi ***with*** *User-*
name = currentUsername,

3.4   Capturing Domain Specification

To ensure the consistency of the provided XUC with the model under verification, we propose a simple domain specification DSL (called *DSpec*) that references all domain elements to be used in the definition of the XUC. Figure 6 shows an excerpt of the abstract syntax of *DSpec*.

DSpec models a simple knowledge representation of the SUV. It is defined as a special kind of structural domain representation that explicitly focuses on domain elements. Notions refers to all events, messages, arguments used in the description of system/context interactions. *Dspec* models are automatically extracted from the system specification models (class diagrams- state machines - sequence diagrams) to prevent errors during manual copy.

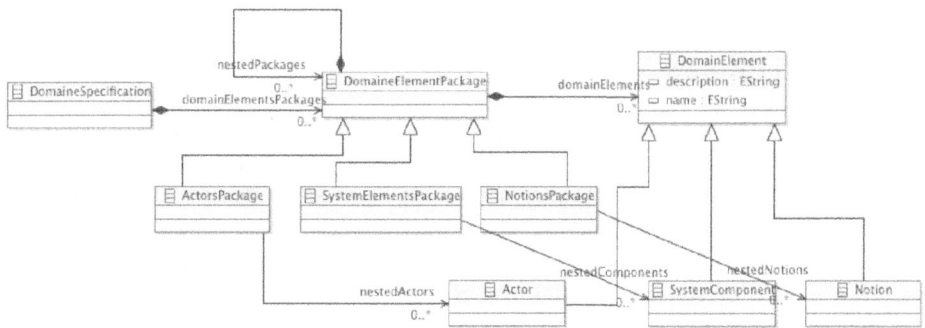

Fig. 6. Excerpt of the Domain Specification metamodel

---

[3] This process is not presented in this paper because of page limitation constraints.

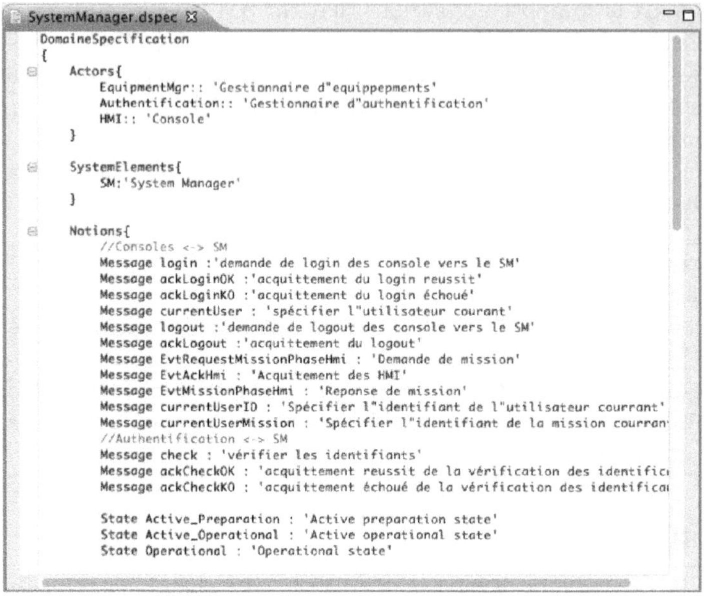

Fig. 7. Excerpt of the Domain Specification metamodel

Figure 7 shows an excerpt of the S_CP domain specification. The XUC editor references domain elements defined in the *DSpec* file to ensure the consistency with the provided XUC models. We have implemented our XUC editor into the Eclipse environment using GMF (for the use case diagram part) and xText to facilitate the description of context scenarios thanks to the features it proposes (syntax highlighting, autocompletion of domain elements names, error marks...). References to the domain elements defined in the *DSpec* file are directly implemented in the grammar file defining the XUC DSL.

4   Experiments and Results

The experiment set-up consisted in verifying real-time properties using CDL and the OBP tool-set [1] on a Intel Core2-Duo desktop machine with 2Go of RAM running a 32 bits Linux Ubuntu 9.10. The context part of CDL models was generated using the approach described in this paper. Properties are then verified using TINA-Selt [12] model checker. This section reports on the verification of a set of operational requirements of the S_CP case study introduced in Section 2.

We first used design models to automatically derive a domain specification in the form of a *DSpec* file. Models used for this step are class diagrams and sequence diagrams provided by our partner in the form of a Rhapsody project. Figure 6 shows an excerpt of the generated S_CP domain specification which consists in the set of actors, system components their corresponding attributes and operations. Generated domain specification is then used as a reference when writing XUCs.

Table 1. Metrics of the CDL generation approach for the S_CP case study

XUC	Number of generated CDL	Average line count	Average of referenced concepts
Login	12	156	14
Initialization	10	98	11
InitHMI	9	127	9
SetRole	4	84	7
Control	25	120	13

Then we specified 5 XUCs corresponding to the use case diagram of Figure 1. Figure 3 shows an excerpt of the constructed XUCs for the *login* use case. After applying our CDL generation algorithm for the *login* XUC. We obtain 12 CDL model representing all extracted control structures for different handlers. For instance, two CDL models can be generated from the *login* XUC shown in figure 1. One for the main scenario without the occurrence of *HmiNotLogged* exception and one considering the exception that includes the *h1* handler steps. Table 1 resumes the amount of generated CDL models, the average of corresponding line count and the average number of referenced domain specification concepts for the S_CP case study.

Figure 8 shows an excerpt of the generated bihavioral models of actors participating in the *login* XUC in the form of UML activity diagrams.

Fig. 8. Excerpt of generated behavioral models

The system model was manually translated into Fiacre code [13]. We used the OBP-toolset [1] to check simple ordering properties such as *ReqS_CP_Init*. Each property is then translated into an observer automaton using OBP toolset.

During our experiments, we noted that the majority of requirements were described in the available requirement documentation. XUC models were constructed, on the one hand, from scenarios described in the design models and, on the other hand, from textual requirement documents. Two major difficulties arose: (i) this description is usually incomplete with regard to properties to check. For instance, some relevant contexts information needs additional interviews with domain experts in order to explicit all context assumption and to clear ambiguities (especially during exceptional scenarios). Furthermore, (ii) some textual requirements can lead to many possible interpretations. Others implicitly refer to an applicable configuration, operational phase or history setup without defining it. Such information, necessary for verification, can only be deduced by manually analyzing design models and requirements documents and/or through discussions with requirements engineers.

The use of XUC as a use case oriented framework to formally and explicitly define contexts and properties overcomes these two difficulties. XUC notation is close to existing artifacts (UML models and textual specification documents) and thus readable by engineers[4]. Feedback from our industrial collaborators indicates that XUC models enhance communication between developers with different levels of experience and backgrounds.

5   Related Works and Discussion

Several works have been proposed in the literature to describe what happens inside UML use cases in order to generate behavioral models including [14,15,9]. Bastide proposes in [15] the integration of user tasks models (called CTT model) to provide an unambiguous model of the behavior of UML use cases. The meta-model resulting from this integration defines the use case main scenario elements. However, exception definition and handlers were not considered in the proposed metamodel. The authors in [14] and [9] propose an approach to translate use case-based functional requirements into activity charts. The source models are use cases diagrams with the support of inclusion and generalization relationships. However the method is restricted to sequences of use cases and not the behavior of each use case.

The work which is most closely related to ours is [16]. In this work, the authors propose an algorithm that transforms dependability-focused use cases with handlers into activity diagrams. The transformation takes textual use case description as source to produce activity diagram models respecting the use case hierarchy source model. Our approach differs in the sense that we go beyond generating activities corresponding to the use case scenarios. We have proposed an algorithmic way to automatically extract formal behavioral models of each participating actor.

The contribution of our approach for formal verification consist in bridging the gap between CDL models and user models. CDL contributes to overcoming

---

[4] UML2 sequence diagrams are directly imported into XUC editor to generate XUC scenarios by means of a pretty-print-like model transformation.

state explosion issue by means of partial verification on the restricted scenarios (specified by context automata). The XUC DSL is proposed to precisely and easily formalize contexts. In CDL, properties are formalized using property description patterns so that they can be linked to one or several contexts.

XUC models describe system/context interactions in a simple and straightforward yet precise way. Interactions are described using simple sentences composed together using a well grounded semantics. Table 1 highlights the number and the complexity of CDL models generated from specified XUCs. Exceptions and their corresponding handlers scenarios are directly specified in XUCs to precisely describe exceptional situations and provide valuable details for formal analysis. XUCs provide a good abstraction level for verification engineers to specify exceptions and explicitly detail their corresponding handlers. We use constrained natural language to facilitate their specification and reduce the gap between requirements and formal tools since formal code is generated automatically from XUCs. During our experiments, we started from specification documents that are described in natural English. Thus, writing XUC models was a straightforward process.

The collaboration with system engineers has motivated them to consider a more formal approach to express their requirements, which is certainly a positive improvement. In some case studies, many textual requirements can be rewritten more easily with property patterns. Thus, XUC permits a better formal verification appropriation by industrial partners since they are editing UML diagrams which they are familiar with. For example, one of our industrial partners affirmed that editing XUC diagrams helped them to produce more precise context descriptions early in the development process. This helped engineers to quickly model check their requirements and to get early feedback on their design models

6 Conclusion and Future Work

The approach presented in this paper automatically generates environment entity behavior directly from use cases and scenarios. Then, we extract the behavior of each actor participating in the activity in a separate activity diagram. The motivation behind this contribution is to facilitate the use of formal verification techniques by providing early context descriptions with enough precision to feed formal verification tools. To the best of our knowledge, there is no similar work dealing with this particular problem.

As a future work, we will extend our work to deal with the rest of activity control nodes in order to produce more precise activity diagrams. Then, we plan to integrate requirement engineering approaches which aims to link high level user goals with operational properties such as that presented in [17]. We believe the combination of model transformations for the generation of precise context descriptions and goal-oriented requirement engineering approaches for elicitation, elaboration and specification of system requirements can considerably improve the integration of formal methods into software engineering activities.

References

1. Dhaussy, P., Pillain, P.-Y., Creff, S., Raji, A., Le Traon, Y., Baudry, B.: Evaluating Context Descriptions and Property Definition Patterns for Software Formal Validation. In: Schürr, A., Selic, B. (eds.) MODELS 2009. LNCS, vol. 5795, pp. 438–452. Springer, Heidelberg (2009)
2. Dhaussy, P., Boniol, F., De Belloy, S.E., Auvray, J., Landel, E.: Using context descriptions and property definition pattern for software formal verification. Modevva (2008)
3. Dhaussy, P., Creff, S., Plllain, P., Leilde, V.: CDL: a context description language, synthax and semantics, ENSTA-Bretagne, Tech. Rep. (2010)
4. Dwyer, M.B., Avrunin, G.S., Corbett, J.C.: Patterns in Property Specifications for Finite-State Verification. In: International Conference on Software Engineering, pp. 411–420 (1999)
5. OMG, UML 2.1.2 Superstructure, pp. 1–738 (2007)
6. Wang, Z., Elbaum, S., Rosenblum, D.: Automated generation of context-aware tests. In: 29th International Conference on Software Engineering, ICSE 2007, pp. 406–415 (2007)
7. Ben Mokhtar, S., Fournier, D., Georgantas, N., Issarny, V.: Context-Aware Service Composition in Pervasive Computing Environments. In: Guelfi, N., Savidis, A. (eds.) RISE 2005. LNCS, vol. 3943, pp. 129–144. Springer, Heidelberg (2006)
8. Stevens, P.: On Use Cases and Their Relationships in the Unified Modelling Language. In: Hussmann, H. (ed.) FASE 2001. LNCS, vol. 2029, pp. 140–155. Springer, Heidelberg (2001)
9. Gutiérrez, J.J., Nebut, C., Escalona, M.J., Mejías, M., Ramos, I.M.: Visualization of Use Cases through Automatically Generated Activity Diagrams. In: Czarnecki, K., Ober, I., Bruel, J.-M., Uhl, A., Völter, M. (eds.) MODELS 2008. LNCS, vol. 5301, pp. 83–96. Springer, Heidelberg (2008)
10. Zhu, H., Jin, L.: Automating scenario-driven structured requirements engineering. In: The 24th Annual International Computer Software and Applications Conference, COMPSAC 2000, pp. 311–316 (2002)
11. Zhu, H., Jin, L., Diaper, D., Bai, G.: Software requirements validation via task analysis. Journal of Systems and Software 61(2), 145–169 (2002)
12. Berthomieu, B., Ribet, P.O., Vernadat, F.: The tool TINA - Construction of abstract state spaces for Petri Nets and Time Petri Nets. International Journal of Production Research 42(14), 298–304 (2004)
13. Berthomieu, B., Bodeveix, J., Filali, M.: The syntax and semantics of Fiacre, Tech. Rep. (2007)
14. Almendros-Jiménez, J.M., Iribarne, L.: Describing Use Cases with Activity Charts. In: Wiil, U.K. (ed.) MIS 2004. LNCS, vol. 3511, pp. 141–159. Springer, Heidelberg (2005)
15. Bastide, R.: An Integration of Task and Use-Case Meta-models. In: Jacko, J.A. (ed.) HCII 2009, Part I. LNCS, vol. 5610, pp. 579–586. Springer, Heidelberg (2009)
16. Mustafiz, S., Sun, X., Kienzle, J., Vangheluwe, H.: Model-Driven Assessment of Use Cases for Dependable Systems. In: Wang, J., Whittle, J., Harel, D., Reggio, G. (eds.) MODELS 2006. LNCS, vol. 4199, pp. 558–573. Springer, Heidelberg (2006)
17. Alrajeh, D., Kramer, J., Russo, A., Uchitel, S.: Learning operational requirements from goal models. In: Proceedings of the 2009 IEEE 31st International Conference on Software Engineering, pp. 265–275 (2009)

Comparing Six Modeling Approaches

Gunter Mussbacher[1], Wisam Al Abed[2], Omar Alam[2], Shaukat Ali[3],
Antoine Beugnard[4], Valentin Bonnet[2], Rolv Bræk[5], Alfredo Capozucca[6],
Betty H.C. Cheng[7], Urooj Fatima[5], Robert France[8], Geri Georg[8],
Nicolas Guelfi[6], Paul Istoan[6,9], Jean-Marc Jézéquel[10], Jörg Kienzle[2],
Jacques Klein[11], Jean-Baptiste Lézoray[4], Somayeh Malakuti[12],
Ana Moreira[13], An Phung-Khac[4], and Lucy Troup[14]

[1] Department of Systems and Computer Engineering, Carleton University, Canada
gunter@sce.carleton.ca
[2] Software Engineering Laboratory, McGill University, Montreal, Canada
{Wisam.Alabed,Omar.Alam,Valentin.Bonnet}@mail.mcgill.ca,
Joerg.Kienzle@mcgill.ca
[3] Simula Research Laboratory, Norway
shaukat@simula.no
[4] Département Informatique, TELECOM Bretagne, France
{Antoine.Beugnard,jb.lezoray,an.phungkhac}@telecom-bretagne.eu
[5] Department of Telematics, The Norwegian University of Science and Technology, Norway
{rolv.braek,urooj}@item.ntnu.no
[6] LASSY Research Team, University of Luxembourg, Luxembourg
{alfredo.capozucca,nicolas.guelfi}@uni.lu
[7] Department of Computer Science and Engineering, Michigan State University, USA
chengb@cse.msu.edu
[8] Computer Science Department, Colorado State University, Fort Collins, USA
{france,georg}@cs.colostate.edu
[9] ISC Department, CRP Gabriel Lippmann, Luxembourg
istoan@lippmann.lu
[10] INRIA, Centre Rennes – Bretagne Atlantique, Rennes, France
jezequel@irisa.fr
[11] Laboratory for Advanced Software Systems, University of Luxembourg, Luxembourg
jacques.klein@uni.lu
[12] Software Engineering Group, University of Twente, The Netherlands
s.malakuti@ewi.utwente.nl
[13] Universidade Nova de Lisboa, Lisbon, Portugal
amm@di.fct.unl.pt
[14] Department of Psychology, Colorado State University, Fort Collins, USA
Lucy.Troup@colostate.edu

Abstract. While there are many aspect-oriented modeling (AOM) approaches, from requirements to low-level design, it is still difficult to compare them and know under which conditions different approaches are most applicable. This comparison, however, is crucially important to unify existing AOM and more traditional object-oriented modeling (OOM) approaches and to generalize individual approaches into a comprehensive end-to-end method. Such a method

J. Kienzle (Ed.): MODELS 2011 Workshops, LNCS 7167, pp. 217–243, 2012.

does not yet exist. This paper reports on work done at the inaugural Comparing Modeling Approaches (CMA) workshop towards the goal of identifying potential comprehensive methodologies: (i) a common, focused case study for six modeling approaches, (ii) a set of criteria applied to each of the six approaches, and (iii) the assessment results.

Keywords: Aspect-oriented Modeling, Object-oriented Modeling, Comparison Criteria, Case Study.

1   Introduction

The Comparing Modeling Approaches (CMA) workshop at Models 2011 continued work begun at the 2011 AOM Bellairs Workshop[1] where (i) a focused case study based on the original Crisis Management System (CMS) case study [1] was developed and (ii) a collection of criteria to compare aspect-oriented modeling approaches with more traditional object-oriented modeling approaches was initiated.

While there are many approaches to aspect-oriented modeling (AOM), from requirements to low-level design, it is still difficult to compare them and know under which conditions different approaches are most applicable. This comparison, however, is crucially important to unify existing AOM and more traditional object-oriented (OO) approaches and to generalize individual approaches into a comprehensive end-to-end method. Such a method that spans from early requirements to low-level design does not yet exist, and it is not readily evident how such a method would actually work in practice. As part of identifying potential comprehensive methodologies, we must be able to compare different AOM approaches with each other and also against more traditional OO approaches on a focused example, and apply the same criteria to each approach.

A focused case study was developed because experiences with the original Crisis Management System case study [2] indicate that the large scope of this case study led different researchers to explore different parts of the system, making it difficult to compare their approaches. The focused case study is called bCMS [3] and describes a single system and a software product line (SPL). bCMS is narrower than the original CMS case study, thus containing only a few pertinent examples of the different kinds of issues that are found when developing complex systems. However, it is now possible to demonstrate the capabilities of a modeling approach on the *entire* focused CMS case study, thus providing a solid basis for discussion, comparison, and evaluation.

The CMA workshop was structured as follows. Authors of six modeling approaches participated in the CMA workshop. Before the workshop was held, the authors of a modeling approach applied their approach to the bCMS case study. The final bCMS case studies are available at the CMA group in the Repository for Model-Driven Development (ReMoDD)[2]. All resulting case studies as well as the comparison criteria document were then distributed among the authors of all modeling approaches, and

---

[1] http://www.cs.mcgill.ca/~joerg/SEL/AOM_Bellairs_2011.html
[2] http://www.cs.colostate.edu/remodd/v1/content/cmamodels2011

each group of authors assessed each modeling approach based on the provided criteria. Hence, six assessments were collected for each modeling approach. These assessments were contrasted and discussed at the workshop, which lead to the refinement, correction, and further development of comparison criteria during the workshop. The improved comparison criteria were applied again to the modeling approaches after the workshop. Each group of authors first applied the new comparison criteria to their own technique and then reviewed the assessment of all other author groups to finalize the assessment.

The following six modeling approaches, listed in alphabetical order, were assessed. The references for each modeling approach constitute the resources used for the assessment.

- **AoURN** (Aspect-oriented User Requirements Notation)
  AoURN is an AOM approach that is applied to the specification and analysis of requirements. Requirements in AoURN are expressed with the help of aspect-oriented goal and scenario models. Goal models capture the rationale for why a specific solution should be chosen for a system while scenario models describe this solution in more detail. The bCMS single system is modeled.
  Resources: [4, 5, 6, 7, 8, 9]

- **AT** (Activity Theory)
  AT is a framework that enables the modeler to abstractly describe a system in its entirety. It provides a common language for a widely diverse set of stakeholders who will interact directly or indirectly with the system, or who will be affected by it. AT facilitates the discussion and discovery of social, contradictory, implicit or explicit intentions that may be present in the broad system usage context, and is useful for very early requirements elicitation. The bCMS single system is modeled.
  Resources: [10, 11, 12, 13]

- **CCA** (The Cloud Component Approach)
  CCA targets architectural design and evolution. A cloud component (CC) is a distributed component which defines the distribution while bindings are established locally to a node. This hides distribution-specific properties that are usually delegated to bindings inside a CC (e.g., quality of service, deployment, security, and protocols). Hence, these properties become non-functional properties of a CC. CCA implements solutions to various concerns as model transformations and applies them at defined variation points. The single bCMS system and its SPL are modeled.
  Resources: [14, 15]

- **MDSE** (Model Driven Service Engineering)
  MDSE may be classified as an OO modeling approach with emphasis on the requirements specification and design phases. It considers services in general as collaborative, partial, and possibly distributed functionalities. Separation between services and components can be obtained by using the concept of service role, i.e., the part a system component/actor plays in a service. The global behavior of several components is modeled to define and understand how a service works. From

these global behaviors distributed component designs are derived. The single bCMS system is modeled.

Resources: [16, 17, 18, 19, 20, 21, 22]

- **OO-SPL** (Object-oriented Software Product Line Modeling)
  OO-SPL is an OO modeling approach based on UML. The structural context information is captured in terms of a domain model using the class diagram notation, including a data dictionary. The behavior information is described in terms of sequence diagrams that model specific scenarios between the key elements of a system, and interacting state diagrams that describe the behavior of a given element as it behaves across multiple scenarios. Furthermore, a feature diagram and OO model fragments, each of which describes the structural and behavioral information for a given variation point, are defined. The single bCMS system and its SPL are modeled.
  Resources: [23]

- **RAM** (Reusable Aspect Models)
  RAM is an aspect-oriented, multi-view modeling approach targeted at high-level and low level software design that integrates class diagram, sequence diagram, and state diagram AOM techniques. As a result, RAM aspect models can describe the structure and the behavior of a concern under study. Reuse of aspect models in RAM is safe and flexible. RAM aspect models define an aspect interface that clearly designates the functionality provided by the aspect, as well as its mandatory instantiation parameters. Safe use of an aspect model is enforced by the RAM weaver, which makes sure that compatible model elements are provided for all mandatory instantiation parameters when an aspect is instantiated. Flexibility is achieved by allowing any model element to optionally be composed or extended. RAM supports the definition of aspect hierarchies. The bCMS single system is modeled.
  Resources: [24, 25, 26, 27, 28, 29]

In the remainder of this paper, Section 2 presents the comparison criteria while Section 3 summarizes the results of the assessment. Section 4 concludes the paper and states future work.

2   Comparison Criteria

This section contains a description of the comparison criteria used for the assessment of modeling approaches. The comparison criteria are grouped into those describing *modeling dimensions* (see Section 2.1) and those related to *key concepts* (see Section 2.2). Where possible, we define each dimension and key concept in these sections. In instances where precise definitions are not generally agreed-upon, we have included examples that demonstrate our intents.

The dimensions that can be used to characterize a modeling technique include the phase of development for which it is most applicable, the language or notation used, etc. In actual fact, a technique comprises many different key concepts that can conceivably be interpreted differently depending on which dimension is being considered. While we recognize this fact, the criteria described below discuss the dimensions and key concepts in a more orthogonal view.

Key concepts related to a modeling technique are those that are targeted for optimization or improvement by the technique. They thus become the criteria by which a given technique can be evaluated or criteria that should be considered when creating a new technique, and their description/definition is critical to common understanding between modelers. Please note that these concepts and their use as criteria can be applied to either a technique or to the model(s) that result from using a technique. Our focus, however, is the assessment of techniques, and not their resulting models.

Questions were developed for each of the criteria to help modelers assess a technique against the criteria. The actual questions associated with the comparison criteria are given in Section 3 along with the assessment answers for each of the six techniques. Given that the assessment aims at comparing aspect-oriented and object-oriented modeling techniques, almost one half of the questions focus on units of encapsulation, modularity, and composability. The questionnaire also includes two questions which are not shown in Section 3 as their answers have already been addressed in Section 1. These two questions ask (i) for the name of the technique and (ii) for references to the resources that were analyzed to assess the technique (e.g., standards, publications, technical documentation, and tools).

2.1 Modeling Approach Dimensions

Phase/Activity. Modeling approaches may be most applicable during certain *phases* of software development, or for specific *activities* of software development. They may also be useful during multiple phases or for multiple activities. For example, the early requirements phase focuses on stakeholder goals and the description and assessment of alternatives. During the architecture or high-level design phase, an architecture is created that describes the overall system structure as well as general rules and constraints imposed on that structure. Examples of architecture are 3-tier, event-based, distributed client-server, distributed peer-to-peer, etc. Activities such as analysis, validation, verification, and evolution tend to crosscut across development phases, although their purpose and targets may differ from one phase to another. For example, model checking can be used as a high-level design analysis technique, whereas performance analysis may be targeted towards low-level design or even implementation phases. Validation ensures that the system is what the stakeholder wants, while verification ensures that the system is built as specified.

Notation/Language. A model must be defined in a well-defined language. In some cases, models may be expressed in a single language, but there are certainly situations that can benefit from the use of languages that are specific to the model viewpoint (e.g., a domain-specific language to define security policies or other system-wide properties). A notation/language for a technique may be able to express the functional elements of a model or it may be able to specifically express quality or other non-functional attributes that are used as criteria to judge the quality of a system, rather than its specific behavior. This ability can aid the modeler when analyzing for specific quality attributes. Techniques to specify and measure such requirements are, e.g., performance specification using the UML MARTE profile followed by system design performance analysis.

A language may have *formal semantics*, i.e., the language is based upon a domain that is well-understood and that allows proofs to be performed, e.g., math or Petri nets, or it is possible to map the language to math, Petri nets, etc. A language with a *rigorous semantics* is a language that is potentially based on a metamodel and can be machine analyzed. Finally, a language that is *not formal* is not machine analyzable.

Units of Encapsulation/Types of Concerns. A modeling approach encapsulates some concepts as units, in order to easily reason about them, manipulate them, analyze them, etc. Examples for units of encapsulation are activities, services, views, aspects, features, themes, concerns, etc. For example, an *aspect* is a crosscutting unit of encapsulation. A *feature* is (usually) a functional unit of encapsulation, as in a feature model. A *concern* is a functional or non-functional unit of encapsulation. A *theme* is an encapsulation of some functionality or crosscutting concern in a system and is considered more general than an aspect.

Furthermore, the units may differ depending on the phase of software development. For example, and not limited to the ones mentioned, units for a requirements phase could be use cases, qualities, and stakeholders, units for design could be classes, aspects, data definitions, and states, and units for implementation could be classes and modules.

Views and Concrete Syntax Supported. A view is a projection of a model for a particular reason. For many models, while both structural and behavioral specifications are part of the model, there can be separate structural and behavioral views of the model, and these perspectives may be described using different languages/notations (e.g., the structural perspective may be described using class diagrams while the behavioral perspective may be described using state machines or activity diagrams). A modeling technique may also use specific views for qualities such as performance, reliability, and safety to support focused modeling and analysis of these qualities.

2.2   Key Concepts

Paradigm. Modeling techniques are based on a paradigm, which is defined as the theories, rules, concepts, abstractions, and practices that constrain how activities and development artifacts are handled or represented. A paradigm imposes a decomposition criterion which is then used to decompose and analyze a problem into smaller problems. Examples are the object-oriented, aspect-oriented, functional, and service-oriented paradigms. The choice of paradigm affects other concepts and dimensions, including tools. For example, in the object-oriented paradigm, modules are classes/abstract data types, while in the procedural paradigm modules are functional abstractions. Tools must be able to perform activities on these module elements.

Modularity. The Separation of Concerns principle states that a given problem involves different kinds of concerns, which should be identified and separated to cope with complexity, and to achieve required engineering quality factors such as robustness, adaptability, maintainability, and reusability. The ideal decision regarding which concerns must be separated from each other requires finding the right compromise for satisfying multiple (quality) factors. A multi-dimensional decomposition, or as it is called multi-dimensional separation of concerns, permits the clean separation of multiple, potentially overlapping and interacting concerns simultaneously, with support for on-demand re-modularization to encapsulate new concerns at any time.

A modeling technique, however, may not support (or indeed need to support) the encapsulation of crosscutting concerns through advanced decomposition and composition mechanisms, but may rather be restricted to basic forms of composition such as aggregation.

Modularization is decomposition into modules according to decomposition criteria imposed by the paradigm. A module is a software unit with well-defined interfaces which express the services that are provided by the module for use by other modules. A module promotes information hiding by separating its interfaces from its internal design (often referred to as its implementation). Some techniques allow modules to be composed with the help of a composition specification. A composition specification may be an intrinsic part of a module or may be encapsulated in its own unit. Hence, the modularity of the composition specification is also of interest, i.e., whether or not it is separated from the modules that are being composed.

Composability. Composition is the act of creating new software units by reusing existing ones (e.g., by putting together several units of encapsulation through manipulating their associated modules). *Basic composition* enables the structuring of modules through traditional means (e.g., aggregation). In addition to basic composition mechanisms, three special kinds of compositions are distinguished: composition of crosscutting concerns, probabilistic compositions, and fuzzy compositions. Furthermore, *implicit composition* does not require the specification of a specific composition operator, e.g., a weaver makes assumptions about how composition is supposed to be realized. On the other hand, *explicit composition* requires a composition operator, e.g., add, replace, wrap, merge, etc.

If a language provides mechanisms for modularization of crosscutting concerns, it must also provide operators for the compositions of these concerns with base concerns. Aspect weaving and superimposition are two examples of such operators. The *composition of crosscutting concerns* can be syntax-based or semantics-based. In *syntax-based composition*, the composition is based on syntactic references to base concerns. This may lead to the well-known fragile pointcut problem, where structural changes in the base concerns may invalidate the compositions. This problem is tackled in *semantics-based composition* by relying on the meaning of the models and the relationships to be captured by the composition rather than the structure of the base concerns or specific naming conventions.

Semantics-based composition may be applied to the identification of locations where composition is supposed to occur (e.g., identification of semantically equivalent patterns) or the composition itself (e.g., in simplifying complex results by recognizing redundant model elements; an example is composing inheritance classes that also have a direct relation – simple composition will result in multiple direct relations, all except the first of which are redundant). The rules that govern semantics-based composition cannot be inferred by a machine unless the formalization of a technique goes beyond its abstract grammar, e.g., if an execution semantics is formally described then behavior equivalence may be determined.

Probabilistic compositions are required if there are uncertainties in the specification of problems. Here, it may be preferable to define and optimize the solutions and the composition of solutions with respect to the probabilistic problem definitions.

Fuzzy compositions are required if a problem can be solved in a number of alternative ways, and it is not possible (or desired) to commit to a single alternative. Here, each alternative may be assigned to a fuzzy set that expresses the degree of relevancy of a solution. Special composition operators are required, which can reason about fuzzy sets.

Techniques may also be classified by whether they support symmetric or asymmetric composition. A composition operator is typically applied to two input models to create another model. If both inputs are of the same "type", then *symmetric composition* is probably supported, and in this case commutativity holds as the order of the inputs does not matter. If the input models are of different "types" (e.g., class and aspect), then *asymmetric composition* is probably supported by the technique, i.e., composition works if A is applied to B but does not work if B is applied to A.

Regardless of whether basic or more advanced composition mechanisms are supported by a modeling approach, assessing the algebraic properties of composition operators such as *commutativity*, *associativity*, and *transitivity* makes it possible to predict what the result of a composition will be. A language treats models uniformly, if it facilitates decomposing a model into a set of uniform and cooperating concerns, and it provides composition operators that manipulate such concerns in a uniform manner. The uniform treatment of the concerns helps to fulfill the *closure property* in the models. If a composition operator applied to any member of a set produces a model that is also in the set, then the set of models is *closed* under that operation. The closure property is a way to standardize the decomposition mechanism and composition operators that are provided by a language. In addition, it helps to increase the abstraction level of concerns by forming a hierarchy of concerns in which the concerns at the higher levels of the hierarchy abstract from their lower level concerns.

Traceability. Traceability is (i) the ability to chronologically interrelate uniquely identifiable entities in a way that is verifiable or (ii) the ability to verify the history, location, or application of an entity (e.g., a concern, a process, or an artifact such as a requirements model element or a module) by means of documented recorded identification.

Traceability can be vertical or horizontal. Using requirements as an example, *vertical traceability* is the ability to trace requirements back and forth through the various layers of development, e.g., through the associated life-cycle work products of architecture specifications, detailed designs, code, unit test plans, integration test plans, system test plans, etc. It is possible to generalize this definition of vertical traceability to refer to abstraction levels above the requirements (e.g., system engineering or business process engineering) and below the requirements (e.g., architecture).

Again using requirements as an example, *horizontal traceability* refers to the ability to trace requirements back and forth to associated plans such as the project plan, quality assurance plan, configuration management plan, risk management plan, etc. This definition can also be generalized. Horizontal traceability may be required during any phase of software development, e.g., at the design level (tracing across different design documents) and at levels above requirements (system engineering or product family domain analysis).

From a composition point of view, traceability includes being able to identify elements in the composed model with their sources in the original models.

It may be argued that traceability is the concern of tools, however, some entities may be explicit in the modeling approach that are, or could be, targeted for traceability.

Mapping from the Previous and to the Next Stage of Software Development. Simply speaking, this is vertical mapping. How do we go from one development phase to another? However, this is not a traceability issue but rather a compatibility issue. It is about whether the concepts of one approach are compatible with another approach that precedes or follows the approach. It may be necessary to coerce the concepts of one approach into those of another or to extend one approach to make it interface properly with another approach.

Trade-Off Analysis. Trade-off analysis investigates the effect of simultaneous changes in one or more key factors in a decision, design, or project. Trade-off analysis offers the ability to choose between a set of alternatives, based on a set of potentially conflicting criteria.

Tool Support. Tools automate formalized parts of one or more activities within and across software development phases (e.g., requirements, design, code, validation, deployment, runtime management, evolution).

Empirical Studies/Evaluation. Empirical studies are broadly classified into controlled experiments, case studies, and surveys.

A case study is an in-depth observational study, whose purpose is to examine projects or evaluate a system under study. Case studies are mostly used to demonstrate the application of an approach in a particular context. For example, in the context of software modeling, the goal of a case study could be to demonstrate the applicability of modeling non-functional behavior (e.g., security) of an industrial case study and reporting lessons learnt during this process.

Surveys are normally conducted to evaluate a tool, methodology, or technique, which has been in use for a while. Usually, data is collected using questionnaires and interviews from a representative population. Once the data is collected, it is analyzed using appropriate descriptive statistics and possibly using statistical tests. Based on the analysis of results, conclusions are drawn and generalized.

A controlled experiment is performed in a controlled environment with the aim to manipulate one or more variables and maintain other variables at fixed values to measure the effect of change (outcome). Experiments usually have two or more treatments, whose outcomes are to be compared. For example, in the context of software modeling, an example of a controlled experiment could be to measure effort required by two techniques, which are developed to solve a particular modeling problem, such as modeling non-functional properties.

2.3   Parking Lot

Several other potential comparison criteria have been identified but at this point have not been adequately discussed to be included in the assessment. During the workshop we ranked these criteria in order of importance. They are, in that order: reusability, scalability, inter-module dependency and interaction, abstraction, usability (readability, understandability), ease of evolution, reduction of modeling effort, completeness, and finally expressiveness.

3   Results of Assessment

3.1   Modeling Approach Dimensions

Table 1. [Phase/activity] During which software development phase is the modeling technique applicable?

	AoURN	AT	CCA	MDSE	OO-SPL	RAM
Early requirements	x	x			x	
Late requirements	x			x	x	
Arch./High-level design	x		x	x	x	x
Low level design			x	x		x
Implementation			x	x		x
Integration						
Deployment			x			
Other		Evolutionary changes	Variability modeling		Variability modeling	

Table 2. [Phase/activity] During which activity is the modeling technique applicable?

	AoURN	AT	CCA	MDSE	OO-SPL	RAM
Validation	interactions of actor and system with AoUCM			Interface compatibility, animation execution		
Verification	interactions of actor with system through scenario definitions			Consistency between interface behaviour and internal behaviour		
Evolution	scenarios as scenario definitions are regression tests		Architecture / Deployment	All model elements		Design
Analysis	stakeholder goals/trade-offs with AoGRL	Relation of key stakeholder groups, the community affected by the system, and the explicit and implicit rules governing their interactions with the system and each other. Analysis is manual at this time.		Properties of flows, activities, interfaces and realizability of choreography		

Table 3. [Notation /language] Please characterize the language/notation

	AoURN	AT	CCA	MDSE	OO-SPL	RAM
Standard				x	x	
Built on standard(s)	User Requirements Notation (ITU-T Z.151)					UML

Table 3. (*Continued*)

	AoURN	AT	CCA	MDSE	OO-SPL	RAM
Non-standard Specific to application domain(s)		x	Component-based architecture for adaptive dis-tributed systems, and components refinement			
General purpose.	x			x	x	x

Table 4. [Notation/language] Is the language/notation

	AoURN	AT	CCA	MDSE	OO-SPL	RAM
Formal Rigorous	x			x	x	x
Not formal		x	x			

Table 5. [Notation/language] If the language/notation is formal or rigorous, it is assumed to be machine analyzable. What can be analyzed (e.g., which quality attributes)?

AoURN	AT	CCA	MDSE	OO-SPL	RAM
scenarios with scenario definitions (regression tests), goal model evaluation and trade-off analysis	n/a	n/a	Properties of flows, activities, interfaces and realizability	n/a	Consistency between views, consistency between aspect compositions specified in different views, control flow

Table 6. [Units of encapsulation/types of concerns] What does the technique encapsulate as a unit?

AoURN	AT	CCA	MDSE	OO-SPL	RAM
scenario concerns, stakeholder goal concerns, quality concerns, features	A human activity that is accomplished through interaction with the system.	Features (as refinements), Cloud components (as distributed components)	Collaboration, activity, composite class, state machine, class	Features, concerns, classes, states, data definitions	Aspects (i.e. design concerns, comprised of structural and behavioural models)

Table 7. [Units of encapsulation/types of concerns] If the units differ over development phases or development activities, please add these details

AoURN	AT	CCA	MDSE	OO-SPL	RAM
typically, goal/quality concerns and features are refined into scenario concerns	n/a	Features from the MVRP (first phase) are dedicated to the refinement of Cloud Component based architectures (second phase).	They do not differ, but are emphasized differently	For the requirements phase, the units used are features and concerns. For the high level design phase, the units used are classes, states and data definitions	n/a

Table 8. [Views and concrete syntax supported] What views are supported by the modeling technique?

	AoURN	AT	CCA	MDSE	OO-SPL	RAM
Structural	x		x	x	x	x
Behavioral	x			x	x	x
Intentional	x	x				
Quality-based	generic support for qualities and non-functional properties	Activity Theory is quite flexibly, so rules/constraints about various system properties such as quality or others can be expressed in natural language.				
Other			Feature composition view / SPL view	Interface behaviour, as projection of internal behaviour		Feature Interaction / Dependency / SPL view

Table 9. [Views and concrete syntax supported] What types of concrete syntax are used by the modeling technique?

	AoURN	AT	CCA	MDSE	OO-SPL	RAM
Textual				x		
Graphical	x	x	x	x	x	x

3.2 Key Concepts

Table 10. [Paradigm] What are the paradigms supported by the technique?

	AoURN	AT	CCA	MDSE	OO-SPL	RAM
Object-oriented				x	x	x
Aspect-oriented	x		x			x
Functional	x			x		x
Service-oriented	x			x		
Component-based			x	x		
Feature-oriented	x		x		x	x
Other	Goal-oriented	Human Activity				

Table 11. [Modularity] How does the language support modularity? (This question deals with how the modeling technique supports modularizing the units of encapsulation identified in Table 6.)

	AoURN	AT	CCA	MDSE	OO-SPL	RAM
Special operators						
1st class language elements	x [1]		x	x	x	x
Domain-specific lang. elements						
Service level agreements						
Interface definitions			x	x		x
Other		Activity				
		System				
		Diagrams				

[1] for hierarchical decomposition, multiple views, and separation of possibly crosscutting concerns

Table 12. [Modularity] If the modeling technique allows composition of modules, can the composition specification itself be separated from the specification of the modules?

	AoURN	AT	CCA	MDSE	OO-SPL	RAM
Yes	x [1]	x [2]	x	x	x	x
No	x [1]	x [2]				

1) For scenario models, the pattern to be matched is separated from the aspectual properties and the composition operators. In goal models, patterns, aspectual properties, and composition operators are all specified together.

2) Activity System Diagrams (ASD) can be composed via networking the outcome(s) of one ASD with any of the elements of another. The network relation is separate from the ASDs it relates. ASDs can also be decomposed hierarchically by relating a Division of Labor item to another ASD. In this case, the composition specification is part of the module specification.

Table 13. [Composability] If the technique does not use composition to create new units, how does it create new units from existing units?

AoURN	AT	CCA	MDSE	OO-SPL	RAM
n/a	n/a	n/a	n/a	n/a	n/a

Table 14. [Composability] What kinds of composition operators are supported by the technique?

	AoURN	AT	CCA	MDSE	OO-SPL	RAM
Explicit	x	x	x	x	x	x
Implicit						x
Basic				x	x	x
Probabilistic						
Fuzzy						
Syntax-based	x		x	x	x	x
Semantics-based	x			x		x
None						
Other				role binding for cross-cutting, partial behaviours		

Table 15. [Composability] If the technique uses composition, how are composition operators defined by the technique?

AoURN	AT	CCA	MDSE	OO-SPL	RAM
URN itself is the composition language. In scenario models, any number of scenario elements may be combined to form composition operators for crosscutting concerns, whereas in goal models, links (contribution, correlation, decomposition, and dependency) may be combined. Basic hierarchical (de)composition is also supported.	Network relation composition is defined as the outcome of one ASD being used in any of the elements (other than object or outcome) of another ASD. Hierarchical decomposition is defined as the relation of an ASD to a specific Division of Labor item in another ASD, that it represents.	Beyond the classical composition of components, the other level of composition is at the feature level, and as each feature is implemented as a model transformation, it can itself be considered as a composition operator.	We use existing composition operators	We use existing composition operators	Algorithmic description of weaving

Table 16. [Composability] If the technique uses composition, is it

	AoURN	AT	CCA	MDSE	OO-SPL	RAM
Symmetric				x	x	x [1]
Asymmetric	x [2]	x [3]	x	x [4]		x [5]

1) at the highest level

2) However, there is no concept of aspect in URN – only the concept of concern which includes crosscutting and non-crosscutting concerns.

3) There is no concept of an aspect in AT or the ideas of crosscutting concerns – the items that can be composed are Activity System Diagrams.

4) when binding roles to classes

5) for the individual views

Table 17. [Composability] What are the composition operators of the technique?

AoURN	AT	CCA	MDSE	OO-SPL	RAM
The basic composition operators are any scenario model element and any link in GRL – these may be combined to form more complex composition operators. In addition, the stub concept in scenario models supports hierarchical (de)composition.	Network relation composition and hierarchical decomposition.	Component composition, and features as composition operators.	Role binding (rb). Aggregation and linking applied to: Role structures in collaborations (rs); activity composition (ac); part composition in composite classes (pc)	Class diagram merge; parallel composition of state machines	Instantiation, i.e. mapping of model elements from one aspect to the other

Table 18. [Composability] What algebraic properties does each composition operator provide?

	AoURN	AT	CCA	MDSE	OO-SPL	RAM
Commutativity	x [1)		x [2)	rs [3), pc [3)	Both operators	
Associativity	x [1)		x [2)		Both operators	x
Transitivity		x [4)	x [2)	ac [3), pc [3), rb [3)		

1) URN composes concerns in waves. A wave is a set of concerns that are applied to the same base model. The next wave is applied to a different base model as it includes the previously applied concerns. In a wave, concerns may be applied in any order, i.e. commutativity and associativity hold. Waves, on the other hand, are not commutative and associative.

2) It depends on how the composition operator is implemented as a feature. Usually, commutativity is not handled (features have to be prioritized), and associativity and transitivity are kept.

3) see Table 17

4) AT network relations do not provide commutativity or associativity, although it could be informally argued that they provide transitivity. Hierarchical decomposition does not provide any of these properties.

Table 19. [Composability] Which composition operators produce models that are closed under the operator?

AoURN	AT	CCA	MDSE	OO-SPL	RAM
All	Both operators	All	All except role structures (which are collaborations)	Both operators	instantiation

Table 20. [Composability] How does the technique support incremental composition?

AoURN	AT	CCA	MDSE	OO-SPL	RAM
Concerns can be activated and organized into waves. Concerns can be applied to other concerns.	It does not.	The methodology provided by the MVRP is based on incremental composition.	By role binding. By incremental aggregation and linking.	Products created by incrementally composing features/concerns with the model of a reference variant	It is possible to weave aspects one by one.

Table 21. [Composability] How does the technique measure the quality of a composition?

	AoURN	AT	CCA	MDSE	OO-SPL	RAM
Resulting model modularity				x		
Resulting model coupling/cohesion				x		
Other	x [1]	x [1]	x [1]	x [2]	x [1]	x [1]

1) no explicit measuring of the quality of a composition

2) consistency, compatibility, absence of errors

Table 22. [Composability] How is a composed model presented to the modeler?

	AoURN	AT	CCA	MDSE	OO-SPL	RAM
Using a new model	x [1]		x	x	x	x
Using an annotated original model	x [1]	x [2]				
Using a set of composition rules			x			
Using a tool	x [1]					x

1) A tool is required to compose concerns. By default, an annotated original model is presented but a new model can also be created.

2) Since composition and modeling are manual at this time, a modeler can simply annotate existing diagrams to show both a network relation composition and hierarchical decompositions.

Table 23. [Traceability] What types of traceability are supported? (For each type, describe the entities that are traced either in the technique (i.e., as part of the process of applying the technique) or in models produced by the technique?)

	AoURN	AT	CCA	MDSE	OO-SPL	RAM
Horizontal	Any model element can be traced with built-in traceability mechanism (typically concerns, stakeholders, qualities, intentional elements, maps, stubs, responsibilities).	Tracing is manual – network relations between ASDs are useful tracings.		All model elements can be traced in a tool	Tracing of features from the product family model to the individual product models; tracing of method calls between the class diagram, sequence diagram and state machine models	Model elements in the composed model can be traced to the aspects in which they originated
Vertical	Any model element can be traced with built-in traceability mechanism but typically an actor in a goal model is traced to a component in a scenario model and a task in a goal model is traced to one or more scenario elements.	Tracing is a manual process - any element of an ASD, hierarchical decomposition between ASDs and network relations between particular elements of ASDs are useful tracing elements.	The MVRP provides decomposition into features, which are refinements of CC models. Therefore, it provides vertical traceability for CC models.	All model elements can be traced in a tool		

Table 24. [Traceability] What capabilities are provided by such tracing?

	AoURN	AT	CCA	MDSE	OO-SPL	RAM
Refinement identification	x	x	x		x	
Composition source identification		x				x
Other		x [1]		x [2]		

1) network relationships
2) model element relationships

Table 25. [Mapping from the previous and to the next stage of software development] How does the modeling technique address moving from the "previous" stage of software development, whatever that might be?

AoURN	AT	CCA	MDSE	OO-SPL	RAM
Mappings and heuristics for the transformation of Activity Theory models to AoURN exist. Use cases can be formalized with AoUCM. Import/Export feature for Requirements Management tools allows (textual) requirements to be linked with AoURN models. Ability to tag model elements facilitates mapping from previous stage.	There really is no previous stage – AT is useful at the very high-level requirements stage.	Not supported by the technique	Early requirements are used to develop role structures and choreographies manually.	As the technique is based on UML, it is possible to use use-cases and use case scenarios for the early requirements phase. Such use-cases will then be connected to the models created by this approach.	We are in the process of defining a strategy to map from requirements models, for example AoURN models, to RAM models.

Table 26. [Mapping from the previous and to the next stage of software development] How does the modeling technique address moving to the "next" stage of software development, whatever that might be?

AoURN	AT	CCA	MDSE	OO-SPL	RAM
Transformation to RAM allows for AoUCM models to be executed in the RAM environment (work in progress). Message Sequence Charts can be generated from AoUCM models. Performance models can be created from AoUCM models. List of responsibilities for a component can be derived from an AoUCM model. Import/Export feature for Requirements Management tools allows design documents to be linked with AoURN models. Ability to tag model elements facilitates mapping to next stage.	Mappings and heuristics have been developed to move to goal modeling, specifically URN, that also includes use case maps.	The CCA output is a CC model that can be transformed into platform specific code, usually for a component framework, using standard code generation techniques.	Semi-automatic transformation to flow-localized choreography and fully automatic transformation from there to code.	Again, as the UML language is used, for moving to the architecture phase, UML architectural models like component, deployment or package diagrams can be created from the current models.	We have already defined a mapping from RAM models to AspectJ code. Our RAM tool can also generate a woven model that is purely OO. From that, an OO implementation can be synthesized using standard code generation techniques.

Table 27. [Trade-off analysis] Does the modeling technique

	AoURN	AT	CCA	MDSE	OO-SPL	RAM
Integrate trade-off analysis as part of the technique and/or tools	x					
Support trade-off analysis by providing easy access to relevant data (if yes, describe the data)				x (properties associated with model element)		
Have no concept of trade-off analysis		x	x		x	x

Table 28. [Tool Support] What activities of the approach are supported by tools?

	AoURN	AT	CCA	MDSE	OO-SPL	RAM
Specification	x			x	x	x
Composition	x		x	x	x	x
Analysis	x			x		
Validation	x			x		
Verification	x			x		x
Model consistency	x			x		x
Transformations	x		x	x		x
None		x				

Table 29. [Tool Support] If a tool is used to visualize a composed model, how is it visualized?

AoURN	AT	CCA	MDSE	OO-SPL	RAM
Graphically using the AoURN language	n/a	Using EMF model editors	Graphically using the language (UML)	The composed model is a UML model, so it can be visualized in a normal UML editor.	Graphically

Table 30. [Tool Support] How do tools help users understand the relationships of units of encapsulation? Which relationships are covered (e.g., unwanted interactions or conflicts, other areas where resolutions are required, or dependencies between units of encapsulation)?

	AoURN	AT	CCA	MDSE	OO-SPL	RAM
Unwanted interactions or conflicts	AoURN allows the specification of a concern interaction graph (CIG) to define precedence rules among conflicting concerns.			Interface validation		Tool could help detect unwanted conflicts using critical pair analysis. This feature is, however, not implemented yet.
Dependencies	AoURN allows the specification of a CIG to define precedence rules among dependent concerns.		Dependencies are explicit in MVRP models.	Type Dependencies		The dependencies are explicitly specified at specification time
Other	AoURN indicates the impact of a concern on other concern with the help of annotations.	Not applicable (no tool support currently exists for this technique)	Not applicable (tool support is currently under development)			

Table 31. [Empirical studies/evaluation] Briefly describe empirical studies or evaluations that have been performed for the technique (provide references wherever possible)

AoURN	Case studies (e.g., original crisis management system [6]; bCMS [9], Via Verde SPL [7]; various smaller systems); proof of concept implementation in jUCM-Nav tool [8]
AT	The technique has been used informally in a case study of a mobile Dengue vector surveillance system in Mexico, where it has shown promise as an elicitation technique effective across diverse groups of stakeholders.
CCA	Two proof-of-concepts implementations were successfully developed to empirically validate the Cloud Component model. The MVRP model is currently being implemented as an eclipse plug-in and, among others, as Java/EMF model transformations.
MDSE	ERTMS (European Rail Traffic Management System - train handover); Safety Module for safety critical motor control; Locker (RFID tag reading in hospital clothes lockers); Bike repair / support; City guide (A mobile city guide and treasure hunt system)
OO-SPL	No empirical studies performed yet
RAM	RAM has been applied to several case studies: - AspectOPTIMA [30][31] (modelling the design of a family of transaction support middlewares) composed of 37 inter-dependent aspect models - CCCMS [27], the design of a car crash crisis management system composed of 23 inter-dependent aspect models - Design Patterns, currently 9 of which are modelled - bCMS [29], simple crisis management system as defined by this workshop, consisting of 14 inter-dependent aspect models. In addition, a detailed survey comparing RAM to 8 other AOM approaches has been conducted. RAM has been taught in a graduate class, and students had to solve one assignment using RAM. However, no controlled experiment or empirical evaluation has been conducted.

4   Conclusions and Future Work

There were several key findings that came out of the workshop. Among these was the fact that a focused case study did in fact allow all the participants to use their approaches on a complete system, not just a part of it. We found that it was thus possible to compare the approaches in a more uniform fashion, using the comparison criteria. We believe that this will also make it possible to recognize areas of possible synergy across the techniques more easily since we can see specific results and artifacts from different techniques for the same modeling activities.

We also found that including SPL and non-functional properties in the case study allowed modelers to apply their approaches to complex system issues, even in the context of a focused set of functionality. This is important because it also highlighted how complex and integrated a set of modeling artifacts can be even for a small system when it includes quality expectations and SPL elements. This depth of application in the techniques we assess is critical to their uniform characterization and will provide information regarding how they can be synergistically combined into end-to-end comprehensive techniques.

Perhaps not unexpectedly, a major element of the workshop involved normalizing our understanding of the comparison criteria. We kept the original criteria structure, dimensions, and key concepts. However, we refined many of the definitions, and discovered that several ideas are not readily generalized into precise definitions. In all cases we attempted to include many examples, in the hope that the examples may serve to define the criteria idea, or that additional examples can be found that will help create a usable definition. In some cases we combined ideas from the original criteria developed at the Bellairs workshop, when we discovered that previous distinctions were not readily evident or useful as we discussed the six techniques we assessed for the CMA workshop. Finally, we added new criteria or extended existing criteria in the context of these assessments to make them applicable to a broader range of techniques, specifically service-oriented and cloud computing techniques.

We expect that the criteria discussed in this paper will enable us to assess other techniques, possibly identifying further adjustments to the criteria. In the longer term, we also expect that by analyzing techniques according to these criteria, we can postulate generalizations that will enable combinations of complete or partial techniques into end-to-end design methodologies. The criteria should help us identify the most applicable techniques for various situations, and thus help modelers and designers choose techniques that will support their work.

A final outcome of the workshop is the repository of its results. The bCMS requirements document developed at the Bellairs workshop, the models from all six modeling techniques developed for the CMA workshop, and the comparison criteria document are available on the ReMODD site to all researchers and practitioners.

We envision three areas of future work. The first consists of a more comprehensive survey of different modeling techniques in the context of the comparison criteria. An outcome of this survey is not only a more uniform platform for comparing modeling techniques, but also the expectation that it will provide a testing bed for the criteria themselves. It is possible that additional refinements to the criteria will come out of this work.

Another area of future work is to use the assessments of the six techniques we have to postulate where they could be synergistically combined into comprehensive, end-to-end modeling techniques. We expect that this work will include the need to generalize parts of the techniques so that they can be combined. As an extension of combining techniques, these end-to-end approaches must be fully defined and justified. Our initial approach to justification will be to apply them to the focused bCMS case study, but we will use other means of assessing their potential wherever possible.

Finally, we intend to refine the presentation of the comparison criteria, in terms of their explanations, definitions, and examples. We will also refine the questions used to perform the actual assessment with the goal of streamlining the useful information for practitioners.

References

1. Kienzle, J., Guelfi, N., Mustafiz, S.: Crisis Management Systems: A Case Study for Aspect-Oriented Modeling. In: Katz, S., Mezini, M., Kienzle, J. (eds.) Transactions on AOSD VII. LNCS, vol. 6210, pp. 1–22. Springer, Heidelberg (2010), doi:10.1007/978-3-642-16086-8_1
2. Katz, S., Mezini, M., Kienzle, J. (eds.): Transactions on AOSD VII. LNCS, vol. 6210. Springer, Heidelberg (2010)
3. bCMS case study document, http://cserg0.site.uottawa.ca/cma2011/CaseStudy.pdf (accessed January 2012)
4. ITU-T: Recommendation Z.151 (11/08): User Requirements Notation (URN) - Language Definition, Geneva, Switzerland (2008), http://www.itu.int/rec/T-REC-Z.151/en
5. Mussbacher, G.: Aspect-oriented User Requirements Notation. PhD thesis, School of Information Technology and Engineering, University of Ottawa, Canada (2010)
6. Mussbacher, G., Amyot, D., Araújo, J., Moreira, A.: Requirements Modeling with the Aspect-oriented User Requirements Notation (AoURN): A Case Study. In: Katz, S., Mezini, M., Kienzle, J. (eds.) Transactions on AOSD VII. LNCS, vol. 6210, pp. 23–68. Springer, Heidelberg (2010), doi:10.1007/978-3-642-16086-8_2
7. Mussbacher, G., Araújo, J., Moreira, A., Amyot, D.: AoURN-based Modeling and Analysis of Software Product Lines. Software Quality Journal (2011), doi:10.1007/s11219-011-9153-8
8. jUCMNav Version 4.3, University of Ottawa (accessed January 2012), http://jucmnav.softwareengineering.ca/ucm/bin/view/ProjetSEG/WebHome
9. Mussbacher, G.: bCMS Case Study: AoURN. ReMoDD, September 20, 2011. ReMoDD (January 16, 2012) http://www.cs.colostate.edu/content/bcms-case-study-aourn (accessed January 2012)
10. Georg, G.: Activity Theory and its Applications in Software Engineering and Technology. Colorado State University Technical Report CS-11-101 (2011)
11. Engeström, Y.: Learning by expanding. Orienta-Konsultit, Helsinki (1987)
12. Georg, G., Troup, L.: Activity Theory Applied to bCMS Modeling. ReMoDD, September 20, 2011. ReMoDD (January 16, 2012), http://www.cs.colostate.edu/content/activity-theory-applied-bcms-modeling (accessed January 2012)
13. Georg, G., Mussbacher, G., Troup, L., Amyot, D., France, R., Petriu, D., Lozano-Fuentes, S.: Unpublished work relating the synergistic application of AT and URN (2012)
14. Lézoray, J.-B., Phung-Khac, A., Segarra, M.-T., Gilliot, J.-M., Beugnard, A.: Cloud Components: Modeling Cloud-like Architectures. Submitted January 2012 to the 6th European Conference on Software Architecture (ECSA)
15. Lézoray, J.-B., Phung-Khac, A., Beugnard, A.: A proposition based on the Cloud Component Approach. ReMoDD, September 19, 2011. ReMoDD (January 16, 2012), http://www.cs.colostate.edu/content/proposition-based-cloud-component-approach (accessed January 2012)
16. Kathayat, S.B., Bræk, R.: From Flow-Global Choreography to Component Types. In: Kraemer, F.A., Herrmann, P. (eds.) SAM 2010. LNCS, vol. 6598, pp. 36–55. Springer, Heidelberg (2011)

17. Kathayat, S.B., Le, H.N., Bræk, R.: A Model-Driven Framework for Component-Based Development. In: Ober, I., Ober, I. (eds.) SDL 2011. LNCS, vol. 7083, pp. 154–167. Springer, Heidelberg (2011)
18. Kraemer, F.A., Bræk, R., Herrmann, P.: Compositional Service Engineering with Arctis. Telektronikk 105(1) (2009)
19. Kraemer, F.A., Slåtten, V., Herrmann, P.: Tool Support for the Rapid Composition, Analysis and Implementation of Reactive Services. Journal of Systems and Software 82, 2068–2080 (2009)
20. Fatima, U., Bræk, R., Castejón, H.N.: Session Initiation as a Service. In: Ober, I., Ober, I. (eds.) SDL 2011. LNCS, vol. 7083, pp. 122–137. Springer, Heidelberg (2011)
21. Arctis Developer Reference, http://arctis.item.ntnu.no (accessed January 2012)
22. Fatima, U., Bræk, R.: Model Driven Service Engineering applied to bCMS. ReMoDD, September 20, 2011. ReMoDD (January 16, 2012),
http://www.cs.colostate.edu/content/model-driven-service-engineering-applied-bcms (accessed January 2012)
23. Capozucca, A., Cheng, B., Guelfi, N., Istoan, P.: bCMS-OOM-SPL. ReMoDD, September 21, 2011. ReMoDD (January 16, 2012),
http://www.cs.colostate.edu/content/bcms-oom-spl (accessed January 2012)
24. Klein, J., Kienzle, J.: Reusable Aspect Models. In: 11th Workshop on Aspect-Oriented Modeling, Nashville, TN, USA (2007)
25. Kienzle, J., Al Abed, W., Klein, J.: Aspect-Oriented Multi-View Modeling. In: 8th International Conference on Aspect-Oriented Software Development (AOSD 2009), Charlottesville, VA, USA, pp. 89–98. ACM Press (2009)
26. Al Abed, W., Kienzle, J.: Information Hiding and Aspect-Oriented Modeling. In: 14th Aspect-Oriented Modeling Workshop, Denver, CO, USA, pp. 1–6 (2009)
27. Kienzle, J., Al Abed, W., Fleurey, F., Jézéquel, J.-M., Klein, J.: Aspect-Oriented Design with Reusable Aspect Models. In: Katz, S., Mezini, M., Kienzle, J. (eds.) Transactions on AOSD VII. LNCS, vol. 6210, pp. 272–320. Springer, Heidelberg (2010)
28. Kramer, M., Kienzle, J.: Mapping Aspect-Oriented Models to Aspect-Oriented Code. In: 15th Aspect-Oriented Modeling Workshop, Oslo, Norway, pp. 1–6 (2010)
29. Kienzle, J., Al Abed, W., Bonnet, V., Alam, O., Klein, J., Jézéquel, J.-M.: bCMS Case Study: Reusable Aspect Models (RAM). ReMoDD, September 20, 2011. ReMoDD (January 16, 2012), http://www.cs.colostate.edu/content/bcms-case-study-reusable-aspect-models-ram (accessed January 2012)
30. Kienzle, J., Duala-Ekoko, E., Gélineau, S.: AspectOPTIMA: A Case Study on Aspect Dependencies and Interactions. In: Rashid, A., Ossher, H. (eds.) Transactions on AOSD V. LNCS, vol. 5490, pp. 187–234. Springer, Heidelberg (2009)
31. Kramer, M.: Mapping Reusable Aspect Models To Aspect-Oriented Code. Study Thesis, Karlsruhe Institute of Technology (2011)

Summary of the Second International Workshop on Models and Evolution

Dirk Deridder[1], Alfonso Pierantonio[2], Bernhard Schätz[3],
Jonathan Sprinkle[4], and Dalila Tamzalit[5]

[1] Vrije Universiteit Brussel, Belgium
[2] University of L'Aquila, Italy
[3] Fortiss GmbH, Germany
[4] University of Arizona, USA
[5] University of Nantes, France
Dirk.Deridder@vub.ac.be, alfonso.pierantonio@univaq.it,
schaetz@fortiss.org, sprinkle@ece.arizona.edu,
Dalila.Tamzalit@univ-nantes.fr

1 Models and Evolution

With the increasing adoption of Model-Based Development in many domains (e.g., Automotive Software Engineering, Business Process Engineering), models are starting to become core artifacts of modern software engineering processes. By raising the level of abstraction and using concepts closer to the problem and application domain rather than the solution and technical domain, models become core assets and reusable intellectual property, being worth the effort of maintaining and evolving them. Therefore, increasingly models experience the same issues as traditional software artifacts, i.e., being subject to many kinds of changes, which range from rapidly evolving platforms to the evolution of the functionalities provided by the applications developed. These modifications include changes at all levels, from requirements through architecture and design, to executable models, documentation and test suites. They typically affect various kinds of models including data models, behavioral models, domain models, source code models, goal models, etc. Coping with and managing the changes that accompany the evolution of software assets is therefore an essential aspect of Software Engineering as a discipline.

Because of this increasing importance, a series of annual international workshops has been set up since 2007 for the MoDSE workshop and from 2008 for the MCCM workshop, with the main objectives of model-driven software evolution (MoDSE) and model co-evolution and consistency management (MCCM). These workshops investigated how model-driven evolution can enforce and reduce critical risks and important costs involved in software evolution, how model-based development enforces and enhances software, and how the manipulation and transformation of models with model co-evolution and consistency management facilitate the natural changes of any software system. To explore and strengthen the interaction and synergy between the active research domains of Software Evolution, Co-Evolution, Consistency Management and MDE, these two workshops in 2010 joined their forces in a common workshop on "Models and Evolution".

J. Kienzle (Ed.): MODELS 2011 Workshops, LNCS 7167, pp. 244–245, 2012.
© Springer-Verlag Berlin Heidelberg 2012

2   Workshop Themes

The objective of the workshop is the discussion of novel research ideas, challenging problems, or practical contributions in the domain of model-driven software evolution, to advance the state of the art concerning how models can facilitate and guide software evolution and how to reduce critical risks and important resources (e.g., costs, personnel, time) involved in software evolution.

This full-day workshop included technical presentation sessions, tool demonstrations, moderated debate sessions with open discussions. The technical presentations were organized in three sessions:

- **Semantics and Versions:** The first session specifically dealt with the identification of changes between different versions of a model concerning its interpretation.
  Contributions discussed basic mechanisms to support a semantics-aware merge in optimistic model versioning (by Petra Brosch, Uwe Egly, Sebastian Gabmeyer et al.), and presented different possibilities to compute semantic model differences for different kind of modeling formalisms (by Shahar Maoz, Jan Oliver Ringert, Bernhard Rumpe).
- **Domain Specific Languages**: The second session was focused on the interdependencies between domain-specific languages and the maintenance of models. Contributions discussed the importance a notation that reflects the transformed elements of the original DSL (by Ingo Weisemoeller and Bernhard Rumpe) and introduced a metamodel dedicated to metamodel evolution description (by Jean-Philippe Babau and Mickael Kerboeuf).
- **Life-Cycle and Evolution:** The third session presented constructive approaches to handle evolution issues in a model-based development process.
  Contributions presented an approach of using concepts from software product lines and feature modeling for evolving multi-version systems (by Hassan Gomaa) and a mechanism for variations to the constraining meta-attributes to enforce of different constraints at different lifecycle stages (Keith Duddy and Jörg Kiegeland).

Full versions of all presented contributions have been made available online (see www.modse.fr).

Acknowledgements. The organizers would like to thank the members of the program committee for acting as reviewers and providing feedback for the improvements of the sububmissions: Arnaud Albinet, Mireille Blay-Fornarino, Jean-Michel Bruel, Jordi Cabot, Rubby Casallas, Antonio Cicchetti, Mateus Costa, Davide Di Ruscio, Anne Etien, Jesus Garcia Molina, David Garlan, Olivier Le Goaer, Ethan Jackson, Gerti Kappel, Udo Kelter, Richard Paige, Mario Sanchez, Eugene Syriani, Ragnhild Van Der Straeten, Hans Vangheluwe.

Towards Semantics-Aware Merge Support in Optimistic Model Versioning*

Petra Brosch[2], Uwe Egly[1], Sebastian Gabmeyer[2], Gerti Kappel[2],
Martina Seidl[3], Hans Tompits[1], Magdalena Widl[1], and Manuel Wimmer[2]

[1] Institute for Information Systems, Vienna University of Technology, Austria
{uwe,tompits,widl}@kr.tuwien.ac.at
[2] Business Informatics Group, Vienna University of Technology, Austria
{brosch,gerti,wimmer}@big.tuwien.ac.at
[3] Institute of Formal Models and Verification, Johannes Kepler University, Austria
martina.seidl@jku.at

Abstract. Current optimistic model versioning systems, which are indispensable to coordinate the collaboration within teams, are able to detect several kinds of conflicts between two concurrently modified versions of one model. These systems support the detection of syntactical problems such as contradicting changes, violations of the underlying metamodel, and violations of OCL constraints. However, violations of the models' semantics remain unreported. In this paper, we suggest to use redundant information inherent in multi-view models to check if the semantics is violated during the merge process. In particular, we exploit the information encoded in state machine diagrams to validate evolving sequence diagrams by means of the model checker SPIN.

1 Introduction

In model-driven engineering, *version control systems* (VCS) are an essential tool to manage the evolution of software models [4]. In this context, *optimistic version control systems* [1] are of particular importance. They provide reliable recovery mechanisms if changes have to be undone and support the collaboration of multiple developers.

An optimistic VCS stores the artifacts under development in a central repository, which may be accessed by all team members at any time. A typical interaction with the repository starts when a developer checks out the most recent version of the model under development. The developer then performs the desired changes on a local copy. Upon completion, the developer commits the modified local version back to the repository. If the performed changes do not interfere

---

* This work was partially funded by the Austrian Federal Ministry of Transport, Innovation, and Technology and the Austrian Research Promotion Agency under grant FIT-IT-819584, by the Vienna Science and Technology Fund (WWTF) under grant ICT10-018, by the fFORTE WIT Program of the Vienna University of Technology and the Austrian Federal Ministry of Science and Research, and by the Austrian Science Fund (FWF) under grants P21698 and S11409-N23.

J. Kienzle (Ed.): MODELS 2011 Workshops, LNCS 7167, pp. 246–256, 2012.

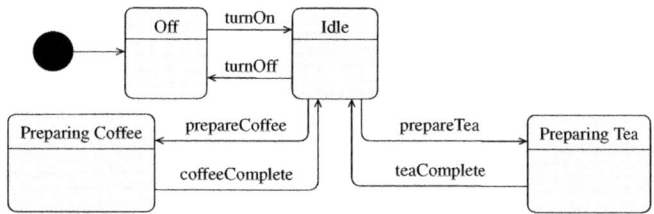

Fig. 1. State machine diagram for the class CoffeeMachine (CM)

with the concurrently introduced modifications of another developer, the merge is straightforward and may be computed automatically. Otherwise, a *merge conflict* [4] is at hand and the divergent versions need to be merged manually. Without adequate tool support, the merged version may result in a syntactically and/or semantically inconsistent version, even though both versions were consistent prior to the merge. Obviously, it is of paramount importance to detect and resolve conflicts as soon as possible to prevent their propagation through multiple development cycles.

Among the many possible merge conflicts [1], the most common are *contradicting changes*. Given two developers working on the same model, this conflict may emerge if both developers commit their changes and either (a) their changes may not be applied in combination (i.e., a *delete/update conflict*), or (b) their changes are not commutable (i.e., an *update/update conflict*). In the latter case, the different ordering of the changes results in different models. In such a situation, often user interaction is required to resolve the conflict. Alternatively, a predefined heuristic-based merge strategy may be applied to automatically generate consolidated, syntactically correct versions. However, it cannot be asserted that the model is *semantically* consistent.

Consider the following example, which describes a semantically inconsistent model caused by an automatic merge of changes. Figure 1 depicts a UML state machine diagram modeling a coffee machine. The upmost diagram S in Fig. 2 shows a possible behavior of the same machine in terms of a sequence diagram. Two software engineers change the sequence diagram at the same time: one includes the message *turnOff*(), resulting in S', the other adds the message *prepareTea*(), resulting in S''. Each change on its own results in a sequence diagram consistent with the state machine. The next step is to merge the changes into a new sequence diagram $\hat{S}$ using an automatic versioning tool, e.g., the one proposed by Brosch et al. [2]. As the messages of a lifeline are represented as an ordered list, an update/update conflict occurs, because both newly added messages are stored at the same index of this list. A conceivable merging strategy is to consider all possible combinations of the two diagrams. This may result in several syntactically correct diagrams. Figure 2 shows two possibilities, $\hat{S}_1$ and $\hat{S}_2$, depending whether *turnOff*() is placed before or after *prepareTea*(). However, making tea after turning off the machine does not make much sense and a modeler would avoid such a solution in a manual merge process.

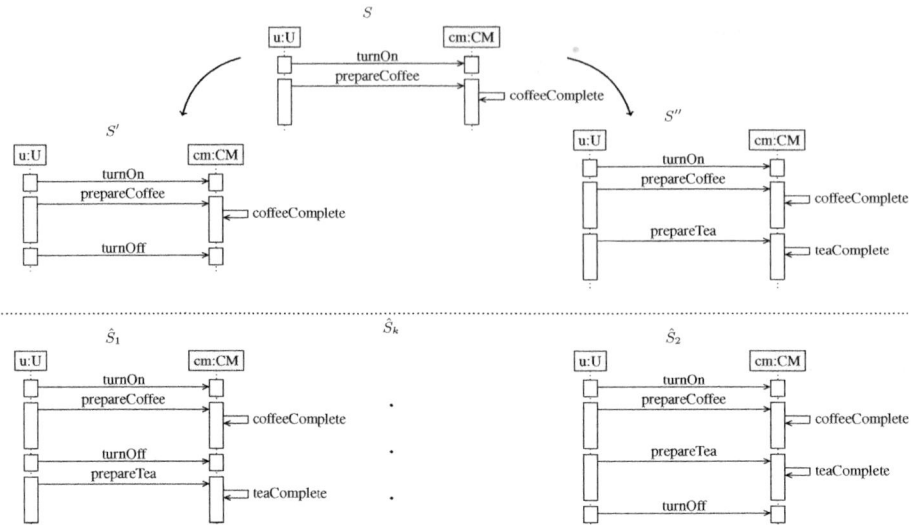

Fig. 2. Versioning scenario for a sequence diagram

At first glance, it might seem necessary to provide additional knowledge, e.g., a specifically tailored ontology, to support an automatic merge process aware of the model's semantics. However, in modeling languages like UML, the required knowledge is distributed over different types of diagrams. Each diagram type provides a view on a specific aspect of the described system. Yet, these views overlap in parts, effectively duplicating certain aspects of the system across different diagrams. For our example, we may figure out that the first merge option, i.e., *turnOff*() before *prepareTea*(), is inconsistent with respect to the state machine diagram, as preparing tea after turning off the machine is not possible.

In this paper, we thus propose to exploit redundant information available in UML models and use the overlapping parts of the diagrams as gluing points to construct a coherent picture of the system. In this way, we are able to assert that the modifications performed on a sequence diagram are consistent with the specification stated in a state machine diagram. For this purpose, we employ model-checking techniques and integrate this approach into the merging component of the model versioning system AMOR [2].

Starting with a review of related work in Section 2, we proceed to present our semantics-aware merging approach in Section 3. We then showcase how the above presented example is solved with our approach in Section 4. Section 5 concludes the paper with a discussion of future work directions.

2   Related Work

The fields of model versioning and model verification are both related to our work.

Model Versioning. In the last decade, more than a dozen model versioning systems have been proposed (see Brosch et al. [1] for an overview). Many existing model versioning systems take advantage of the graph-based structure of software models. As a consequence, conflicts resulting from contradicting changes are more precisely detected, sometimes even automatically resolved. Since changes are rarely introduced independently of each other, think of refactorings for example, some approaches analyze the set of composite changes to recognize the user's intention, and try to derive suitable resolution strategies when conflicting versions are checked into the repository [2,6]. However, the semantic aspects of models are mostly neglected by current model versioning systems. To the best of our knowledge, only two approaches consider semantics in the context of model versioning.

The first approach suggests the usage of *semantic views*, which are constructed by a manually defined normalization process that removes all duplicate representations of one and the same concept from the original metamodel [13]. When two divergent versions of the same base model are committed to the repository, the two versions are normalized and compared to determine possible conflicts. Although the normalization procedure integrates a semantic layer into the model versioning process, the actual comparison of the normalized models is still performed on a syntactic level.

Another elegant technique, which employs *diff* operators to compare models, is presented by Maoz et al. [10]. A *diff* operator $diff(m_1, m_2)$ expects two models, m_1 and m_2, as input and outputs a set of so-called *diff witnesses*, i.e., instances of m_1 which are not instances of m_2. For example, two *syntactically* different models m_1 and m_2 are *semantically* equivalent if each instance of m_1 is an instance of m_2 and vice versa. While [10] focuses solely on the semantic differencing aspect of model versioning, we aim to advance to a semantics-aware model merging process that is supported by an inter-diagram based consistency verification technique.

Model verification. Decoupled from the above sketched research field of model versioning systems, various works propose the verification of the syntactical consistency of models, many of which focus on the verification of UML diagrams (e.g., as done by Egyed [7] and Maoz et al. [11]). The verification process may be enhanced by the addition of semantic information. For example, Cabot et al. [5] verify the behavioral aspects of UML class diagrams annotated with so-called *operation contracts*, which are declarative descriptions of operations specified as OCL pre- and postconditions. The class diagram and the operation contracts are thereby transformed into a constraint satisfaction problem, which is solved with respect to a set of consistency properties expressing, e.g., the applicability or the executability of an operation. A formal verification technique for UML 2.0 sequence diagrams employing linear temporal logic (LTL) formulas and the SPIN model checker [8] to reason about the occurrences of events is introduced by Lima et al. [9].

In contrast to these single-diagram verification techniques, multi-view approaches assert the consistency across a set of diagrams. Proponents in this area are, among others, the tools HUGO [14] and CHARMY [12]. HUGO verifies whether the interactions of a UML collaboration diagram are in accordance with the corresponding set of state machine diagrams. The tool automatically translates the state machine diagrams to PROMELA, the input language of SPIN, and generates so-called "never claims" from the collaboration diagrams. The generated artifacts form the input for SPIN, which performs the verification. While HUGO operates on UML diagrams, CHARMY provides a modeling, simulation, and verification environment for software architectures (SA), which share many commonalities with UML. SAs describe the static and behavioral structures of systems with component, state transition, and sequence diagrams. Again, CHARMY translates the modeled artifacts to PROMELA and calls upon SPIN to either locate deadlocks and unreachable states in the state machines, or to verify temporal properties of the system.

In contrast to the standalone, snapshot-based verification procedure implemented by CHARMY and HUGO, our approach integrates the consistency verification procedure into the model versioning process to enable the semantics-aware merging of models.

3   Semantics-Aware Model Versioning

To detect semantic merge problems as described above, we propose to use a model checker like SPIN [8] within the merge process. The idea is to generate possible merge results and to check for each if it is consistent with the behavior defined by the corresponding state machine. We first give a short definition of the modeling language concepts needed, and then introduce our approach in detail. In particular, we consider a simplified subset of the UML state machine and sequence diagrams.

3.1   Definitions

For our purposes, a *software model*, $\mathcal{U}$, consists of a set $\mathcal{M}$ of *state machines* and a *sequence diagram* $\mathcal{S}$, defined as follows: A state machine $M = (Q, T, \tau, q_0, A)$ is a deterministic finite automaton, where

- Q is a set of *states*,
- T is a set of *transition labels* (or possible *input symbols*),
- $\tau : Q \times T \to Q$ is the *transition function*,
- $q_0 \in Q$ is a designated *initial state*, and
- $A \subseteq Q$ is a set of *accepting states*.

A sequence diagram $\mathcal{S}$ is a pair $(N, \overline{\mathcal{L}})$, where N is a set of *messages* and $\overline{\mathcal{L}}$ is a set $\{\mathcal{L}_1, \ldots, \mathcal{L}_n\}$ of *lifelines*. A lifeline, $\mathcal{L}$, in turn, is a triple (M, L, tr), where

- $M \in \mathcal{M}$ is a state machine,
- L is a finite sequence $(n_1, \ldots, n_m)$ of elements of N and
- $tr : N \to T$ is a bijective function, mapping each message to a transition label of the corresponding state machine.

A model $\mathcal{U}$ is *consistent* iff, for each lifeline $\mathcal{L} = (M, L, tr)$ of $\mathcal{S}$, there exists a path $(tr(n_1), \ldots, tr(n_m))$ in the state machine M, where $L = (n_1, \ldots, n_m)$.

3.2   Versioning Scenarios

Our versioning scenarios involve concurrent modifications on a sequence diagram. The state machine diagrams remain unchanged. A modification concerns one or more messages, each being of either of the following three types:

- *insert*: a message $n \in N$ is inserted at any index of a lifeline;
- *delete*: a message n is removed from a lifeline; and
- *update*: a message n is replaced by $n' \in N$ different from n.

Concurrent changes may result in different sequence diagrams. It is then up to the versioning tool to merge these changes into a new version of the diagram, which must be syntactically correct and consistent with the state machine diagrams.

Merging sequence diagrams is done as follows: For each lifeline, any possible sequence of messages originating from both diagrams is syntactically correct, but possibly inconsistent with the behavior defined in the corresponding state machine diagrams.

3.3   Semantics-Aware Model Merging

We propose to integrate the model checker SPIN [8] to support the generation of merged sequences. SPIN is a software verification tool. It takes as input a software abstraction, or model, encoded in SPIN's input language PROMELA and relevant properties of the software model in LTL. SPIN can be run in two modes: In *simulation mode*, where the PROMELA model is executed, and in *verification mode*, where the LTL formula is checked for satisfiability with respect to the PROMELA model.

For our basic definition of a software model, we propose a simple encoding that allows to check for the consistency between a sequence diagram and a set of state machines by running SPIN in simulation mode, which is much faster than verification mode and sufficient for our purpose. The state machines are encoded as deterministic finite automata and the sequence diagram as a set of arrays containing transition labels of the respective automata. The verification task in this case is to check if each word (i.e., array of transition labels) is accepted by its automaton.

The workflow of the merging process, as depicted in Fig. 3, is as follows:

0. The set $\mathcal{M}$ of state machine diagrams is encoded in PROMELA automata. Other than for sequence diagrams, this encoding is done only once, as the state machine is considered fixed in our application scenario.
1. The versioning operations *diff* (comparison) and *conf* (conflict detection) are executed on the original sequence diagram S and the two modifications S' and S''.
2. The versioning operation *merge* is performed based on the output of Step 1 and a merge strategy. In order to produce a syntactically correct sequence diagram, the merge strategy defines conditions on the possible orderings of the merged messages on a lifeline. A possible strategy is one that orders

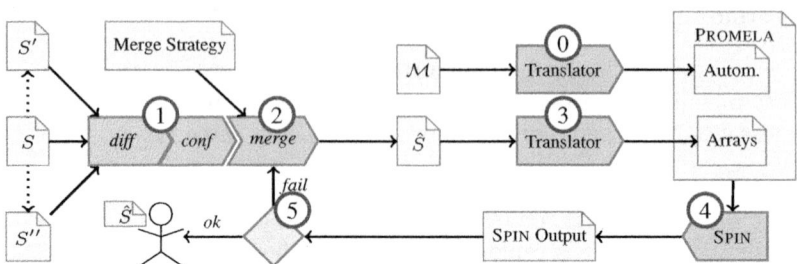

Fig. 3. Workflow of the merge process

messages in a first-come, first-serve manner, or one that allows any possible combination. A strategy may allow more than one possible sequence diagram as result of the merge. In this case, the choice is made deterministically.

3. The output of *merge*, i.e., a syntactically correct sequence diagram $\hat{S}$, is encoded as a set of PROMELA arrays in the form of $(tr(n_1), \ldots, tr(n_m))$, describing each lifeline as a word from the input symbols of the automaton encoded in Step 0.

4. The PROMELA code is fed into SPIN, which checks if each of the words generated in Step 3 is accepted by the respective automaton. It returns either a success message or the state and transition where the verification failed.

5. If the SPIN output does not contain any error message, the current merged sequence diagram $\hat{S}$ and the SPIN output are returned to the user. Otherwise, the procedure continues until a fixed-point at Step 2 is reached with a new merged sequence diagram $\hat{S}$ different from the previous ones.

For the encoding we make use of the following elements of PROMELA [8]:

- `active proctype`: defines a process behavior that is automatically instantiated at program start;
- `label`: identifies a unique control state (we also use the prefix `end`, which defines a termination state);
- `mtype`: a declaration of symbolic names for constant values;
- `array`: a one-dimensional array of variables (we use arrays of `mtype` elements to encode words checked by the automaton);
- `if`: a selection construct, used to define the structure of the automaton; and
- `goto`: an unconditional jump to a label, also used to define the structure of the automaton.

The PROMELA encoding of a state machine is performed as follows:

- The state machine is encoded as `active proctype` that contains all the necessary elements of the state machine.
- Each transition label $t \in T$ is encoded as an element of `mtype`. The additional element `acc` is added to model transitions to the `end` state.

- Each $q \in Q$ is encoded as a label marking a state of the `active proctype`. The additional state `end` is added.
- The state q_0 is placed at the beginning of the respective process in order to be executed at process initiation.
- τ is encoded as a set of `if` conditions inside each PROMELA state q. For each $t \in T$ such that (q, t) is defined by τ, the current symbol of an input sequence (which is, as described below, the encoding of a lifeline) is compared to t. If the condition holds, a `goto` statement jumps to state $\tau(q, t)$.
- Our sequence diagram semantics does not require a lifeline to terminate with a specific message, so all states are accepting states. We thus place a transition `goto end`, if the current symbol equals our additional transition label `acc` into each state except the `end` state.

A lifeline is encoded as an array `S` of `mtype`. Each field of `S` with index i contains the `mtype` element $tr(n_i)$ where n_i is the i-th element of the sequence L.

The PROMELA code is executed as simulation. It prints a success message if the word encoded in the array is accepted. In this case, the lifeline is consistent with the corresponding state machine. Otherwise it aborts when it hits a transition label that is undefined in the current state.

We have implemented the outlined approach based on the Eclipse Modeling Framework (EMF)[1]. In particular, the presented language excerpt of UML has been specified as an Ecore-based metamodel. The transformations of state machines into PROMELA automata and sequence diagrams into PROMELA arrays have been implemented as model-to-text transformations using Xpand[2]. The implementation is available at our website: `http://www.modelevolution.org/prototypes/semantic-merging`.

4 Application Scenario

We illustrate our approach using the example from Section 1. First, we translate the state machine of Fig. 1 by means of the encoding presented in the previous section as follows:

- The state machine is defined as `active proctype` named `CoffeeMachine`.
- The transition labels of the coffee machine, along with an additional label `acc`, are contained in `mtype`.
- Each state of the coffee machine is represented by a label, such as `Off` or `Idle`, and an `end` state is added. The start and end states of the coffee machine are summarized in label `Off`.
- For each state, all defined transitions are encoded using `if` and `goto` statements.
- A counter is added to keep track of the current index of the input word.

---

[1] `http://www.eclipse.org/modeling/emf`
[2] `http://www.eclipse.org/modeling/m2t/?project=xpand`

Listing 4.1. State machine encoding in PROMELA

```
 1  mtype={turnOff,turnOn,prepareCoffee,coffeeComplete,prepareTea,teaComplete,
 2        acc};
 3
 4  active proctype CoffeeMachine() {
 5  byte h = 0;
 6  mtype CM[4];
 7
 8  CM[0]=turnOn; CM[1] = prepareCoffee; CM[2] = coffeeComplete; CM[3] = acc;
 9
10  Off:
11    printf("Off\t %e\n", CM[h]);
12    if
13    :: CM[h] == turnOn -> h++; goto Idle
14    :: CM[h] == acc -> goto end
15    fi;
16  Idle:
17    printf("Idle\t %e\n", CM[h]);
18    if
19    :: CM[h] == prepareCoffee -> h++; goto PreparingCoffee
20    :: CM[h] == prepareTea -> h++; goto PreparingTea
21    :: CM[h] == turnOff -> h++; goto Off
22    :: CM[h] == acc ->   goto end
23    fi;
24  PreparingCoffee:
25    printf("PreparingCoffee\t %e\n", CM[h]);
26    if
27    :: CM[h] == coffeeComplete -> h++; goto Idle
28    :: CM[h] == acc -> goto end
29    fi;
30  PreparingTea:
31    printf("PreparingTea\t %e\n", CM[h]);
32    if
33    :: CM[h] == teaComplete -> h++;   goto Idle
34    :: CM[h] == acc -> goto end
35    fi;
36  end:
37    printf("end!\n")
38  }
```

The sequence diagram contains one relevant lifeline, the instance cm of the coffee machine, which is encoded as array CM of mtype: For each message n_i received by cm, CM[i]= $tr(n_i)$. Recall that tr returns an element of the set of transition labels and that those are encoded as elements of mtype.

The resulting encoding of the state machine with the initial version S of the sequence diagram is shown in Listing 4.1. It is easy to see that the above code eventually reaches the end state. Replacing the array CM by the two modified sequence diagrams S' and S'', encoded in the same manner, the code also reaches the end state. However, on the merged sequence diagram $\hat{S}_1$, shown below, the model checker will give up when it reaches the Off state trying to match CM[4].

```
6  mtype CM[7];
7  CM[0]=turnOn; CM[1]=prepareCoffee; CM[2] = coffeeComplete; CM[3] = turnOff;
8  CM[4] = prepareTea; CM[5] = teaComplete; CM[6] = acc;
```

On the other hand, the second merged sequence diagram $\hat{S}_2$, given below, is consistent. Hence, in our merging workflow, $\hat{S}_2$ will be returned to the user.

```
6  mtype CM[7];
7  CM[0] = turnOn; CM[1] = prepareCoffee; CM[2] = coffeeComplete;
8  CM[3] = prepareTea; CM[4] = teaComplete; CM[5] = turnOff; CM[6] = acc;
```

5   Conclusion and Future Work

In this paper, we proposed to use a model checker to detect semantic merge conflicts in the context of model versioning. Model checkers are powerful tools used for the verification of hardware and software. A model checker takes as input a model of a system and a formal specification of the system and verifies if the former meets the latter. We applied this technique to check the semantic consistency of an evolving UML sequence diagram with respect to state machine diagrams that remain unchanged. When contradicting changes occur, a unique automatic merge is not possible in general. However, additional information on violations of the model's semantics allows to identify invalid merge results. Hence, a more goal-oriented search for a consistent merged version is supported.

Our first experiments on this approach gave promising results, but for the full integration into the versioning process several issues have to be considered which we discuss in the following.

Extension of the Language Features. So far, we considered only a restricted, simplified subset of the UML metamodel. In this setting, the execution semantics of the considered diagrams is quite unambiguous. With the introduction of more advanced concepts, several questions concerning the execution semantics will arise, which are not covered by the UML standard and need detailed elaboration in order to translate them to the formalisms supported by the model checker. When including these language features, we expect to fully exploit the expressiveness of LTL for the needed assertions.

Integration in the Merge Component. We use the information obtained by the model checker not only to verify the consistency of two diagrams, but to support the merge process as necessary when models are versioned in an optimistic way. At the moment, only the fact that the model checker failed to verify the provided encoding is propagated back to the merge component. We plan to build an analyzer which is able to deduce constraints from the output of the model checker. These constraints can then be used to create an alternative merged version.

Visualization of the Conflicts. For reasons of usability, the representation of conflicts is of paramount importance. In particular, we conjecture that conflicts have to be reported in the concrete syntax of the modeling language [3]. Therefore, we propose a mechanism based on UML profiles to include merging information directly into the model. We plan to extend this mechanism to report semantical problems in the concrete syntax.

Benchmarking. Finally, we need more test cases to evaluate our approach. In particular, it will be interesting to learn about precision and recall in various merging scenarios as well as to study scalability with growing model size.

References

1. Brosch, P., Kappel, G., Langer, P., Seidl, M., Wieland, K., Wimmer, M.: The Past, Present, and Future of Model Versioning. In: Emerging Technologies for the Evolution and Maintenance of Software Models. IGI Global (2011)

2. Brosch, P., Kappel, G., Seidl, M., Wieland, K., Wimmer, M., Kargl, H., Langer, P.: Adaptable Model Versioning in Action. In: Modellierung. LNI, pp. 221–236. GI (2010)

3. Brosch, P., Kargl, H., Langer, P., Seidl, M., Wieland, K., Wimmer, M., Kappel, G.: Conflicts as First-Class Entities: A UML Profile for Model Versioning. In: Dingel, J., Solberg, A. (eds.) MODELS 2010. LNCS, vol. 6627, pp. 184–193. Springer, Heidelberg (2011)

4. Brosch, P., Langer, P., Seidl, M., Wieland, K., Wimmer, M.: Colex: A Web-based Collaborative Conflict Lexicon. In: IWMCP @ TOOLS 2010, pp. 42–49 (2010)

5. Cabot, J., Clarisó, R., Riera, D.: Verifying UML/OCL Operation Contracts. In: Leuschel, M., Wehrheim, H. (eds.) IFM 2009. LNCS, vol. 5423, pp. 40–55. Springer, Heidelberg (2009)

6. Cicchetti, A., Di Ruscio, D., Pierantonio, A.: Managing Model Conflicts in Distributed Development. In: Czarnecki, K., Ober, I., Bruel, J.-M., Uhl, A., Völter, M. (eds.) MODELS 2008. LNCS, vol. 5301, pp. 311–325. Springer, Heidelberg (2008)

7. Egyed, A.: UML/Analyzer: A Tool for the Instant Consistency Checking of UML Models. In: 29th Int. Conf. on Software Engineering, pp. 793–796. IEEE (2007)

8. Holzmann, G.J.: The Spin Model Checker: Primer and Reference Manual. Addison-Wesley Professional (2003)

9. Lima, V., Talhi, C., Mouheb, D., Debbabi, M., Wang, L., Pourzandi, M.: Formal Verification and Validation of UML 2.0 Sequence Diagrams using Source and Destination of Messages. ENTCS 254, 143–160 (2009)

10. Maoz, S., Ringert, J.O., Rumpe, B.: A Manifesto for Semantic Model Differencing. In: Dingel, J., Solberg, A. (eds.) MODELS 2010. LNCS, vol. 6627, pp. 194–203. Springer, Heidelberg (2011)

11. Mens, T., Van Der Straeten, R., D'Hondt, M.: Detecting and Resolving Model Inconsistencies Using Transformation Dependency Analysis. In: Wang, J., Whittle, J., Harel, D., Reggio, G. (eds.) MODELS 2006. LNCS, vol. 4199, pp. 200–214. Springer, Heidelberg (2006)

12. Pelliccione, P., Inverardi, P., Muccini, H.: CHARMY: A Framework for Designing and Verifying Architectural Specifications. TSE 35(3), 325–346 (2008)

13. Reiter, T., Altmanninger, K., Bergmayr, A., Schwinger, W., Kotsis, G.: Models in Conflict – Detection of Semantic Conflicts in Model-based Development. In: MDEIS @ ICEIS 2007, pp. 29–40 (2007)

14. Schäfer, T., Knapp, A., Merz, S.: Model Checking UML State Machines and Collaborations. ENTCS 55(3), 357–369 (2001)

Model Based Architecting and Construction of Embedded Systems (ACES-MB 2011)

Stefan Van Baelen[1], Sébastien Gérard[2], Ileana Ober[3],
Thomas Weigert[4], Huascar Espinoza[5], and Iulian Ober[3]

[1] KU Leuven - DistriNet, Belgium
Stefan.VanBaelen@cs.kuleuven.be
[2] CEA - LIST, France
Sebastien.Gerard@cea.fr
[3] University of Toulouse - IRIT, France
{Ileana.Ober,Iulian.Ober}@irit.fr
[4] Missouri University of Science and Technology, USA
weigert@mst.edu
[5] Tecnalia, Spain
Huascar.Espinoza@tecnalia.com

Abstract. The fourth ACES-MB workshop brought together researchers and practitioners interested in model-based software engineering for real-time embedded systems, with a particular focus on the use of models for architecture description and domain-specific design, and for capturing non-functional constraints. Six presenters proposed contributions on a systematic transition from systems modeling using SysML to software modeling using UML, verification of initial architecture models against requirements using consistency checking techniques, techniques to check the validity of refinement relation between abstraction levels, constructing rapid prototypes to assess the behavioral design characteristics, new abstraction layers to describe operating system and mixed-signal issues, and a model-driven approach for parallelizing software programs. In addition, a lively group discussion tackled these issues in further detail. This report presents an overview of the presentations and fruitful discussions that took place during the ACES-MB 2011 workshop.

1 Introduction

The development of embedded systems with real-time and other critical constraints raises distinctive problems. In particular, development teams have to make very specific architectural choices and handle key non-functional constraints related to, for example, real-time deadlines and to platform parameters like energy consumption or memory footprint. The last few years have seen an increased interest in using model-based engineering (MBE) techniques to capture dedicated architectural and non-functional information in precise (and even formal) domain-specific models in a layered construction of systems.

J. Kienzle (Ed.): MODELS 2011 Workshops, LNCS 7167, pp. 257–261, 2012.

MBE techniques are interesting and promising because they allow to capture dedicated architectural and non-functional information in precise (and even formal) domain-specific models, and they support a layered construction of systems, in which the (platform independent) functional aspects are kept separate from architectural and non-functional (platform specific) aspects, where the final system is obtained by combining these aspects later using model transformations.

The fourth workshop on *Model Based Architecting and Construction of Embedded Systems* (ACES-MB 2011) brought together researchers and practitioners interested in all aspects of model-based software engineering for real-time embedded systems. The participants discussed this subject at different levels, from requirements specifications, model specification languages and analysis techniques, embedded systems product lines, model synthesis, to model based verification and validation.

2   Workshop Contributions

6 full papers had been accepted for the workshop, see the ACES-MB 2011 workshop proceedings [1]. A synopsis of each presentation is given below. Extended versions of articles [6] and [4] are included in this MoDELS 2011 workshop reader.

[2] addresses the integration of system modeling and software modeling for embedded systems, which are software intensive systems that consist of both hardware and software components. A systems modeling approach to create structural and behavioral models of the total system using SysML, and the systematic transition to software modeling using UML is been described.

[3] states that designing cyber-physical systems is a challenge originating from the multidisciplinary and mixed-signal requirements. In order to handle this challenge, many design languages have been developed, but none is able to connect different application domains adequately. A new system based view for cyber-physical system design is been proposed, which can be easily adapted by MARTE or SysML as it uses a model based design technique. Instead of defining another UML profile, the paper presents an intuitive idea for the development of cyber-physical systems by refinement, and introduces new abstraction layers that help to describe operating system and mixed-signal issues. Using new abstraction layers, it is now possible to support all views of the platform based design by using one consistent language. The approach explicitly distinguishes between the physical system and the computational system.

[4] describes a model-driven approach that aids the developer in parallelizing a software program. Information from a dynamic call tree, data dependencies and domain knowledge from the developer are combined in a model transformation process. This process leads to a model of the application where it becomes obvious which parts of the application can be executed in parallel.

[5] states that during the development of software intensive systems, typically several models of this system are designed, representing the system structured by different concerns. While these approaches help to cope with complexity, the need of relating the models to one another arises. A major task is to keep model

specifications consistent and traceable through special relations. The relation of interest for this paper is the refinement relation between abstraction levels. The paper describes a technique to check the validity of these refinement relations with respect to formal behavior and interface specifications of design items. For evaluation, the proposed refinement technique is being applied to an industrial example modeled with a contract-based methodology.

[6] argues that the electric and electronic architecture (EEA), which is built up during the concept phase of automotive electronics development, has fundamental impact on the success of a vehicle under development. The complexity of upcoming architectures requires novel approaches to support system architects during the design phase. The paper describes a model-based generic approach which allows verifying an EEA with regard to its requirements by using techniques of consistency checks during an early design phase, including the handling of incomplete models. In this case, it offers the possibility to automate consistency checks and facilitates an automatism for optimization and design space exploration to check different realization alternatives of an initial EEA. Automatic report generation of results serves for documentation.

[7] describes an approach for constructing rapid prototypes to assess the behavioral characteristics of real-time embedded software architecture designs. Starting with a software architecture design nominally developed using the concurrent object-oriented design method COMET, an executable Colored Petri Net (CPN) prototype of the software architecture is developed. This prototype allows an analyst or engineer to explore behavioral and performance properties of a software architecture design prior to implementation. This approach is suitable both for the engineering team developing the software architecture as well as independent assessors responsible for oversight of the architectural design.

3   Summary of the Workshop Discussions

The workshop was divided into 3 sessions: system and software development and modeling, system and software architecture, and a plenary discussion session. During the 2 technical sessions, specific discussions on each paper have been held. In the plenary discussion session, a group discussion was held on broader questions and recurring issues that were raised during the session presentations. The following integrates and summarizes the conclusions of the discussions.

Traceability

A discussion was being held about the usefulness of traceability between models at different abstraction levels. Traces can be defined between a variety of model elements, such as system components, events, functional elements, and non-functional descriptions. It is often easy to generate traceability, at least in a model-driven approach where traceability information can be generated during the model transformation execution. But it is hard to decide how to use traces in a meaningful manner and where to generate useful traces, since one can easily end up with a huge number of inter-model traces that are hard to be used efficiently afterwards. Therefore methodological guidance is needed on what and where to trace. Semantic information could be added to the traces (e.g., by labelling traces) in order to generate semantically rich traces to increase the usability of the tracebility information.

Ontologies, Metamodels and UML Profiles

For expressing domain concepts and dependencies, domain experts can either build ontologies using dedicated ontology languages, develop domain-specific modeling languages (DSMLs), defining the metamodels and mappings (transformations) between the metamodels, or define UML profiles, defining the set of annotations for labelling and enriching UML elements). Each of these approaches can have their specific benefits in a particular situation. Although the definition of a DSML is not always straightforward, the actual definition, extension and usage of a metamodel is usually meant only for domain experts, and not for application engineers.

Domain-Specific Languages for the Automotive Industry

The acceptance of EAST-ADL, a domain-specific language defined specifically for describing automotive applications, is very low in the automotive sector while AUTOSAR instead is heavily used. One of the reasons could be the inappropriateness of the concrete syntax used by EAST-ADL. One could think on building a new concrete syntax on top of the existing abstract syntax, but it is not clear whether it is only the issue of concrete vs. abstract syntax, or whether the abstract syntax of EAST-ADL is not sufficient.

Acknowledgements. This workshop was supported by the IST-004527 ARTIST2 Network of Excellence on Embedded Systems Design (http://www.artist-embedded.org), the research project EUREKA-ITEA EVOLVE (Evolutionary Validation, Verification and Certification, http://www.evolve-itea.org), the research project EUREKA-ITEA VERDE (Validation-driven design for component-based architectures, http://www.itea-verde.org), and the research project EUREKA-ITEA OPEES (Open Platform for the Engineering of Embedded Systems, http://www.opees.org).

References

1. Van Baelen, S., Gérard, S., Ober, I., Weigert, T., Espinoza, H., Ober, I. (eds.): Fourth International Workshop on Model Based Architecting and Construction of Embedded Systems. CEUR Workshop Proceedings, vol. 795. CEUR, Aachen (2011)
2. Gomaa, H.: Towards integrated system and software modeling for embedded systems. In: [1], pp. 9–22
3. Slomka, F., Kollmann, S., Moser, S., Kempf, K.: A multidisciplinary design methodology for cyber-physical systems. In: [1], pp. 23–37
4. Sackmann, M., Ebraert, P., Janssens, D.: A model-driven approach for software parallelization. In: [1], pp. 39–53

5. Weber, R., Gezgin, T., Girod, M.: A refinement checking technique for contract-based architecture designs. In: [1], pp. 55–69
6. Adler, N., Graff, P., Müller-Glaser, K.D.: Model-based consistency checks of electric and electronic architectures against requirements. In: [1], pp. 71–83
7. Pettit IV, R.G., Gomaa, H., Fant, J.S.: Modeling and prototyping of real-time embedded software architectural designs with colored petri nets. In: [1], 85–98

Model-Based Consistency Checks of Electric and Electronic Architectures against Requirements

Nico Adler[1], Philipp Graf[1], and Klaus D. Müller-Glaser[2]

[1] FZI Research Center for Information Technology, Karlsruhe, Germany
{adler,graf}@fzi.de
[2] Institute for Information Processing Technology,
Karlsruhe Institute of Technology (KIT), Karlsruhe, Germany
klaus.mueller-glaser@kit.edu

Abstract. The electric and electronic architecture (EEA), which is built up during the concept phase of automotive electronics development, has fundamental impact on the success of a vehicle under development. The complexity of upcoming architectures requires novel approaches to support system architects during the design phase.

This paper describes a model-based generic approach which allows verifying an EEA with regard to its requirements by using techniques of consistency checks during an early design phase. This includes handling of incomplete models. In this case it offers the possibility to automate consistency checks and in future work facilitate an automatism for optimization and design space exploration to check different realization alternatives of an initial EEA. Automatic report generation of results serves for documentation.

Keywords: electric and electronic architectures, model-based engineering, automotive, verification, requirements.

1 Introduction

Electric and electronic architectures (EEAs) in the automotive and avionic domain build a complex network of a multitude of embedded systems. In the automotive domain we already see an amount of up to 70 networked electronic control units (ECUs) in current upper class vehicles [1, 2]. Various innovations, e.g. driver assistance systems, and new technologies, e.g. FlexRay, cause that the EEA of vehicles gets more complex, including numerous technical and functional aspects. Driven by customer demands for more safety, comfort and infotainment, this bears growing challenges for upcoming development activities [3].

The Original Equipment Manufacturer (OEM) must find new ways to control and manage the rising complexity of an EEA. In addition different variants of the EEA, as a single product can have several equipment concepts, increase the difficulty to analyze, whether an EEA meets all requirements [4, 5]. Moreover new international standards like ISO 26262 [6] increase quality requirements and efforts to verify an EEA regarding functional safety.

J. Kienzle (Ed.): MODELS 2011 Workshops, LNCS 7167, pp. 262–275, 2012.
© Springer-Verlag Berlin Heidelberg 2012

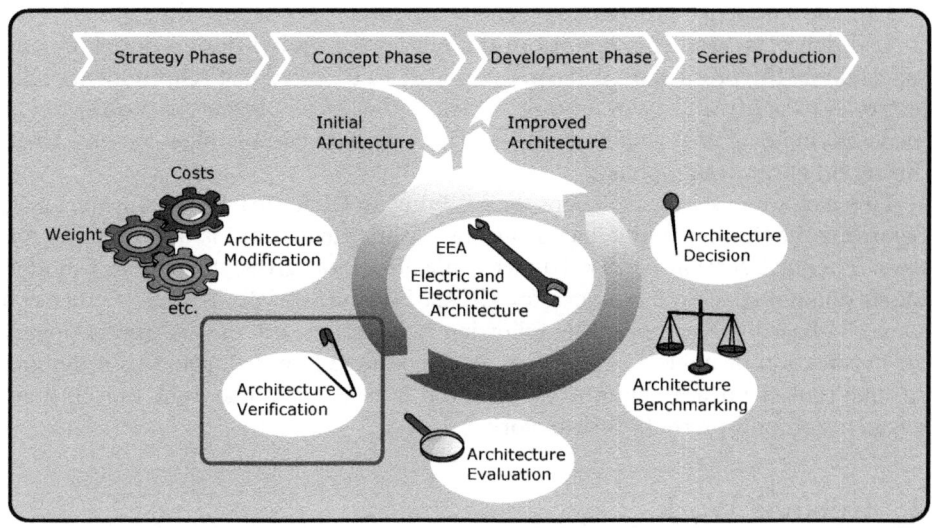

Fig. 1. Simplified product life cycle in context of model-based engineering for EEAs[7]

Within a simplified product life cycle, as shown in Fig. 1, the *concept phase* deals with functionality, convenience, risk and profitability of the vehicle [8]. The result must be a concept that meets the main requirements of a vehicle. During the *development phase* the OEM implements the variants of the solution from the *concept phase* into prototypes. This deals with the technical feasibility of alternative solutions. Further phases follow and are out of the scope of this work.

During the *concept phase* about 80 percent of lifecycle costs will be determined, although the *concept phase* itself is only about 6 percent of the total incurred costs [9, 10]. After finalization of the *concept phase* subsequent changes in the EEA are either associated with enormous costs or may not be feasible anymore. Inconsistencies, which cannot be eliminated, in the worst can put the project's success in risk. Therefore, it is a necessity to perform optimizations and verification already during the *concept phase*.

A simplified iterative process for developing an EEA can be described using a cycle with five steps, as shown in Fig. 1. During *architecture modification* system architects try to improve an existing initial EEA concerning different criteria. This can be done by optimization or by design space exploration. In the second step, the *architecture verification*, it must be proved, if the modified architecture meets all requirements. This is a very challenging and time-consuming task and can be accomplished using consistency checks. Subsequently the EEA has to be evaluated. This can be done using a cost breakdown structure to get the total system costs with regard to product lifecycle [11]. To find the most acceptable solution and to achieve an *architecture decision*, different realization alternatives are benchmarked against each other.

The development process for vehicle architectures is usually spread over several departments. This results in difficulties for global design decisions and especially in the proof of overall consistency of an EEA against requirements. Objective is to verify and demonstrate, which (sub-) areas present or could present inconsistencies against requirements, so that measure can be taken to solve them during an early design phase.

This paper focuses on a concept for verifying an EEA during the concept phase regarding requirements and specifications automatically and is organized as follows: The next section briefly defines verification and gives an survey of model-based domain specific languages for EEAs. Section 3 briefly relates verification to model-based engineering. The following two sections present our methodology for verification of model-based EEA. A discussion of the adaption to a domain specific toolset for a first prototype is given in Section 6. The final section gives a conclusion and presents future work.

2   Related Work

Verification of an EEA is one of the significant points during development. Boehm describes the basic objectives of verification and validation (V&V) early in the product life cycle with identification and solving of problems and high risk issues [12]. The V-Model-XT V1.3 describes: 'verification is to ensure that selected work results meet their requirements'. Therefore a definition of verification procedures and setting up the necessary verification environment must be done [13].

Different commercial tools support requirements management such as IBM Rational DOORS[1] or Geensoft Reqtify[2], etc. A survey of requirements management tools is provided by the International Council on Systems Engineering[3] (INCOSE). Some of the main requested objectives of requirements management tools are exemplary traceability, change management and tool integration[14]. For traceability also links to the system design are relevant. This is only possible within an integrated model.

EEA modeling supports system architects as models abstract complex problems. Different approaches and projects for the model-based description of especially automotive EEA exist, e.g. the project Titus [15], the language EAST-ADL [16], which emerged from the project EAST-EEA, and the EAST-ADL2 [17], which emerged from the follow-up project, and AUTOSAR [18].

A survey of languages, tools and applications for integrated model-based development and a number of european projects in the automotive domain can be found in [19]. Exemplary lightweight extensions of the Unified Modeling Language (UML) like MARTE and SysML profile are presented. Also general-purpose tools for grahical UML2 modeling such as Papyrus[4] are mentioned.

---

[1] http://www.ibm.com/software/awdtools/doors, 2011.
[2] http://www.geensoft.com/en/article/reqtify, 2011.
[3] http://www.incose.org/productspubs/products/rmsurvey.aspx, 2011.
[4] http://www.papyrusuml.org, 2011.

Another model-based approach for the description of EEAs is the 'Electric Electronic Architecture - Analysis Design Language' (EEA-ADL) [20, 21]. This data model also forms the basis of the architecture modeling and analysis tool PREEvision [4]. It combines most of the previously presented approaches within a tool and was used for the following described implementation. PREEvision Version 3.1 provides five abstraction layers. *Product goals* consisting of requirements with customer features and feature functionality network constitute the first abstraction layer. Artifacts of this layer are text elements, which represent atomic features or requirements for the architecture. The underlying layers are: *logical function architecture, system software architecture, hardware architecture* consisting of component architecture with network topology, electric circuit and wiring harness, and the *geometrical topology*. Cross layer links between model artifacts can be modeled using mappings. Apart from modeling EE relevant content, the EEA-ADL provides the opportunity to deposit attributes for costs, weight etc. This makes the model suitable for applying metrics and performing architecture evaluations. For analysis of an EEA an integrated, graphically notated metric framework can be used [22]. To perform consistency checks an integrated consistency rule model editor is given. Rules for consistency checks can be modeled in a graphical way. Simple rules for checks can be set up easily, but for complex ones with lots of constraints, inputs and multiple involved abstraction layers, this approach is too limited. Another disadvantage is that the provided rule modeling is limited as only the boolean logic operator AND can be used. Consistency checks have to be generated within the consistency rule model and afterwards synchronized with the architecture model. This is very time-consuming, especially for building up and testing complex rules. The created consistency checks can be started only manually. Therefore it is not straightforward to use this methodology for a desired semi-automatism for optimizing an EEA as the checks must be started individually depending on the actual optimization state.

Some of the presented domain specific languages offer an import and export of requirements from requirements management tools. The combination of these tools offers to map requirements within the model-based domain specific language to the corresponding artifacts and consistency checks.

3   Checking EEA-Consistency in the Context of Model-Based Engineering

The quality of verification for EEA models is only as good as requirements are described, the according consistency checks are derived from these and realized as executable rules. A consistent model is mandatory, which ensures that all EE relevant data including requirements are available and up-to-date. During the concept phase with consideration of model-based engineering, models are not complete and different sub-parts exist at different detail levels. Therefore model-based verification of constraints has as an additional requirement to secure that verification rules also work with incomplete models. Incomplete requirements and specifications either from OEM or suppliers have to be taken into account. However absolute maximum ratings of datasheets or specifications can be pre-calculated or estimated from previous series to perform first consistency checks.

Inconsistency at any point shall not abort verifying as any information about existing consistencies and also about inconsistencies against requirements are beneficial. With automated reporting the results must be captured so that during the development process different versions can be traced and reproduced. Guidelines or regulations of standards must be used as a basis for documentation templates. This for example is requested by ISO 26262.

It has to be ensured that consistency checks do not apply changes to the EEA data model. The deposited rules are only allowed to retrieve data out of an immutable model.

4   Overview of the Constraint Verification Approach

Starting point for model-based verification is an integrated EEA data model, which is filled with any available and relevant information, as shown on the left-hand side in Fig. 2. This can be done using a model-based domain specific language such as the examples presented in Section 2.

Within this model the EEA has to be specified and requirements must be defined or imported from requirements management tools. During the development process requirements can further be detailed. The requirements linked to the EEA data model are relevant for the verification. For the requirements layer textual described and hierarchical constructed requirements are suggested. To structure requirements, requirements packets should be used. Layer internal mappings are used for building up a network of requirements and also requirements packets. In further steps requirements can be mapped for traceability to the corresponding consistency checks.

For automatic verification five different functional blocks are provided, as shown on the right-hand side in Fig. 2, and are described in the following subsections: *consistency check blocks* with the checking rules for verification, *model query blocks* concerning data acquisition, *logic unit*, *requirements block* and *report generation block* for documentation.

4.1   Consistency Check Block

From each requirement or requirements packet at least one consistency check must be derived and implemented as an executable rule. As a decision criterion, the complexity to check the requirement or requirements packet can be used. Therefore the architect has to analyze all requirements separately.

Verification can relate to different abstraction layers in an EEA data model. For consistency checks, the corresponding artifacts, including their attributes and their mappings between different abstraction layers, are required. This input data for the consistency check can be provided by outsourced data acquisition using model queries and is described in the following subsection.

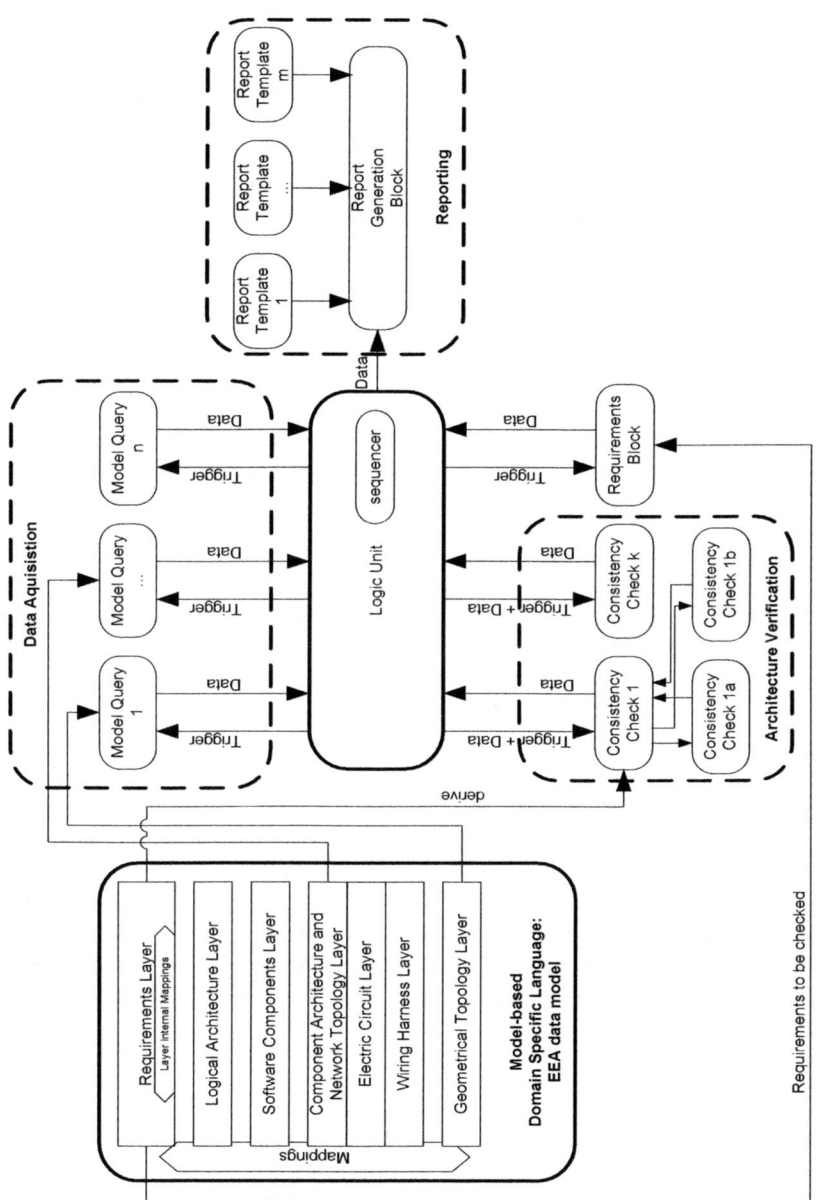

Fig. 2. Approach for verification of EEAs against requirements

The multitude of incoming model data from the model queries has to be preprocessed. This includes sorting and filtering data, furthermore structuring of model data which belongs together. Another task is to capture the required corresponding attributes of model artifacts.

The crucial point to verify the EEA is the execution of the consistency check. This is composed of a sequence and examination rule. The sequence is partitioned into *consistency checks that cannot be performed* and *consistency checks that can be performed*. It is advisable to inspect if all relevant data for performing the check are available. If any information is not available, the consistency check cannot be performed. At this point results of not possible checks must be collected and stored for postprocessing and preparation for reporting. If the consistency check can be performed, the examination rule describes what shall be checked and in fact represents the derived requirement or requirements packet. Instructions for checking on consistency or inconsistency can be implemented using a specific algorithm. The algorithm examines the available data and executes the rule.

Results of the consistency check are lists or tables. Additionally the degree of a possible violation of a rule can be estimated. Subsequent post-processing is used mainly for preparing the data in a structured way for reporting.

4.2   Model Queries Block

Expert knowledge demonstrates that great effort for verification consists of data acquisition and structuring. Model queries can be used for data acquisition and should be based on the corresponding EEA data model. This ensures that model queries are correct.

Different consistency checks may require the same model artifacts. The reuse of existing model queries can significantly reduce the overhead of setting up new checks. Hereby model queries can be used for different consistency checks which need the same model artifacts, or the artifacts are part of the model query result and must be extracted by the consistency check block. Therefore, an approach has to be found to avoid redundancy so that model queries are implemented only once. To provide results of model queries to different consistency checks, the model queries must be connected to a *logic unit*. The *logic unit* forwards the model query results to the corresponding *consistency check blocks*.

4.3   Logic Unit

The *logic unit* is the central block. It acts as a sequencer and is connected to all other blocks by input and/or output ports. The ports are used to transmit different kind of data. Two port modes are differentiated: *trigger mode* is used for data request and *data mode* is used for transmission of data consisting of header and payload. For both port modes, it is possible to directly connect an input port to one or more output ports. Additionally incoming data or triggers can be split and/or combined.

Data preprocessing for paths coming from model queries to consistency checks is not provided, because preprocessing can distort results with possible data losses. To avoid this, preprocessing of model query results has to be implemented directly in the *consistency check blocks*. However data preprocessing is applied for the path coming from output ports of consistency checks to report generation. Therefore the *logic unit* is further connected with the report engine. After final preparation of verification results, the *logic unit* transfers data together with report filename to the report generation block.

The execution of the verification is started by the *logic unit*. Thus the *logic unit* needs information about which requirements should be verified. For this, a *requirements block* as a further block is incorporated.

4.4   Requirements Block

The *requirements block* is used to insert a collection of demanded requirements which have to be verified. Therefore the corresponding requirements from the *requirements layer* are mapped to the block. The *logic unit* retrieves them as a data input and triggers the derived consistency checks. No mapped requirements means that all consistency checks have to be executed.

4.5   Report Generation Block

Reporting for documentation is an important tasks to reproduce and capture results. Reporting can be differentiated into documentation for internal or external use. Therefore, an individual configurable template based approach must be provided, as in different departments they have to fill in different forms or bring a different proof respective to standards or recommended practice.

For internal use, there is also the need of documentation, but the key factor is to design an EEA which meets all the requirements as soon as possible. Therefore additional identified information can be documented.

The *logic unit* must decide at runtime, which results have to be sent to the *report generation block* to fill the corresponding placeholders in the templates. Result export to other tools must also be performable. For this purpose e.g. a XML Schema Definition (XSD) can be implemented using the templates. This offers a wide range to interface other tools for further processing of results. Therefore the generation of documents shall be delivered through a suitable report engine, which can access the prepared templates.

5   Execution of Verification

The sequence for model-based verification is shown in Fig. 3. In the vertical 'swimming lanes' (columns) the five different functional blocks are presented. Starting point is the *logic unit*. The *logic unit* requests the *requirements block* for information about which requirements should be checked by using a trigger.

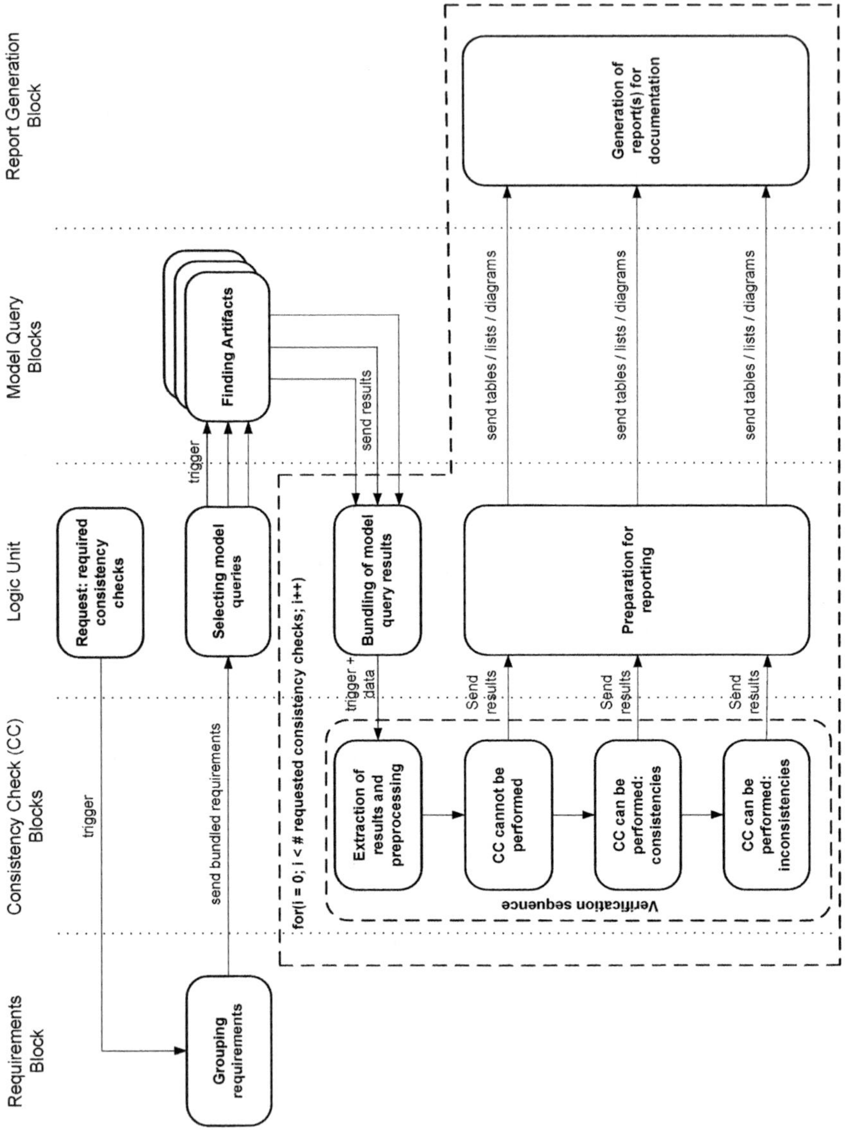

Fig. 3. Execution of verification against requirements

The bundled requirements are sent to the *logic unit* which selects the model queries to be executed for the corresponding consistency checks. The results in form of lists or tables are sent back to the *logic unit*. The model queries are executed only once, because during verification the EEA data model is not modified. At this point a loop starts. For every requested verification, the *logic unit block* bundles the demanded model queries results and sends them to the corresponding *consistency check block*. The verification sequence starts and therefore the examination. Relevant results of the consistency check are sent to the *logic unit*, which forwards them after potential preparation for reporting to the *report generation block*.

6   Prototype Implementation in PREEvision

Integrated consistency checks require an integrated model as described in Section 2. PREEvision is a software tool that allows persistent modeling and evaluation from requirements down to topology and was used for the first prototyping the concept described before.

As a simple example we demonstrate the approach with a consistency check derived from the requirement 'All ECUs with the attribute *isPartOfActiveVariant = true* and *availability in crash* is set to *low, medium* or *high* must be allocated to corresponding *installation spaces!*'

For preparation an exemplary EEA within PREEvision was modeled. This consisted of *component layer* with *ECU* artifacts, the *topology layer* with *InstallationLocation* artifacts and added *HardwareToTopology-Mappings* between the two abstraction layers. The requirement was inserted in the *requirements layer* of the EEA data model. The metric framework of PREEvision was used for the following described implementations.

6.1   Model Query Blocks

Afterwards we identified which artifacts from different abstraction layers are relevant for performing the consistency check. In this case the involved *ECU* artifacts from the *component layer* including the attribute *availability in crash* are relevant. This formed the first model query. Further we needed all *InstallationLocations*. This formed the second model query. The last model query finds all existing ECU mappings from the component into the *topology layer*.

For the model queries, the integrated rule model in PREEvision was used which is based on the corresponding EEA data model. It allows to model rules in a graphical way. Complex patterns to match can be defined, using not only the *source-object* and its properties, but also *objects* and *LinkPairs* between the *objects*, as shown on the left-hand side in Fig. 4 for the rule diagram *ECUtoInstallationLocationMappings*. A further restriction was added to the example by using one of the *attributes* of the *ECU*, thus the *isPartOfActiveVariant* was set to boolean value *true*.

The generated rules for the three required model queries could be used within the metric framework. The results after execution of the model queries are tables or lists, as shown on the right-hand side in Fig. 4. These can be further processed by the consistency checks.

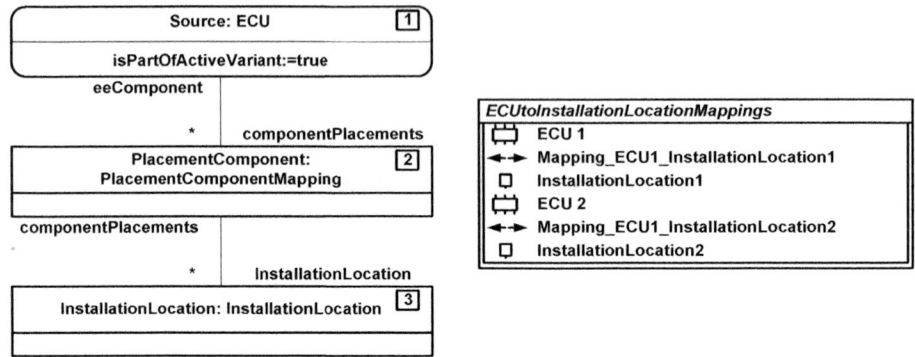

Fig. 4. Rule diagram for the model query (left) and results (right)

6.2 Consistency Check Blocks

For the *consistency check block* a Java-based calculation block within the metric editor was used. With this approach we access EEA model artifacts and their attributes using Java as a programming language instead of the graphical rule modeling as for the model queries. Being more flexible, it allows to construct simple to very complex consistency checks. The results of the *model query blocks* are used as their input.

It is also possible to construct hierarchical consistency checks using several calculation blocks. For example this can be used to subdivide a requirement or requirements packet into several consistency checks. In this case trigger and data paths have to be looped through the parent *consistency check blocks*.

6.3 Logic Unit

The *logic unit* was implemented using a calculation block and was connected with all other blocks using data flows. It contains an allocation table of model queries to the corresponding consistency checks. The execution sequence was implemented and internal trigger and data paths were connected. It is possible to individually improve existing consistency checks or to add new ones. Extension of any kind can be performed easily, as existing model queries, etc. can be reused and only the allocation table in the *logic unit* has to be updated.

6.4   Report Generation Block

For the *report generation block*, we used the open source templating *Apache Velocity Engine*[5], which is integrated in the PREEvision metric framework. Velocity permits to use a simple template language to reference objects defined in Java code. As the output format for the first prototype we chose HTML for the generated files. This allows graphical layout of results and ensures traceability using hyperlinks. Using velocity templates we formed the basic structure of the graphical appearance including a navigation bar. Placeholders in the velocity templates were filled with the data coming from *consistency check blocks*, looped through the *logic unit*. To obtain better overview of the identified inconsistencies we export the corresponding diagrams to PNG-file format automatically and include them in the reports.

7   Conclusion and Future Work

In this paper we have presented an approach that makes it possible to automate verification for electric and electronic architectures using consistency checks in a model-based way already during concept phase. The methodology is generic and even incomplete models can be checked. This is a significant step to support the system architect concerning reduction of development time and ensures EEA being consistent against requirements. Integrated reporting serves for documentation.

The developed methodology and its implementation in PREEvision has shown to work in our first prototype. An analysis and application of the approach in EAST-ADL is being considered. Also, adapting to an existing standard for expressing constraints, the Object Constraint Language (OCL) which is included in the Unified Modeling Language (UML), could be analysed.

Future work will mainly focus on expanding the approach to architecture evaluation using metrics for calculating quality of the EEA. This ability can be used for benchmarking different EEA realization alternatives. In further steps, the approach can be extended to (semi-) automatic optimization and design space exploration. For generating new EEA realization alternatives a strategy for design space exploration must be found. For this purpose, the automatic verification can deliver useful information about the degree of compliance to requirements for a new generated EEA realization alternative.

Application and evaluation of the approach with a real-world EEA model is planed for a case study, but will require the cooperation with an Original Equipment Manufacturer (OEM) to bring in the real-word application as its intellectual property.

---

[5] http://velocity.apache.org, 2011.

Acknowledgements. This document is based on the SAFE project in the framework of the ITEA2, EUREKA cluster programme $\Sigma!\,3674$. The work has been funded by the German Ministry for Education and Research (BMBF) under the funding ID 01IS11019. The responsibility for the content rests with the authors.

References

[1] Larses, O.: Architecting and Modeling Automotive Embedded Systems. Doctoral dissertation, Stockholm (2005)

[2] Reichart, G., Haneberg, M.: Key Drivers for a Future System Architecture in Vehicles. Convergence International Congress & Exposition On Transportation Electronics, Society of Automobile Engineers (SAE), Detroit (2004)

[3] Hillenbrand, M., Heinz, M., Adler, N., Müller-Glaser, K.D., Matheis, J., Reichmann, C.: ISO/DIS 26262 in the Context of Electric and Electronic Architecture Modeling. In: Giese, H. (ed.) ISARCS 2010. LNCS, vol. 6150, pp. 179–192. Springer, Heidelberg (2010)

[4] aquintos GmbH: PREEvision Version 3.1 Manual. aquintos, Karlsruhe (2010)

[5] Burgdorf, F.: Eine kunden- und lebenszyklusorientierte Produktfamilienabsicherung für die Automobilindustrie. Doctoral dissertation. Karlsruhe Institute of Technology, Karlsruhe (2010)

[6] International Organization for Standardization: ISO 26262 Road vehicles - Functional Safety Part 1-10, Switzerland (2011), www.iso.org

[7] Adler, N., Gebauer, D., Reichmann, C., Müller-Glaser, K.D.: Modellbasierte Erfassung von Optimierungsaktivitäten als Grundlage zur Systemoptimierung von Elektrik-/Elektronik-Architekturen. In: 14. Workshop Methoden und Beschreibungssprachen zur Modellierung und Verifikation von Schaltungen und Systemen (MBMV) 2011. OFFIS - Institut für Informatik, Oldenburg (2011)

[8] Kuster, J., Huber, E., Lippmann, R., Schmid, A., Schneider, E., Witschi, U., Wüst, R.: Handbuch Projektmanagement. Springer, Heidelberg (2008)

[9] Voigt, K.I.: Industrielles Management - Industriebetriebslehre aus prozessorientierter Sicht. Springer, Heidelberg (2008)

[10] Bürgel, H.D., Zeller, A.: Controlling kritischer Erfolgsfaktoren in Forschung und Entwicklung. Controlling 4 (1997)

[11] Blanchard, B.S., Fabrycky, W.J.: Systems Engineering and Analysis. Pearson Prentice Hall, New Jersey (2006)

[12] Boehm, B.: Verifying and Validating Software Requirements and Design Specifications. IEEE Softw. (1984)

[13] V-Modell-XT Version 1.3, Part 7: V-Modell Reference Mapping to Standards (2009)

[14] Hoffmann, M., Kühn, N., Weber, M., Bittner, M.: Requirements for Requirements Management Tools. In: Proceedings of the 12th IEEE International Requirements Engineering Conference, Kyoto, Japan (2004)

[15] Eisenmann, J., Köhn, M., Lanches, P., Müller, A.: Entwurf und Implementierung von Fahrzeugsteuerungsfunktionen auf Basis der TITUS Client/Serverarchitektur. In: VDI Berichte, Nr. 1374, Systemengineering in der Kfz-Entwicklung. VDI-Gesellschaft Fahrzeug- und Verkehrssicherheit (1997)

[16] The East-EEA Project: Definition of language for automotive embedded electronic architecture approach. Technical Report, ITEA, Deliverable D3.6 (2004)

[17] The ATESST Consortium: EAST ADL 2.0 specification. Technischer Bericht, ITEA (2007), http://www.atesst.org/

[18] AUTOSAR, Automotive Open System Architecture (2010), http://www.autosar.org

[19] Passerone, R., Damm, W., Ben Hafaiedh, I., Graf, S., Ferrari, A., Mangeruca, L., Benveniste, A., Josko, B., Peikenkamp, T., Cancila, D., Cuccuru, A., Gerard, S., Terrier, F., Sangiovanni-Vincentelli, A.: Metamodels in Europe: Languages, Tools, and Applications. Design & Test of Computers 26(3), 38–53 (2009)

[20] Matheis, J.: Abstraktionsebenenübergreifende Darstellung von Elektrik/ Elektronik-Architekturen in Kraftfahrzeugen zur Ableitung von Sicherheitszielen nach ISO 26262. Doctoral dissertation. Karlsruhe Institute of Technology, Karlsruhe (2010)

[21] Belschner, R., Freess, J., Mroßko, M.: Gesamtheitlicher Entwicklungsansatz für Entwurf, Dokumentation und Bewertung von E/E Architekturen. In: VDI Bericht, Nr. 1907, pp. S511–S521. VDI-Verlag, Düsseldorf (2005)

[22] Gebauer, D., Matheis, J., Kühl, M., Müller-Glaser, K.D.: Integrierter, graphisch notierter Ansatz zur Bewertung von Elektrik/Elektronik- Architekturen im Fahrzeug. In: Moderne Elektronik im Kraftfahrzeug IV: Energiebordnetz - E/E-Architektur HW/SW-Assistenzsysteme. expert, Essen (2009)

A Model-Driven Approach
for Software Parallelization

Margarete Sackmann, Peter Ebraert, and Dirk Janssens

Universiteit Antwerpen, Belgium
{margarete.sackmann,peter.ebraert,dirk.janssens}@ua.ac.be

Abstract. In this paper, we describe a model-driven approach that aids
the developer in parallelizing a software program. Information from a
dynamic call tree, data dependencies and domain knowledge from the
developer are combined in a model transformation process. This process
leads to a model of the application where it becomes obvious which parts
of the application can be executed in parallel.

1 Introduction

In the past, it was unnecessary to write programs that have the potential for
parallel execution since most processors contained only one processing core and
programs were therefore executed sequentially. Now, however, multiple processors are getting more and more popular, even for smaller devices such as routers
or mobile phones, and it is crucial that the possibilities offered by the parallel
processors are used well.

Despite this trend towards parallel processors, most programmers are still
used to a sequential style of programming. It is difficult for them to judge where
parallelization is both feasible and worthwhile. Even for programmers who are
used to parallel programming, it is often less error-prone to start out from a
sequential program rather than designing a parallel program from scratch, as
errors that arise from the parallel execution can then be distinguished from other
programming errors. In this paper, we propose a model-driven approach that aids
the programmer in deciding where good opportunities for parallelization are in
a program.

The starting point is the source code of a program from which a model of
the behavior of the program is derived. This is done by profiling the execution
of the program. In the resulting model, the developer may add information
about the sequential order that may be required among program parts. Model
transformations are then used to derive a parallel model of the application, taking
into account both the information derived from profiling and the information
added by the developer.

2 Related Work

A popular way to parallelize programs is Thread Level Speculation (see for
instance [1] or [2]). In this compiler-based approach, the program is parallelized

J. Kienzle (Ed.): MODELS 2011 Workshops, LNCS 7167, pp. 276–290, 2012.
© Springer-Verlag Berlin Heidelberg 2012

during execution. The parallelization is speculative which means that in some cases a part of the execution has to be repeated since there are dependencies that were not taken into account. This approach seems unfit for systems where resources such as energy are scarce, since parts of the application have to be executed more than once to take effect.

Other approaches, for instance [3], require specific hardware. The speedups for floating point operations are close to optimal, however porting the application to different platforms is not possible.

When trying to parallelize applications for different hardware platforms, an approach that focuses on the software is a better solution. Examples are Embla 2 [4] which links back the profiling information of the program to the source code to help the user identify possibilities for parallelizing the code. iPat [5] is an Emacs assistance tool for parallelizing with OpenMP. However, it is entirely text-based and provides no visual aid to the developer.

In [6], a model transformation process is used to generate parallel code. The difference to our approach is that information about possible parallelism in the program has to be added to the code as compiler directives. Via various model transformations, code can then be generated for different hardware platforms.

An approach that helps to extract a parallel model of the application is the Compaan/Laura approach [7]. It gives a more complete view of the program than the approach presented here since the extracted model is representative for any input data. However, it requires a massive restructuring of the code and an initial idea about the program behavior to help with this restructuring.

3   Approach

We propose a toolchain that focuses on the software so as to ensure portability of the code to different hardware platforms. The approach is based on model transformations and provides a visual interface to the developer. Several models of the application are used throughout the toolchain to represent the application at different levels of abstraction and with different levels of detail. The advantage in this context is that the approach is not bound to the profiling tools we use and that details that are not important for the parallelization can be hidden. The resulting parallel model can be used to parallelize the source code or to schedule the application on a multiprocessor platform. Parts of the application are represented as nodes in a graph, and dependencies between them – implying precedence relations – as edges in that graph. Thus, the developer gets a visual aid that helps him to understand the data and control flow in the program. The toolchain will be illustrated on the Fast Fourier Transform (FFT) application of the MiBench benchmark [8].

In Figure 1, an overview of the transformation process from source code to parallel model is given. In the next section, the different models that are used throughout the transformation, i.e. call trees, call graphs and the parallel model, are introduced. In Section 5, the transformation from source code to a parallel model of the application is explained. Section 6 shows how to implement the model transformation in practice. The results of the transformation process for the FFT application are given in Section 7 and ideas for future work are explained in Section 8. We also explain some of the limitations of the approach, that can arise for instance from variable reuse or structural problems in the original program. Some conclusions are presented in Section 9.

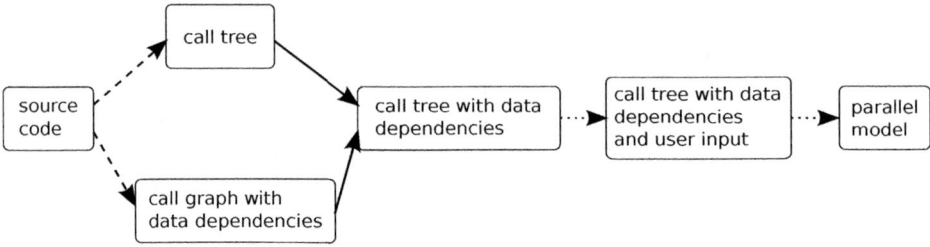

Fig. 1. The transformation process. Dashed lines stand for the use of a profiler. Solid lines represent a parsing and transformation step. Dotted lines represent model transformations.

4   Models Used during the Transformation

In this section we present the models that can be seen in Figure 1: the parallel model that is the goal of the model transformation, the call tree model and the enriched call tree model with data dependencies and dependencies added by the developer that is used during the model transformation.

To abstract from implementation details, we chose to represent the program at the level of functions. This means that a single function execution is the smallest part of the application that can be discerned in the different models. In case that is too fine-grained, several functions can be grouped into coarser-grained modules. If a finer grain is required, functions have to be broken up: If the user for instance suspects that a loop could be parallelized, then the calculations that are done within the loop body should be put into a separate function.

4.1   Parallel Model

The goal in the transformation process is to derive a model of the program that shows which parts of the application can be executed in parallel. The Parallel Model (PM) that is the outcome of the transformation process is a graph-based model. The nodes represent function instances that occur during an execution of a program. The edges in the parallel model represent a precedence relation between functions. An edge from function instance f_1 to f_2 means that f_1 has to start execution before f_2. The more important information in this model is however the lack of edges or a path between two functions. If there is no path between two function instances, they can be executed in parallel. This information can then be used for scheduling or to insert code to parallelize the program, for instance with OpenMP. A second type of edge, which we will call a subgraph edge, represents a stronger precedence relation. A subgraph edge from function f_1 to function f_2 means that f_1 and all its successors, i.e. its children, their children and so on, have to finish execution before f_2 can start execution.

The information provided by the subgraph edges can be used to get a greater flexibility of the model when the software has to be executed on different platforms with varying numbers of processors. In case the number of processors is small, a function f that is the source or target of a subgraph edge can be combined with all its successors into a subgraph that is scheduled as a whole. For a larger number of processors, the subgraph edges can be replaced by regular edges and more nodes can be distributed over the parallel processors.

4.2 Call Trees

To derive the parallel model, we start by analyzing the program code. One way to analyze the relation between the different functions is to track the calls from one function to another. This can either be done statically on the whole source code, or dynamically at run time. We chose for dynamic analysis, since it represents the actual execution of the program. During program execution, a profiler tracks which functions are called in which order. The resulting model, the call tree, is specific to a single execution of the application. Therefore, this approach works best for applications that always have a similar behavior (i.e. the same function calls are executed even if the actual data on which the calculations are performed is different), for instance Digital Signal Processing (DSP) applications such as digital filters or matrix multiplications. An advantage of using dynamic call trees is that functions that are not used during execution (and thus do not have to be distributed on the parallel platform) are not considered. Recent research has shown that in many circumstances dynamic analysis is better suited for parallelization than static analysis (see for instance [9]). A disadvantage of using dynamic analysis is that programs may be executed differently based for instance on the input. In that case, a system scenario [10] approach, where different types of execution behaviors are identified can be used.

Call trees can be represented as graphs, where the nodes are function instances and the edges are calls between the function instances. An excerpt of the call tree that is derived from the FFT application can be seen in Figure 2.

As can be seen in Figure 1, besides function calls we also add data dependencies and dependencies added by the developer to the call tree in our toolchain. A data dependency edge from a function f_1 to a function f_2 means that f_1 reads or writes data that is also read by f_2. This implies that at least some part of f_1 has to occur before f_2. Otherwise, a correct outcome of the program cannot be guaranteed. f_1 and f_2 can consequently not be executed in parallel. At the moment, we use the Paralax [11] compiler to automatically detect the data dependencies. It logs for each data element that is used in the program, such as arrays or integer variables, which functions access this data in which order.

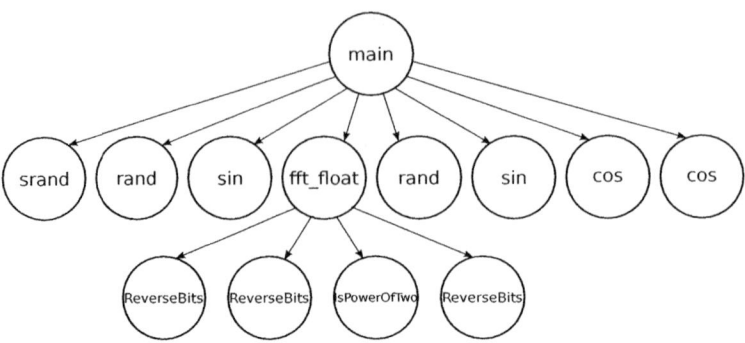

Fig. 2. Part of the call tree of the FFT application

This is done by tracking accesses to the address space of the data. Paralax also logs the access type, i.e. whether it is a read or write access. The read accesses are the critical ones and therefore the ones that are included into the model. The functions accessing a specific piece of data are identified by their call path, so that if a function is called from several other functions, a data dependency is only added if the whole call path matches. The data dependencies can be automatically included in the call tree model via a model transformation. To avoid loops, data dependencies are only added from a function f_1 to f_2 if f_1 occurred earlier in the call stack than f_2. The position in the call stack is recorded while obtaining the call tree and is a function attribute in the model transformation.

The third type of edge can be added by the user, in contrast to the function calls and data dependencies that can be detected and combined into a model automatically. The user can add edges between two function instances that are called by the same function instance. In Figure 2, the user can for instance add edges from the srand function instance to rand. An edge from f_1 to f_2 should be added if the execution of f_1 has to be finished before the execution of f_2 can start. Again, this implies that f_1 and f_2 cannot be executed in parallel. These extra edges can for instance be useful when the profiling tools could not detect all data dependencies due to the use of pointer arithmetics.

It could be argued that using call graphs rather than call trees would reduce the number of nodes. This approach is taken in [11], which we use to profile data dependencies. In a call graph, all instances of a function are combined into a single node. The problem with this approach is that the information contained in a call graph is not detailed enough. Consider for instance the call graph in Figure 3. The information that is included in this call graph is too limited to be able to parallelize the application properly. Many different executions can correspond to a call graph. In Figure 4 two call trees are shown that would both result in the call graph of Figure 3. For the parallelization step that is described in the following chapter it is important however, that the exact instance of a function that calls another function is known.

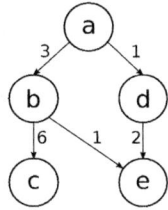

Fig. 3. A call graph

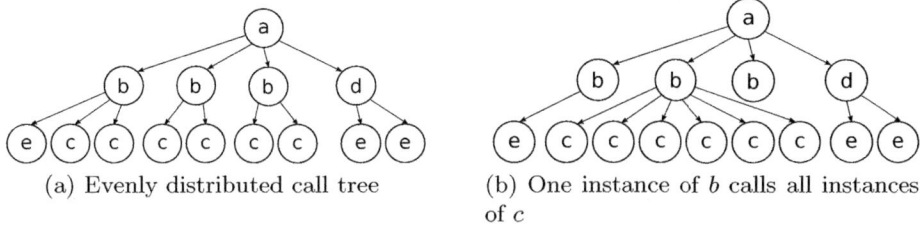

(a) Evenly distributed call tree   (b) One instance of b calls all instances of c

Fig. 4. Two possible call trees for the call graph in Figure 3

5 Transforming Source Code into a Parallel Model

In this section, the transformation process from the source code of an application to a parallel model of this application is described. The starting point is a dynamic call tree of the application (see 5.1) that is then enhanced with additional edges that represent data dependencies (5.2) and domain-specific knowledge of the user (5.3). The automatic transformation into the parallel model is described in Subsection 5.4. In Subsection 5.5, the usage of special edges that represent a dependency between subgraphs in the parallel model is explained.

We assume that, if a function f calls a function g, then there are no further computations (only possibly calls to other functions) in f after g returns. This form can be easily established in the source code: in case there are computations in f after the call to g, then these can be put into a new function h, and a call to h is added in f after the call to g.

5.1 Pruning the Call Tree

The size of a call tree can be quite large. Even for simple programs, thousands of functions are called. However, many of these functions are library calls or other functions that the user does not have control over. Therefore, we concentrate on functions that either are part of the source code that the developer programmed, or that are called from within that source code.

Example 1. In Figure 5 a loop from the `main` routine of the FFT application is shown. The functions `sin` and `cos` are called inside a loop. Even though these functions were not implemented by the user, they can be responsible for a large amount of execution time. Additionally, the user can add code to parallelize the different calls to these functions. Therefore, these functions are included in the call tree, but the functions that are not visible in the source code are not included (for instance functions that are called by sin).

```
for ( i =0; i <MAXSIZE; i++) {
    RealIn [ i ]=0;
    for ( j =0; j <MAXWAVES; j++) {
        if  (rand ()%2) {
            RealIn [ i]+=coeff [ j ]*cos (amp[ j ]* i );
        }
        else {
            RealIn [ i]+=coeff [ j ]*sin (amp[ j ]* i );
        }
    }
}
```

Fig. 5. Standard library functions called within a program

Even when leaving out calls to library functions, the number of function instances can be overwhelming. Therefore, only the functions with the largest instruction count are picked. Although this instruction count can vary on some processors with specialized computation units and may also be different for different compilers, this number is in general a good indicator on the expected execution time. This way, the user can later concentrate on parallelizing those parts of the software that make up the largest part of the execution time.

5.2   Data Dependencies

Besides the calling relation between functions, there exist other relationships between functions that can require them to be executed sequentially. If two functions for instance change the value of the same variable, then they have to be executed in a given order. However, these data dependencies are not visible in the call tree. Adding data dependencies that are later taken into account when producing the parallel model prevents race conditions that might occur when the program is parallelized.

As we work with models of the application, adding precedence relations between functions simply means adding directed edges in the graph representation of the model. Therefore, different profilers can be used to derive the data dependencies. Even profilers that can extract different dependencies between function instances could be used to include more edges in the call tree.

5.3   User Input

Since it is possible that some dependencies that will prohibit a parallelization are not included in the dependencies from the call tree and the data dependencies, the developer gets to add precedence relations that were not discovered by the profilers. Sometimes, as in the case of the FFT application, not all dependencies can be recognized by the profiler for instance due to the use of pointer arithmetics. In that case, the user has to add these dependencies by hand. Simply allowing the user to add edges between any two nodes of the graph would, however, not result in a very good parallel model. A call tree can be rather large and the user is bound to make mistakes if he is allowed to add edges unrestrictedly. In addition, parallelizing function instances that are called from the same function can be realized rather easily and without having to rewrite parts of the code. Therefore we chose a step-by-step approach, where only a part of the call tree is presented to the user in each step.

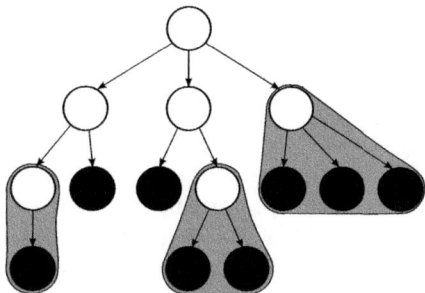

Fig. 6. A call tree where all leaves are shown in black. The subtrees marked in gray consist of one parent node and its children nodes that all have to be leaves.

A subgraph that consists of a parent node and its children nodes is presented to the user in each step. The children nodes all have to be leaves of the call tree, as illustrated in Figure 6. If there is a dependency between two children nodes of the subgraph, the user adds an edge between these nodes. In case that the user does not add any precedence relations for some children, it is assumed that these children nodes can be executed in parallel.

5.4   Transformation to a Parallel Model

In the automatic step from the enhanced call tree to the parallel model of the application, all the information from the profilers and the developer is combined. A model transformation is used to build up the parallel model of the application, while at the same time deleting nodes from the call tree in a bottom-up way.

Before presenting the first subgraph to the user, all nodes of the call tree are copied to a new graph, the parallel model PM, without however copying the edges. The edges are inserted step-by-step, as the subgraphs are modified by the user. Redundant edges are not copied to the parallel model. An edge between nodes f_0 and f_1 is redundant if there is a directed path from f_0 to f_1 that consists of edges of the same or a higher importance. The call tree edges are the least important edges and the data dependencies are the most important edges.

We chose to keep all data dependency edges in the transformation from the call tree to the parallel model. This is not strictly necessary to get a parallel model of the application. However, it is better to keep the data dependencies intact if this parallel model is used for scheduling where the data communication is important, such as embedded systems. If the data on a data dependency edge is for instance very large, it is better to schedule the functions on both ends of this data dependency on the same processor to avoid a large overhead for communication.

After copying the edges of the call tree subgraph in the manner just described to the parallel model, all children nodes of the subgraph are now deleted in the call tree. That way, it is ensured that for each function f, the subgraph with f as the parent node is presented to the user at some point.

5.5   Subgraph Edges

In the parallel model PM one needs to be able to see which subgraphs were already considered, i.e. for each node it needs to be obvious which function instance it was called from. This is best explained by way of an example.

Example 2. Imagine a subgraph with parent node p that has a child c. According to the transformation algorithm, the edge from p to c is copied to PM. In a later step, p and another node q are the children in a subgraph with parent t as shown in Figure 7(a). The user now indicates that q has to be executed after p as indicated by the dotted line in the figure. If no information is kept that p and c formed a subgraph earlier, then edges will now go from p to both c and q in the parallel model, indicating that c and q can be executed in parallel. This is shown in Figure 7(b). However, this is impossible to implement in practice without rewriting a part of the code.

This is why subgraph edges are allowed in the parallel model. These edges can be removed in a later step and replaced with the regular edges in the parallel model, but are useful during the transformation phase. For the example that was just discussed, the parallel model in Figure 7(c) is the result of using a subgraph edge. All nodes inside the dotted circle on the right p' have to be executed before all nodes inside the dotted circle q' on the left. The subgraph edge is indicated by a dashed arrow.

We could of course also allow users to specify that c and q in the example in Figure 7 can indeed be executed in parallel. However, in practice this will most likely be difficult to realize. It would force the programmer to ensure that q can be executed in parallel with c, but only after some of the computations of p are already done. While our approach is more conservative, it allows for an easier adaptation of the source code and will lead to less errors.

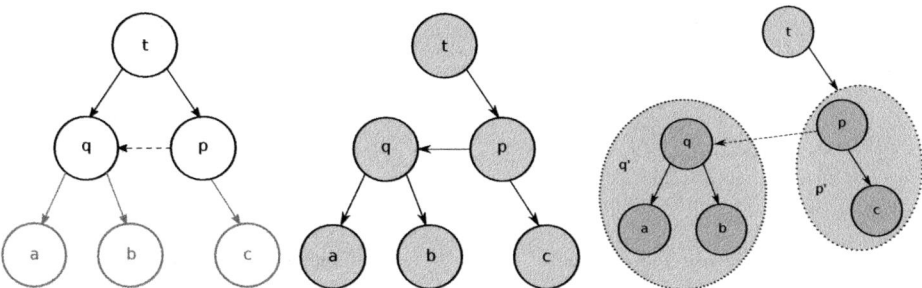

(a) A call tree with a precedence relation from p to q. The parts that are in gray are already deleted from the call tree, but are shown here to indicate the precedence relations in the subtrees with parents p and q.

(b) Transforming the call tree into a parallel model without subgraph edges. Here, it seems as if q and c could be executed in parallel.

(c) Transforming the call tree into a parallel model using a subgraph edge. In this case, all parts of p' are executed before any nodes in q' can start execution.

Fig. 7. Using subgraph edges to prevent undesired parallelism in the parallel model after the transformation from a call tree

Subgraph edges can e.g. be useful if the parallel model is used for scheduling, but the number of nodes in the call tree is much too large compared to the number of processors. In that case, subgraphs can be seen as a single node.

An optional model transformation step allows to replace subgraphs and subgraph edges with nodes and regular edges to adapt the granularity of the parallel model.

Example 3. An example is given in Figure 8, where h represents the subgraph that consists of h_0 and its successors. The edges that lead away from h_0 have to be redirected. For that, all leaves within h have to be found. In Figure 8 this would be nodes h_1, h_3 and h_4 since they have no outgoing edges. The subgraph edges going out from h_0 will each lead to three outgoing edges from h_1, h_3 and h_4 respectively. Finally, the subgraph edges can be deleted. The result of replacing the subgraph edges of h_0 in Figure 8 is shown in Figure 9.

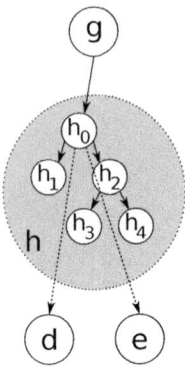

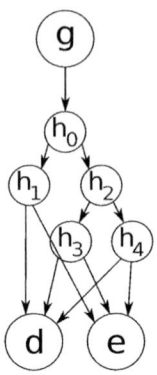

Fig. 8. Subgraph edges in the parallel model

Fig. 9. Replacing the subgraph edges in Figure 8

6   Implementation

We implemented the above approach in a toolchain that goes from the software source code via call trees to a parallel model of a software application.

The call tree is represented graphically within the AToM^3 [12] modeling tool. Each edge type – function call, data dependency and user-defined dependency – has a different color, so that the user can keep track of what kind of dependency an edge represents.

The first type of edge is a function call. To derive these edges, the toolchain uses a modified version of the Callgrind profiler [13] that is part of the Valgrind tool suite [14]. The adaptations were necessary to filter out the functions that do not appear in the source code of the application. In addition, Callgrind had to be modified to produce a call tree as an output rather than a call graph. The call tree that is produced as the output of the modified Callgrind tool is then parsed into a Python file that can be opened in AToM^3. In the parsing step, we allow to adapt the granularity of the call tree by transferring only the function instances with the largest instruction count to the Python file.

The second type of edges are data dependencies. They are derived from the output of the Paralax [11] compiler. Data dependencies in Paralax are dependencies between different call paths. For a data dependency between call path $f_1, \ldots, f_n$ and call path $g_1, \ldots, g_m$ that is found by the Paralax compiler, an edge has to be inserted in the call tree between each instance of f_n and each instance of g_m in the call tree, provided that the predecessors of f_n resp. g_m are instances of $f_1, \ldots, f_{n-1}$ resp. $g_1, \ldots, g_{m-1}$.

Example 4. Consider the call tree in Figure 10. Assume that there is a data dependency from call path $a \rightarrow b$ to $a \rightarrow c \rightarrow d$. Then, two data dependencies would be added, from b_1 to d_1 and d_2. There will be no data dependency from b_1 to d_3, since the call path of d_3 does not match with the one described by the

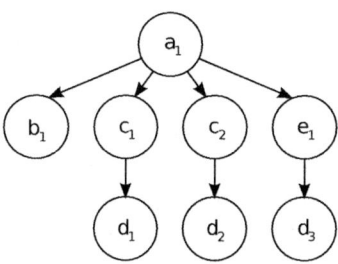
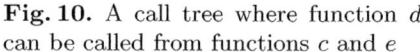
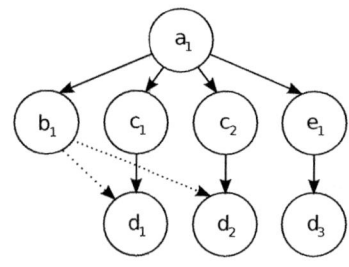

Fig. 10. A call tree where function d can be called from functions c and e

Fig. 11. Adding the data dependency from call path $a \rightarrow b$ to $a \rightarrow c \rightarrow d$ in Figure 10

call path $a \rightarrow c \rightarrow d$. The resulting call tree with the added data dependencies is shown in Figure 11.

The last type of edge is a user-defined edge. As explained above, these user-defined edges can be added one subgraph at a time. In each step, a subgraph of the call tree is highlighted. This subtree consists of a function instance p and all its children that all have to be leaves in the call tree. The user can add missing dependencies by drawing edges in the model. The position of each function instance in the call stack is given, so that the developer can see in which order the different function instances were actually executed during the profiling.

Once the user inserted all edges in a subgraph, he can indicate this with the click of a button and wait until the next subgraph is highlighted. The edges of the current subgraph are then copied to the parallel model in the manner described above. All children of the subgraph are then deleted along with the edges leading to and from them. A rule that determines for each node if it is a leaf of the call tree is invoked, so that the parent of the call tree will now be marked as a leaf. Then, the next subgraph is highlighted and so on.

After all nodes of the call tree have been deleted there is an optional step for replacing the subgraph edges. This is done in a top-down way, meaning that the subgraph edges closest to the root node (usually the `main` function) are replaced first so that the granularity of the model can be adapted.

7   Results

The approach was tested on the FFT implementation of the MiBench benchmark. In order to get usable results, we had to divide the loop that computes the FFT in the program into function calls. Although this was done within a few minutes, it shows a limitation of our approach that is due to it using functions as the smallest entities.

During the transformation phase, it was shown that it is a good idea to present the model to the user instead of just relying on the information given by the profiling tools. When we profiled the FFT application, the dependency that arises from filling the input signals with random numbers as seen in Figure 5 to using these signals in the actual Fast Fourier Transform was not detected by the Paralax profiler.

From the resulting parallel model, it became apparent that the best opportunities for parallelization are in two loops. The first loop is the inner loop of the actual Fast Fourier transformation (the outer loop has data dependencies) and the second loop is the one shown in Figure 5. These two loops make up more than 50 percent of the execution time. This shows that our approach can indeed help the developer in identifying the program parts where parallelization will bring the largest benefit.

The code was parallelized by inserting OpenMP [15] directives according to the parallel model. To parallelize the loop that computes the FFT, it was enough to add a simple line of code that allows the concurrent execution of the loop. Parallelizing the loop that initiates the input signals for the FFT is more difficult. As seen in Figure 5, there is a conditional execution within the loop. Therefore, the code had to be changed into the form seen in Figure 12. This already gives a slight improvement in the sequential execution of the code. This new for-loop can then be parallelized. Note that in order to get the same results as with the sequential version of the code, it has to be ensured that the random numbers are used in the same order. Therefore, they are stored beforehand in a separate array. Creating this array takes about one quarter of the total execution time of the parallelized program. When executing the program on an Intel Core i3 processor (dual core model with hyper-threading technology), the overall speedup when parallelizing both loops in the manner just described was 2.5.

```
for ( i =0; i <MAXSIZE; i++) {
    RealIn [ i ]=0;
    for ( j =0; j <MAXWAVES; j++) {
        x = rand ()%2;
        RealIn [ i ]  += x*coeff [ j ]*cos (amp [ j ]*i )+
                        (1−x )*coeff [ j ]*sin (amp [ j ]*i );
    }
}
```

Fig. 12. Modifying the code in Figure 5 so that there is no conditional statement in the for-loop

We also tested the approach on a Motion-JPEG implementation [7]. In addition to the pipeline parallelism for decoding the different blocks in a picture, five more opportunities for parallelization were found, four of which are task-level parallelism. The speedup when introducing OpenMP directives was minimal as all parallel portions in the program have a very small execution time. On an embedded system with less processing power the parallelization can however still prove useful. As two of these possibilities for parallel execution were found within the pipeline, this example also shows that with our approach we can find code sections that can be executed in parallel at different levels of detail.

8   Future Work

When testing our approach on a medical imaging software, it became apparent that pipeline parallelism is difficult to detect with our approach. In the case of the medical imaging software, a 4-stage pipeline is used. Each pipeline stage writes on an array that is then read by the next stage. Since the data dependency profiler does not distinguish between function instances, dependencies are added from each stage 1 function instance to each stage 2 function instance that occurred after it in the call stack. This makes the model very cluttered and the developer might not be able to see the possible parallelism. There are two possible ways to overcome this: the first is to adapt the profiling for data dependencies so that it works at the level of function instances rather than functions. However, this might lead to a large overhead for the parser. The second possibility would be to allow the user to indicate whether a data dependency should be added between all function instances or only those that follow each other in the call stack.

The approach can be easily extended to include other profiling information about dependencies between different functions. Our approach already considers dependencies that can be left out in the parallel model if alternative paths exist in the model (the function calls), and dependencies that are always copied from the original call tree to the parallel model. Therefore, it would be straightforward to include other dependencies without having to adapt the graph transformation algorithm.

The model transformation itself is independent of the programming language that is used. However, the profiling tools that we use at the moment limit our approach to programs written in C or C++. It would be interesting to see how difficult it is to adapt the approach to a different programming language like Java or Python, and especially to see how much effort is necessary to write new parsers to get the profiling information into the correct format for the transformation tool.

9   Conclusion

In this paper, we proposed a model-driven approach to help developers parallelize sequential software programs. Profiling results are combined with domain-knowledge of the user to transform source code into a parallel model of the application. We believe that by abstracting away the implementation details we can assist the developer significantly in the parallelization process. By providing the developer with an abstract model of the software that already includes function calls and data dependencies, the developer gets a graphical representation of his program that hides irrelevant details. As the developer can add precedence relations, a parallel model can be derived. It can for instance be used for scheduling the application on a multi-processor platform or adding compiler directives for parallel execution into the source code.

References

1. Quiñones, C.G., Madriles, C., Sánchez, J., Marcuello, P., González, A., Tullsen, D.M.: Mitosis compiler: An infrastructure for speculative threading based on pre-computation slices. In: 2005 Conference on Programming Language Design and Implementation, PLDI (2005)
2. Steffan, J.G., Colohan, C., Zhai, A., Mowry, T.C.: The STAMPede Approach to Thread-Level Speculation. Transactions on Computer Science (2005)
3. Chen, M.K., Olukotun, K.: The Jrpm System for Dynamically Parallelizing Java Programs. In: 30th Annual International Symposium on Computer Architecture (ISCA 2003) (2003)
4. Mak, J., Faxén, K.-F., Janson, S., Mycroft, A.: Estimating and Exploiting Potential Parallelism by Source-Level Dependence Profiling. In: D'Ambra, P., Guarracino, M., Talia, D. (eds.) Euro-Par 2010. LNCS, vol. 6271, pp. 26–37. Springer, Heidelberg (2010)
5. Ishihara, M., Honda, K., Sato, M.: Development and Implementation of an Interactive Parallelization Assistance Tool for OpenMP:iPat/OMP. IEICE Transactions on Information and Systems (2006)
6. Assayad, I., Bertin, V., Defaut, F.-X., Gerner, P., Quévreux, O., Yovine, S.: JAHUEL: A Formal Framework for Software Synthesis. In: Lau, K.-K., Banach, R. (eds.) ICFEM 2005. LNCS, vol. 3785, pp. 204–218. Springer, Heidelberg (2005)
7. Stefanov, T., Zissulescu, C., Turjan, A., Kienhuis, B., Deprettere, E.: System design using kahn process networks: The compaan/laura approach. In: Proceedings of the Conference on Design, Automation and Test in Europe (DATE) (204)
8. Guthaus, M.R., Ringenberg, J.S., Ernst, D., Austin, T.M., Mudge, T., Brown, R.B.: Mibench: A free, commercially representative embedded benchmark suite. In: Proceedings of the Workload Characterization 2001 Workshop (2001)
9. Tournavitis, G., Wang, Z., Franke, B., O'Boyle, M.F.: Towards a holistic approach to auto-parallelization. In: 2009 Conference on Programming Language Design and Implementation (PLDI) (2009)
10. Miniskar, N.R., Hammari, E., Munaga, S., Mamagkakis, S., Kjeldsberg, P.G., Catthoor, F.: Scenario based mapping of dynamic applications on mpsoc: A 3d graphics case study. In: SAMOS Proceedings of the 9th International Workshop on Embedded Computer Systems: Architectures, Modeling and Simulation (2009)
11. Vandierendonck, H., Rul, S., de Bosschere, K.: The paralax infrastructure: Automatic parallelization with a helping hand. In: Parallel Architectures and Compilation Techniques (PACT) (2010)
12. de Lara, J., Vangheluwe, H.: Using AToM3 as a Meta-CASE Tool. In: 4th International Conference on Enterprise Information Systems (ICEIS 2002) (2002)
13. Weisendorfer, J., Kowarschik, M., Trinitis, C.: A tool suite for simulation based analysis of memory access behavior. In: Proc. of the 4th Int. Conference on Computational Science (ICCS 2004) (2004)
14. Nethercote, N., Seward, J.: Valgrind: A framework for heavyweight dynamic binary instructions. In: Proc. of ACM SIGPLAN 2007 Conference on Programming Language and Design (PLDI 2007) (2007)
15. Chapman, B., Jost, G., van der Pas, R.: Using OpenMP. The MIT Press (2007)

Author Index